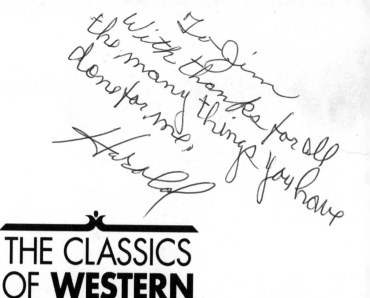

THE CLASSICS
OF **WESTERN**
SPIRITUALITY

THE CLASSICS OF WESTERN SPIRITUALITY
A Library of the Great Spiritual Masters

The Spirituality Of The German Awakening

EDITED, TRANSLATED, AND INTRODUCED BY
DAVID CROWNER AND GERALD CHRISTIANSON

PREFACE BY
MARTIN E. MARTY

PAULIST PRESS
NEW YORK • MAHWAH, N.J.

Picture credits for this volume: The pictures which appear on the front cover and within this volume are taken from the following sources: Theodor Fliedner from the Fliedner Cultural Institute at Kaiserswerth; Johann Hinrich Wichern from Martin Gerhardt, *Johann Hinrich Wichern: Ein Lebensbild,* 3 vols. (Hamburg, 1927–1931), vol. 1, frontispiece; August Tholuck from Leopold Witte, *Das Leben D. Friedrich August Gottreu Tholuck's,* 2 vols.(Bielefeld and Leipzig, vol. 1, 1884, vol.2, 1886), vol. 1, frontispiece; Friedrich von Bodelschwingh from Martin Gerhart, continued by Alfred Adam, *Friedrich von Bodelschwingh: Ein Lebensbild aus der deutschen Kirchengeschichte,* 2 vols. (Bethel bei Bielefeld, 1950, 1958), vol. 2:1, frontispiece.

Book design by Theresa M. Sparacio

Cover and caseside design by A. Michael Velthaus

Library of Congress Cataloging-in-Publication Data

The spirituality of the German awakening / edited, translated, and introduced by David Crowner and Gerald Christianson ; preface by Martin E. Marty.
 p. cm.
 Texts by August Tholuck, Theodor Fliedner, Johann Hinrich Wichern, and Friedrich von Bodelschwingh.
 Includes bibliographical references (p.   ) and indexes.
 ISBN 0-8091-4108-6; ISBN 0-8091-0549-7
 1. Pietism—Germany. 2. Christian life—Lutheran authors. I. Crowner, David. II. Christianson, Gerald. III. Tholuck, August, 1799–1877.
BR1652.G3 S65 2002
284.1′092′243—dc21

2002012196

Published by Paulist Press
997 Macarthur Boulevard
Mahwah, New Jersey 07430

www.paulistpress.com

Printed and bound in the United States of America

Contents

CONTENTS

CONTENTS

Translators/Editors of This Volume

DAVID CROWNER (Ph.D., Rutgers, 1967), whose scholarly interest is in modern German culture and literature, retired from Gettysburg College in 2001 as professor of German language and literature. He is the author of *German for Mastery* and coauthor of *Impulse*. He has taught and traveled extensively in Germany, and helped build an international program at Gettysburg College as faculty coordinator of service learning.

GERALD CHRISTIANSON (Ph.D., University of Chicago, 1972) is Central Pennsylvania Synod Professor of Church History at Gettysburg Lutheran Seminary. He is the author of *Cesarini, the Conciliar Cardinal* and coeditor of several books on Nicholas of Cusa, including the forthcoming primer on Cusanus from Paulist Press, coedited with Christopher Bellitto and Thomas Izbicki. Both Crowner and Christianson were raised in pious Scandinavian Lutheran circles and have lived in Gettysburg since 1967.

Author of the Preface

MARTIN E. MARTY is the Fairfax M. Cone Distinguished Service Professor Emeritus at the University of Chicago, where he taught for thirty-five years in the divinity school, the history department, and the commitee on the history of culture. His main scholarly interests had to do first with the history of religion in America and later, more recently, with comparative studies of human rights, ethnonationalism and religion, issues of health and faith and ethics, and most notably The Fundamentalism Project of the American Academy of Arts and Sciences. Long an editor and still a columnist at the *Christian Century*, he edits the newsletter *Context* and contributes a weekly e-mail editorial for the Martin Marty Center at the University of Chicago. He is a Lutheran minister. His honors include the National Medal of Humanities, the National Book Award, and the Medal of the American Academy of Arts and Sciences. He has written over fifty books, most of them on American religion.

For Pat and Carol

Love is patient.
1 Corinthians 13:4

Preface

The path to spirituality in our time necessarily follows the path of action. That was a contention of Dag Hammarskjøld, who spent daylight hours serving the United Nations and his moonlight hours writing the semi-mystical *Markings*.

Hammarskjøld's claim seems to be borne out in the careers of great spiritual leaders of the twentieth century; Dorothy Day, Martin Luther King Jr., Thomas Merton, Pope John XXIII, and Dietrich Bonhoeffer are names that come to mind at once as examples.

They together embody Charles Péguy's observation that "everything begins in mysticism and ends in politics." By "mysticism" he evidently did not mean what technical observers mean by the term. His accent was on what popular culture today would call spirituality. By "politics" he also did not mean only the sphere we often reduce to ballots, campaigns, and parties. His concern was for that to which politics points, the *polis*, the human city, served also through voluntary activity.

Keeping mysticism and politics or holiness and action together is difficult in a time in which publics are both invited to wallow in consumerism at the market *and* to be soulful or spiritual. Spirituality then means not getting their hands dirty by mingling in congregations, communities, institutions, organizations, or the mucky world that surrounds us.

Keeping mysticism and politics or holiness and action, as here defined, *together* is precisely what the four characters in the drama that unfolds on the following pages do. In part because they do, they will sound especially unfamiliar, almost idiosyncratic, to those who expect spiritual writing to help distance them from the world of human need and public disorder. The editors have selected examples of their writings, including transcribed talks and sermons, that show these writers being attentive to physical as well as spiritual need, to codes and rules for community at the same time as they stress intimate discourse with and experience of God.

Other reasons for the unfamiliar character of what follows have less to do with genre than with fashion. It has long been in fashion for turn-of-the-millennium Westerners to familiarize themselves with voices from the Himalayas, Africa, the Native American worlds, from what to so many look like exotic and esoteric cultures. Within the West millions have by now become familiar with profound spiritual writing from the hands of Saint Francis of Assisi and medieval Catholic mystics, a few of them even from Germany (as our four authors were). Thus Meister Eckhart and Hildegard of Bingen have become favored contributors to the spiritual life of today's seekers.

The company of—get ready, these are not household or churchhold names!—Friedrich August Gottreu Tholuck, Theodor Fliedner, Johann Hinrich Wichern, and Friedrich von Bodelschwingh—is not familiar from *The New York Times* bestseller lists or a candidate for anyone's "top forty" of anything. Unfamiliar (but not idiosyncratic) they certainly are.

They are from nineteenth-century Germany? So were Friedrich Nietzsche, Karl Marx, and other great bearded antitheological god-killers. So were David Friedrich Strauss and Ludwig Feuerbach, anti-theological (=God) theologians. But Tholuck, Fliedner, Wichern, and Bodelschwingh, contemporaries of numbers of these, while in no cases professional theologians, all were at home with "God-talk" and found God very much alive and close, a demanding and promising Presence.

Where will one hear names like theirs? Try the phone book's Yellow Pages and try to connect them with German culture. Look for the nearest Germania Club. Almost nowhere did such entities survive the stigma that modern German culture received during and after two world wars in which Germans were the main enemies. And if one located such a club, there is almost no chance that any member would be anything but bemused if asked about the identity of these four.

Try the church yearbook, then, and call upon contemporary embodiments of their Lutheran ethos and thrust. If you find a pastor or layperson who knows any of them, you have stumbled upon an antiquarian or someone who has boned up for *Trivial Pursuit.*

Like so many who might have so much to say to persons and issues of our day, this quartet has faded from public consciousness. They demand rediscovery, and they will need it if they are to address any in our time. I am happy to note that David Crowner and Gerald Christianson, by introducing well their translations, "firsts" in our culture, of representative writings by the four, will give them a chance to make their case, as if for the first time or, quite likely, for the first time. I hope that people who read Buddhist texts and the writings of Spanish mystics will be tantalized enough to move into their world and give them a chance.

Whenever one invites others to a world that has been unfamiliar, there is a temptation to over-introduce it. For example, there are linguistic nuances. Being faithful translators, Crowner and Christianson have to translate "O" at the beginning of many paragraphs into "O" in the English, thus preserving a Germanism or a German Pietist construct unfamiliar and perhaps uncongenial to people who did not grow up on Lutheran chorales or German translations of Psalms. After a few encounters with "O," one no longer notices it or sees it as a barrier.

The world that we dare not over-introduce out of respect for readers who can find their own way and for authors who have a right to their own way will strike some readers of spirituality texts as out of place or off-putting. Eyes glaze over—mine did, until I decided either to pass over long lists of biblical texts or actually to look up and read a few; they are relevant!—when Bible passages, codes of conduct, and other serial apparent distractions get in the way.

Then I remembered how patient we have come to be with spiritual writings by medieval Catholic women mystics who were also abbesses or other leaders of communities, and who webbed their spiritual discoveries and passions with codes and rules for the conduct of those in such communities. Or the preoccupations of Dead Sea Scrolls scribes with the details of daily living in a community that expects the End soon. Or the rules for monasteries in Asia or the material preoccupations that come with the *Spiritual Exercises* of Loyola. On those terms, these four authors can quickly win their place.

Beyond the German and Lutheran contexts, the linguistic peculiarities, and the spiritual-material, transcendental-mundane mixes, there are still other barriers. These writings come from schools of thought that carry a name as stigmatizing as Puritanism became in many sectors of the culture: Pietism. Even heirs of Pietist movements shun the term. It connotes withdrawn, timid, backs-to-the-audience prayer folks who are crabby toward others and over-scrupulous but still prideful about themselves and their ways.

However Pietist movements from the eighteenth and nineteenth centuries got their bad names, the negative connotations do not always apply to all Pietists. Yes, these four authors are unmistakably at home with the Pietists' Bible, but they are not cramped by it. Yes, they are all pietistically prayerful, but their praying is mainly intercessory. That means it is of a character that suggests "loving your neighbor on your knees," and they get up from those bent knees to take on worlds of injustice that need mercy.

Some of their inventions, especially the deaconess movement in evangelical Protestantism, prison ministries, the Rough House and halfway houses for ex-criminals and prostitutes, the sub-communities, conventicles that look like house-churches, their forms of congregating that countered the establishment but did not lead them to break with the order around them—all these live on today. Sometimes these appear in direct descendancy from these unrecognized and unacknowledged German Pietists, and sometimes these draw upon parallel lines from other movements, especially in the British Isles and the United States, that shared the ethos of our four spiritual writers. Readers who confront them are likely to be drawn more deeply into the world of the transcendent, which here means of God, and also the world of the imminent, which here means the neighbor.

PREFACE

To say that Tholuck, Fliedner, Wichern, and Bodelschwingh lived in a time of transition would be to locate them with most other Western spiritual writers. The Black Death, crusades, feudal warfare, economic upheaval, displacement of peoples—all these surrounded medieval and often other such figures. It is always interesting to ask what specific contextual questions surround figures. In the first half of the nineteenth century what today we call the Industrial Revolution was bringing its promise and threat, its contributions to new ways of living and its desolations.

As social reformers these pious folks rolled up their sleeves, got their hands dirty, took observation tours, got on the stump for sermons and off the stump for action, made and raised funds, always with an eye on the needs of people left behind, always with a voice for the fortunate ones who stayed ahead but could help others. Sermons, letters, the equivalents of today's Internet and e-mail communications, were carriers of their spiritual jottings and reasoned concerns. The Enlightenment that preceded them in culture and the Romantic movements that followed it and surrounded them are reflected here. Widespread transatlantic expressions of religious "awakening" or "revival" or "renewal" or "conversions" enriched their hopes and their repertory of options.

Not a few readers are likely to say, after encountering them and absorbing their contributions, that they have also enlarged ours.

MARTIN E. MARTY
Fairfax M. Cone Distinguished Service
Professor Emeritus at the
University of Chicago

Foreword

The purpose of this book is to acquaint the reader with the remarkable faith and work of four figures of the nineteenth-century Awakening in Germany: August Tholuck (1799–1877), Theodor Fliedner (1800–1864), Johann Hinrich Wichern (1808–1881), and Friedrich von Bodelschwingh (1831–1910).

The strategy we use is to let Tholuck, Fliedner, Wichern, and Bodelschwingh speak for themselves. Aside from our introductions to the four figures and our prefaces to their texts, the writings are theirs. Our intent is to let the reader experience their spirituality directly and thereby discover how they understood their faith and their commission to serve the world. Hence, the texts are chosen not primarily for their documentary or scholarly interest—although these factors play a role—but for their value in bringing to life the spirit of the authors and the vitality of their heritage. At the same time we want the selections to illuminate the tradition in which the figures stand and illustrate historical continuity despite differences of emphasis. In these sources one may also catch glimpses of wider developments in an era that was both tumultuous within Europe and, according to Kenneth Scott Latourette, "The Great Century" outside Europe because it witnessed significant missionary expansion.

Since each of our four representatives penned large amounts of material, the challenge was to choose those writings that would best serve our aims. We sought to produce balanced portraits by reviewing as much of their production as possible. We then selected diverse pieces they had written for a variety of audiences at a variety of times. We also chose from a variety of genres, such as reports, sermons, speeches, essays, and poetry. Another criterion was that the selections could be regarded as characteristic because they gained widespread fame as testified by their numerous editions or printings. From these varied materials, like a patchwork quilt, the spirituality of our figures emerges, not just their complexities, ambiguities, and ironies, but also the problems they faced, the principles they articulated, and the legacy we have inherited from them.

The origin of this book goes back many years. While not discounting the fact that both of us, born in widely separate areas, were raised in a significantly similar ethos influenced by the Awakening transplanted to America from Scandinavia, the first thoughts of this project derived from concurrent sabbaticals and a subsequent study tour for college and seminary students, when the two of us crisscrossed the territory in Germany bounded by Kaiserswerth, near Düsseldorf, and Bethel at Bielefeld. We knew of the venerable institutions at these places and began to pursue the story of their founders—Fliedner and Bodelschwingh, respectively—to complement our familiarity with the Inner Mission movement and its foremost proponent, Johann Hinrich Wichern, as well as our interest in the influential professor of theology, August Tholuck, who preceded them all.

Although we knew that these representatives of the Awakening were related to the spirituality of the Pietist tradition, we soon discovered that a considerable amount of research focused on the classical Pietist era of Spener, Francke, and Zinzendorf, while comparatively few studies continued the story with the Awakening in the nineteenth century. Consequently, individuals such as Tholuck, Fliedner, Wichern, and Bodelschwingh had received little attention, and when they did, they were rarely quoted directly.

Thus evolved our decision to help bring their fascinating lives, faith, and work to the attention of a broader audience. Though in their lifetimes these men were widely known in Germany and abroad, they are by no means household names even in Germany today, and outside of their country very few people have ever heard of them. One reason for this unfamiliarity is that few of their writings are available in translation. We are pleased that with this volume we are able to break new ground for the English-speaking world. If our work helps to create renewed interest in Tholuck, Fliedner, Wichern, and Bodelschwingh, if some readers are intrigued by the larger-than-life individuals we present, grapple with their challenging spirituality, begin to discover the impact of the Awakening on the life of church and society in the twenty-first century, and, like the figures in this volume, are struck by the massive, unresolved, urban-industrial problem of blighted lives, then we will be satisfied that our endeavor has more than met its goal.

The special pleasure of working together on this volume is that the two of us—one representing church history, the other German literature and culture—found a common interest and delight. Our specialized disciplines proved to possess their own merits, but, far from raising artificial barriers, enhanced their individual integrity as each of us supported, questioned, contradicted, yielded to, and in general, entered into dialogue with the other.

Among the many who encouraged and helped us along the way are colleagues at Gettysburg College, especially former provost Baird Tipson, and Gettysburg Lutheran Seminary, especially former president Herman G. Stuempfle Jr., as well as Sara Mummert, who assisted us in obtaining materials, and Kim Breighner, who provided technical support. The Fliedner Archive in Kaiserswerth, Germany, offered invaluable assistance with its materials. We are deeply grateful to Bernard McGinn, editor of this distinguished series, for his support and direction. Finally, we thank Martin E. Marty, not only because he has written the Preface for this volume but also because he brings us back to the beginning, when some long years ago he inspired consideration of Johann Hinrich Wichern.

Notes on the Translations:

All the selections are fresh translations and with few exceptions appear in English for the first time. We have retained the authors' use of **bold** for emphasis and have included their occasional footnotes, citing their authorship in our endnotes. We have also retained the authors' use of parentheses around their biblical references. For ease of reading we have inserted our own additional biblical references in brackets rather than in endnotes.

General Introduction

SPIRITUALITY AND AWAKENING

For individual Christians, spirituality and the experience of awakening have shared an intimate relationship since the early church, but the common ground for Friedrich August Gottreu Tholuck, Theodor Fliedner, Johann Hinrich Wichern, and Friedrich von Bodelschwingh is the Awakening, a movement whose diverse but related expressions of spiritual renewal coursed through Germany during the nineteenth century. By spirituality we mean one's attitude toward and sense of connectedness with the world that arise from one's religious faith and are shaped by one's religious tradition. Spirituality also involves the complex of practices both formal and informal, corporate and individual, by which one nurtures and manifests this attitude that reflects the essential character of one's life—practices that relate not only to the inward journey, but also to outward social and interpersonal relations. The heart of a specifically Christian spirituality is a person's awakening to faith and the restoration of a broken relationship with a loving God, who calls us to show this love toward our neighbor. To borrow a phrase from Tholuck's foundational exposition of Awakened spirituality, awakening is the "lesson learned about sin and the reconciler."[1]

The primary passages in the New Testament that employ forms of the verb *to awaken* suggest the metaphor of awakening from sleep and can imply resurrection, arising from the dead. The first, Romans 13:11, summons the reader to awake from sin since dawn is near and salvation is at hand, and also to watch, since this is a necessity throughout the Christian life. The second, Ephesians

5

5:14, quotes a passage of unknown origin (perhaps an early Christian hymn) that contrasts dark and light, death and life. The mandate here is to walk in the light and avoid works of darkness, suggesting illumination as well as awakening from sin.[2]

Throughout the centuries various individuals have used *awakening* to describe an experience of renewal, but only in modern times has the term been applied to an entire movement. Forms of the German word for "awakening," *Erweckung*, as something more than an individual experience, first appeared around 1750 in the writings of the Pietists and Moravians.[3] Gerhard Tersteegen (1697–1769), one of the most important hymn-writers of Pietism, lamented the frequent complaints "among called and awakened souls."[4] The strident Swabian Pietist Immanuel Gottlob Brastberger urges that Christians, in their daily struggle against the devil, "ought to be awakened" by tearing themselves away from the world.[5] Some later Protestant theologians designated awakening as the first step in the "order of salvation," followed by conversion and sanctification.

Awakening as applied to a movement has served the scholarly world as a convenient term since about 1800, and despite its infrequent use by the representatives who appear in this volume, the term helps identify them. In the most general sense it embraces those manifestations of revival in the eighteenth century called the Great Awakening in North America and the Evangelical Revival in Britain, and in the nineteenth century the *Reveil* (Awakening) in Switzerland, France, and the Netherlands, and the *Erweckungsbewegung* (Awakening movement) in Germany and Scandinavia. In this volume we use the term to denote the specific manifestation in nineteenth-century Germany of the broader movement that should be read, in Martin Marty's judgment, "as the Protestant version of an alternate to the old Catholic Christendom" of the Latin Middle Ages when the church took an active hand in the direction of society. For this reason Marty wonders whether without an understanding of the movement we can comprehend how Protestant churches could have survived to face the crises of the twentieth century.[6]

Yet despite a growing number of individual monographs no adequate general history of the German Awakening has yet appeared.

Some of the best work comes from chapters appended to histories of the Pietist movement that preceded it. Much of this work also assumes that the Awakening reached its peak around 1830 and waned after the Revolution of 1848, when Wichern gave his famous speeches at Wittenberg. From the material gathered here a different picture emerges, not only of a movement that continues throughout the whole century, but of one that finds a common denominator in the drive to add a definitive expression of social action to an awakened spirituality, best illustrated by the frequently used phrase "faith active in love."

The centrality of this theme, especially in response to desperate human needs brought about by the Industrial Revolution, does not exclude concurrent emphases on new beginnings, personal engagement with the Bible, and similar experiences, but it has not received sufficient attention in the literature thus far. "Faith active in love" confronts us at every turn in the sources we present, from Tholuck's stress on mission, to Fliedner's diaconate, to Wichern's comprehensive design for an Inner Mission, and to Bodelschwingh's caring institutions at Bethel. Consequently, if readers find more historical context here than they might have expected in a volume dedicated to spirituality, it is because these Awakened leaders chose to employ their reflection on the Christian gospel in service to a specific world at a specific time.

PIETISM

The specific religious world into which the Awakening arrived was deeply influenced by Pietism, the great movement of renewal that flourished in the eighteenth century. Pietism, however, remains a problem in modern research on two fronts: the origin of the movement itself and its precise relation to the Awakening. Some, such as Albrecht Ritschl, whose evaluation was not entirely neutral, traced the origins of Pietism to late medieval, especially Franciscan, mysticism. In his view Pietism represents a kind of this-worldly asceticism, a Protestant alternative to Catholic monasticism.[7] Other more recent scholars believe that in its classical form Pietism was a non-separatist, churchly, and reforming movement with roots in the sixteenth-century Reformation, especially regarding the priesthood of all believers. F. Ernest Stoeffler represents a growing consensus when he offers this broad definition: the movement goes back to Martin Bucer's mediating theology between Luther and Calvin; it manifested itself first in English Puritanism and the Dutch Reformed and appeared in Lutheranism through Philipp Jakob Spener (1635–1705) and August Hermann Francke (1663–1727); it was radicalized by such figures as Gottfried Arnold (1666–1714), romanticized by Johann Heinrich Jung-Stilling (1740–1817) and Johann Caspar Lavater (1741–1801), and appropriated by Moravians, Church of the Brethren, Swedish Mission Friends, Wesleyan Methodists, and the Evangelical Awakening in North America.[8]

Highly popular and edifying works nourished the development of Pietism on the continent, in Scandinavia, and in England. One of the earliest and most enduring was *On True Christianity* (1605) by Johann Arndt (1555–1621). Even in today's world of mass marketing its record of fifty editions in the first seventy years is astounding. At the heart of Arndt's argument is this principle: "The proof that one is a true Christian does not consist in knowing and hearing God's Word, but in doing it."[9] Arndt's contemporary in the Netherlands, the theologian Wilhelm Amesius (1576–1633), struck a similar chord in 1629 with his *Medulla Sacrae Theologiae (The Marrow of Sacred Theology)*, a book that was widely used in the education of theological students. It begins with the sentence "Theologia est doctrina Deo vivendi," which expresses a concept basic to all he had to say: Theology deals primarily not with assertions about God, but with the knowledge of how to live for him.[10]

This concern about how to live the faith turned attention away from dogmatic theology and toward personal experience, for if a demonstration of one's rebirth lies in how one lives, then experience—one's own as well as that of others—takes on great instructive value. An excellent example of this pedagogical temper was *The Practice of Pietie* by Lewis Bayly (1565–1631), published in England in 1610. For seventy years this Puritan volume was probably the most widely read edifying book in the English language, to say nothing of its many translations.[11] Another example is Heinrich Müller's

Heavenly Kiss of Love, or the Practice of True Christianity Flowing from the Experience of Divine Love (1659).[12] This Baroque-style title is illustrative of many works that reflect the persistent interest in the practice of piety and illustrate the emphasis on experiencing God with the heart and feelings rather than with the intellect. The presence of these works in the libraries of the Awakened in the nineteenth century testifies to their long-lasting influence.

The focus on how to live, a faith fueled by the inward gaze, and the Baroque theme that this world is a vale of tears gave credence to the stereotype that Pietists were drab, legalistic individuals who defined Christianity in moralistic prohibitions. This evaluation appears in a German conversation encyclopedia of 1817:

> The essential peculiarities that the Pietists retained as the product of their more than twenty-year struggle with the Orthodox were: a strict, almost gloomy morality which rejects dancing, games, and other traditional forms of entertainment as the devil's workshop; the belief that rebirth into a holy life comes from a sudden breakthrough of grace; high estimation of the usefulness of every devotional practice, for which the initiated, mostly common people, gathered in private homes; and a mistrust of those who thought differently.[13]

In general, however, Pietism was neither life-denying nor turned in on itself, but vitally involved in the world, influencing politics, economics, the arts, language, and, above all, education.[14] In Prussia, Pietist schools were by far the most advanced educational institutions. Far-flung missionary activity gave Pietism an international dimension, and because of the focus on issues other than dogma and confessional differences, the movement acquired an ecumenical outlook. Pietism's vitality came in part from being in harmony with the needs of the times. In Stoeffler's view,

> It was a day of practical concern, of horizons expanding in all directions, and Pietism had caught the spirit of the new day. It was venturesome, relatively unfettered by the past,

oriented toward life's vital concerns, and vibrant with spiritual and emotional dynamic. The result was that it helped to deal the deathblow to the old orthodoxy and to give a new complexion to Lutheran faith and piety.[15]

Characteristic of the Pietists was their emphasis on three principles: the fruits of faith rather than disputes about dogma; rebirth as the event upon which a fruitful faith is contingent; and sanctification as the effect of living the faith. Underlying these emphases was the preeminence of the Bible in directing one's spiritual life. Although Christianity had often espoused one or more of these principles, they combined to become a focus of faith and life, and acquired the identity of a movement—detractors labeled it Pietism—during the late seventeenth and early eighteenth centuries.[16] The most significant stimuli were the powerful writings and exemplary work of Philipp Jakob Spener, recognized as the founder of Lutheran Pietism, and August Hermann Francke, who created an influential center of the movement in Halle.

Those who desired to pursue the practice of piety did not always find conducive structures within the church, so they employed a method introduced by Spener: devotional meetings known as *Collegia pietatis* held regularly for the purpose of mutual inspiration, teaching, and guidance. For the most part the goal was to achieve renewal within rather than in competition with the established church. Like-minded Christians gathered in homes to pray, share personal experiences, and study the Bible along with other edifying works. The small size of the groups encouraged every individual to participate but also had a wider effect: it allowed the laity to have a greater voice than before, and thus gave concrete expression to Pietism's belief in the priesthood of all believers. These circles, or *conventicles*, spread widely and served as a seedbed for the Awakening as well as a bulwark against the Enlightenment.

ENLIGHTENMENT

Even as Pietism was at its peak another movement—one that related to the German Awakening in a very different manner—was in its ascendancy. This was the Enlightenment *(Aufklärung)*, which flourished in Germany from approximately 1730 to 1780. One herald of the dramatic change in the intellectual climate, Christian Wolff (1679–1754), taught at the very university where the Pietist leader Francke exerted widespread influence by turning dry theological learning into devout study of the Bible and practical Christianity. Wolff went a step further. In applying and popularizing the thought of Gottfried Wilhelm Leibniz (1646–1716), he separated the study of philosophy from theology so that philosophy could be pursued on the basis of reason. It is no coincidence that Halle, founded in 1694, was the first German university at which academic freedom became the norm.

The combined influence of French Rationalism, English Empiricism, and German Idealism, led by Leibniz's gradually permeating philosophy, stimulated the new approach, which encouraged the application of rational inquiry to all fields of human endeavor. Early support for this approach and the allied focus on the temporal world came from the rapidly expanding realm of the natural sciences, where experimentation, observation, and logical thought were rewarded with one astonishing success after another. One symbol of this confidence was Edmond Halley's (1656–1742) accurate calculation of the return of the comet that now bears his name. Achievements such as this, together with a renewed confidence in the power of reason and the senses, proved invigorating and fostered a spirit of optimism, while the dispassionate nature of scientific inquiry contributed to a temper of tolerance.

The new excitement over science also became a most important source of skepticism, and neither the Bible nor Christianity was immune from the new spirit of inquiry. The results, if not devastating, were unprecedented. Leading the list of the emerging threats to the church in the early nineteenth century were de-Christianization and de-confessionalization, both prompted in large measure by skeptical Rationalism.[17] This, and not the Enlightenment as a comprehensive scientific and cultural phenomenon, was the issue. Even so, belief in the rationality of the universe and in the power of reason to comprehend it did not necessarily lead individuals to dismiss or oppose

Christianity. Nevertheless, already in the eighteenth century prominent voices such as David Hume (1711–66) cast doubt on the existence of God and on other traditional doctrines.

Nothing, however, could compare with the sensation caused by David Friedrich Strauss (1808–74) and his controversial book *The Life of Jesus* (1835). Ironically, it was written in Württemberg, a province known for its tenacious groups of Pietists, but it threw down a challenge: submit the Bible to the historical-critical method like other books. Ludwig Feuerbach (1804–72) applied this "higher criticism" in *The Essence of Christianity* (1841) to prove that God is the projection of human self-consciousness, and Karl Marx in *Das Kapital* (volume 1, 1867) took Feuerbach a step further by claiming that religion is a societal delusion, an opiate of the people.

Further signs of the disturbing changes taking place were a series of religious conversions in reverse by such luminaries as Strauss himself[18] and the young Friedrich Engels (1820–95) who, as a devout confirmand, had addressed a poem to his friend, Jesus:

> O come with all your blessedness,
> Arrayed in God's own gloriousness,
> And help me choose you only!
> Lovely, splendid, unregretted
> Is the joy when our voice raises
> Up to you, our Savior, praises!
>
> You came to bring release to people,
> to set them free from death and evil,
> to save and bring your happiness.
> When again you come from heaven,
> you'll cause on earth a transformation,
> for each will get his share, no less.[19]

At age eighteen, however, he issued a kind of personal declaration of independence in his "Letters from Wuppertal," another hotbed of Pietism, under the pen name Friedrich Ostwald. These contain a ringing attack on the Pietists because of their world-negating mysticism and hypocritical condemnation of any who lacked their brand of piety.

According to a contemporary church historian, Philip Schaff, who later emigrated to America, the storm caused by Strauss's *Life of Jesus* divided Protestants into two camps, the "critical" and the "evangelical." The former tended to join Strauss and reject Christianity's claim of supernaturalism. The latter showed a cautious acceptance of the new historical method and supported a "Mediating Theology" *(Vermittlungstheologie)* between traditional Christian beliefs and the new intellectual currents.[20] Among these theologians was August Neander (1789–1850), Schaff's own mentor and a church historian who had converted from Judaism, inspired by the highly influential theology of Friedrich Schleiermacher (1768–1834).[21]

Even the proponents of Mediating Theology, however, saw the attempt to dismiss traditional Christianity by those they labeled Rationalists as an attack from the outside. Moreover, the perception that the outcome of the struggle would be a turning point in history imbued Awakened spirituality with a sense of urgency. Thus, in view of its strong reaction to Rationalism, the Awakening can be seen in part as a rallying cry of the faithful to arouse the spirit and energy necessary to combat the powerful new foe, stem the tide of apostasy, and "re-Christianize" society.

Yet, to say that the Awakening was simply a reaction to the Enlightenment is to overemphasize the negative and define the movement only in relation to its opponents.[22] This approach misses the Awakening's more positive features and the ones most often used by its advocates to define themselves, such as its fresh reading of the Bible and history—both viewed as a revelation of God—and its works of mercy and mission to society. In addition, the Awakened were not as far removed from the Enlightenment as many believed. In their skepticism of traditional church structures, as well as in their organization of new initiatives, they shared a spirit of rational inquiry that does not simply accept the status quo. Like the leaders of the Enlightenment, the Awakened desired liberation from strictures of the past and were optimistic about what could be achieved. Both camps espoused more individual autonomy, more personal responsibility, and a greater sense of individual worth. The ecumenical spirit of the Awakening was also related, if only indirectly, to the scientific method's dispassionate and unified view of the world, and the Awakening's emphasis on the practice of faith and on the importance of experience corresponds to the Enlightenment's delight in empirical proof. In the main, however, the Awakened were too preoccupied with their opposition to the new intellectual spirit to contemplate what they might have held in common with their antagonists.

GERMANY AND THE FRENCH REVOLUTION

Since the Awakened regarded the Enlightenment as their nemesis, they also opposed its momentous political expression, the French Revolution of 1789. They resisted not because they disapproved of its ideals, for they too could see the virtue of liberty and equality, but because they regarded the moral and spiritual decay brought about by the Rationalists as the underlying cause of the Revolution. After all, Rationalism had come from France, and the Awakened found it distasteful to envision the model of the French Revolution in the political landscape east of the Rhine.

On the one hand, the Revolution, as well as the following War of Liberation from Napoleon (1813–15), inspired many Germans to hope for an end to autocratic power. The Wartburg demonstration in 1817, the gathering of twenty to thirty thousand Germans at the Hambach Castle in 1832, and the abortive Revolution of 1848 all testified to a liberal presence in the land. Yet the Awakened were only part of a larger populace not inclined to emulate the French example for a variety of reasons. Many Germans assumed they were better off than the French to begin with. In addition, their political concerns differed from those of the French. Unlike pre-revolutionary France, Germany lacked a unified, broad base of citizens—whether agrarian, proletarian, or burghers—who could advocate change and mobilize wide support. Another issue was how to coerce change, not from one seat of power, as in Paris, but from two competing centers, one in

Vienna and one in Berlin. However, the overarching political challenge throughout most of the nineteenth century was how to create a unified German nation out of thirty-nine separate and independent political units.

A further development that reduced the allure of revolution came from Berlin. While fundamental constitutional change in Germany was often thwarted, enlightened civil servants such as the astute statesman Karl Reichsfreiherr vom und zum Stein (1757–1831) introduced forward-looking, liberalizing political, economic, and social reforms in Prussia as early as 1806. These changes were not the result of pressure from the masses but were an incremental revolution "from the top down." Later in the century Bismarck also instituted reforms, hoping to defuse the liberal opposition by supporting certain grievances of the industrial workers. Bismarck often said that Germany needed a certain amount of "state socialism," which amounted, in his words, to "practical Christianity."[23]

In this atmosphere the Awakened were hardly sympathetic to revolution. Nor were they outsiders, but members of a church that served as an official arm of an individual realm. Berlin, the seat of Prussian authority, was predominantly Protestant, and the monarchs of the time—Friedrich Wilhelm III (1797–1840), Friedrich Wilhelm IV (1840–61), and Wilhelm I (1861–88)—were pious Lutherans. In fact, Friedrich Wilhelm IV, who exhibited a mixture of politics and Pietism, stressed that his office was of divine origin and, borrowing a biblical verse, declared, "I and my house—we wish to serve the Lord."[24] As a result of longtime cooperation with the monarchy, the advantages derived from ecclesial appointments, and shared values between an educated clergy and the aristocracy, the church was predisposed to participate in an alliance of "throne and altar."

Finally, Tholuck, Fliedner, Wichern, and Bodelschwingh were all born into devout Lutheran families in which they inherited the view that God had ordained the estates of family, church, and state. Thus, given the general political environment, the relationship of church to state in Prussia, and their personal backgrounds, the four figures in this volume rejected strident calls for radical change and supported monarchy and state. This perspective naturally influenced the way they put their faith into action.

AWAKENED CIRCLES

By the turn of the century in Germany a remarkable number of intellectual currents flowed together.

> In the two decades before and the two after 1800, Germany may have witnessed more changes in every sphere, may have borne more high drama and known more creative personalities and ideas than in any comparable interval: Kant's critical revolution, the audacious philosophies of the Idealists, the rainbow of writers and literary schools, *Sturm und Drang, Klassik,* Romanticism, the French Revolution, Goethe, Napoleon, the War of Liberation.[25]

Hidden within this creative ferment was a latent resource out of which would emerge the Awakening: the pious circles that met for Bible study, devotions, earnest conversation, and mutual support. Some of these were new and others, as we saw earlier, were still alive from the days of Pietism. They are the first public manifestations of the movement, but their precise role brings us to a second major question of modern research: the relationship between Pietism and Awakening. Some scholars deny any close connection because of the disruptions of the Enlightenment and argue that the Awakening arose *sui generis.*[26] Still others find that the transition from one to the other took place without a significant break.[27] Recent scholars see elements of truth in both views. They emphasize that each movement exhibits its own personality but also stress the important bridges between Pietism and Awakening, especially the preparatory role of the circles.[28]

Although conventicles had formed an integral part of the Pietist experience, a new tendency toward consolidation and cooperative action took place in Basel, where Johann August Urlsperger formed the German Society for Christianity *(Deutsche Christentumsgesellschaft)* in 1780.[29] The Basel Tract Society followed in 1803, the

Basel Bible Society in 1804, and the Basel Mission in 1815. Their publications and ministry at home and abroad brought them international fame and inaugurated the nineteenth century as a century of mission. The fact that Christian Krafft (1787–1845), a Reformed minister, and Karl von Raumer (1783–1865), a layman, emerged as prominent leaders alerts us to several significant features of the early Awakening: the role of laity, the openness to ecumenical cooperation, and the importance of the established churches, rather than the free churches, as the centers where the movement first took root.[30]

Basel is only one center of the lively circles leading to the Awakening. The movement manifested itself in a variety of ways and in a variety of regions with the nature of each circle depending on the religious character of its locale. Three regions are especially significant for our story: Wuppertal in the northwest, Württemberg in the southwest, and Prussia (including Pomerania, Silesia, and Berlin) in the northeast.

The arrival of the fervent preacher Gottfried Daniel Krummacher (1774–1837) in Elberfeld in 1816 marks the beginning of the Awakening in Wuppertal, although the continuing presence of the Quiet in the Land *(Die Stillen im Lande)* indicates how beginnings often meld with continuities. In Kaiserswerth, not far from Elberfeld, another young pastor with a pious background, Theodor Fliedner, brought his ministry to a tiny, struggling congregation in January 1822. Friedrich Wilhelm Krummacher (1796–1868) joined his uncle Gottfried Daniel in Elberfeld in 1834 and quickly gained fame as a fiery preacher. His published sermons were much in demand, an admirer observed, as far away as "the log cabins" of frontier America. Krummacher became a favorite of the crown prince, who appointed him court preacher in Potsdam,[31] but he garnered a different response from the young Friedrich Engels, who gave this unflattering description in his "Letters from Wuppertal":

> Then he runs around in all directions in the pulpit, leans over the sides, pounds on them, stomps like a steed in battle, shouting at the same time so that the windows rattle and people in the street wince....Krummacher's mighty voice sounds forth through all the weeping as he

paints before the entire gathering innumerable diabolical scenes of damnation.[32]

Nevertheless, both the Krummachers and their famous critic testify to a lively style of piety in a traditionally "quietist" region.

Württemberg, where piety was "by instinct and tradition warm, intense, and emotional," served as a temporary but formative home for Philip Schaff as well as utopian groups such as the Harmony Society.[33] A half-generation later in the same region Bad Boll became a mission center headed by the Blumhardts, whose convictions, not far removed from Schaff's, grew into a vision close to that of Wichern's. Johann Christoph Blumhardt (1805–80) and his son Christoph Friedrich (1842–1919) stressed the visible realization of the kingdom of God and the liberation of humanity from undeserved suffering.[34]

Few circles, however, had as much influence as the Kottwitz circle in Berlin. Baron Hans Ernst von Kottwitz, known for his genial personality and incisive mind as well as for his connections in high places, emerged as leader of the Berlin Awakening between 1816 and 1819.[35] No one could ask for a better portrait of Kottwitz, who became a paternal figure for the young, restless searchers around him, than the one drawn by Tholuck in *The Lesson Learned About Sin and the Reconciler.* He describes Kottwitz as the gentle, insightful, and inspiring "Father Abraham" who declares: "A great day of resurrection is dawning. Hundreds of young people are being awakened everywhere by the Spirit of God."[36]

The baron's elevated social position was also decisive. Yet, although he put aspiring students of little means, such as Tholuck and Wichern, in touch with the aristocracy, Kottwitz remained aware of the lower classes and their needs. A native of Silesia, Kottwitz had observed the social problems created there by the early industrial age and made more intractable by the French occupation. In 1807 he founded a work program in Berlin and later added a boarding house, hospital, and school. As many as nine hundred persons were at one time or another affiliated with the program. He also took an interest in the child-labor problem and in the founding of public schools.[37]

In his concern for society the old baron was ahead of other aristocrats as well as many of his young followers. Yet, unlike Wichern, who later championed organized works of mercy, he advocated withdrawal as the means of renewal. He may have derived this apparently paradoxical attitude from a Quaker friend, Carl Heinrich Albinus (1754–1823), one-time war minister in Berlin, whose grave, according to Tholuck's moving description, Kottwitz took his students to visit.[38]

A Pietistic Club, as some called it, gathered on Sundays and Wednesdays at the baron's, Thursdays at Tholuck's, and Saturdays at Neander's. The group read scripture and other edifying works, discussed their interpretations, and sang hymns. Tholuck said he experienced "the definite consciousness that Christ had come alive in the same way in everyone who was present." Another participant, Ludwig von Gerlach, offered this description:

> We concentrated extremely hard on the Christian faith and Christian life as we saw it in the Awakened of that time and in the Community of the Brethren—or as some now say "Pietists"—so that repentance, a living, heartfelt faith, brotherly love, a duty to profess one's faith, a loving, evangelizing, intentional drive to win people over, and a deep moral earnestness…came to the fore, while in contrast, dogmatic specificity…receded into the background.[39]

Eventually the Kottwitz circle established a wide network of contacts besides Tholuck, Wichern, and von Gerlach. This included several future leaders such as Moritz August Bethmann-Hollweg, Ernst Wilhelm Hengstenberg, and Richard Rothe. Philip Schaff, who came by way of Württemberg and met Kottwitz through Tholuck, assimilated the evangelical emphasis of the Awakening he witnessed here and the sacramental emphasis of Prussian High Orthodoxy, in which a newly invigorated Lutheran confessionalism joined an ecumenical outlook. These two strands Schaff worked into the Mercersburg Theology he espoused in North America.[40] Thus, although critics abounded, Kottwitz and his circle left an indelible mark on an entire generation and on both sides of the Atlantic.

LIBERATION, INDUSTRIALISM, AND THE REVOLUTION OF 1848

For all its regional variations, the Awakening emerged almost everywhere in Germany at the same time. The primary reason is the German War of Liberation against Napoleon (1813–17). The disasters that culminated in the humiliating defeat of the Prussian army at Jena in October 1806 and the triumphant entrance of Napoleon into Berlin prompted a religious revival—combining Christian, patriotic, and Romantic elements—in which the seeds of Awakening began to grow.[41]

The influence of these interrelated elements can be seen in Baron von Stein's reform program during the French occupation.[42] This effort tapped into the popular belief that the war represented a struggle against the powers of darkness and that the demise of Napoleon promised God's new day for Germany.[43] Another sign was the activity of Friedrich Ludwig Jahn. Convinced that physical fitness and democracy went hand in hand, he introduced the *Turnverein* in 1810 to stir patriotic sympathies along with physical exercises. His movement became so popular that his followers, including a large contingent in the United States, referred to him as "Father" Jahn.[44] In the same year the poet-patriots Adam Müller and Achim von Arnim founded the Christian German Round Table Society *(Christlich-deutsche Tischgesellschaft)* in Berlin.[45] The society's rejection of Rationalism and the French Revolution is reflected in Müller's blunt appraisal of the situation in Germany.

> I see in the general fanaticism for the illusion of an absolute state, an absolute law, and an absolute Reason nothing but a groping and grasping by an unhappy humanity for a personal God from whom it has fallen away.[46]

GENERAL INTRODUCTION

The decisive German victory at Leipzig in October 1813 and the national celebrations culminating in the Wartburg Festival of 1817 seemed a vindication of these feelings, even though a number of years would pass before a widespread awareness of national identity would unite the separate German states.

The movement known as Romanticism contributed significantly to these sentiments. In part a reaction against the Enlightenment, which had affirmed the authority of reason and held out the possibility that people could live harmoniously "in the best of all possible worlds," Romantics preferred the self-expression of the individual consciousness and emphasized respect for the past and the value of belonging to a distinct culture.[47] These were manifest, for example, in the vocal and orchestral music of Beethoven; in the *Sturm und Drang* works of Goethe and Schiller, who celebrated individual freedom, political idealism, and the importance of sensibility; in the Grimm brothers, who collected folktales and compiled a massive German dictionary; and in a renewed interest in the Reformation as a German event.

The Wartburg Festival in 1817 celebrated the 300th anniversary of this event and prompted reflection about the future of the Evangelical Church, particularly the relative merits of the Lutheran *Confessions* and the need for ecumenical cooperation or even church unity.[48] At the center of this debate was the most bitterly opposed of the Prussian reforms, the unification of Lutheran and Reformed churches. Reactions to the imposition of the Prussian Union and Liturgy (*Agenda*) by Friedrich Wilhelm III, also in 1817, covered a wide spectrum but most had in common a reevaluation of Lutheranism in a new Germany. In Prussia, Pomerania, and Silesia a revived interest in Luther was combined with nationalism and Idealism in men such as Wichern and Bodelschwingh, who attacked the union's supposed Rationalist, anti-confessional theology, while Bavaria and Franconia witnessed a turn toward churchly piety, a development that became known as New Lutheranism and is best exemplified by Wilhelm Löhe. In Saxony, the home of Luther, Claus Harms issued a new version of the 95 Theses as a call to return to Lutheran fundamentals. The Prussian Union also drove a dissident group into exile in North America and eventually to the creation of the Lutheran Church—Missouri Synod. Thus, besides the issues of nationalism and Romanticism, the Awakened in this period, including the figures in this volume, most urgently had to face the issue of Lutheran identity.

Yet, of all the conditions that "awoke" the evangelical movement, none had greater impact than the Industrial Revolution and the resulting need to win over the rapidly expanding masses of urban laborers who, though ostensibly members of the church, no longer identified with it. One key development in Germany's economic growth following the War of Liberation was the inauguration in 1834 of a German Customs Union *(Zollverein)* that created a free trade zone among eighteen of Germany's independent states. Less dramatic, but perhaps more important, was Prussia's acquisition of the Ruhr District with its extensive coalfields and huge potential to become an industrial giant.

The human cost of the new industrialism, which struck many Awakened Christians with great force, leading them to compassion for the dislocated and impoverished, was the result of interrelated developments. Enormous growth in population accompanied a shift away from an agrarian society not only in Germany but also throughout Europe. From 1815 to 1850 the German population increased almost 40 percent, from 24,800,000 to 34,400,000.[49] At the same time, expanding industries drew increasing numbers of people to urban areas. Between 1800 and 1850 Hamburg, the site of Wichern's early work, grew by 32 percent, from 130,000 to 171,000. In the same years Munich almost tripled—from 40,500 to 110,000—and Dortmund, in the heart of the Ruhr industrial region, exploded from 4,000 to 22,100.[50] Furthermore, the transformation accelerated at a rapid pace; what took 150 years in England was achieved in Germany in barely one-third the time.[51]

The resulting surplus of workers in urban areas combined with the profit motive and the factory system led to miserable conditions: long, strenuous working hours, low wages, the necessity for women and children to work, no help in case of sickness or injury, no security in old age, and squalid living conditions. One indication of the harshness of life is that the first child-labor law in Germany, not enacted in Prussia until 1839, prohibited employment of children under nine years of age and limited work for those under sixteen to ten hours a day. As a result of all these difficult circumstances families deteriorated, the number of orphans multiplied, and prostitution increased. For the church this meant that urban parishes grew to enormous size. Tholuck recalled the dilemma of a Hamburg pastor who asked how he could minister to 30,000 members. The University of Leipzig replied that Jonah succeeded in tending a flock of 120,000 at Nineveh.[52]

In sum, industrialism reoriented civil society, redefined social relations, and effected new habits of thought, especially by exporting the crisis of religion to the proletariat. The agrarian world of the eighteenth century in which Pietism had flourished was no more. In its place nineteenth-century industry brought accelerating socioeconomic change accompanied by new and escalating human needs—a most auspicious time for a new birth of faith active in love.

These socioeconomic developments added to liberal pressures for reform and set the stage for dramatic events in the year 1848. Rumblings first heard during the War of Liberation heralded the storm ahead. The intervening struggle had unleashed several liberal demands—freedom of trade, freedom of speech and religion, and equal status before the law—that appealed most to professionals, tradesmen, and merchants but were yet unfulfilled. To exacerbate the situation, Prussia and Austria had responded by imposing censorship and restricting the right to assembly.

Hopes for fundamental change first appeared in 1848 beyond the borders of Germany. At the end of February an insurrection in Paris brought down the monarchy and quickly spread to other capitals. On March 13 Vienna rose and drove out Prince Metternich, Prussia's great rival. On March 18, less than a week later, the revolution reached Berlin, and to the dismay of King Friedrich Wilhelm IV it broke out under his window. He reacted, according to William Shanahan, as if Adam had fallen a second time.[53] Although the king issued a proclamation "To my beloved Berliners," he could not stem the tide, at least not immediately.[54] Among the consequences was the departure of Ernst von Bodelschwingh, Friedrich's father and minister of the interior since 1845. The elder Bodelschwingh was an advocate of Baron von Stein's reform program and an admirer of Fliedner's institutions at Kaiserswerth.[55] His exit from office probably intensified the fears of the younger Bodelschwingh and Wichern, who visited the Bodelschwingh home as a student, that order and stability were on the verge of collapse.

For all the turmoil it created, the abortive Revolution of 1848 led not to a new government but to an equally futile constitutional convention in Frankfurt in March. The old order was restored as early as November, prompting the historian G. M. Trevelyan to remark that 1848 was "the turning point at which modern history failed to turn."[56] Nevertheless, the events of that year left a deep impression on the church. Many saw the revolution as a threat to divinely established order. Wichern acknowledged these concerns, but he also saw opportunity. Events had proved that the church desperately needed a ministry to the whole of society that was more than piecemeal and that adopted a notable liberal principle, the right of free association, in order to elevate the new ministry above traditional church structures. Combining these two elements—the need and the associative principle—Wichern's dramatic speeches at the Wittenberg *Kirchentag* (church conference) in October provided a vision for Inner Mission. Anxiety over the revolution provided an attentive audience.

AFTER WITTENBERG

Historians of an earlier generation tended to end the story of the German Awakening in 1848, believing that Wichern's appearance at Wittenberg was the climactic event of both his career and the movement. Evidence from the sources in this volume, while enhancing the significance of the Wittenberg speeches, also suggest that the Awakening flourished throughout the nineteenth century and into the first years of the twentieth. In Sidney Ahlstrom's judgment, the Awakening began a process of recovery which was sustained during the entire century, until it finally joined with the so-called neo-Orthodox impulse of the early twentieth century.[57]

If this continuity prevails in the realm of theology, it is even more apparent when we consider social action as a leading characteristic of Awakened spirituality.

Naturally the movement was confronted with new circumstances such as the ever more intense challenge of Rationalism. The earlier threat posed by Strauss's *Life of Jesus* paled in comparison to the message of Friedrich Nietzsche's madman who storms into the marketplace crying "God is dead! We have killed him, you and I."[58] Similarly, Darwin's theory of evolution in *The Origin of the Species* (1859) proved equally unsettling and in an earlier form provoked some acerbic comments from Fliedner. Paradoxically, the missionary enterprise inspired by the Awakening was beginning to pay rich dividends outside Europe, leading to a "great century" of Christian expansion.[59]

The church itself posed another challenge. Many pastors did not get involved in the socioeconomic changes taking place around them, and their lack of involvement did nothing to cause the growing number of urban laborers to regard the church as relevant to their plight.[60] The working class, as some have observed, was not atheistic; it was alienated. One estimate indicates that outside the regions where the Awakening flourished, as few as 3 percent attended church on a regular basis, while others swelled the ranks of those who practiced a new habit: attendance only for baptisms, confirmations, and weddings.[61]

At the same time we cannot overlook those who attempted to identify with the cause of the poor and achieve some measure of social justice by entering politics. Friedrich Naumann (1860–1919), who once worked at the Rough House *(Das Rauhe Haus)*, Wichern's home for boys near Hamburg, looked beyond the paternalistic model of the Inner Mission to change conditions from below and campaigned for election to the Weimar Assembly. Still another Wichern associate, Adolf Christian Stoecker (1835–1909), had worked in the Berlin City Mission. Convinced that social and political reform must offer more than the Inner Mission's emphasis on charitable aid to the individual, Stoecker left the ministry to found the Christian Socialist Workers' Party in 1878.[62] Later in the century Theodor von Wächter (1865–1943), a theological student raised in the Pietism of Württemberg, joined the Social Democratic Party, Stoecker's hated rival. When Wächter stood for election in 1893 on the grounds that a Christian and a Social Democrat were compatible, his Consistory denied him candidacy as a pastor.[63] Wichern himself never went so far as to enter politics, but Bodelschwingh did. The beloved "father" of Bethel bei Bielefeld, not far from the centers of burgeoning industry, gained a seat in the Prussian Diet in 1903.

During all this time the charitable institutions associated with the Awakening, rather than engage directly in politics, continued to expand their programs and hone their skills in ameliorating the ills of the day. The success of the *Kirchentag*, which met in different cities after Wittenberg in 1848, derived from its nature as a voluntary gathering apart from the state churches. Wichern and the Central Committee of the Inner Mission held regular Congresses—thirty-one by 1901—to further the cause of help and healing through nurseries, homes, asylums, Sunday Schools, and the like.[64] Bodelschwingh's Bethel offered still another model: a single institution with substantial resources concentrated in a limited area, and one that could retain considerable flexibility when confronted with the vagaries of the twentieth century.

AWAKENED FAITH

The German Awakening did not give the world a defining personality who might have guaranteed it a wider audience. Nor did any one theologian emerge as its singular voice. Tholuck comes closest, and Karl Barth, the great theologian of the early twentieth century, gives him high praise as an evangelical alternative to Schleiermacher, although Barth remains ambivalent about Tholuck's emphasis on experience as a category of the Spirit's revelation.[65] Thus, rather than extracting a systematic theology from a single theologian, we must consolidate a few key principles from the recurring themes within the works of our four figures.

Tholuck, Fliedner, Wichern, and Bodelschwingh, who for us have the advantage of covering the entire course of the Awakening and its century, shared many significant characteristics. As Fliedner's *Almanac* amply demonstrates, they valued Bible-reading, sobriety, thrift, a work ethic, healthy exercise, education, generosity to others, and associations for study and service.[66] They stressed self-discipline in all walks of life whether these were works of charity, ordinary commerce, or the Prussian military. They encouraged risk-taking in new ventures of mission at home and abroad, a willingness to sacrifice their own interests for those of their neighbors, a sensitivity to the challenges of the needy, and a joy in telling their story. After looking at such evidence, Erich Beyreuther concludes that, in comparison to Pietism, the Awakening was more open to the world, to history, and to nature; that it had a greater capacity for the enjoyment of creation; that it more actively promoted community; and that it added to these the value of patriotism.[67]

Beyond these habits, our four representatives of Awakened spirituality consistently articulate six key principles: (1) The need of all is to be awakened to salvation; (2) the proof of the Gospel is not found in rational argument but in the power of Christian experience; (3) the kingdom of God comes both temporally and eschatologically; (4) this kingdom is manifested in community, especially in the church as the community of believers; (5) this community is nurtured through proclamation and Bible study; and (6) the necessary response to God's love is service to others—a principle not sufficiently stressed by scholars in the field, but one that puts a special stamp on the movement.

The first conviction is "the one thing necessary" to which our authors frequently refer. It is the need for awakening to the new life in Christ through heartfelt repentance and continual renewal of faith. Although our four representatives infrequently use the term *awakening*, they express the experience in the traditional Lutheran terminology of one's personal confrontation with sin, grace, and atonement. Fundamental is God's love freely offered, in Tholuck's phrase, through the "drawing of the Father to the Son."[68]

Second, the Awakened were not concerned to show that these principles could meet all the intellectual objections of the Rationalists. The proof of the gospel is based on its power to reconcile sinners and imbue them with Christ's awakening grace.[69] Similarly, the Awakening had less interest in the liberal view that people were "born free" than that one experienced freedom as a gift of God to those who submitted in faith.[70] In this context the Awakened did stress experience and earnest feelings more than rational thought, although these were not simply an expression of one's inner self but a response to the objective fact of God's saving grace.

That an awakened experience of faith is more than an assertion of subjectivity is further demonstrated by the importance of proclaiming the kingdom of God. This proclamation has an eschatological emphasis as well as a summons to awakening and service as signs "that the kingdom is a hand." Eschewing utopian measures, whether these are millennial communities or the French Revolution, the Awakened learned from Neander to envision the gradual incursion of the Spirit into every corner of life, even where—as Wichern insisted—the most destitute and degraded are found.

The church is of central importance to the Awakening as the gathering of believers into community, for the community is a reflection of the kingdom on earth and the crucible for preaching and service to the world. Generally, the Awakened remained faithful to the system they inherited, advocating reform within the state church, even though they frequently expressed their desire for a people's church *(Volkskirche)*. At the same time, Awakened circles and institutions modeled a greater role for laity as well as the potential for associations outside traditional church structures.

These central commitments are communicated by writings and witness of various kinds, but the vast sermon literature, devotional works, and biblical commentaries from our four representatives demonstrate that Awakened spirituality is a biblical spirituality. While resistant to extreme forms of the historical-critical method as practiced by Feuerbach and Strauss, they were far from literalists and cautiously incorporated a developmental view of the church and the Bible. More important than debate over methods, however, was the belief that the Bible is a vibrant and prophetic voice and that engagement with the text is engagement with the living Lord.

SERVING SOCIETY IN LOVE

A final, critical element of Awakened spirituality is the impulse to serve the needy of society. This spirituality does not draw one away from this world into a world beyond, or from full humanity into disembodied soul. In Rowan Williams's words,

> "Spirituality" becomes far more than a science of interpreting exceptional private experiences; it must now touch every area of human experience, the public and social, the painful, negative, even pathological byways of the mind, the moral and relational world. And the goal of a Christian life becomes not enlightenment but wholeness.[71]

The Awakening's pursuit of wholeness is founded on two related Reformation concepts: the priesthood of all believers and vocation. The Awakened emphasize that not only the clergy but also every faithful person has a ministry to church and society. This ministry manifests one's faith through *vocatio*, one's "calling" as a Christian to labor for the neighbor's needs and to labor specifically within the three structures by which God orders creation—church, state, and family. Vocation, then, is more fundamental than one's occupation, although the two are connected, and its inspiration and final goal is love.

Since Awakened spirituality is enmeshed in service, we should not be surprised to learn that, while scholars have paid increasing attention over the last two decades to the origins and development of poor relief in Europe, Gerhard Ulhorn wrote the first modern history of Christian charity at the suggestion of Theodor Fliedner during a conversation one summer evening in Kaiserswerth. Ulhorn argued that the Reformation brought about a major change in poor relief, and several modern scholars such as Carter Lindberg agree. Lindberg writes that in the late Middle Ages the amelioration of human need was linked to a "quantifiable salvation process" that depended on private donations. To Luther, on the other hand, salvation is not a reward for works, even when they are church-related works. Instead, poor relief grows out of worship *(Gottes-dienst)* in the literal sense that worship is "God's service" *(Gottes Dienst)*. In this "liturgy after the liturgy," human reason and human skill are the tools for communal solutions to social problems.[72]

The remarks by Bodelschwingh at the cornerstone laying for a new church at Bethel summarize these principles in such a fashion that they take on the character of a personal creed:

> I know that I am one with all my co-workers in the field of carrying out acts of Christian love. We *all* want one faith that is *active in love* and that is not satisfied with propositions that are learned by heart. We *all* want a Christianity that does not consist of words, but of deeds....We serve in love solely to transform godless, unhappy and embittered people into God-fearing, happy, cheerful, thankful people, to the glory of God and for the good of the Father-land....That is what Wichern and Fliedner wanted, nothing more, and we all sit at *their feet.*[73]

What at first glance looks like a simple explanation is a deceptively complex argument. Fundamental to this argument is that Bodelschwingh holds "temporal" and "spiritual" concerns together.[74] Caring for a neighbor's physical needs can create the opportunity to address his or her spiritual needs, and the health—understood broadly—of society depends in great measure on spiritual health. J. F. Ohl, who helped popularize the Inner Mission in America, was explicit:

> Social ills are in part due to social mal-adjustments which can to an extent be corrected by legislation, and in still greater measure to the wicked ways of individuals themselves.[75]

Bodelschwingh touches on this theme when he refers to the manifestation of faith, the nature of Christianity, and three goals of service that bridge the physical and spiritual: transforming the godless into the God-fearing, the unhappy into the happy, and the embittered into the thankful. To these he appends two more purposes that go beyond the individual: the glory of God and the good of the country. Finally, the legacy one has received from Wichern and Fliedner encourages, even obligates, one to serve.

Bodelschwingh's declaration is typical. Our four representatives did not expound on the topic in finely argued treatises but rather found their favorite argument in the biblical exhortation to rescue others out of gratitude to Christ for having rescued them. Of all the key elements of Awakened spirituality this principle, celebrated as "faith active in love," deserves a special place.

While this may differ from the late medieval view of "charity" that sprang from the principle *fides caritate formata* (faith formed by love) and the desire to atone for one's sins, one should not expect Awakened social action to satisfy all the standards of modern welfare. To extend Scott Hendrix's recent suggestion that the Reformation was an "attempt to reroot Christian faith in European culture," the figures in this volume perceived that Christianity had to be rerooted in the realities of their time.[76]

Thus, unlike more modern notions, but no less than the Middle Ages or the Reformation, they believed that Christians engage in social improvement in order to help bring about awakening.[77] The care of the soul motivates the care of the body, and social improvement depends upon faith. This may sound naive to modern ears, but to Wichern social action is based on a concern for the individual, and since grace shapes character, society benefits when morally stronger, more productive individuals serve within it.

A LEGACY OF SERVICE

Despite whatever limitations one might ascribe to this concept of service, the Awakening made several significant contributions, especially when one recalls that the "poor box," the giving of alms, and the asylum were the common standards until then and that no one had mobilized the service sectors that we take for granted today. Nursing was in its infancy, the Red Cross was unknown before 1864, and world health organizations were unheard of.

The first contribution is the legacy of the institutions themselves. Fliedner built hospitals and schools, founded a diaconate, and managed an increasingly large complex of institutions at Kaiserswerth. Wichern went a step further to organize a mission to the whole of German society, and Bodelschwingh combined a form of Wichern's Rough House with a form of Fliedner's diaconate to establish a comprehensive care-giving institution.[78]

Second, Awakened social action significantly increased opportunities for women. Although Fliedner and Bodelschwingh worked within a patriarchal system, they insisted on theological grounds that women had a legitimate place in the working world and gave single, often lower-class women skills and meaningful places in society, supported by a community of their sisters, the deaconesses. The Awakening set a pattern for years to come by giving women entrance to nursing, social work, and education.[79]

Furthermore, the figures in this volume also adopted a relatively enlightened attitude toward the poor. In the nineteenth century a proletarian was one who had no skill or other means of support—someone close to a vagabond.[80] Wichern thought the best avenue back into society was training for a trade so that eventually one could become self-sufficient and a contributor to the common welfare. Bodelschwingh went so far as to identify with his "brothers of the road" and thus offered them a measure of dignity as human beings in their own right.[81] He and the others offered the same dignity to the sick, the orphaned, and the mentally ill.

In addition, the Awakening established voluntarism as a means by which the church could adapt to the demands of industrial society.[82] From Fliedner's fund-raising journeys, to Wichern's insistence that Inner Mission remain a people's movement outside the church hierarchy, to Bodelschwingh's appeal to open one's purse, the call to service demanded human and monetary resources beyond state and church support and necessitated the creation of voluntary, interdenominational institutions.

Most important, the social-service institution—for lack of a better term—became and still remains a major form of the church's ministry in Europe and America. Martin Marty identifies four of these forms and observes that they originated in the late eighteenth and early nineteenth centuries: the denomination, the parish church as a social center, the missionary movement, and the Sunday School.[83] From what we have learned about the Awakening, we can add another, the social-service institution, that continues to flourish in retirement homes, hospices, day-care centers, counseling services, and the like.

Beyond these five contributions the Awakening's most notable accomplishment is something more than new methods and institutions. As Kenneth Clark concludes:

> The early reformer's struggle with industrialized society illustrates what I believe to be the greatest civilizing achievement of the nineteenth century, humanitarianism....Nowadays, I think we under-estimate the humanitarian achievement of the nineteenth century. We forget the horrors that were taken for granted.[84]

Some values have been with us for a long time. A spirituality of experience has existed since the beginning of Christianity. Compassion for one's fellow creatures is characteristic of all ages. Visions of the kingdom, whether in the future or the here-and-now, have been common. The church as a guiding force in society was a hallmark of the Middle Ages. But to the nineteenth-century German Awakening we owe a spirituality that fostered human kindness, grounded it in an awakened faith, and gave it the shape of loving service to society.

Notes

1. See this work in the Tholuck section below.

2. See also Matthew 15:1–13, the parable of the wedding guests who are to watch for the bridegroom; and John 11:11–13, the raising of Lazarus, where Jesus compares resurrection to rising from sleep.

3. Matthijs Dirk Geuze, "Some Remarks on Revival, Its Terminology and Definition," in *Erweckung am Beginn des 19. Jahrhunderts,* ed. Ulrich Gäbler and Peter Schram (Amsterdam, 1986), pp. 23–32, here 23–27. See also Ulrich Gäbler, "'Erweckung'—Historische Einordnung und theologische Charakterisierung," in Ulrich Gäbler, *"Auferstehungszeit": Erweckungsprediger des 19. Jahrhunderts. Sechs Porträts* (Munich, 1991), pp. 161–86; R. Seeburg, "Erweckung," in *Realencyklopädie für protestantische Theologie und Kirche,* vol. 5 (Leipzig, 1898), pp. 486–88; W. Eisenblätter, "Erweckung," in *Historisches Wörterbuch der Philosophie,* ed. Joachim Ritter, vol. 2 (Basel, 1972), cols. 732–33; and August Langen, *Der Wortschatz des deutschen Pietismus,* 2d ed. (Tübingen, 1968), p. 33, with extensive bibliography. For general overviews of the movement in English see the Suggestions for Further Reading herein. A brief account in German is Erich Beyreuther, *Die Erweckungsbewegung* (Göttingen, 1977), which first appeared under the same title in Kurt Schmidt and Ernst Wolf, eds., *Die Kirche in ihrer Geschichte: Ein Handbuch,* vol. 4, pt. R (Göttingen, 1963). See also W. Wenland, "Erweckungsbewegung," in *Die Religion in Geschichte und Gegenwart,* 2d ed., vol. 2 (Tübingen, 1928), cols. 295–304; and Erich Beyreuther, "Erweckungsbewegung," in *Die Religion in Geschichte und Gegenwart,* 3d ed., vol. 2 (Tübingen, 1958), cols. 621–29.

4. Gerhard Tersteegen, *Crumbs from the Master's Table,* trans. Samuel Jackson (London, 1837), p.32. The original was *Geistliche Brosamen, von des Herrn Tisch gefallen, von guten Freunden aufgelesen, und hungrigen Hertzen mitgetheilt: Bestehend in einer Sammlung verschiedener Erweckungs-Reden weyland von Gerhard Tersteegen zu Mülheim an der Ruhr gehalten,* 2d ed. (Solingen, 1772).

5. Immanuel Gottlob Brastberger, *Evangelische Zeugnisse der Wahrheit zur Aufmunterung im wahren Christentum* (Reutlingen, 1758), p. 341.

6. Martin Marty, *The Modern Schism: Three Paths to the Secular* (New York, 1969), p. 40.

7. For a review of the literature from L. Tiesmeyer to Erich Beyreuther, including Ritschl, see Martin Greschat, "Die Erweckungsbewegung: Versuch einer Übersicht anhand neuerer Veröffentlichungen,"

Westfälische Kirchengeschichte 66 (1973): 98–99. See also idem, "Zur neueren Pietismusforschung," *Westfälische Kirchengeschichte* 65 (1972): 220–68; idem, ed., *Zur neueren Pietismusforschung* (Darmstadt, 1977); Hans Schneider, "Der radikale Pietismus in der neueren Forschung," *Pietismus und Neuzeit* 8 (1982): 15–42; Martin Brecht, "Spätpietismus und Erweckungsbewegung," in Gäbler and Schram, *Erweckung*, pp. 1–22; and Gustav Adolf Benrath, "Einige Bemerkungen zur Zeitschriften-Literatur der Erweckung," in Gäbler and Schram, *Erweckung*, pp. 197–204.

8. F. Ernest Stoeffler, *Continental Pietism and Early American Christianity* (Grand Rapids, 1976), p. 9; idem, *The Rise of Evangelical Pietism* (Leiden, 1965), chap. 1; Dale Brown, *Understanding Pietism* (Grand Rapids, 1978), pp. 15–16.

9. Johann Arndt, *Vom Wahren Christentum* (Berlin, 1712), trans. Peter Erb, *True Christianity* (Mahwah, New Jersey, 1979).

10. Stoeffler, *The Rise of Evangelical Pietism*, p. 135.

11. Lewis Bayly, *The Practice of Pietie* (London, 1610). The first German edition, *Praxis Pietatis*, appeared in Basel in 1628.

12. Heinrich Müller, *Himmlischer Liebeskuss oder Übung des wahren Christentums fliessend aus der Erfahrung göttlicher Liebe...* (n.p., 1659).

13. "Pietismus," in *Conversations-Lexicon oder encyclopädisches Handwörterbuch für gebildete Stände*, vol. 7 (Stuttgart, 1817), p. 576.

14. See, for example, Harold Berman, *Law and Revolution: The Formation of the Western Legal Tradition* (Cambridge, 1983), p. 31, for the influence of Pietism on laws pertaining to slavery, labor, and welfare.

15. F. Ernest Stoeffler, *German Pietism During the Eighteenth Century* (Leiden, 1973), p. 246.

16. Koppel Pinson, *Pietism as a Factor in the Rise of German Nationalism* (New York, 1934; reprinted New York, 1968), p. 12 n.2, believes that "the word Pietist originated in 1689 as a term of ridicule directed against the members of Francke's *Collegia biblica.*"

17. For a succinct summary, see Sylvia Paletschek, *Frauen und Dissens: Frauen im Deutschkatholizismus und in den freien Gemeinden 1841–1852* (Göttingen, 1990), pp. 247–48; and the introductory chapter, "Restoration and Reaction," in Karl Kupisch, *Die deutschen Landeskirchen im 19. und 20. Jahrhundert*, vol. 4, R2 of *Die Kirche in ihrer Geschichte: Ein Handbuch*, ed. Kurt Schmidt and Ernst Wolf (Göttingen, 1966).

18. Franklin Baumer, *Religion and the Rise of Scepticism* (New York, 1960), p. 132.

19. Friedrich Engels, quoted in Karl Kupisch, *Vom Pietismus zum Kommunismus: Zur Jugendentwicklung von Friedrich Engels*, 2d ed. (Berlin, 1965), p. 28.

20. Klaus Penzel, "Philip Schaff: A Centennial Appraisal," *Church History* 59 (1990): 209.

21. Horst Stephan, *Geschichte der evangelischen Theologie in Deutschland seit dem Idealismus*, 3d ed., ed. Martin Schmidt (Berlin, 1973), pp. 134–37.

22. Gäbler, *"Auferstehungszeit,"* pp. 162–63.

23. W. H. Koch, *A History of Prussia* (New York, 1978; reprinted New York, 1993), p. 279.

24. Ibid, pp. 227–28. Richard Gawthrop, *Pietism and the Making of Eighteenth-Century Prussia* (Cambridge, 1993), p. 4, emphasizes the role of Pietism in "the acceptance of an ideology of unconditional service to the state." John Groh, *Nineteenth-Century German Protestantism: The Church as Social Model* (Washington, D.C., 1982), observes "an unwritten Protestant charter" between church and state that was intended as a model for all institutions. For general treatments, see A. M. C. Waterman, *Religion, Economics, and Revolution: Christian Political Economy, 1798–1833* (Cambridge, 1991), and Helmut Walser Smith, *German Nationalism and Religious Conflict: Culture, Ideology, Politics, 1870–1914* (Princeton, 1995).

25. Andrew Weeks, *German Mysticism from Hildegard of Bingen to Ludwig Wittgenstein: A Literary and Intellectual History* (Albany, 1993), p. 215.

26. Beyreuther, *Erweckungsbewegung*, pp. 25–26; idem, "Erweckungsbewegung," col. 621; Martin Schmidt, *Pietismus*, 2d ed. (Stuttgart, 1978), p. 161; Friedrich Wilhelm Kantzenbach, "Orthodoxie und Pietismus," in *Evangelische Enzyklopädie* (Gütersloh, 1966), p. 17.

27. Martin Brecht, "Spätpietismus und Erweckungsbewegung," p. 6.

28. Gäbler, *"Auferstehungszeit,"* pp. 162–63; Greschat, "Die Erweckungsbewegung," pp. 106, 136–37.

29. Brecht, "Spätpietismus und Erweckungsbewegung," pp. 7–8. Horst Weigelt, *Pietismus-Studien*, vol. 1, *Der spener-hallische Pietismus* (Stuttgart, 1965), stresses Urlsperger's role in the transition from Halle Pietism to Awakening.

30. Erich Beyreuther, *Der geschichtliche Auftrag des Pietismus in der Gegenwart: Drei Fragen an Pietismus und Kirche* (Stuttgart, 1963), p. 38. On Raumer, see Horst Weigelt, *Erweckungsbewegung und konfessionelles*

Luthertum im 19. Jahrhundert, untersucht an Karl v. Raumer (Stuttgart, 1968).

31. Robert Bigler, *The Politics of German Protestantism: The Rise of the Protestant Church Elite in Prussia, 1815–1848* (Berkeley, 1972), pp. 433–38.

32. Friedrich Engels, quoted in Kupisch, *Vom Pietismus zum Kommunismus*, p. 32.

33. Anne Taylor, *Vision of Harmony: A Study in Nineteenth-Century Millenarianism* (Oxford, 1987), p. 5. Taylor describes Württemberg as a region where "religion lay like lees in wine."

34. Frank Macchia, *Spirituality and Social Liberation: The Message of the Blumhardts in the Light of Württemberg Pietism* (Metuchen, 1993), especially pp. 95, 145.

35. Peter Maser, *Hans Ernst von Kottwitz: Studien zur Erweckungsbewegung des frühen 19. Jahrhunderts in Schlesien und Berlin* (Göttingen, 1990), p. 148, believes that the "breakthrough" to the Awakening in Berlin occurred at a New Year's Eve gathering in 1816 when Bethmann-Hollweg, who would chair the first *Kirchentag*, experienced a conversion. Maser's is the most important book on the beginning of the Awakening to come out of the current generation.

36. See Tholuck, *The Lesson Learned About Sin and the Reconciler*, below.

37. Peter Maser, "Ein Modell diakonischer Arbeit in der frühen Erweckungsbewegung. Vorbild für die innere Mission," in Gäbler and Schram, *Erweckung*, pp. 169–82. W. R. Ward, *The Protestant Evangelical Awakening* (Cambridge, 1994), p. 354, observes that these "massive blows...gave evangelical religion the best opportunity it ever received."

38. Maser, *Kottwitz*, pp. 66–69.

39. Ludwig von Gerlach, quoted in ibid, p. 151.

40. Penzel, "Philip Schaff," p. 211.

41. Maser, *Kottwitz*, pp. 139, 222–26.

42. Greschat, "Die Erweckungsbewegung," p. 146. For the reforms see Kerr D. Macmillan, *Protestantism in Germany* (Princeton, 1917), pp.173–74.

43. Arlie Hoover, *The Gospel of Nationalism: German Patriotic Preaching from Napoleon to Versailles* (Stuttgart, 1986), surveys numerous sermons from the War of Liberation to demonstrate the role of the clergy in promoting nationalism. See also Bigler, *The Politics of German Protestantism*, pp. 430–31; and Pinson, *Pietism as a Factor*, p. 59. Sydney

37

Ahlstrom, "Religion, Revolution and the Rise of Modern Nationalism: Reflections on the American Experience," *Church History* 44 (1975): 492–504, here pp. 496–97, defines nationalism as "'a state of mind' that began to gain quasi-religious fervency only in the later eighteenth century" but argues that it first took definitive shape in America.

44. Koch, *A History of Prussia*, p. 192.

45. Beyreuther, "Erweckungsbewegung," col. 625.

46. Adam Müller, "Von der Notwendigkeit einer theologischen Grundlage der gesamten Staatswissenschaften," in *Die deutschen Romantiker*, vol. 1 (Salzburg, n.d.), p. 450.

47. In an extensive literature, see Bernard Reardon, *Religion in the Age of Romanticism: Studies in Early Nineteenth Century Thought* (New York, 1985). Walter Conser Jr., *Church and Confession: Conservative Theologians in Germany, England, and America, 1815–1866* (Macon, 1984), stresses the importance of Romanticism in renewing the belief that the church is a divinely established institution.

48. Maser, *Kottwitz*, pp. 237–38.

49. Wolfgang Mickel, ed., *Geschichte, Politik und Gesellschaft*, vol. 1 (Berlin, 1988), p. 167.

50. W. Buchholz and W. Köllmann, eds., *Raum und Bevölkerung in der Weltgeschichte*, vol. 2 (Würzburg, 1955), p. 225, quoted in Mickel, *Geschichte, Politik und Gesellschaft*, p. 183.

51. Koch, *A History of Prussia*, p. 279.

52. Macmillan, *Protestantism in Germany*, p. 239.

53. William O. Shanahan, *German Protestants Face the Social Question*, vol. 1 (Notre Dame, 1954), p. 161. Although published a half-century ago, Greschat, "Die Erweckungsbewegung," p. 143, believes that "this seminal work lays the foundation for all further work."

54. Koch, *A History of Prussia*, p. 197.

55. See the conversation between the young Friedrich von Bodelschwingh and his father concerning their attitudes toward rich and poor in Friedrich von Bodelschwingh, *Ausgewählte Schriften*, ed. Alfred Adam, 2 vols. (Bethel bei Bielefeld, 1955, 1964; reprinted 1980), vol. 2, pp. 85–86.

56. In contrast, R. W. Postgate, *Revolution from 1789 to 1906* (London, 1920; reprinted New York, 1962), p. v, argues that 1848 "did mark a turning point in history, and the essence of the change was in truth that the working class replaced the middle class as the active revolutionary force."

57. Sydney Ahlstrom, *A Religious History of the American People* (New Haven, 1972), pp. 521–22. See also Greschat, "Die Erweckungsbewegung," pp. 143–46. For the work of Roman Catholics, see Paul Misner, *Social Catholicism in Europe: From the Onset of Industrialization to the First World War* (New York, 1991).

58. Baumer, *Religion and the Rise of Scepticism*, chap. 3: "The Death of God." Shanahan, *German Protestants*, p. 34, concludes that "nothing compared with the Industrial Revolution in extending the crisis of religion to the masses." See also Kupisch, *Die deutschen Landeskirchen*, pp. 69–70.

59. This gives both title and theme to Kenneth Scott Latourette, *The Great Century in Europe and the United States of America, 1800–1914* (New York, 1941), vol. 4 of *A History of the Expansion of Christianity* (New York, 1937–45).

60. This is the conclusion of Oliver Janz, *Bürger besonderer Art: Evangelische Pfarrer in Preußen 1850–1914* (Berlin, 1994).

61. Kupisch, *Die deutschen Landeskirchen*, pp. 91–93. See also Hugh McLeod, *Piety and Poverty: Working-Class Religion in Berlin, London and New York, 1870–1914* (London, 1996).

62. Ronald Massanari, "True or False Socialism: Adolf Stoecker's Critique of Marxism from a Christian Socialist Perspective," *Church History* 41 (1972): 487–96.

63. Gerd Wilhelm Grauvogel, *Theodor von Wächter: Christ und Sozialdemokrat* (Stuttgart, 1994).

64. Andrew Landale Drummond, *German Protestantism since Luther* (London, 1951), pp. 216–17.

65. Karl Barth, *Protestant Theology in the Nineteenth Century: Its Background and History* (New York, 1959; reprinted Valley Forge 1973), p. 509. See the interesting observation by Maser, *Kottwitz*, p. 241, that Barth "more or less takes to a logical conclusion what the Awakening introduced," but that his chapter on Tholuck shows how he retained "a simultaneous fascination with and rejection of it."

66. See the selection from Fliedner's *Almanac* below.

67. Beyreuther, *Erweckungsbewegung*, p. 26.

68. See Tholuck's sermon of this name below.

69. Penzel, "Philip Schaff," p. 209.

70. See Richard Helmstadter, ed., *Freedom and Religion in the Nineteenth Century* (Stanford, 1997), pp. 87–88. Helmstadter's "Introduction" argues that the subject is far more complex than usually thought—a

caution to those who would draw a straight line from the Reformation through Awakening to National Socialism.

71. Rowan Williams, *Christian Spirituality: A Theological History from the New Testament to Luther and St. John of the Cross* (Atlanta, 1979), p. 2.

72. Carter Lindberg, *Beyond Charity: Reformation Initiatives for the Poor* (Minneapolis, 1993), pp. vii, 21, 169; idem, "The Liturgy After the Liturgy: Welfare in the Early Reformation," in *Through the Eye of a Needle: Judeo-Christian Roots of Social Welfare*, ed. Emily Hanawalt and Carter Lindberg (Kirksville, 1994), pp. 177–91.

73. Martin Gerhart and Alfred Adam, *Friedrich von Bodelschwingh: ein Lebensbild aus der deutschen Kirchengeschichte*, 2 vols. (Bethel bei Bielefeld, 1950, 1958), vol. 2, pp. 143–44.

74. This was also the case with the helping institutions at Halle: Kurt Aland, "Pietismus und die soziale Frage," in *Pietismus und moderne Welt*, ed. Kurt Aland (Witten, 1974), pp. 111, 133.

75. Jeremiah F. Ohl, *The Inner Mission: A Handbook for Christian Workers* (Philadelphia, 1913), p. 204.

76. Scott Hendrix, "Rerooting the Faith: The Reformation as Re-Christianization," *Church History* 69 (2000): 558–77, here p. 575. Hendrix better accounts for the goals of the Reformers—as well as the Awakened—than the controversial thesis of Gerald Strauss, "Success and Failure in the German Reformation," *Past and Present* 67 (1975): 3–63, that we must attribute the "rooting" of reforms such as Bible-reading and catechetics more to Pietism than to the Reformation.

77. Shanahan, *German Protestants*, p. 87.

78. Leif Grane, *Die Kirche im 19. Jahrhundert: Europäische Perspektiven* (Göttingen, 1987), pp. 160–62; Maser, *Kottwitz*, pp. 240–41; Shanahan, *German Protestants*, p. 88. The observation of Klaus Pönnighaus, *Kirchliche Vereine zwischen Rationalismus und Erweckung: Ihr Wirken und ihre Bedeutung vornehmlich am Beispiel des Fürstentums Lippe dargestellt* (Bern, 1982), that Wichern's design for the Inner Mission only provided an umbrella organization for already-existing efforts, does not detract from his vision or his accomplishment.

79. Paletschek, *Frauen und Dissens*, pp. 153–54. See also Catherine Prelinger, *Charity, Challenge, and Change: Religious Dimensions of the Mid-Nineteenth-Century Women's Movement in Germany* (New York, 1987).

80. Koch, *A History of Prussia*, p. 264.

81. See, for example, Bodelschwingh, *Ausgewählte Schriften*, vol. 2, p. 433.

82. Martin Marty, *Religion and Republic: The American Circumstance* (Boston, 1987), p. 45, notes, "The Great Awakening of the eighteenth century may best be seen as the moment when the revolution toward voluntaryism occurred." "Voluntaryism" is the technical term Marty uses to designate the practice of supporting religion by voluntary association and effort.

83. Martin Marty, "When the Forms Began," *Dialog* 4 (1965): 21–26.

84. Kenneth Clark, *Civilisation: A Personal View* (New York, 1969), p. 329.

AUGUST THOLUCK

Introduction

Friedrich August Gottreu Tholuck (1799–1877) leads our presentation of four great figures of the German Awakening because he, more than anyone else, was its spokesperson. He gave voice to, and practiced, the views, faith, and spiritual life that define the movement. Furthermore, he takes his place as our introductory figure because he is regarded as *the* theologian of the Awakening, and as such, in the words of one of the most respected theologians of the twentieth century, Karl Barth, "there was no one beside him."[1] During his lifetime Tholuck became so widely known that a letter from the United States addressed to "Mr. Tholuck, Europe" was delivered to his home in Halle, Germany.[2]

Remarkably, at only twenty-four years of age Tholuck burst onto the scene with the publication of his first work, *The Lesson Learned About Sin and the Reconciler, or The True Consecration of the Skeptic* (1823). This fruit of Tholuck's own intense spiritual struggle captured the imagination of Christians everywhere, and even though the first edition was published anonymously, Tholuck soon began receiving gifts, letters of gratitude, and growing acclaim. Many readers reported the work to be a turning point in their lives. *The Lesson Learned* achieved enormous international success and came to be regarded as the seminal document of the German Awakening.

Two attributes account for this early achievement by a young man who had hardly started his teaching career: his uncommon intelligence and his passion to excel. Tholuck, who was born in Breslau, Germany, on March 30, 1799, took up intellectual pursuits at an early age. As a boy he used paper and paste to create a fantasy world for which he invented countries, rulers, and universities. He kept a historical record of this fictional world and even wrote a weekly international newspaper for it.[3] By the time he was thirteen years old he had read between two- and three-thousand volumes, and by seventeen he could write reasonably well in nineteen languages, including Spanish, Russian, Hungarian, Chinese, and his favorite, Arabic.[4]

45

Tholuck's stepmother was unsupportive. She did not appreciate the boy's life of the mind, was annoyed at the cost of his schooling, and was angered when he neglected his chores. Her antagonism was coupled with physical punishment from his father. The more oppressive the parental atmosphere grew, the more the boy retreated, became bitter and frustrated, and suffered from loneliness. At the same time, Tholuck was troubled by his unfulfilled yearning for the comradeship and stimulation of close, like-minded, friends. Moreover, he was repeatedly bothered by illness. These combined frustrations led to occasional periods of despair and even drove Tholuck to the brink of suicide several times when he was thirteen and fourteen years old.[5]

On his stepmother's insistence Tholuck had dropped out of school at age twelve to work for his father, who was a goldsmith, but neither Tholuck's insatiable intellectual curiosity nor his weak eyes suited him for this career. Instead, his love of languages led him to an early, deep interest in the Orient, which, in turn, contributed to the spiritual struggle that continued throughout his youth. In his speech upon graduation from secondary school he ranked Manu, Zoroaster, and Confucius above Moses, Jesus, and Mohammed, and he characterized Christianity as banal compared to the wisdom of the East. In 1833 Tholuck reflected on his earlier difficulties:

> Even in early boyhood infidelity had forced its way into my heart, and at the age of twelve I was wont to scoff at Christianity and its truths. Hard has been the struggle I have come through, before attaining to assurance of that faith in which I am now blessed.[6]

Thus, when Tholuck went to study in Berlin in 1816, he brought with him a complex of unresolved religious questions. Buoyed by his newly acquired fluency in Arabic and planning to take up oriental philology, Tholuck decided to study under the retired Prussian diplomat and well-known orientalist Heinrich Friedrich Diez (1751–1817).[7] The decision proved to be momentous, for this retired gentleman practiced a warm, Lutheran piety, and this piety led Tholuck to a series of experiences and friendships that in 1818–19 awakened in him a new faith.

He became acquainted with some of the nearly twenty circles of pious individuals who met regularly to deepen and activate their spiritual life. Particularly in the influential Community of Brothers and Society for Christianity[8] Tholuck encountered goals and structures that would carry over into the Awakening:

> the practice of an intense personal piety; the organizing of the pious into a centralized association crossing national and church boundaries; ecumenical tolerance; interest in mission; the spreading of written material; and the education of the young.[9]

Tholuck was especially inspired by his contact with Baron Hans Ernst von Kottwitz (1757–1843), the devout "'Patriarch' of the German Awakening in northern and eastern Germany,"[10] whose theology, piety, and service to others influenced an entire generation of young men. Later, Kottwitz would serve as the model for "Father Abraham" in Tholuck's *Lesson Learned About Sin and the Reconciler*. Furthermore, having transferred from oriental studies to theology, Tholuck came under the influence of another great mentor, the church historian August Neander (1789–1850), whose motto was *pectus est quod facit theologum*—"the heart makes the theologian."[11] Tholuck met weekly with Neander and developed a personal friendship with this prominent theologian, whose stress on Christianity as more than a system of dogma, as the power of God in human lives, found warm reception in the student.

Soon Tholuck became involved in a number of initiatives that, in typical Awakening fashion, sprang up outside the Evangelical Church, exhibited missionary zeal, and gave outlet for an active faith. These include teaching in Berlin at Johannes Jänicke's missionary school from 1821 to 1826; serving as director of the Central Bible Society from 1821 to 1825; assuming the position of secretary for the Mission to the Jews in 1822; acting as representative of the London Society in 1823; and, as of 1824, publishing the periodical *The Friend of Israel*. Tholuck's motivating principle echoed a central theme of the Awakening: faith active in love. In a sermon delivered in Halle a few years later he declared:

If we want to walk in the footsteps of our Savior on earth, we cannot do things only for ourselves. We are on earth also to do things for others. To conquer sin and reduce suffering—that is why *He* came to earth, and whoever wants to walk in his footsteps says: this, too, certainly belongs to my responsibilities on earth, to reduce the sin and suffering around me as far as my hands reach.[12]

Tholuck's most important contribution to the Awakening came as a result of his career as a professor of theology, first in Berlin (1821–26), and then—except for two years (1827–29) in Rome as court-appointed preacher—for the remainder of his life at the University in Halle. As a theologian Tholuck was greatly indebted to Schleiermacher, whose view he echoes in arguing that religion is more than moral behavior. Religion he defines as, "namely nothing other than the **felt connection between God and life,** the feeling of the dependency of the mortal spirit on the immortal."[13] Yet, regarding the Christian faith Tholuck generally held orthodox Lutheran views on such matters as original sin, the two natures of Christ, grace, reconciliation, and redemption. However, the Pietist influence is evident in his strong emphasis on "the subjective, experiential side of Christianity: the recognition of sin, conversion, and rebirth in Christ."[14] Tholuck espouses a faith that is heralded by rebirth, felt intimately, and expressed outwardly by the sanctified life. In *Conversations About the Foremost Questions of Faith in Our Time* (1846) one of Tholuck's characters says:

> We call out with Paul, "Thus we are justified through faith; we have peace with God through our Lord Jesus Christ." We call out with John, "We know that we have gone from death to life." We can provide the year—some of us the month and the hour—of our birth, when a new faith, a new love and hope began in us, through which our entire inner being was satisfied in every way.[15]

Tholuck's biblical, Christocentric theology put him squarely at odds with German Rationalism, the dominant intellectual approach of the day. When Prussian Minister Altenstein, sympathetic to Tholuck's countervailing Awakened views, appointed Tholuck in 1826 to the theological faculty at the Fridericiana Halle-Wittenberg, the many Rationalist professors raised strong opposition. Nevertheless, Tholuck persevered.

Although Tholuck was firmly opposed to Rationalism, he was sympathetic with people who desired "to assign reasons for their belief, and justify it scientifically in a conflict with the doubts which had been raised on every side against it."[16] Thus, in the spectrum of nineteenth-century responses to Rationalism, Tholuck occupies a place in the middle as a "mediating theologian" who values both faith and reason. Faith, he argues, is not derived from rational thought, but from a change in one's relationship to God, and he reiterates Augustine's view: "I believe in order that I may understand."[17]

One might consider placing Tholuck in the conservative confessionalist wing because he clearly defends the Evangelical Church and its confessions. However, this would be to overlook moderating elements such as his ecumenicity and his non-judgmental attitude toward other denominations. On one occasion, for example, he said in regard to missions:

> Up until this moment the enemy has not yet succeeded in destroying the loving respect with which missionaries from four different countries and six to eight denominations have been working together for conversions in East India, the New World, and South Africa.[18]

Clear evidence of his ecumenicity was his participation in London in 1846 in the founding of the Evangelical Alliance, an international organization of evangelical Christians of various denominations.

The influence of Tholuck's career was determined by his unremitting question: What is the ultimate purpose of studying theology? In one of his sermons to the students and faculty in Halle he raised the issue as follows:

> How is it now, my academic colleagues, if I reach into your hearts with this question: "Have I strived for the

knowledge of religious truth merely in order to **know** it, or in order to **do** it?"[19]

Tholuck was, of course, intent on doing it, on practicing what he preached, and, correspondingly, his legacy is not as a scholar but as a mentor, or, to use Barth's phrase, as "the theological personality."[20] Here, in the field of personal, pastoral care, lay Tholuck's strength, and from it came his great contribution to the Awakening.

A major factor in creating this reputation was his appeal with students, to whom he became known as the *Studentenvater.* He had no children by his first wife, who died after a marriage of only eighteen months, and none by his second wife, Mathilde, but as if making up for that lack, the Tholucks kept their home open to students, visitors, and guests. Tholuck met formally and informally with students in and outside of his home, conversed with them, held regular Bible studies with them, and offered support and guidance. Over a span of fifty years he was the spiritual mentor to generations of students, about which Tholuck's biographer, Leopold Witte, comments: "This relationship has scarcely an equal in the history of the German universities."[21]

Tholuck's distinction as theologian and pastor of the Awakening also derived from his outstanding preaching. In 1839, in recognition of his great pastoral talent, Tholuck was named university pastor, and from then on he preached regularly to the students and faculty. The theologian Martin Kähler, one of Tholuck's better-known students, explains why the sermons had such a profound impact:

> [H]is outstanding significance as a preacher brings one to that place where scholarship and spiritual edification are merged in a profound way. Thus, probably no one else of his day exerted as direct an influence on his contemporaries as he, and with such comprehensiveness and versatility.[22]

Many contemporaries reported the great power of his sermons. One of them, Karl Heinrich Sack, who studied Tholuck's collected sermons of 1834–42, cites Tholuck's compelling imagination and his "erudite, magnificent eloquence that is expressive and often moving."[23] Sack notes that Tholuck is able to draw on his prodigious knowledge of exegesis, church history, biography, philosophy, and literature. Generally his sermons do not reflect a systematician who traces out doctrine in expository prose. Rather, Tholuck communicates "a personally experienced faith in the gospel, a spiritual view of the Savior and his deeds, the feeling of having received mercy and peace."[24] With this approach Tholuck became the model of a new and stimulating manner of preaching that characterized the Awakening. Karl von Raumer (1783–1865), a leader of the Awakening in Bavaria, pronounced Tholuck one of only two theologians (E. W. Hengstenberg being the other) who were qualified to train students to preach because they themselves could preach well.[25]

Correspondingly, the published works of Tholuck that met with the most success are those related to his edifying activities. These works consist mainly of his very popular commentaries, all of which were reprinted in numerous editions: Romans (first edition 1824); the Gospel of John (1827); the Sermon on the Mount (1833); and Hebrews (1836). His study of the Old Testament in the New Testament, which appeared in 1836, was also popular, and his devotional book, *Hours of Christian Devotion* (first edition 1839), was a best seller. Tholuck's collected works were published in eleven volumes from 1866 to 1873.

The readings on the following pages present a cross-section of Tholuck's most influential and popular writings: first his very personal account, *The Lesson Learned About Sin and the Reconciler*; then two of his sermons; and finally, two examples of his devotional literature. The selections illustrate central themes in the faith and work of this foundational figure in the German Awakening.

Personal Testament

The Lesson Learned About Sin and the Reconciler, or The True Consecration of the Skeptic

EDITORS' INTRODUCTION: This engaging narrative, which Tholuck wrote in 1823 when he was only twenty-four years old, quickly achieved enormous popularity and was considered a major work in its time. By 1851 the book had already reached its seventh edition, from which the translation here has been prepared. *The Lesson Learned About Sin and the Reconciler, or The True Consecration of the Skeptic,*[1] is a deeply personal account in epistolary form of the spiritual growth of two young men. Like the *Confessions* of Saint Augustine, the account is neither strictly autobiographical nor a theological essay but a combination. It is Tholuck's testimony of his conversion, that is, as the title indicates, the lesson he learned and eagerly wants to share. Given the depth of feeling in *The Lesson Learned,* the work is noteworthy for its moderate approach to Christianity that eschews the extremes of orthodoxy and rationalism.

We present two key sections of the much longer work. The first is the opening of chapter 1, which introduces the two main characters with their unsatisfied hopes and longings. One, called Guido, represents Tholuck himself; the other, Julius, is a figure like Tholuck's lifelong friend Julius Müller, to whom Tholuck dedicates this work. While Julius's letters trace his path to a religious rebirth and the decision to transfer from philology and history to theology, Guido, in contrast, becomes increasingly distraught in his quest for truth. In spite of his earnest study of theology and philosophy, his religious doubts deepen.

We pass over the remaining letters in chapter 1 in order to present chapter 2 in its entirety. Chapter 2 is Guido's long letter detailing his spiritual journey out of skepticism, capped by his intense experience of a Christian community where he finds his spiritual center and the joyful calm of feeling the Lord's presence. We meet, in particular, the focal person of the community, its "Father Abraham," a portrayal of Tholuck's contemporary Baron Hans Ernst von Kottwitz, whose gentle spirit and insightful counsel exert an enormous influence on the young men.

Section One
About Sin

CHAPTER ONE

Early on Guido and Julius became close friends because of their similar dispositions. While other boys with whom they were acquainted were satisfied to finish the assigned homework and turn to childish pleasures, both of them were drawn by an irresistible urge to higher realms of intellectual life. Even though an earthly fog floated in front of their tender eyes, hindering their understanding by preventing a view into the distances and heights, the air of worldly wisdom called them up to mountains with clear vistas. As the mystical melody of emotions rang in the depths of their hearts—a melody that rings within every soul that is moved, and lures it home—they followed its beckoning, magical tones that called them down into the depths of religion. Often, until they were weary, they pursued the shimmer of the arts that flashes across and gilds ordinary life.

They hated only one thing: the ordinary. Their noble spirits were charged with energy, inviting, as it were, an electrical wand that would discharge the power. But none came. No Emmaus, no fields of spring flowers, no groves of Academe were in the vicinity of their school. The new wisdom to which they applied themselves had established itself on the crumbling ruins of the ancient Stoa and on withered plots in the gardens of Epicurus. The director of the gymnasium, an aged man, revered the pineal gland as the seat of the spirit and had often speculated whether the creator should not have given the human being a third hand or foot instead of a heart. His job was teaching religion. Day after day he unfailingly dragged into class the skeleton he had constructed, often shaking the bones so that the students were filled with dismay.

The rest of the teachers—philologists—were no better; of all the words they knew they had not a single life-giving word. The preachers in the young men's hometown were in part orthodox, in part neologists; both kinds were dull and spiritless. What they possessed of religion was cold lava picked up from distant volcanoes. Consequently, the flame in the souls of these young men who were eager for fuel bent vainly to the left and right. Not finding any fuel, the flame flickered fainter and fainter.

Early on, one great question had stirred their young hearts repeatedly—the question that so often forces itself upon persons of the world during quieter hours and that they brush aside again and again, until on life's final sickbed it resounds in their breasts like a goddess of revenge for their wasted days: **for what purpose was I born?** Even at their young age this question led the two friends to more serious writings and reflections, because it seemed criminal to these high-minded youth to dismiss the question without an answer. However, since no one was at hand to nurture their awakening religious needs, their answers to the great question varied, depending on the different books or people with whom they associated.

At one time the right thing—the nobler pleasures of life, as they called it—seemed to consist in striving as hard as possible to pluck every flower that presented itself in public life, in socializing with friends, and in the study of the arts and sciences. At another time they could see objectively that the one goal of life cannot be pleasure, especially since people of the lower classes from whom the finer pleasures are withheld could, with the same undeniable right as everyone else, demand freedom for the crude outbreaks of their desires. Consequently, the young men concluded it was more accurate to identify the purpose of the individual as working for the welfare of one's fellow human beings. However, when they recognized that the nature and power of that work depend on the kind of heart one has, then sanctification of one's disposition had to rank as life's ultimate goal.

But what is sanctification, they asked? If sanctification is denial and renunciation, then it is like a line that extends forever and ever, and which, the longer it is propelled ahead by an inner energy, the faster it extends itself. If my life and my "I" have become ever thinner and more transparent by denying everything—not only what I have, but also what I am—then I will have reached the goal of my sanctification when I have reached the end of my **being.** Might I not hazard the bold thought that this lauded sanctification is a corrosive that, after it has consumed that which is evil, penetrates through the living bones, for it knows no other enemy than freshness and life?

Many people who came to the young men told them the goal of life is the height of knowledge, that is, a joyful observing and a splendid conceptualizing and categorizing of life's multifaceted activities. However, they soon rejected these advisors who, splitting up the stream of the human family, wanted to lead only the ONE narrow branch of the stream up beyond the clouds, while letting the waves of the other immeasurable branch roll slowly onto desolate shores in the fogs of time. It was all too clear to the friends that whatever the goal of life, it must be the same for **everyone,** and would not the fundamental purpose of all being have to be their goal, too?

Thus both young men had matured for the academy, enriched with basic knowledge and endowed with sound, correct judgment. Yet they were unhappy and felt impoverished because they neither wanted, nor were able, to conceal from themselves that the longing for calm—this remnant of the divine image in humans—had not yet been satisfied. With melancholy and deep distress they surveyed the long road of life that lay behind them, full of dashed hopes and unfulfilled wishes, full of errors and transgressions. With secret trembling they looked at the flood of their turbulent inner desires, at the cataracts of their unbounded passions, at their anchorless inner life, at the fleeting clouds of their decisions, at their principles, which were stationary for only days or hours. And yet! Is there a life without a center? No more than a world without God.

Then the two went their separate ways. **Guido** went to the university of **X** to study theology; **Julius** went to **Y** to study philology and history. The morning of their farewell was a moving one. It was a bright spring day. The sun had already risen and was bathing gloriously in the boundless blue expanse. The meadow on which they saw each other for the last time was the very one on which, as nine year olds, they had once knelt and called on God to make them pious. "Well," said **Julius,** "who knows whether some day on the same meadow we might celebrate the answer to our childhood prayer!" "Who knows," responded **Guido,** while sobbing on his shoulder. "I'm looking into the future with troubled eyes! O, **Julius,** if the lower region of our life's Etna, the age of boyhood and youth, has brought us so much pain, how is the cold region of manhood and old age to make us any happier? Calm will scarcely have entered the much-stirred heart before the old man tumbles into the crater."

"I do not doubt," answered **Julius,** "that we will find what we are seeking, but I do not yet see any way out. I also say: O, wanderer, from where do you come? O, wanderer, where are you going? I do not know. But I do see the heavens full of stars, and the human heart full of anticipation. So let us here, in the presence of the All-knowing, make a covenant to wrestle and struggle until we have achieved the peace for which our souls thirst. Let us faithfully and without wavering follow the voice in our hearts which calls us—sometimes softly, sometimes forcefully—to follow!" With these words they embraced and went their separate ways.

Guido began his theological studies with great zeal. He went to lectures given partly by neological teachers, partly by supernaturalist teachers. In these lectures he became acquainted for the first time with all the doubts the new age had stirred up against Christianity. While earlier he had spread his efforts to the most diverse disciplines, expecting that he would find equal satisfaction for his longing in all of them, he now limited his energy to theology in particular. Here he saw a vast field open up, and he wished above all to attain certainty about Christianity. None of his teachers satisfied him. Some spoke so coldly and with such disinterest about the persons of the New Testament that even though he did not believe in its divine origin at all, he nevertheless found something greater and nobler in it than the teachers did. He was most outraged when the very thing that ought to lift humanity above the earthly is itself pulled down to the earth. He was of the opinion that even if Christianity were not true, one nevertheless ought to allow it a mysterious appearance of holiness so that it could have an effect on the spirit, just like artificial pollen on unformed leaves.

Other teachers wanted to uphold the teachings of Christianity through a series of historical proofs. Each proof, as these teachers admitted, had little weight in itself, but taken together they had adequate power of persuasion. However, precisely those doubts, which bothered him, remained unresolved, and knots that did not trouble him were untangled with a tediousness that made him weary. Yet another teacher at the university based his entire system on the Confessions and tried to beat down every contradiction and difficulty that presented itself to the scholarly young man through the demand for inflexible literalness in an unconditional submission to belief.

Theology could hold him no longer; it appeared to him like a coarse barbarian who, accustomed to food of a paltry nature, was unable to satisfy guests who presented themselves from the classical world of beautiful Hellas yet defiantly swung his club at anyone who refused to pay the bill. Furthermore, the barbarian appeared to betray his servile origin and unworthy existence when, with an over-friendly beckoning and flirtatious look, he asked worldly wisdom to grant him a few feet of land from the territory out of which he had already taken the most beautiful acreage from the rightful owners. **Guido** wanted to drink from the **spring** itself, not out of paltry cups.

Therefore, he turned to what he recognized as the queen of human sciences: philosophy. How wondrously his spirit was drawn in various directions when he entered this circle of knowledge. The searching youth recognized that he had now set foot upon a path where to go halfway would mean not to venture at all. Whoever puts one's hand to the chain of logical speculation must follow wherever it leads, whether into the light of day or the dark of night. Scornfully he therefore passed by the systems he regarded as vacillating between willing ignorance and full, even if deadly, truth. He compared them to comets, unaligned to any planetary system. He searched out only **those** intellects as leaders with whom he had everything to gain because they had the courage to lose everything. So he let

Parmenides, Spinoza, Schelling, and Schleiermacher pass instructively before his mind.[2] Each called out the same great words to the carefully listening soul, each one, though, in his particular voice.

After **Guido** had finished the earnest, uninterrupted journey through these intellectual worlds, he stood thoughtfully, as though in an unfamiliar, dark region. Suddenly he noticed in horror what he had often imagined in dreams: how his spirit indeed had been abandoned to an **eternal fall.** He recognized all too clearly that the end of all speculation is the **denial of all finite being.** He had posed the question to himself, **what** am I?, and obtained knowledge about the infinite variety of what he was. He had gone further and asked himself, **who** am I?, and with this question had lost himself. He had inquired about the origin of the world, and the finite world of appearances had redirected him to God. He had inquired about God, and the infinity of his being had redirected him to the world. So all finite being was a shadow that no one casts, an echo that no one causes. **Guido** was feeling the endless fall!

But there was yet another pole in his spiritual life besides that of logical deduction. He had moments of deep reflection and indescribable stillness in his life when he heard the breathing of his spirit, and he could overhear the dialogue of an unfamiliar spirit with his own. In the "you" and "I" he tasted a primitive feeling of life that no absolute universal was able to bestow. And often when the magic lantern of pantheism blended all the colors of good and evil so that the one, like the other, was flattened into a dull gray, then, as if awakening from slumber, the noble young man would call out: Does this mean that the first and innermost and eternal word of my life is a delusion?

Where, then, is truth? If this speculation is truth, he said to himself, why does it kill, annihilate me? **Can we seek and love a truth that annihilates us?** Should not food come from the animal? If it is truth, why has it vanished again and again, even though since the time of the Indian Vedas[3] it has been found so often? Why is it always found by only a few, and of these why do even fewer hold onto it? Does this not occur because human beings seek not merely shadows in the world but something that casts the shadows? Is it not because they shudder to see the entire world and themselves pass before themselves as shadows? Again: what is it that drives my intellect irresistibly forward in its deductions until it has annihilated God, the world, and itself through its syllogisms? And when the weak-hearted threaten to overturn the results of that logical speculation in order that their pathetic huts do not collapse on what they have scraped together, what is the irresistible power that again and again leads people back to the old truths? Which boldness is greater, the one by which the intellect denies God, the universe, and self, or the one by which the heart believes in them? **And is the greatest boldness the best?** These were the questions that, like storm-tossed waves, hurled his head and his heart against each other as if they were two ships with only one captain and threatened to break them apart. It is true that he continued his studies untiringly, but instead of coming closer to an outcome in this powerful struggle, he merely saw the opposing forces grow month by month and, as a result, the heat of battle intensify.

His friend **Julius** had not written to him frequently. The main content of the few letters was that he had begun to read the Bible diligently, that he had found it difficult to convince himself of its teachings, but that he had understood the necessity for a positive religion. He had learned this through studying history, as well as through the wonderful effect of Christian morality on persons who conformed their lives entirely to the Bible.

Suddenly, a year before he left the university, **Guido** received a letter from his friend after having heard nothing from him for a long time. **Julius** announced that he had undergone a great change. He called it a **rebirth.** The letter's entire language and manner of expression were different. A number of things were unclear to **Guido,** and since **Julius** had also stated his positions regarding several doctrines of Christian faith with great interest and conviction, **Guido** communicated frankly and extensively his many doubts and hesitations. Moreover, he conveyed his anxiety that **Julius,** in his excessive enthusiasm, had intended to unite himself with a Juno but actually united with a cloud and therefore would produce chimeras like Ixion.[4]

The next letter brought new, unexpected news. **Julius** had switched to theology. At the same time he assured **Guido** that he need not worry at all about chimeras. His heart, the friend wrote, had learned from experience what truth is, from an experience as certain as none other can be. He wrote that his constant longing for clarity had not abandoned him now, for it had led him to the study of theology. He now wished to understand in terms of logical necessity what he had experienced as fact, and he recommended that above all **Guido** should take up in his studies the investigation of evil. Were he to pursue this seriously, a new light would soon break forth from his studies.

Guido was greatly surprised, on the one hand, by the joyful, exuberant spirit that his soul mate's letter revealed and by the deeply rooted calmness in his soul, of which everything seemed to testify. On the other hand, he was surprised at the hints **Julius** gave in reference to a number of Christian doctrines, which formerly his friend had seen in a completely different light. In the last few days he himself had fallen into the despair of great skepticism. He had given up forever finding the truth, and in this state of deep discontent had written to his friend.

CHAPTER TWO

After a few weeks had gone by **Julius** received another letter from **Guido** which bore witness that what divine grace had initiated in his soul was being brought to marvelous completion. The letter read:

Dear Julius, Beloved in Christ!

Those who await the Lord receive new strength, so that they rise with wings like eagles, so that they run and do not get exhausted, so that they walk and do not tire [Isa 40:31].

This expresses my joyful situation! I am happy and my soul praises God its Savior, who led it out of darkness into light and set its feet on a sure path. I said I must lie down and will never rise, but you shamed my fear and made me walk in confidence. I said I am a blade of grass, blown in the wind. If the wind tears it loose, who will bring it back again? I am a bent reed. If a storm comes, I will be completely broken. But you, Lord, comforted me in my loneliness, and spoke to me in my distress like a friend. Therefore I will praise you forever and ever and proclaim your praise to a great congregation. Yes, it has gone well with me. Peace I have found, and rest for my soul.[5]

Your letter, dear **Julius,** is new proof for me that one and the same spirit rules both of us because every single one of your words spoke so deeply to my own innermost experience. Between the mirrors of our hearts stands the sun. It reflects in both of them, shining out of one into the other.

When I bring to mind all the confessions and professions of Christians of all centuries and times, as well as yours and mine, an almost frightening awe of the holy stream of life overwhelms me. Down through many centuries this stream has poured itself into innumerable exhausted and empty hearts, reflecting everywhere the great image of the same sun. If in your confession and the confessions of Christians in the most distant regions I recognize myself down to the smallest detail, while the non-Christians next to me cannot see beyond the end of their noses, why should I not believe that we have entered into a higher realm of things, where human spirits come into direct contact with each other in God, where in God's light they can see their own heart and the hearts of all others?

Since I last wrote to you the course of my inner life has been as follows. At first I tried to get an overall picture of God's great plan of salvation. I found how the fallen human race took with it into its sunken state the marks of a higher knowledge, like the crown put into the grave of a departed king. I found in the first two brothers how the church of God's children and the congregation of the evil one had already split apart [Gen 4:8–16; Heb 11:4]. It is a useful concept, appearing often in **Augustine** and **Luther,** that the church of God and that of the children of the world were modeled on the first pair of brothers, and, so to speak, accepted the two as their heads. Augustine, **City of God,** I.15, c.1:

Scripture tells us that Cain founded a city, whereas Abel, as a pilgrim, did not found one. For the city of the saints is up above, although it produces citizens here below, and in their persons the City is on pilgrimage until the time of its kingdom.[6]

See also Luther's *Lectures on Genesis* [Weimar edition, vol. 42, pp. 221–22].

I found how a kernel of piety persisted through even the most depraved generations, just as the Milky Way, poured into the dark expanses, lends a glow of light even in the gloomiest of times. I also found how, while the peoples of earth generally sink into bondage to sin and idolatry, a holy sound of God keeps on ringing to the pious remnant, a song of angels for the lonely, devout shepherds in the fields [Luke 2:8–14].

I discovered how we find ultimately in Abraham the forefather of all who want to believe. I saw that by means of his entire life he provided the earthly example of hating one's own soul, of losing one's own life, and of the crucifixions and resurrections of the spiritual champion. That is why the promise is first connected with his seed. I found how after this seed has developed into a people, the entire race receives as its own possession the ladder of heaven upon which, in order to connect fallen human beings with the sacred world of the spirit, the people of God ascend and the messengers of God descend [Gen 28:12]. I found how the people received the law, which made a Savior necessary, and the prophets who made the people long for him. I found how all the history, guidance, and institutions of the people provide in the dim mirror of this physical world a hint of the spiritual and of what lies in the future. I learned how this spirit finally enters the world as an inner theocracy in order to become the model and intimation of the glory on the other side, so that we can see in the dark glass how, in its transfiguration, the inner kingdom of God will emerge visibly and in splendor [1 Cor 13:12].

Furthermore, I found in this new covenant of God such glorious and awe-inspiring prospects regarding the perfection of the whole plan of God for humanity. I found the goal for the entire development of humanity so marvelous beyond all measure that I was astonished and asked myself apprehensively: You worm, are you really included in this kingdom whose boundaries reach from the

steps of God's throne all the way down to the bottom of the abyss—
and everything is glorious?

The one who had the Spirit without measure appeared among
us so that we could become one with him as he is one with the Father.
This is the will of God, and what can withstand it? The visible and its
shackles? O, even the visible longs for deliverance from its bonds by
means of the glorification of the children of God [Rom 8:22–23].
Satan and his spirits? O, they are, as Augustine says, only the antithe-
sis in God's great pronouncement of resurrection whereby its effect
increases all the more.[7] The will of those who hate the light? O, the
All-knowing, who can bestow his grace in as many forms as the heavens have suns, will certainly know in what form to set this grace
before the stubborn heart so that it cannot remain closed.

How often I enthusiastically focused my contemplation upon
the marvelous conclusion of the eleventh chapter of the Epistle to
the Romans, which, for the person who takes the context into
account, is not the main pillar of the doctrine of divine predestina-
tion, but a sword. The train of thought is obviously this:

> Since the Jews rejected the gospel, the Gentiles were
> given the opportunity to enter the kingdom of God. Yet
> one day God will show the same mercy to them that he
> has shown to you, for God has allowed all people unbelief
> so that in the end he can show mercy to all! O, how deep
> are the riches of God's grace, wisdom, and knowledge
> with which he is able to draw the most diverse people by
> the most diverse means unto himself. How unfathomable
> for the limited human eye are the manifold ways by which
> he rescues fallen souls! (Again and again the perverse
> impulses of our self-centeredness tear us away from the
> source of divine grace, so again and again God must think
> of other ways to meet us in a, so to speak, veiled form.)
> For who has ever given him advice regarding his designs?
> Who can say that they, with justification, can demand
> anything of him? He, the ground of all being, has given
> existence to everything. He who points the way to himself
> leads everything back to himself. He is the goal toward

which all creation strives, because in him alone are satisfaction and fullness [Rom 11:25–36].[8]

Let me set down here the splendid remarks of Chrysostom regarding this passage (**Homilies on the Epistle to the Romans, 11:33**):

> Going back to the creation of the world, he considers God's plan of salvation from the beginning up to the present moment, and, contemplating the manifold ways in which God leads his creatures to salvation, he is seized with wonder and breaks out with this exclamation. He is in devout astonishment that God not only **desired** to achieve, but was **able** to achieve, opposites through opposites.[9]

At times my spirit prayerfully contemplated the "then comes the end" of which Paul writes (1 Cor 15:24), that is, the moment when hell and death will be no longer but when God will be all in all; when the blemishes in the spiritual world will be wiped away and the division will be overcome; when the Son will have finished his reign and will deliver it to the Father of the **pure and blessed** spiritual world; and when the alternating from night to day ceases and everything is everlasting light. Then, however, looking into my own heart I found only death and night, and I often became very despondent.

Yet I, too, wanted to become **glorified.** I wanted to see in **myself** the glory of a child of God. Therefore, I began to wrestle in prayer. I began more earnestly to observe, examine, inspect, sift, clarify, and compare all my words and deeds. I took note of what still had to be eliminated from my life. I wrote down the failures and transgressions that each day brought to my inner life. Even so, my soul found no peace. I stopped feeling that Jesus was my friend and became cold and indifferent. Perhaps I was standing at the edge of a deep abyss and did not know it. How often a person hurries along a narrow trail between a steep cliff and a deep abyss as though one were on a broad, smooth path. God it is who hides the abyss from us. If he did not, we would be lost.

Who rescued me in my time of need? More about that later. For now let me continue telling about the rescue itself. It became clear to me that I had set out on a false path of salvation, taking things into my own hands, and had not yet understood reconciliation. I had neglected to turn my eyes to the certainty of my salvation, which lay outside and beyond me in his will. To find out how gracious he is to me, I had examined only my love for him and had used its meager size to measure the greatness of his mercy. As I saw afterward, this is, in essence, the Roman Catholic view of the doctrine of atonement, in which sanctification precedes reconciliation. This view inverts the order of salvation, and consequently never lets a person find peace. As a result I had acquired at that time—and I cannot really explain why—a dislike for Luther, preferring to read Tauler and Thomas à Kempis.[10]

It is indeed true that the redemption of Jesus Christ, all of God's grace, and eternal heaven itself are of no help to me as long as he is not there for **me,** and he is only there for me through faith and love. However, in order for me to believe in his grace and to love his love again, his grace and love must be there first. Truly, a Christ must be in world history, and Christ must really have done what is sufficient for my salvation. There must be an objective redemption of the world from which my faith in my own redemption can draw strength.

This conviction explains why even our reformers, as I now see, insist so earnestly on the Christ **for us,** through whom alone the Christ **in us** can become whole. That is why our Melanchthon writes:

> Away with the speculations of Augustine or others! When you hear that we are justified by faith, do not think justification occurs because faith is a virtue in us, which attracts God's good will, nor because this virtue produces still others. Rather, whenever you hear the word *faith* remember that faith is something offered to us **from outside.**[11]

We can never use our love of God to measure how things stand with our pardon, says Melanchthon, because then we would never be justified, **because we never love enough.** Even though our new person begins in this life, sin nevertheless still clings to us. Therefore, we must focus on the fact that we are righteous not on account of the new being in us, but on account of the mercy in God.[12]

In this evangelical way we are led away from ourselves entirely and, conversely, into God. Away with anxiety-ridden reflection and brooding about yourself! Instead, look courageously and joyously into the abundant sun of grace. In no other way can you become free of yourself. Fallen humanity regains its glory as Orpheus [regained] Eurydice. Without looking back at her he must lead her out of sin's night. If he looks back she becomes a shade again.[13]

Legalistic Christians—the lesser sort—will pharisaically lay their virtues and self-denials on the balance scales and weigh them against those of everyone else, judging and condemning everyone except themselves. Of course, they consider themselves saved, and they attribute no small part of this to themselves and to the love they return. The pinnacle of all Christian holiness—true humility—is unattainable for them. If, on the other hand, they are of the better kind, they certainly will not degrade all others in comparison to themselves, nor will they insist on their right as the redeemed.

However, if these Christians discover no loving response within themselves, they will be shaken all the more frightfully by anxiety and despair. Perhaps the precious stone does lie in their house; yet they cannot find it because the windows of proper evangelical understanding are closed. They believe that love of their Lord must express itself in nothing but strong emotions. They do not know that simply the self-conquering will that serves quietly is the greatest expression of love.

Consequently, they wish to extract from the soil with artificial machinery the spring water that is fresh only when it springs forth naturally. They wish to pick grapes on the banks of an asphalt sea. They will either imagine pious emotions, which they do not really have, or, what is even more common, construct out of good deeds a rickety ladder to the bosom of their Savior, where they could find rest even without such a ladder.

So it is that through this reversed, and therefore erroneous, order of salvation—as would be the case with any such doctrine—people are of necessity forced to self-deception and arrogance. I am coming to see more and more clearly that Abraham really **honored** God because he **believed** what appeared unbelievable according to the normal way of thinking, which meant, as we know, acknowledging that God can do things beyond human comprehension [Rom 4].

Just as love for the divine does not begin with faith in what is already in us—because nothing is yet there—so, too, we must, whenever experiencing a cold moment in the ensuing Christian life, rekindle that life through faith not simply in what God has done within us—my humility itself can draw a veil over that—but faith in the mercy he has shown outside of and beyond me. We have, the apostle therefore says, free access through Christ to the free grace of God (Rom 5:2), so that we can approach, and draw from, the springs of grace at any time. Thus Calovius explains Romans 3:25, "he had passed over former sins,"[14] as follows:

> Persons who have experienced redemption begin a new life as though they would never sin again, because the **desire** to sin, **pleasure** in the ungodly, is not in them. Yet the deeply rooted inclination breaks forth powerfully again and again and overtakes them. Repeatedly they must seek the peace of God through Christ, and thereby new strength as well. Thus, "former sins" are all the sins which precede every hour of grace when one feels anew the forgiveness of sins through Christ's reconciliation.[15]

Thus, I also now recognize the nature of the holiness and purity attainable here on earth. We always prefer to be holy angels rather than holy humans. We are Nebuchadnezzars who demand that forgiveness of sins and grace build our palaces so that we can stand at the battlements and declare: "This is the great Babylon that I have built as a royal residence through my great power and in honor of my magnificence." However, the wisdom of God ordains that we are driven from our thrones now and then, and our bodies lie out under the dew of heaven until we praise the one who lives eternally, whose dominion lasts forever and ever [Dan 4:28–33].

> The truly pardoned are those who go about as if they had a noose around their necks, who are ashamed of the mercy shown them, and who, like the wheelwright Willigis, because he became archbishop of Mainz, are afraid they might forget their origins.[16]

This is probably an additional reason why the Savior does not hurry to a convert more quickly and pull the weeds out by the roots.

Only one demand is made of us in connection with holiness, but even that demand is made easy by the provision that accompanies it: **"Sin will no longer have dominion over you, for you are no longer under the law, but under grace"** (Rom 6:14). Truly a **"for"** that none but the pardoned will understand! Let me give you the commentary from our great Augustine's splendid **Propositiones ad ep. ad Rom.,** where he says:

> If this happens (when divine grace is imparted to a person who is under the law), certain desires of the flesh will remain behind, which, as long as we are in this life, will compete with the spirit in order to lure it into sin. However, because the spirit is firmly grounded in the grace and love of God it stops sinning, since we sin not through the evil desire itself, but through acquiescence (Opp. T. III. ed. Bened. *Propos. XIII. ad ep. ad Rom. 3:20*).

After one has committed sin for a long time and scarcely suffered from it, there comes the time when one must suffer from it more and more even though committing it no longer. Before, sin was alive in me and I was dead. Now I have become alive, but sin does not die immediately; a portion remains. Yet the time is coming, yes, it is coming, when he who is called the Lord of Salvation and the Prince of Life will lead me through death to an undefiled inheritance. There will be no suffering or crying there, and all tears will be dried. O, would that you were already here, you sacred time! O, how my soul longs for you and your clarity!

Given the forgoing, all self-examination by a true evangelical Christian consists only in asking oneself: **What do you love?** It does not consist of moaning and groaning about one's many sins, but in turning in childlike joy to the one on the cross. Earlier it was inconceivable to me that such a doctrine would not lead to frivolous indulgence in sin. Yet through my own experience my belief has become just as rock-solid that only this order of salvation brings about godlike holiness. The same Luther who says, "We obtain the forgiveness of sins through faith alone, not through love, and through faith alone are we justified, because being justified means being born through the new spirit," was also well aware of the fire, small as a mustard seed, deep within such a faith. Luther often revealed it so powerfully that one could easily see the difference, indeed the great difference, between faith of the heart and faith of the lips. With his direct, dynamic voice he describes faith in this way:

> **Faith is a living, carefully considered trust in God's grace, so certain that a person would die a thousand times for it.** Such trust in, and knowledge of, divine grace causes one to be joyful, confident, and cheerful toward God and all creatures. This the Holy Spirit brings about through faith.[17]

Elsewhere, the same Luther:

> Faith is a tremendous, living thing; **it is not a sleepy, lazy idea.** It does not hover about or float on the surface of one's heart like a goose on the water, but it is like water heated over a fire. The water remains the same, but now it is warm instead of cold, and thus very different water. So it is that faith, which is the work of the Holy Spirit, produces a different disposition, mind, and heart, thus making a totally new person.[18]

Furthermore, in his book of sermons he testifies about true faith:

> Saint Luke and Saint James say so much about works in order that you cannot go out and say: "Yes, now I'm going to believe," and then fabricate a delusion that merely floats on the heart like foam on beer. No, no, faith is a vital, crucial thing, makes us totally new, transforms our hearts and turns us completely around. It goes to the core and causes there a total renewal of the entire person. Thus, if heretofore I have seen a sinner, I now see by that person's different course of conduct, different nature, different life, that that person believes. Faith is such a great thing; that is why the Holy Spirit has Luke and James address the issue of works, because these are the evidence of faith. So when we see people without works we can easily draw the conclusion and say: they have heard about faith, but it did not sink in. If you want to remain arrogant, greedy, and angry, and still chatter a lot about faith, then Saint Paul will come and say: "Well, well, dear friend, listen; the kingdom of God does not consist of words, but of power and life; it is something to be done, not something to be achieved by chattering" [cf. 1 Cor 4:20].[19]

But now, my **Julius,** I'm going to proceed to a description of something that has had a more decisive influence on my life and thought than the system of theology and my studies. I have become acquainted with a community of true disciples of Christ. Before I myself came to know Jesus, I had heard people talking about these individuals now and then, referring to them as mystics, bigots, or Pietists. I very carefully avoided them because I, more than anyone else, dreaded a narrow-minded view of life, one which, so I thought, squeezed the breath and vitality of a lively person into a corset, put handcuffs on the bold spirit of aspiring young people, and cast the color of death over their faces as well as their actions. I thought that under such confining, dismal views the great, marvelous flower garden of scholarly endeavor would have to shrink to an ordinary vegetable garden for the kitchen; the full, wide, undulating Eden of

70

nature to a gloomy, confined patch within cloister walls; and the vast, shining heavens above me to the vault of a catacomb.

Occasionally I would run into Otto, but having heard that he, too, belonged to the group of narrow-minded people, I carefully avoided him. Later on, when I began to come closer to Christ and when P. and others often jokingly called me a mystic, it occurred to me on occasion that perhaps those other people and I were pursuing the same goal. I watched Otto more carefully, and the tremendous sincerity and gentleness I noticed in him almost convinced me that his entire being mirrored that third person whom I, too, loved.

So I looked for the charming young man. One evening I found him alone out in his small yard. In a few minutes I had opened my heart to him, and he fell into my arms. "So," he exclaimed, "you are a disciple of the Lord!" My response was, "I ask and plead that I might be one, and at the same time be your brother in Him." He drew me to his heart and then we told each other our experiences.

He had been led on a path entirely different from mine. He had never actually doubted the principles of faith, but, at the same time, he had never attached any great importance to them. He had never been fundamentally worldly, but neither had he been decidedly spiritual. While in this state he became acquainted with a man who, since then, has also become the guiding light of my life.

This venerable old man has been living here for a few years in a Sabbath such as those in heaven will celebrate, namely, a state in which the most blissful calm and the most blissful activity of love have become one. Until he had reached a very old age he had always been extremely busy—both traveling and making extended stays—with works of love toward God and humanity. The places that saw him most often were those of misery and distress because he knew of nothing more loving than to dry tears. With this purpose in mind he even traveled around in a number of German territories. Wherever his influence and means extended to larger initiatives, he improved hospitals and prisons. Wherever his activity in large-scale projects met with opposition, he turned to helpless individuals and offered himself as a friend.

He was of the opinion that great physical misery oppresses the human spirit so much that one hardly ventures to look to what is above. Therefore, he first dried the tears of earthly suffering from those who were miserable in body and spirit before showing them the wounds of their souls. After they had learned to love him as their benefactor, they were more willing to listen to what he had to say about the wounds of their souls and about the One who helps. In this way, thanks to him, many who were physically and spiritually poor no longer had to eat their physical or spiritual bread with tears. He had also acquired a little knowledge of simple medical treatments and, just as everything else he did served the One, he was able to use these, too, at the sickbed in order to open a path to the souls of those who were suffering. Often he sat for weeks at the bedside of those in great pain without saying anything about the suffering of their souls. He won their hearts only through submissive, quiet acts of humble love. Then, however, when a ray of hope would begin to shine on the physical life of the sick, he would occasionally begin to speak of the happiness of those who had a heavenly friend beyond this life who would receive them when they died. Often this had sparked a glimmer of hope, bringing warmth to the tired soul who then wanted to find out more about the friend beyond, and a number had passed away with a passionate longing for him.

In carrying out this work the blessed servant of God had traveled about various parts of Europe for a great many years, stopping here and there for periods of time, using everywhere the apostolic privilege of weeping with those who weep [Rom 12:15]. The public knew nothing of this activity. His motto was "Avoid attention."[20] He regarded works of love as a balsam that, when exposed, loses its fragrance and power. When he had helped someone, he, like his Savior, loved the words: "Go, and be sure not to tell anyone!" [Matt 8:4].

It never failed that some people who did not understand his way of life considered him a Samaritan, or said to him: "You have a devil in you!" His customary, simple reply was: "I'm not a Samaritan, and I don't have a devil" [John 8:48–49]. Occasionally it also happened that a Shimei would curse him and call him a troublemaker. If a third party wanted to react and avenge the insults, he responded, "Let him curse, for the Lord bid him do it" [2 Sam 16:5–14].

So it was that this disciple had followed the narrow path to the end of his pilgrim journey. In sunny hours he could already see shimmering in the distance the land toward which he was going. He wanted to rest for a short time in order to approach his heavenly rejuvenation with strength and youthfulness. Therefore he decided to stay here in our city for the remaining days of his pilgrimage and have his foster son, who lives with him, lay his pilgrim garment to rest.

This was the man (we always call him our **Abraham**) whom Otto had been encouraged to see. Otto had heard the rumor that the man was a Herrnhuter.[21] Otto had never been able to stand the Herrnhuter, partly because he assumed they had an effeminate weakness and partly because he thought they disdained scholarship. So he went to the man reticently. The aide who received him at the door repelled as much as attracted him. The man's tender and gentle nature seemed to betray too transparently the Herrnhuter in him, yet Otto was jealous of the divine calmness that graced a countenance worn down by grief.

First Otto had to be alone with this man for a while because the patriarch was not yet available. Otto struck up a conversation by mentioning the military exercise being held at that moment, but in a couple of minutes the aide lifted the conversation to a spiritual plane, speaking of the wars of passion **within** us from which all outward wars arise. Otto switched to the subject of his journey, but here, too, he hardly noticed how the discussion turned to the beyond and to the journey to our eternal home. He was not accustomed to this. He would like to have convinced himself that the man was trying to initiate a talk about conversion in a forced way. However, it was all too clear to him that these turns in the conversation were totally unforced and were the product of the deepest inclinations of this man's heavenly soul. The more he studied the features of the aide's countenance during their conversation, the more he perceived a heavenly nobility, which elicited and commanded respect. He was surprised to see before him in a contemporary, in a man of the middle class, what he thought had been realized probably only in a Plato.

Now it was announced that the noble old man himself had arrived. Otto proceeded to the room with his heart pounding rapidly because he was afraid that this man's attention would be focused even more on spiritual things and the beyond—and, hence, so would the conversation. It would be a painful situation for him, since only in rare moments of his life up to now had he lifted his thoughts above the temporal world. He found the patriarch alone with another young man. The room was unusually plain. The patriarch himself, a venerable man of almost seventy years, appeared to him like a figure out of a higher world. In **his** countenance, too, were the marks of hidden grief, but it was as if an uninterrupted smile of triumph were spread over them. His eyes gleamed from a mysterious fire such as Otto had never seen in a mortal. Often his eyelids closed over that glow, as though the soul wanted to close itself off from the earthly world and open itself only to the inner one. In his speech there was no sentimental sweetness, but a masculine nobility, which testified to a great and powerful soul.

The conversation dealt only with things of ordinary life, but above it was intermittent illumination like the gentle sheet lightning, which comes from another realm. Otto noticed in particular the warmth of love as the old man's interest increased as soon as they spoke of individuals who were suffering in any way. It was as if he had been sent to earth by God as a representative to impart relief and comfort to all.

When Otto was about to leave at the end of this first visit, he was asked whether he had already arranged for lodging. His answer was no. So, humbly and gently, as though Otto had a favor to bestow, the old man invited him to stay at his house and share in his simple meals. People who are unfamiliar with higher things always have an uneasy feeling when they are with a higher person. It is as if in that person their own conscience or the gaze and judgment of God himself were at their side. Consequently, in spite of being deeply stirred by the old man's indefinable, heavenly nobility, Otto would rather have declined the offer. However, he had no excuse such as the ones people always invent when the spirit of God wants to touch their hearts, and he had to stay.

He stayed in this Emmaus for three weeks, and during this time his rebirth occurred. In Otto's case the rebirth did not come in an earthquake that has to shake the firm foundations of a temple of idols, since his love of self and the world did not have very deep roots. It came very gradually during these weeks through a growing feeling of the majesty and peaceful grandeur of a truly Christian life. More and more this feeling replaced the indifference in his heart with humility and love.

From morning until evening he saw how the Sabbath that the disciple chose was none other than the one God celebrates, out of whose blessed peace streams of love flow unceasingly, and in this outpouring he finds his peace. People came with their various needs: helpless children who were granted schooling and food; feeble old people for whom space was found in hospitals; the sick and ailing to whom medicine and nourishing food were given; unemployed laborers who needed shelter; poor students wishing free board and study fees; people troubled about the salvation of their souls requesting advice and comfort; joyful believers who came for strengthening. Otto never saw the door open without knowing that whoever came brought nothing but wanted to be satisfied in body or in spirit. And the one who had long ago given up living for himself was never fatigued and never discontented. The same sympathy and the same warmth for every single one! Love was his motto. Love flowed from the hem of his garment [Matt 14:36].

Otto was reminded of the words of holy scripture about being transformed into the image of Christ. Up to now he had regarded this as an oriental figure of speech that he did not know how to interpret except that one should be as righteous as Christ. However, from the copy of the image he was learning to understand the original; the disciple was casting light on the master. It really seemed to him as though in the patriarch he were seeing the living Christ. Suddenly the sight of this sanctified life provided him with explanations and expositions of the scripture, which no book had given him.

O, how Otto's story gave wings to my soul! It is true that I had had daily discourse with the spirits of Augustine, Melanchthon, Luther, Francke,[22] and Spangenberg,[23] but now to **see** such a disciple!

Otto was at once willing to take me to him, and what I have learned up to now in this circle of Abrahamites—and, **Julius,** I say it once more—goes beyond books and doctrine!

I want to tell you something only about my first two visits and about the one yesterday, the most important of all. When I went there the first time, a few younger brothers were still present, and the very old disciple, seated in their midst, really did look like a patriarch. **Julius,** human words cannot express what I experienced there because it emanated from a higher region! It was as though a soft, holy breeze emanated from the disciple and spread over all who were present. Whether we talked about sacred issues or ordinary ones, everything was sanctified because everything was spoken as if in the presence of the invisible one who is near. We also alternated between seriousness and childlike, innocent humor, which the venerable man himself loved, although the humor was only a fleeting cloud against the deep blue, tranquil sky.

Among those present was one who did not share the spirit, but in this hour he was incapable of resisting the spirit that had come over the others, and even **his** words took on a touch of the eternal. The discussion also turned to unbelieving preachers. The disciple related whatever good things he knew about them but remained silent about anything else, reproving only complete unworthiness. This he would do, however, with holy judgment, so that it seemed to me that if the respective persons had been standing before him they could not have endured the earnest, melancholy look in his eyes.

After several hours of conversation he got up and invited us to take a walk, and we went. The conversations kept ringing inside me like the peal of bells and, overwhelmed, I called out: "If here on earth this is already the blissfulness of Christians being together, can the blessedness of a future day be greater still?" The disciple heard my words, took my arm, and appeared as if he wanted to speak, but remained silent and in that sacred silence we walked along fields of grain toward the evening sun as it was sinking lower and lower.

My thought was: O, you holy patriarch, would that every young person and I could be at your side like this, walking securely toward the everlasting sun! Finally I could not repress my overwhelming emotions. I embraced the noble man and exclaimed: "O, how blessed must be the soul that has matured to the state of perfection in which you live, my father!" A grave look came over his countenance, and I saw melancholy and dignity in his eyes. "My dear friend," he said, "in order that you won't be bitterly disappointed, don't let yourself be deceived by the first instance of brotherly love. I noticed earlier how the first experience of being together as brothers in Christ made a deep impression on you. You thought you could find a spotless bride of the Lord in a Christian community, and you believe that today you have really encountered one. Of course, who would want to deny that where the Lord is you can feel the movement of the Spirit, and he was in the midst of us today. But even a sanctified human being remains a **human being.** If I should confess to you about myself I have nothing to say except that I am a sinner who wants to attain salvation through grace. My sanctification is my daily request for forgiveness through which my proud heart becomes more and more gentle and my lofty spirit less and less haughty. Therefore, my very dear friend, do not speak about reaching perfection. Only One was perfect, the One whom we are to love more than we love anyone else. And as to life with others in Christ, O, do not forget that we must become holy human beings before we are holy angels. Yes, it is true, sometimes in the company of other Christians you will receive the gift of a Sabbath feeling. And why shouldn't you, since the Lord so expressly blessed this kind of company? But as in yourself, so in every other person you will still find the human being."

I must admit to you it was painful for me that the level-headedness and deep humility of the man tempered the heat of my feelings. O, I sighed, how deeply the human being must have fallen if even the soul who has served the Lord so long still has to struggle so hard against things below! I wanted to learn even more from his words. I told him my story and yours, and asked whether many experiences of our time might not indicate an outpouring of the Holy Spirit, the results of which would be very great.

The disciple responded to this with great interest and answered: "My beloved friend, take what I am going to say now as the bequest of an old man who will soon depart from the world.

Take it as the lesson taught me by a long life of experience and extensive acquaintance with thousands of people from various regions and ranks. Before my journey home I would like to lay this message upon the heart of many a young theologian who is called to stand in the great time now approaching, for the greater the time, the greater the need for the cunning of the serpent and the innocence of the dove [Matt 10:16]. Thus I am speaking to you as if you yourself might soon be at an academy and become one of the instruments of the great days that are before us.

"The work of God's spirit in these days is greater than you or most people imagine. Yes, a great resurrection morning is dawning. Hundreds of youth are being awakened everywhere by the spirit of God. Everywhere the converted are entering into closer union. Even scholarship is becoming the servant and friend of the Crucified. Also, civil authorities, albeit in part still hostile to this great transformation, are acting favorably in many places out of fear that the transformation might have an influence on politics, and where they do not act favorably, the forces of light are all the stronger. Many an enlightened preacher is already proclaiming the gospel in its power. Many who are still hidden will come forward. I see the dawn, yet my eyes will not behold the day itself from here, but rather from a higher place. You will live to see it! O, would that you do not reject the words of an old man who, out of sincere love, wishes to give you a hint regarding this great time!

"The more divine a power is, the more frightful its perversion. Therefore, in telling about the end times when the gospel is spread across the entire earth, the scripture does not present merely the confrontation with the ever more powerful opposition of the enemy but also with the ever greater art of deception within the kingdom of light. In life there is a shadow side to every truth, with the darkest shadow accompanying the greatest truth.

"Above all else watch out that the tempter does not practice his crafts in the congregation. There will be those for whom the simple gospel is not enough. It frequently happens that when a soul has received forgiveness of sin and felt the blessed results for a short while, the soul apparently thinks it is too simple merely to accept grace upon grace for one's evil, inconstant heart. The individual wants to go beyond that, but every step beyond is also a step away from the Savior. There is no thorough cure for the proud, self-willed heart other than renewing every day and every hour that by which one first came to Christ. If there are steps in the spiritual life, then every single person begins at the same place, on the bottom step. Nevertheless, you may see members of the congregation who do not find it important to humble themselves every day as much as they did on the day of their conversion, nor do they find it important to remember throughout their lives that they have been pardoned only through the righteousness of another. My dear friend, whenever you see such members you can be sure they do not yet know the true frailty of our nature!

"May you yourself, however, pray in an ever more childlike spirit that the free grace of your Lord might never become unimportant to you. Rather, being brought up through grace, may you learn to discern daily from a new facet of this grace that it is the ever-flowing fountain of life. Above all, flee from the error of those who want to become children of God so that on the basis of the glory they have attained they can measure themselves against the children of the world. I mean those who seek the life only for the sake of light, who want to be seized only for the sake of figuring it out. Never will such people truly find the life or be seized, for God is jealous and wants to be loved for his own sake. We receive understanding only as something that belongs to and accompanies righteousness.

"You will hear a great deal of complaining about narrow-mindedness and about the zeal to condemn. Do not join the conversation unless you know the nature of what is being criticized. You might find groups where tongues wait to catch the person they can attack; where people prefer to hunt for what is missing from everything rather than praise what is present; where they pick at the scab before the wound is healed; where they trample in the mud the imitation jewel and its setting rather than replace the imitation with a diamond; where their shallow words create reality, rather than the reality the words. If you find such people you might criticize along with them, but guard against condemning in a narrow-minded way the narrow-minded people who are quick to condemn. You do not know which heart even among them might be precious to the Lord, and which he soon will cleanse of its impurities. Do not try to ingratiate yourself with the lukewarm by inveighing against these errant brothers and sisters. Instead, cast light on the virtues that the Lord has given them, too, and do not be afraid of calling yourself their brother.

"Pietism is going to be greatly discredited. Indeed, it has been already. But do not simply launch an uncritical attack on what the world identifies by that name. If so, the world will rejoice at the trick it has played on you because you yourself were included under that name and, in the world's eyes, you were attacking yourself. O, might you much rather acknowledge each time with the simplicity of a child that you, too, must take this name upon yourself with the meaning the world gives. The reason for this, my dear friend, is that very often you will discover that what people are referring to as narrow-mindedness and the zeal to condemn is nothing but the spirit of godly simplicity which desires only the One Thing and desires all else only if it is in the One Thing. Christians who love only the One in everything and love nothing they cannot love in and for Him must of necessity appear narrow-minded to the world, since the world has not found its all in the One.

"Furthermore, Christians must condemn what the Word of God has already condemned. Their love is no weakness. They cannot call out 'Peace, peace!' where there is no peace. Yet if they condemn, it is not they who condemn, but the Word of God. Moreover, they do not enjoy condemning, for it is more blessed to bless than to condemn. Therefore, my dearly beloved, let your heart be purified of all self-interest through the healing grace of Jesus, and let the eyes of your soul be illuminated.

"Then you will not have the kind of narrow-mindedness that is repudiated even before the throne of the Lord. You will not discard what the world offers you—art, knowledge, entertainment, and whatever else—but you will let it be purified by the Spirit, who is a refiner, and use it thus sanctified. Neither will you condemn where the Lord has not condemned, but will be happy when you can bless. You will often feel a calm, comforting peace in your heart

80

when you let an unnecessary reprimanding word die on your lips out of love for the One who allows even the coarsest sinner to taste his grace. Happy are the Christians who always follow the disciplining spirit, the spirit that so often in life obliges them to keep silent instead of speaking, especially when they are about to repudiate someone! At the same time, never let yourself be overcome by the fear of associating with people in order to avoid the urge to condemn. On the other hand, you should not give in to an innocuous good nature, which often can have the appearance of godly humility without having the humility itself. Rather, at those times when the Spirit witnesses to your spirit that you must speak on its behalf, then you reprove simply and distinctly what the Word of God has reproved. Your heart will ache since you would prefer to praise rather than criticize. No doubt you will also utter a sigh for the person whose work you had to reproach. Nevertheless, you cannot call out 'Peace!' where the Spirit declares war on the flesh.

"Do not look down on any human greatness, neither on talent nor abilities of any kind, but also guard against overestimating them. I see a time coming, and it is already here, when gifted people will raise their voices for truth. But woe to the time that merely flirts with those voices, rather than taking their **words** to heart!

"There will come a time when the world will declare an armistice with Christ, since after a few decades there will not be many people in the various parts of Germany who will not want to be called **Christian**. Learn how to distinguish between the spirits! [1 John 4:1]. You will encounter some individuals who enjoy wisely presented Christian ideas, whether in the fine arts or in speech, and you will meet others who can show that what is Christian is the underpinning of thrones and the substance that binds states together. You will come across those who can identify the triune God and redemption in peoples and nature everywhere, and those who attend edifying circles and keep up with ascetic periodicals. While you should not reproach such people for what they say and do, these practices alone do **not** make them your brothers or sisters in Christ.

"'The wisdom from above is pure, peaceable, gentle, open to reason, full of mercy and good fruits, impartial and without hypocrisy' [Jas 3:17]. 'Those who belong to Christ crucify their flesh along with its passions and desires' [Gal 5:24].'Let those who have wives live as though they had none, and those who weep as though they did not weep, and those who rejoice as though they did not rejoice, and those who buy something as though they do not possess it' [1 Cor 7:29–30].'Those who want to follow me must deny them-selves, take up their cross daily, and follow me' [Matt 16:24; Mark 8:34; Luke 9:23]. These are a few signs by which you can distinguish between true and false spirits. Yet you certainly cannot expect any-one to fulfill these words to the full extent. No, no! But how gratify-ing to see at least the beginnings! At the same time, wherever you find these sure signs, do not ask apprehensively about the pilgrim clothing of the creed in which the Christian is journeying through this world. The disciple will lay it down with the body, but humility and love will continue to the other side. You know that up until his final breath the disciple whom the Lord loved let this be his sermon: 'Little children, love one another' [cf. 1 John 3, 4]. Remember that the most reliable means by which you can establish godly love is to lead fellow Christians to close, familial love of one another.

"Community in godly love is simultaneously the touchstone and litmus test of Christianity. Community is not possible in its true form without true love of the Lord, and, in addition, community sep-arates out everything odd and artificially idiosyncratic that so readily attaches itself. At the same time it is an enemy of all lukewarmness. Everyone has a different gift of grace, so each person can learn from the other, just as we all can learn from Christ. Wherever Christians live isolated from one another you will very often find peculiarities, and no doubt lukewarmness and sluggishness, too. However, those who find joy in being together should allow the various spirits their varied developments, as long as all converge in Christ. The soul of a Luther should not be poured into the mold of a Zinzendorf,[24] but by the same token, one should not expect the gentler soul of a Zinzen-dorf to take on a ruggedness that simply is not in its nature. Then, too, it is a great abuse—one that you will see more and more—when people excuse as peculiar or idiosyncratic something that is not just superficial but grows out of a bitter root in the heart.

"The sum of my words is: **humility and love.** O, when I am no longer here below, and you, my dear friend, find yourself in better times, may these weak words of mine come back to you and guide you!"

In the meantime dusk had fallen, and only the red glow of the sun illuminated the edge of the horizon. We had come to a churchyard. The disciple led us to a grave. "Here," he said, "is buried one of the most faithful servants of Christ, whose works on earth consisted of nothing but suffering. I knew him intimately; I learned much at his sickbed." While saying this he uncovered his head and looked silently at the rays of the setting sun. I do not know if he was praying, but I do know that **I** was praying as I looked into that sanctified countenance upon which rested the peace and joy of a morning beyond. And all of us around him were praying.

A few days later I wanted to attend one of his evening devotions. Prior to that we had spoken briefly about their benefit. He had said the following: "The outer church, as a nursery garden for the inner church, is a holy and divine institution. Yet if the gospel is not preached from the pulpit, and if even the hymns do not proceed in the Spirit of the Lord, then it is impossible for the soul who is seeking edification to be satisfied. Thus, it is in the nature of things that like-minded souls will gather for common prayer and song, just as other groups of like-minded souls will gather for dance and play.

"However, even if the gospel is preached in the churches, the Christian soul does not celebrate just **one** Sabbath. Every day is consecrated to the Lord, so the urge will be felt daily to gather for edification. For instance, a father can feel the need to impress more deeply upon the hearts of his family particular points about the Christian life. Of course, it is quite possible that here, too, a shadow will accompany the light; perhaps more importance will be attached to these gatherings than to those in church, even though the location does not make the difference; perhaps during or after such gatherings people will make one-sided judgments about others. If so, it would be better to play cards. Yet, since the Lord once promised his blessing to gatherings of two or three, he will certainly be able to use enlightened servants to prevent possible abuses."

After this we went to the prayer hour. All the members of the house and a few of their acquaintances had gathered in a small room. First we sang a hymn. Then in a dignified voice the old man read an awakening sermon from a Christian periodical. He never took the liberty of speaking his own words. He always said: "As long as we have printed sermons by esteemed teachers the layperson does not need to hear any others. Besides, the prayer of a broken and humble heart often has a much greater effect." Then we sang a hymn whose last verse was:

We who all have gathered here together,
join our hands to pledge as one,
bound by what you suffered, to hold ever
true to you 'til life is done.
And to show that this our song of honor
fills your heart with beauty and with pleasure,
say, "Amen," and add your call:
"May God's peace go with you all."

Then he closed with a prayer. I cannot believe, **Julius,** that a human being can be as close to God as the old disciple was in that prayer! It was not enthusiasm that characterized his words, but **submissiveness.** His soul seemed to become nothing but humility before the presence of the Most Holy. The prayer ended: "Simplicity focuses only on the one thing in which everything else is found. Simplicity clings only to the eternal magnet. O, you magnet of all hearts and souls, make our souls, too, so simple that they seek nothing but your heart."

After that we all went our separate ways. Naturally I took home more from this prayer hour than I often do from church. I had the clear sense that Christ had come alive in the same way in everyone present. It was the feeling experienced by a living member of a body when it feels united with the other living members under one head [1 Cor 12:12; Eph 4:15–16; Col 2:18–19]. But I cannot say that this awareness spoiled my memories of gatherings in large sanctuaries. I merely experienced the natural difference we feel when we move from a company of souls where we rightly **expect** the best to one where we **know** we are at one with them.

Since those two times I have frequently been in the circle of the Abrahamites and have always felt the presence of the Lord. I found that the disciple himself was not at all the same every time; sometimes great joy filled his countenance, other times sorrow. Yet the foundation of the heaven in his soul remained constant, and in the darkness of his sorrow the full moon shone tenderly.

The first time I saw him cheerless I was very worried. I was worried that even the cedars of Lebanon could fall! But soon I saw how, as the star acquires its brightness from the night, so the Christian from sorrow. Once when I told him about this he replied, "So it is, my dearest friend! Every sorrow is truly a ladder to heaven because it reaches from the earth, where it begins, to the heavens in whose blessedness it ends [Gen 28:12]. This is true of temporal as well as of spiritual concerns. For what they both test is our **faith.** They test our belief that we actually are reconciled children, eternal heirs of an everlasting glory of which neither transitory suffering nor transitory sins can make us unsure. Only the suffering Christian knows that this faith is an anchor line leading behind the curtain into the holy place. Since the grace of the Lord enables his disciples to stand for years in the storms of earth with their heads amid the clouds, his disciples acquire, as a result, the decisiveness and firmness of action that the person of the world does not possess. Therefore, let us be no less thankful for the gloomy hours of life than for the sunshine. Thanks to him, we are, in spite of all sunshine and gloom, elevated above all change."

My visit yesterday turned out to be especially important. When I think of it, tears still come to my eyes and my heart beats faster. Yesterday afternoon I went to his place and found Otto alone with him. Immediately an especially solemn dignity radiated toward me from his entire person. "Today," he began, "we are setting a long imprisoned soul free to go to the home where it is anxiously awaited. My dear Anton is lying on his deathbed. If it is all right with you, we wish to bid him our last farewell today."

Toward evening the patriarch set out with us in order to witness the departure home of the blessed man's soul. On the way he told us that this individual had maintained his faith during nine years of suffering. For nine years an abscess had made it impossible for him to do any work and had kept him in bed for the last four. Every day during this period he had to look for his subsistence from unseen hands. During his long affliction his wife fell ill, and when she died he lost the only person who faithfully had cared for him. Occasionally his pains were mild, but usually they were severe. Yet the entire time he had remained a stranger to grumbling because his prayer had been only for the same measure of patience as suffering.

We arrived at his cottage and found a circle of brothers already in the small room. They wanted to wait until the suffering spirit's wings were unbound. At the head of the man's bed sat his only daughter. Although she had been crying, now she was not, but was looking with quiet joy at the countenance of the dying man. He was lying peacefully on his bed. His face was haggard and emaciated, its features serious, and he had folded his hands on top of the cover. However, when he saw that the disciple had come, his serious features were suddenly cloaked in a wonderfully lovely smile such as I have seen only on those who have actually departed. He tried to sit up and say: "Soon, soon I will be better able to say thanks, dear…," but the disciple closed his mouth with a kiss, so that his words of praise would stop.

The disciple sat down at his side and rested his hand in the man's folded hands. "Do you feel more relief today?" he asked. Anton answered: "The physical pain has left me, but my soul is reflecting seriously on all my wrongs and transgressions. Now that I am just at the point of passing over to the other side, the nine years of suffering lie before me concentrated in a single point. Thanks to Him I have never grumbled during this time about the difficult path. However, neither have I ever truly considered the infinite greatness of the blessing granted my hardened heart because of it. That is what stands so vividly before my soul at this moment of departure. Thus I now want to testify that I owe the complete surrender of my heart to this nine-year infirmity alone. Here I had to learn what it means to deny one's own will and make one's will the will of him whose ways here on earth are beyond knowing [Rom 11:33]. I was freed from myself, from people, and from the world: from the world, because it granted me only pain; from people, because up until the time that I became acquainted with you, my brother in the Lord, I had to rely totally on unseen hands; from myself, because so many temptations arose during the frightful loneliness and pain, and I became so deeply acquainted with every recess of my corrupt heart that it was purely and simply the reconciling grace of my Lord that was able to hold me high above the sea of my misery. But now I have reached my goal."

He sank back exhausted and remained quiet for a while. Then he once again raised himself, and with a countenance that shone brighter and brighter he said: "I feel that the final moment is approaching when I will depart from the dark chamber. I am laying down my pilgrim garment and shall be clothed in incorruptibility [1 Cor 15:53]. Lord Jesus, O, would that I could now exclaim from my cottage to the world: How blessed the one who crosses over in your name! I praise you for everything!"

We all sat silently for a time at the side of the one who was silent. The features of his face gradually relaxed into a smile, and his previously dull eyes took on more and more of a sparkle. Behind him sat his daughter, whose smile expressed a heavenly sadness, as though she were the angel who was to lead him out of the dark chamber. The dying man requested that we sing a deathbed hymn. The final verse was this:

> So now it's time to lay aside the dwelling
> which housed the faithful spirit of the Lord,
> and into which Christ's love was richly poured,
> who purifies it now, all dross expelling.
> Released, the cheerful spirit takes to flight,
> as thoughts about its dwelling fade from sight.

After that the disciple rose majestically, like an angel at the throne of God, and, bending over the man who was passing away, prayed softly. All our hearts were praying along with him, for they had already been in uninterrupted prayer the entire time. Then the long eyelashes of the infirm man closed over his brightly shining eyes, and we waited the final moment. His throat rattled; then stillness. He breathed loudly again; stillness again. Then he called out loudly: "I have conquered through the power of the Lord!" [Rom 8:37; 1 John 5:9]. Then his eyes closed forever.

A profound, solemn stillness lay over all those present. In the silence tears flowed from everyone. Such an awesome feeling pulsed through our hearts that it was as though invisibly the spirits of his and our departed brothers and sisters who were to take him to his Lord had entered our midst. It was as though the gates of heaven had opened and fragrances of life wafted toward us. For a time we simply sat next to each other, enjoying the communion.

Then we got up to leave. It was already late in the evening. Otto and I accompanied the disciple to his home. He was particularly solemn. Yes, he walked along in the darkness next to us like a transfigured person who is already wearing the crown. Overwhelmed by indescribable emotion, we called out as we parted from him: "We will go to no other; he alone has the words of eternal life" [John 6:68]. "Amen!" said the old man, "and when we die, we shall have a blessed journey home." While looking up toward heaven he laid his hands on our heads. Then he kissed us and left.

Julius! Whoever believes in Christ is risen indeed, and has gone from death to life!

Eternally in Him,
Your Guido

Sermons

The Blessing of Dark Hours
in the Christian Life:
A Missionary Sermon on Luke 22:31–32

EDITORS' INTRODUCTION: In this sermon, delivered in Halle and published in 1838,[1] Tholuck expresses concern over the inadequacy of the church's effort to spread the gospel. He aims to persuade his hearers to be engaged vigorously in bringing salvation to others, even by becoming foreign missionaries. Yet what can motivate Christians to take up the task of strengthening their brothers and sisters and planting the cross in distant lands?

Tholuck finds a model in a chain of events in the life of the apostle Peter: the dark hour of his denial of Christ; Christ's rescuing care for him; and then his spectacular record in winning new believers. Emphasizing the experience of "being sifted," Tholuck analyzes the stages that take the apostle from darkness to empowering light. The crux of Tholuck's sermon are his words: "Yes, beloved, the world would be full of missionaries if all those who have been helped out of their dark hours by the prayers of the Redeemer desired to bring him thank-offerings of their love, as Peter did."

Unfortunately, we can only imagine Tholuck's moving style of delivery that made him a celebrated preacher. Nevertheless, his clear and sometimes passionate prose demonstrates a personal warmth in contrast to what he considered the dry scholasticism of orthodoxy and the impersonal rationalism of the Enlightenment. In delivering the sermon Tholuck could not help but recall that as a student in Berlin his life's aim was to become a missionary. However, in 1820 a number of circumstances, chiefly a serious, recurring lung ailment, compelled him to change his career plans.

Why are we so lukewarm in spreading the saving faith? We can cite a variety of reasons. Without a doubt, a primary one is that we do not always keep our eyes on what the Lord's grace has done for us. Therefore, let us today take to heart the words of our Savior that, while reminding us of the miracles of divine grace we have experienced, also challenge us to bring salvation to our neighbors.

We base our meditation today on the words the Lord speaks to Peter in **Luke 22:31–32:**

> But the Lord said, "Simon, Simon, behold, Satan has desired to have you so that he might sift you like wheat. But I have prayed for you that your faith should not cease, and when you have once turned back, strengthen the others."

Guided by these words we will consider together: THE BLESSING OF DARK HOURS IN THE CHRISTIAN LIFE, and, specifically,

I. Their blessing in the life of Peter, and
II. The blessing they are to bring into our own lives.

Since we want to consider the blessing of dark hours in Peter's life, let us turn our attention first **to the dark hour,** then **to the praying Savior,** and finally **to the disciple who is sifted.**

Once when a wise Greek, Aesop, was asked how God occupies himself, his answer was: He lowers what is high and raises what is low. One can say that this answer did not come from flesh and blood, for it is a statement confirmed in every way by the history of God's kingdom, and also in a peculiar way comes true in the story of the apostle Peter. On the one hand, we see the great distinction of this disciple whom the Lord calls the bedrock on which he intends to build his church [Matt 16:18]. On the other hand, we are shocked by the weaknesses and stumblings reported about this very disciple more than any other. Thus, it would seem that Jesus deliberately chose none other than Peter in order to show that he could make something out of nothing. So it was for the people Israel.

Why else did he choose them—that stubborn folk—other than to show that he could make something out of nothing?

The apostle Peter belongs to the type of persons from whom the best and worst can come, whose lives continually alternate between the greatest extremes—now heaven, now the abyss. Such a life has many dark hours because it is continually fluctuating from night to day. Yet one hour more than all the others in his life is **the** dark hour, the one to which the Savior had alluded with anxious intimation several days earlier, just as he had alluded to the betrayal by the other disciple. It is good that he points out these things ahead of time because, as a result, we can see that he did not err. He knew in advance about the betrayal by the one, as well as the fall of the other, yet he still took them into his circle of disciples. Hence the one's betrayal and the other's fall must have been included in the plan of salvation and could not spoil God's design for redemption.

Dear friends, you have observed in Old Testament prophecies that, similar to the rising sun, the closer the time of fulfillment, the clearer the prophecy. You can see the same in the Lord's prophecies: the one about his own suffering, the one about Judas, and the one about Peter. In the betrayer's case, you can trace it from the moment Jesus says, "Have I not chosen twelve of you, and one of you is a devil?" up to the words, "He is the one who will dip into the bowl with me" [John 6:70; Matt 26:23]. In the case of Peter we first see it where we read in our text: "Simon, Simon, behold, Satan has desired to have you so that he might sift you like wheat." Then we read: "Peter, I say to you, the rooster will not crow today until you have denied knowing me three times" [Luke 22:34]. "Satan has desired to have you so that he might sift you!" That is how the Word of the Lord reads.

O, how evil appears much more terrible to us when we do not regard it simply as the weakness of our own flesh and blood, but when the finger of the Lord lifts the curtain and points to a mysterious, dark power that desires weak mortals in their weak hours and laughs whenever one falls. Satan has desired me! O, how this ONE thought should have directed the disciple's eyes deep, deep into himself. Of course, he did not yet know where to be on guard. Ah, entrances for the dark power were indeed on all sides of his weak heart. Then he even hears the Lord's prophetic voice say to him: "You will deny me three times." Nevertheless, when the hour does come the disciple falls—and with a great fall.

But how, you ask, how, indeed, could he fall? Friends, I do not want to say that we, too, would have betrayed him in that hour or so would have each one of the disciples. But this I will say: In how many an hour of tribulation have we, too, called out, "Just **one** more time, just **this once,** Lord! Show that you are my God and I will never be annoyed with you again." Then he shows us he is our God, the hour of tribulation comes again, and, like Peter, we are annoyed with him, and like Peter we fall. O, the human heart is a stubborn and cowardly thing. Who can fathom it?

"But I have prayed for you!" says the Lord, and so let us look at **the praying Savior.** He prayed for Peter because Peter belonged to those who were his own. He prayed for him because Peter had accepted with all his heart the word the Savior had spoken to him, and through that word had become the Lord's possession. "You are pure," he said to them, "but not everyone" [John 13:9–11]. "You are now pure," he says, "for the sake of the word I have spoken to you" [John 15:3]. That word was the holy seed that had fallen deep into Peter's heart, too. Therefore he was able to call out, "Lord, where shall we go?" [John 6:68]. The Lord was able to pray for a person who had experienced the power of the Word like that, and for such a person the hour of temptation turned into the hour of sifting.

The words of the Lord sound strange: "Satan has desired to have you that he might sift you." We might have expected: "that he might **corrupt** you." Sifting is beneficial for the human being. Has Satan, the archenemy, turned into a **friend** of humankind? Our German translation actually says more than the original text, and yet it is not wrong.[2] The original reads: "Satan has desired you, that he might **winnow you back and forth,**" that is, tempt you, harass you. You see, this is the intent of the archenemy with such tempting. His only interest is attacking the human being. However, where actual **grain,** grain that has kernels, is winnowed in this way the winnowing is also a sifting in which the chaff blows away. This is what **God's grace** does. In the same way, every apparent destruction is a **sifting,** every failure a purification, every death a new **dawn,** not simply for Peter, but for every single Christian who has the **holy kernel** within. Friends, as often as you feel the winnowing fork remember this: the Savior prayed for you, and the result of the winnowing will be the sifting!

Now let us look together at **the disciple who was sifted.** In Peter resides a vigorous fire that breaks out at every opportunity. He is always the first to speak, always the first to act. This kind of fire enables a person to have a great impact on others. Yet such a person is no better than anyone else, because the Lord distributes natural gifts such as this diversely. However, out of regard for Peter's talent the Lord named him the "rock-solid man" upon whose shoulders his church should rise.

Side by side with great, natural attributes such as this stand great defects. As a rule, natural fire is coupled with arrogance. Since the impact of these fiery people on the public **is** great, they think they **are** great. It takes a great deal to declare self-confidently like Paul, "I have worked harder than all of them," and yet at the same time confess truthfully, "I am the least among the apostles" [1 Cor 15:9–10].

However, this same disciple has yet another failing that the human eye would consider even more reprehensible: his fire alternates with hours of weakness. We see it later in Antioch, when, out of mortal fear, he denies what he really knows. But the weakness of having merely a reticent spirit is exceedingly less pernicious than arrogance. You see how in Antioch he willingly lets himself be chastised by Paul, and not until after such humiliation does he really become strong again [Gal 2:11–14].

Thus, in the case of Peter, the dark hour of sifting is intended first and foremost to stamp out arrogance. Of course, the right strength entered the sifted disciple at the same time as humility. Three times the words of denial cross his lips, the rooster crows, the gates of the high priestly palace open, the judged and condemned Son of God steps out. Peter, how do you feel now? He feels as though a heinous deed committed in the dark of night is suddenly bathed in the light of the moon. He was able to hide his conscience deep within his heart, but then his conscience, in the person of Jesus, stepped directly in front of him and he cannot hide it. "And Jesus," it says, "turned around and **looked at him**," and, it continues, "Peter dashed out of the courtyard and cried bitterly" [Luke 22:61–62].

He is wandering about in a lonely field. O, you, too, are certainly acquainted with those moments when the cover-up of self-deception lies close before your eyes, and **one** word of scripture, or of a friend, or a direct flash from the conscience suddenly tears open the veil. Then you could sit down and bathe yourself in tears all day, and see everything around you in a new light. In such hours when the skies suddenly clear, you recall all sorts of things from earlier times that you had not thought of before; you begin to hear again all the faded tones of earlier admonitions and warnings. So it is that Peter first remembers the word about the rooster crowing when he sees that glance. So it certainly is that when he is wandering about in loneliness **this** word appears again before his awakened soul: "Simon, when you have once turned back, then strengthen the others!" Yes, in his loneliness he certainly must have called out in tears: "Lord, forgive me just one more time. Once I have turned again, I will strengthen the others. I want to tell them of the self-deception of sin, of your wondrous glance, of the wondrous blessedness it brings to condemn oneself as soon as one has a Savior."

The story shows us that the dark hour sifted the disciple and bore fruit for his own inner being. "And if everyone else takes offense at you," he had said earlier, "I will never take offense" [Matt 26:33]. What does he say when at the last farewell the Lord asks him, "Simon, son of John, do you love me?" "Lord, you know that I love you." He no longer trusts himself to pass judgment on himself and pronounce it, but the **Lord** is to pronounce judgment [John 21:15–19]. Self-confidence is broken, arrogance is cut down, and human weakness has become divine power.

Yet beyond Peter the hour of sifting bore fruit a hundredfold, a thousandfold. At the celebration of Pentecost the same disciple laid the foundation for the new community. Because of his words three thousand people were added in one day. For Christ's sake he let himself be whipped, and he left the high council with joy that he was "worthy of suffering disgrace for the sake of Jesus' name" [Acts 5:41]. He carried his preaching about Christ into the distant Orient and to the capital city of the Roman Empire. He fulfilled literally the saying of the Redeemer about "whoever does not take up the cross and follow me," because he followed the Lord all the way to the cross and died the death of the Lord, as had been prophesied about him (John 21:18).

O, you saints and beloved of God, what feelings does this story arouse in your souls? See, O see what blessing **your** dark hours can also achieve for the Savior. Yes, beloved, the world would be full of missionaries if all those who have been helped out of their dark hours by the prayers of the Redeemer desired to bring him thank-offerings of their love, as Peter did.

Inasmuch as I am talking about dark hours in the Christian life, let me explain how I perceive them. There are two different kinds. First, there are dark hours in the Christian life when the sun has set, but the moon, or at least the distant evening star, is still in the sky. These are the hours when outward needs are pressing, and the comfort of the gospel is far off; hours when, as the scripture expresses it, the countenance of the Lord is veiled; hours like those when David calls, "Lord, be merciful to me, for I am weak; heal me, Lord, for my whole body trembles with fear, my soul is very fearful; O Lord, why so long?" [Ps 6:2–3]. All of you are certainly acquainted with this hour, are you not? And you know well, do you not, that in such hours it sometimes becomes difficult to believe in hope against hope, and you have sometimes seen yourself standing in spirit at the edge of the precipice at which Peter stood.

Yet these dark hours are by no means the most terrible. These nights are not terrifying as long as the evening star gleams from afar. However, there is another sort of dark hour, when the night is total, when not only does the **Lord** hide his countenance, but **Satan** reveals **his.** He steps before the frightened soul and speaks to it of defiance, denial, and betrayal. "Say farewell to God," he calls out, "and pray to me. Then I will give you the riches of the world and its splendor" [cf. Matt 4:8–9]. This was the hour when Job cursed the day he was born [Job 3:1]. This was the hour in which Asaph called out: "Is it to be in vain that my heart has lived uprightly, and I have always washed my hands in innocence? I would almost have said so, like the godless, but behold, by saying this I would have condemned all your children who have ever lived" [Ps 73:13, 15]. That was the hour in which Judas rose from the table and went out into the night [John 13:21–30].

Is it not true that one or the other of you has experienced hours when Satan is desirous of you, when only a very, very thin thread still connects you with your Lord, and Satan puts his knife to it, intending to sever it? The Lord had prayed for you, so Satan did not sever the connection. Then comes the loud call: "Soul, I did this for you; what are you going to do for me?" "Simon, Simon when you have once turned back, then strengthen the others." O, in one way or another you have all become Peter's companions in his dark hour and his sifting. Through the power and prayer of your Lord you have emerged from the hours of night as newborn children. O, walk then in Peter's footsteps and strengthen the others!

O, you congregation of Christians gathered here, may what you have learned from your hours of need, affliction, despair, and temptation—and I see multitudes of those hours coming—appear before your soul at this moment. However, may the manifold offering of aid, which is yours, appear before your soul at the same time. Also, in the name of the eternal love to which you once swore you would bring your thank-offering, I exhort you with the words of the Lord: O, bring thanks by doing what you can to strengthen the others in faith, your weak friends here in your country, here in your families, and the even far weaker persons of other lands who do not know the name of Jesus. How pleasing to the Lord are such thank-offerings. You can see this from the admonition he gives Peter.

Perhaps the Lord has chosen a few in your midst personally to strengthen those who are his among the people in distant lands. The spirit will provide you with a holy witness of your calling. When the dark hours are over, when the clouds within you have passed, when the sun glistens again, when in humility you throw yourself in the dust as the least of all his children, not worthy to bear the title of disciple, then tenderly, yet firmly, a heavenly voice will say to you: "Go forth and bring my little sheep out of the unbelieving world into my flock."

To others among you, while you are drying your tears after the dark hours, the same voice will say, "Open your mouth, spare not your voice, and call aloud to my children who bear my name that, although they are alive, they are still dead [Rev 3:1]. Call aloud to them, 'Arise, you who are sleeping, so that Christ can enlighten you'" [Eph 5:14]. O, my friends, **only a humble preacher of God's Word can proclaim it in a genuinely fruitful way,** because forbearance, patience, and a tirelessly searching love belong to fruitful preaching of the Word. This love comes only from the experience of how eternal love tirelessly searched for **us** until we were found.

However, you who remain here in your own country and make it your concern to strengthen your closest neighbors, do not forget the unbelievers in distant places. Even up to this hour the lukewarmness of our Christians for missionary work bears witness that the call of the Lord, "Strengthen the others!," has not yet penetrated the hearts and minds of the congregations. Even if hundreds of individuals give their contributions, and some even set out to distant lands, our Christianity is covered with disgrace as long as entire congregations do not rise up to labor at the holy task. Think back on how the word about the cross sped across the earth in the first two centuries. In two centuries the fire of the first love had raised the banner of the cross in all the countries of the vast Roman Empire. Not thousands or hundreds of thousands but millions were saved in the name of Jesus. And now? For three centuries we have called ourselves **evangelical** Christians, yet the evangelical message has hardly gained a foothold in even four or five foreign countries. Friends, mission work must become the concern of **congregations,** as it was in the early church. Preachers, church leaders, and congregations—they must pursue it as a task of the church.

We, as members of congregations, are not severed, isolated parts, but, through God's grace, members of the **congregation** over which Christ is the head, and whose abode, until one day the congregation stands gathered before his throne, is the whole wide world. Therefore we can no longer view the task of our office complete and our Christian calling fulfilled if we have an eye and a heart only for the needs of those who live within **our** city walls and in the closer association of **our** church community; if only **there** we preach the gospel, feed the hungry, clothe the naked, and assist in church and school; if we do only individual acts individually. Through faith we are numbered among the royal priesthood whose blessed task is to preach in the entire world the virtues of him who called us out of darkness into his wondrous light!

Are we asking too much if we desire that every congregation calling itself Christian should take to heart as its own concern this matter of Christ's kingdom? Are we hoping too much if we expect that once more each congregation should send into the harvest at least one person who would carry out in its name the vocation of strengthening the others? Is the challenge too great if we hold before you the example of the first Christian congregation in Jerusalem, whose members were all joined in loving friendship and therefore gave testimony with great power to the resurrection of Christ, and among whom no one said of one's possessions, "They are mine!"? [Acts 4:32–35].

What could, what would, happen if the spirit of Jesus Christ were poured out over our congregations so that they turned back the way Peter did, so that they recognized the love of Christ as he did!

So, dear friends, know your calling! Keep the goal before your eyes! Hear the admonition of the Lord! Now that God's Spirit has brought these words near to you, do not delay with your deeds. And when, at the close of this gathering, you offer your contribution for the unsaved, may your mite be evidence that the sacred task of missions has become a great concern of your heart and from now on you will recognize that the call of the Lord is directed to you: "You who have turned from darkness to light, rise, and strengthen the others!" Amen.

AUGUST THOLUCK

The Drawing of the Father to the Son

EDITORS' INTRODUCTION: Tholuck preached this sermon to his congregation of students and faculty at the University of Halle.[1] His probing message and the manner in which he appeals directly to his listeners working in the fields of philosophy, history, law, medicine—indeed all disciplines at the institution—give the reader a sense of Tholuck's earnest yet spirited style, which contributed to his fame as a preacher.

Tholuck opens the sermon, in effect, with the theological question of how a person comes to Christ. His answer consists of his commentary on John 6:43–45 in which he presents and explains one of his fundamental theological positions: that God the Father takes the initiative of reaching out to every human being to draw that person to the Son.

How is one aware of this initiative of the Father? His presence pervades all realms of temporal life. The tug of the Father occurs through nature, human history, but above all—and here Tholuck cites Augustine—through the individual's conscience, which is the voice, or, more broadly, the image of God within the person. One need only be receptive in order to recognize and follow the Father's gentle but constant tug, though one has the freedom not to heed the calling present in everything that one experiences.

My devout friends, do you not find it painful that the words "my Savior," "my Redeemer" cross many thousands of lips, and yet if you were to ask someone face to face, "Dear soul, how do you really know that you are saved by him?," you would be met with silence? And it is just such people—the ones you find to be most like this—who argue most about Christ. They cannot find Christ in what the scriptures report about him or in what the church believes about him.

We are reminded of the words the Lord spoke when he once heard such people arguing. These words are so important at a time when people are disputing religious matters so much and understanding so little, arguing and writing so much but experiencing so little. I am referring to the declaration of the Lord that we read in John 6:43–45:

> Jesus answered and said to them, "Do not murmur among yourselves. No one can come to me unless the Father who sent me draws that person, and I will awaken that person on judgment day. It is written in the prophets, 'They will all be taught by God.' Whoever hears and learns it from the Father comes to me."

In approaching this text with you I would also like to call out: "Take off your shoes because we are stepping onto holy ground!" [cf. Exod 3:5]. What a high mystery of grace into which we are led. The one who created us wants to lead us with the strong and yet tender pull of his Spirit to no one else but his Son!

Clearly, this coming to Christ of which Jesus speaks is not merely an outward coming; all those whom he addresses obviously had come to him by foot. Therefore, he must be speaking about coming to him with the heart. In another declaration—namely, when he says, "I am the bread of life. Whoever comes to me will never hunger, and whoever believes in me will never thirst again" [John 6:35]—he presupposes that no one can come to him who does not hunger and thirst. Therefore, we are talking about a coming to him in whom a person begins to taste and enjoy him as a **redeemer**. He says no one can come to him in this way who has not been **drawn** by the Father, that is, as he further explains, whoever has not been **taught** by the Father, whoever has not **heard** and **learned** from the Father. Now, in the light of truth, we want to get better acquainted with **this drawing of the Father to the Son.**

Judging by appearances, it is a gift of grace for a few chosen ones, yet in truth it is as universal and far-reaching as the air. It pervades nature and the course of human life. It pervades

the spirit and heart of the human being. The Father draws, but we do not follow; the Father teaches, but we do not learn.

Judging by appearances, it is a gift of grace for a few chosen ones, yet in truth it is as universal and far-reaching as the air. Like a sacred mystery the phrase wafts over us, "the drawing of the Father to the Son." Who does not sense something of a mystery in these words? One does not understand them; one experiences them. The deeper, or should I say, the more mysteriously a person experiences them, the more they give the impression of being a gift of grace that others do not have, purely and simply because the Father has not **drawn** the others.

He has not drawn them because they, as we can say with certainty, are not at all attuned to such experiences. When we see the unbelievable indifference of all the others toward the mystery of godliness, when we see how very happy and content people are in the world without the Father and the Son, then we can say that such people appear to be of an entirely different order. It seems unbelievable to us that the only reason they do not know anything about the mysteries of godliness is because they do not **want** to know. It is unbelievable that the reason so many do not experience the drawing of the Father lies simply in the fact that they do not **let** themselves be drawn.

Just as we are certain that everyone who comes to the Son has been drawn by the Father, so, too, we are certain that others do not come simply because the Father did not draw them. Is this not the obvious meaning of the Lord's declaration? When Jesus says to them, "Do not murmur among yourselves. No one can come to me unless the Father draws that person," is he not making the obvious distinction between those whom the Father draws and those whom he does not? Does it not really sound as though he wanted to say to them: "You good people, what good does your working and disputing do? If God shuts the little door, truly you will never open it" [cf. Luke 11:7]?

That is how it seems. Yet, if that is what was meant, does not plain, cold scorn lie in these words? Who, however, can bear scorn from Christ's lips? Who can hold back the question: If that is what he meant, then why do we read, "And he rebuked their unbelief" [Mark 16:14]? Why then does he again and again enter into the midst of those who cannot open the little door that the Father has closed? You see, this word of the Lord makes us anxious.

But did he himself not give us the key? If the drawing by the Father is nothing but the teaching and instruction, and if it says, "Whoever listens to the Father and **learns from him,**" is it not apparent that there can also be a teaching by the Father when one does **not learn,** and a drawing when one does **not let oneself be drawn?** If this is so, can we still doubt that the phrase, "unless the Father draws that person," makes no distinction at all between those whom he draws and those whom he does not? When he says, "Whoever listens to the Father **and learns,** comes to me," does he not make it clear that the Father indeed always teaches, but people do not learn; that the Father indeed always draws, but people do not let themselves be drawn?

We note, of course, that the Reformed Church's doctrine of election causes the most salutary distress, and millions still profess it from the heart. According to this doctrine one half of the fallen world is drawn to the Son through the free mercy of the Father, so that they become a mirror of his unearned mercy. The other half is turned over to its fate through the Father's justified anger over sin, so that they become a mirror of what sin truly has earned. Indeed, tremendous power is undoubtedly exerted by sermons about this awesome omnipotence that arbitrarily grasps out of the mass of those who are being lost the chosen ones to be saved.

However, the Word of God preaches too mightily and too incontrovertibly about a God who is the Savior of all, and of a salvation whose light reaches equally as far as the shadow of sin that covers all humankind. God's Word proclaims that from eternity humanity has been **directed toward Christ,** that the creation of the world itself rests on him. If, as the apostle Paul says, God chose us in Christ before the foundation of the world was laid—thus, before paradise and the fall into sin—then Christ is the fundamental principle, the hub around which the entire development of the human race turns. Then everything must be reckoned according to him. Then the drawing of the Father to the Son must go as far as humanity goes, must be as broad and universal as the air above.

It is so universal **it pervades nature and the course of humankind. It pervades the spirit and heart of the human being.** O, would that I could awaken in you, first of all, the awareness that he whom you call your Father in heaven is actually so close to his people that he can draw them with his hand, that he can address them with his voice. O, would that you believed that his heaven is not enclosed, nor his throne beyond the clouds. His spirit is nearer to you than you are to yourselves.

I do not yet want to speak to you about this mysterious tugging within the depths of the human heart, of this drawing that you carry around with you and that preaches to you from within: Reconcile yourselves to God. Let me first speak to you about the drawing of the Father that **pervades nature** and the **course of humankind.**

Indeed, as far as nature is concerned, if you listen to what people say about its pleasures it would appear as if nature, rather than directing humanity toward a redeemer, makes one unnecessary. Is it not nature that, with its quiet magic, knows how to captivate human beings so that they, with hearts moved by storm and troubles, throw themselves on its expansive breast and find **reconciliation** there? Yet, if we investigate more closely what people call the reconciling power of nature, am I mistaken, or should I not regard the sermon that nature preaches in the most sacred hours of its pleasure to be a gospel, a sermon of repentance rather than of reconciliation? When people who never get away from the noise of the workaday world step into the temple of nature, perhaps alone, their world finally becomes quiet. It is true that nature—this grand nature—is just one large workshop. However, it does its work so quietly, and with such unchanging regularity.

We sense this and are thrown back on ourselves. The first impression is comforting, but does this impression not at the same time shame and chastise, when a person begins to reflect on it and ask: Why, then, is it not calm within me? Why does not that same quiet regularity rule in me if I say about myself that I, created in God's image, am supposed to follow in freedom the eternal laws of our Creator, just as nature follows them in eternal necessity?

These are thoughts that would occur to people if they stopped to think, but they plunge thoughtlessly ahead. They come home thoughtlessly and talk as if they have achieved reconciliation, which, however, lasts scarcely a few hours. They do not realize that the enjoyment of nature certainly does not make reconciliation with God unnecessary for the human spirit. On the contrary, the experience makes the need tangible, for in the presence of nature we become conscious of the fact that something is missing.

However, deeper and more serious reflection is required if we are to discover what is missing and find out from nature what the prophet has noted: **Sin and sin alone is the ruin of humankind** [cf. Isa 59:1–15]. **This** sermon, and with it the drawing of the Father to the Son, speak more loudly and more perceptibly through history and the course of humankind. Is not the history of all humanity, the history of each household, the fate of each human life, a drawing of the Father to the Son that preaches to us we need a Redeemer? Do the prophet's words, "Why do the people complain in life? They grumble **against their sin**" [Lam 3:39], appear to say too much, as if each and every misfortune would be eliminated from human life if sin were eliminated from it? Is he really wrong in saying this? Certainly not. Take away sin, and the earth would be a paradise in spite of all the weaknesses and foibles of our life on earth, yes, in spite of plagues and earthquakes, sickness and death.

If you think about all the tears that have been shed on earth since the angel placed himself with his sword before the paradise of innocence, are the tears not for the most part tears over sin and its results? Consider the wounds that are not caused by the sins of humanity but by the fragile features of human nature and the physical world, agents in the struggle against humanity and destroying the creations of its hands. Yes, consider the two angels of anger, which we fear most intensely: sickness and death. How much easier we could bear all this if only sin had not entered the world. Just imagine how much easier it would be to bear all this if people loved one another as they should, if those who weep no longer had to pour out their tears for themselves alone, if all humanity were of the same heart! And should it not be this way? Yet not only this.

How much do not our sins indeed have something to do with **even these** evils—sickness and death—that seem to stand entirely outside our control! Do we not still hear in folk sagas the memory of times when in a simple, natural life the poison of sickness was almost unknown, and the grim angel of death who now breaks off buds in the morning and tears off blossoms at noon came only as the reaper who, at the very end of day, cuts down the mature grain to store it in the barn? It is written that death came into the world through sin [Rom 5:12]. Apart from what happened at the beginning of the human race, O, how sin now plays a great part in **hastening** death! O, how sin now whittles away at human life in order to make it even shorter than our frail nature already is without it! Truly, a voice continues to pervade the course of humanity, proclaiming to us that **the sin of the people is their own ruination,** and this voice draws and directs us from the Father to the Son!

Yet, this drawing extends in vain through nature, human destiny, and everything that is outside the human being, as long as it does not push and pull deep within. Hence, as quietly, illuminating, and warm as a ray of sunshine, the **drawing from the Father to the Son also goes through the human spirit and heart.** You, whose professing is in the academy, regardless of what faculty to which you belong, will discover in your deeper studies how all thinking about humanity pushes and drives the spirit unceasingly until it has reached the center of all things, God. However, you will also discover that the thinking spirit can rest with no other God than the one whose hidden glory lies exposed in the countenance of Jesus Christ.

You who investigate the laws of thinking in their unavoidable logic must have experienced more than anyone how the keystone of all the world's wisdom is missing as long as it has not found its final goal in God, in the Spirit that first set aglow the light of our thoughts! Furthermore, you must have realized that human thought has uncovered the lost signature of God that lies hidden in the human spirit only since the Word of God became flesh and gave us a name for the unknown God.

You who have applied your studies to a no longer existing world of beauty and warfare must have recognized that this world disappeared only because it did not possess the highest revelation of divinity, and you can comprehend even the noblest struggle of this world only if you recognize it as a struggle for the light and life that revealed itself to the world in the Son. You who turn your intellect to those statutes through which community and civil law exist among people, you must have recognized how all civic community finds its culmination in the spirit of Christian morality, and law finds its highest perfection in love. You must have seen how all of the activity of the lawgiver with his staff of Moses cannot make a people truly happy from the outside as long as their hearts have not become gentle under the mild shepherd's staff of Jesus Christ so that they serve the law with joyfulness and out of their own inner motivation.

You who investigate the healing powers of nature in order to strengthen and maintain the body, the holy temple of the Spirit, you must have perceived what a ghostly thing life itself is unless the life-breath of the eternal is found in it. You must have experienced what an empty corpse the body is to which you dedicate your life and work if it is not the temple of an immortal resident. And you must have experienced how the horrible larvae of death become the face of an angel only if you can see it in the light of the one who took away the power of death.

Thus, the drawing of the Father to the Son goes through the human spirit in such a way that one could almost say that in all realms of human thought it is more difficult to **avoid** the God revealed in Christ than to **find** him. One might say that all the disciplines are only satellites around the eternal sun of the Spirit, from which, in various degrees, they receive the light in which they circle. For the soul who hears God's teaching in his or her own heart, these endeavors are only sermons on the indispensability of the redemption, which has become ours in Christ Jesus.

O, the restless, never satisfied human heart whose yearning is as great as its struggles! We are shaken by the inner voice of judgment that we call the conscience when it reproaches us for our squandered days, our broken promises, our sins of youth, and the hidden offenses of our desire. Then we perceive that the voice of our conscience was simply the voice of the Father wanting to lead us to the Son, who is the sacrifice for our sins! It is true that now and then we have tried to listen to the voice of our conscience with only half an ear. We have tried to compromise with it, tried to drown it out. We dared to do this when we took it to be the voice of our own heart. But will we still risk this after we have realized it is the voice of the Father, who wants to lead us to the Son? How holy the voice of the conscience becomes in light of the pronouncement that no one can come to the Father unless the Father draws that person!

So, does anyone here have a heart full of self-accusations that cannot be silenced, or a conscience burning with fires that cannot be extinguished? Does anyone here need an advocate? There, my friend, stands the advocate to whom, through the anxieties of your own conscience, the drawing of the Father moves you! We had regarded the unsatisfied longing that gnawed at our hearts day and night as unsettled nerves. We had regarded it as a nervous twitching of our own heart, and we had tried to rout it, like people chasing flies, by means of raucous laughter and a great deal of joking, by the noise of parties and riotous living. Now we hear: It was the voice of the Father who was looking for his child! "Listen, you heavens and earth, hear this: an ox knows its master and a donkey its master's crib; but Israel does not know, my people do not understand" [Isa 1:2–3].

Is not, as a great thinker once said, the restlessness that does not become calm other than in God **the remnant of the divine image in the human heart?**[2] Why else does our heart remain restless and unsatisfied by everything outside of God, other than because it is created for God? Eventually our heart will find in the Son of God the peace the world cannot give. Then it will recognize that the voice of longing which remained unsatisfied as long as Christ was not in the heart was nothing but the sacred activity of the Father that draws people to the Son! Naturally the heart looked here and there for such a long time without knowing what was actually missing, and it did not find out until the missing thing was given in Christ. After we found in him what was missing, how clear it became to us that every pulse of the beating heart, every convulsive twitching of the troubled conscience—all this was only a drawing through which the Father wants to lead us to the Son.

Yes, truly, **the Father draws us, but we do not want to follow; the Father teaches, but we do not want to listen!** If the drawing by the Father goes to the Son, then it really does reach as far as the air of his heavens. Then all who are excluded from the mysteries of godliness are excluded only through their own fault. How much more depressing is the thought that in all ages it has looked as if the mystery of salvation were a gift for only a chosen few, when in actuality God's choosing reaches as far as humanity.

O, would that the power of human speech, that the strength of the Spirit from God would stand by me so that you might believe the Word of Jesus, because you **cannot** believe it unless it moves your heart, unless you heed it. And the Word of Jesus is this: The tugging of the Father's love that desires to lead you to the Son goes through everything you experience, both within and outside of you.

You see a poor child in the woods and the wilds. First it stops, then it runs, now right, now left. The child's eyes do not see the path that leads home, while behind and above it and on every side a father's voice calls. Yet the child's ears do not hear it. This is the human being amid the voices of God calling from the heights and the depths, from within and without! You children of the heavenly Father, today, when you hear his voice, do not harden your hearts! O, if you now go out into nature, do not close your ears to the great question that it puts to you: O friend, why is it not as calm within you as it is within me? If you walk out into nature and its sacred stillness leads you back into your own heart, then, in the presence of its harmony, your awareness of your own unrest and inner turmoil will begin to awaken.

O, might the history of humanity, might the little segment that is filled with your own history, become the object of serious contemplation. What does not the small circumference of one's own life preach to a person as soon as one learns to ask the question: What could life be like if my own sin and the sin of others had not confused and warped it? Just think what life could be like if people looked for the drawing of the Father, through which, ever anew, he wants to draw them to the Son.

You disciples of learning, your studies themselves must become an act of worship. Be sufficiently aware that you are beyond dedicating yourselves to intellectual work simply for the sake of transitory ends, for honor and office, for if you carry out your work with your eyes on God, then it can lead you to God in every instance! Truly, you have not yet recognized the sacred significance of learning as long as it seems impossible to you to do it as an act of worship. And that unrest, that unsatisfied longing, that weariness your heart feels would appear to you in a different light than it has up to now: it is the Father drawing you. And when you regard your unfulfilled yearning in this light, you will no longer grasp at any other helper in need than the all-fulfilling one to whom the Father wants to draw you.

We have the Word of Christ that tells us there is an inner voice in one's own breast that is the drawing of the Father. The more blessed the results if we listen to it; the more serious the responsibility if we remain deaf. The longing of your heart, the voice of your conscience has already been a sacred one even if you regarded it only as the voice of your own heart. How much more exalted it becomes when, according to Christ's declaration, we regard it as **God's** voice, as something pointing to Christ! We have drowned it out, listened with only half an ear, and compromised with it, because we viewed it as the voice of our own heart. However, if the one who speaks to us in truth through the admonition of our conscience as well as through the longing of our heart is the one who someday will judge us, then who among us cannot say, "Lord, speak! Your servant hears!" [1 Sam 3:9].

Yes, my God, I know that humanity finds its path to you in no other way than by your hand. O merciful Father, grasp your weak, poor child by the hand, and I will go where you lead me. I know it is an act of unlimited mercy for you to lower yourself to us, to teach us in our own hearts what will give us peace! Therefore I am so afraid not to listen when you speak! No, I want to be attentive, attentive like an obedient child whenever you direct your voice to me, and I want to be led by you. I know that wherever you want to lead me is good.

Devotional Literature

Where the Spirit of the Lord Is, There Is Freedom

EDITORS' INTRODUCTION: What is a Pietist, and what is piety? Tholuck addresses these questions in the course of giving counsel to Christians who are scorned as "Pietists." First, he assures the reader that those who identify with Christ should be prepared for undeserved disdain. Nevertheless, Tholuck continues, one can distinguish between proper and improper piety, and there are indeed those who, because of their sanctimony, rightfully deserve to be called hypocrites. Then he describes a second category of piety that is not above criticism. It is the understandably flawed practice of new Christians who are over-zealous in outward works. A third kind of faulty piety is that of narrow individuals who seem to reject the world entirely and for whom piety becomes a preoccupation.

In the second part of his essay Tholuck turns to a definition of proper piety. The pivotal element is that one must serve freely from the heart. The text for this assertion is 2 Corinthians 3:17, which Tholuck appropriates for the title of this devotional reading: "Where the spirit of the Lord is, there is freedom."

This piece is drawn from Tholuck's extremely popular book, *Hours of Christian Devotion*, which was first published in 1839 and went through numerous editions.[1]

What is a **Pietist?** By others' definition
it is the Christian type whose obvious contrition
and earnest discipline make other folks resist.

But is this accurate? No, this is just describing
the one who is a shell, whose pious deeds are hiding
an empty heart inside, that is, a **formalist.**

Matt 6:17–18. "But when you fast, anoint your head and wash your face so that you do not appear before people with your fasting but before your father who is hidden; and your father, who sees into what is hidden, will reward you openly."

1 Tim 6:5. "Avoid those depraved of mind and devoid of truth, who think that godliness is a business."

2 Tim 3:5. "Those people have the appearance of a godly life, but they deny its power. Avoid such people."

Col 2:16–17. "So let no one trouble your conscience about food or drink, or about specific holidays, or new moons, or Sabbaths. These are only a shadow of what is to come; but the body itself is in Christ."

2 Cor 3:17. "For the Lord is the Spirit, but where the spirit of the Lord is, there is freedom."

Rom 8:14. "For those who are led by the Spirit of God are God's children."

It is always the same: whoever wants to be a friend of the Lord Christ must also accept disdainful looks from the world. Just as the ocean gives up its dead, so the world expels those who have died to it. The pious prophets experienced this when they were treated like fools with insult and humiliation (Heb 10:33; Matt 5:12). The Lord Christ experienced this when he had to listen to others say he had the devil in him and was a Samaritan (John 8:48).

Furthermore, "If they have called the father of the house Beelzebub, how much more the members of the household?" (Matt 10:25). "The disciple is not above the master, and the servant not above the lord" (Matt 10:24; John 13:16). If the Lord could not avoid the abuse of evil names—he, the model of all wisdom and love—neither will we, using all our wisdom and love, be able to escape. O, I ask you, dear Lord, only to preserve me from cleverness of the flesh so that I might not achieve a false peace with the world.

I know well how easily it can be bought. You scratch my back, and I'll scratch yours, and everything will be just fine. And:

> If you want life that's trouble-free,
> just seal your lips at what you see.

Whoever wants to live this way may, indeed, enjoy peace and quiet in the world. Yet, regardless of who wants to strike a deal like this, I do not like it. No, like Moses I prefer much more to suffer "derision with the people of God than to have the temporary pleasure of sin" (Heb 11:25). I know that the disgrace one bears for your sake, dear Lord, is a noble disgrace upon which the Spirit of glory rests (1 Pet 4:14). They can call me what they like, but I know, Lord, that I bear a glorious name through you, a new name that the world does not know (Rev 2:17).

Once again people have invented a new name, and everyone ridicules the person as a **Pietist** and sanctimonious hypocrite whose piety inches forward on the narrow path a few centimeters further than one's own. A sanctimonious hypocrite? This is supposed to be a person who has only the appearance of sanctity but denies its essence. And do they really think we are **hypocrites?** What is so unusual about the fact that in our day there are Christians whose hearts are not upright before God, but who make an outward practice of sanctity, putting on pious clothing without having a pious heart inside? Even the first Christian church had its Anannias and Simon the Magician [Acts 5:1–11; 8:14–24]. If nothing is perfect on earth, why should we be surprised that in the great net that is the church of Christ you can find good fish and foul, and in the great house of Christ you can find vessels of dishonor along with vessels of honor (Matt 13:48)? Consequently, among the variety of people who are committed to the Lord Christ today, there may naturally be people who take to heart what the proverb says: "Be one-half saint, and rogue the other, and you'll have years of health and vigor." But we know well what the **Lord** says about such hypocritical sanctimony. We read: **they already have their reward** (2 Tim 2:20). They have looked for their honor and gain among **people**, and have found them, so they already have their reward.

However, one must admit to the world that pietism has a home not merely with the **hypocrites**. In the case of Christians who really are concerned about their salvation, the world might sometimes cry out with justification that in their piety these people are doing **too much**. Although such talk is fundamentally foolish, since there can never be too much good, I must note that even where hearts are upright before God it does happen that some Christians turn out to be narrow, morose persons, taking their spiritual pulse, worrying about their days, measuring steps, and anxiously clinging to the Christian cloak right down to the hem of the garment. Since **this** Christianity, which has not one joyful, fresh, and free **beat of the wing,** cannot be the right one; since **this** Christianity, which makes narrow instead of broad, outward instead of inward, sad instead of joyful, cannot be the right one, we might justifiably call this narrow form **pietism,** but in translation we mean nothing other than a **false kind of piety.**

Piety is supposed to be the **fountain** of life, but some will come along who make it the single **business** of life. Piety is supposed to be the **soul** of everything we do, but some will come along who make it the **object** of everything we do. Piety is supposed to be the **center** of life, but some will get the idea of making it the entire surroundings.

Once the eye has begun to turn too far from the center and look toward the surrounding area, then an additional seduction can occur. The Christian life is obviously supposed to be a tree with not only vigorous roots but also with healthy limbs and branches. Some might think foolishly that where the limbs and branches are not growing on one tree as they do on another, something is wrong with the roots. They imagine they have to trim their own limbs and branches and those of the others until they are the same. They think if, perhaps, a branch growing on one tree is lacking on another, they have to graft branches that the roots themselves did not produce. However, just as with trees in the yard, where limbs and branches do not grow the same on one tree as on another even if they all grow from healthy roots, so the roots of faith do not produce only limbs and branches that are the same. Hence, grafting, cutting, and trimming are of no use, since nothing matters at all unless **the growth comes from the roots.** If the clock is not running right, it makes no difference how much you fiddle with the hands as long as the works are not as they ought to be. It is written, **"Where the spirit of the Lord is, there is freedom"** (2 Cor 3:17). Since there is no freedom in all this attention to outward works, we are dealing with a **false** kind of piety which some chide as **pietistic.**

Meanwhile, it is necessary for us to **differentiate between the spirits** [1 Cor 12:10], for, as the outward symptoms of a variety of illnesses can be the same even though the symptoms stem from a variety of causes, so it is here. First, distinguish whether the **narrow** person who makes piety the single **business** of life and shuts out all other activities still belongs to **milk**-Christianity and therefore does not live from a heart refreshed by grace, but rather from one that is **too full.** This happens when it pleases divine grace to snatch many an **unsuspecting** soul out of Egypt and slavery and set them down in the middle of the promised land, which is the way that divine providence especially likes to treat strong and fiery natures like Paul and Luther. Such are the persons who previously hated the Holy Land passionately and to whom the land of Canaan, seen from the fleshpots of Egypt, seemed to be nothing but one great, dark territory. If divine grace suddenly places such people on Carmel's heights, then their eyes see even in the mountains and valleys of Egypt only deep night and fog, as though not a single ray of the sun can find a small path. Civil institutions and laws, the social intercourse of the world, its fine arts and sciences, all its loving and living appear to be one long night and deceit or, at most, a miserable Martha-task that is much too unbecoming for Mary-souls.

If all their life they have forgotten entirely the one thing needful, now they want to catch up all at once. If they have dashed about in outward activity long enough, now they cannot get enough spirituality. Consequently they speak about spiritual things continuously, pray and preach continuously, and constantly rebuke the evil world. Since, as a result, they often cannot find time for the responsibilities of daily life placed upon them by nature, family, and relatives, and cannot keep up with the mighty onslaught of spiritual things, they find themselves criticized as being "weak." Is this any wonder? If for such souls the new life has not arrived as a gentle rustling but in storm and earthquake, why should there not be rubble and dust? How are the old and the new supposed to strike a balance immediately and suddenly get along with each other?

> How can the goblet's rim hold back the wine
> That surges up in sparkling, bubbling foam?

Therefore do not interfere too hastily, do not pour cold water on such holy fires! The best medicine for an illness of this sort is **time.** This person has, like a child, been born into a new world because God's grace has transferred the individual into the kingdom of his dear Son. Childhood—this is the unopened blossom, the time when the entire spiritual being lies enclosed at first in the bud of powerful **feeling.** O, guard against wiping the morning dew from the flower with too hasty a hand. The longer the dew lies, the stronger the blossom grows, and no one needs to interfere so nervously. The noonday sun will come on its own and draw the dew away. The spiritual child grows toward adulthood, the blossom unfolds, the milk-years recede, and, as adulthood approaches, the capacity for reflection emerges from the strong emotions.

Then it becomes obvious—and the reflective individual cannot miss the fact—that the practices and outward forms of piety would circumscribe life all too narrowly, that if piety were the single **object** and single **work** of life, the **cloister** would have to become our **world.** If the eye directs its gaze on all the forms in which life around us stirs, then we cannot miss the fact that especially in the realm of our **Christian** world nothing remains entirely untouched by the light illuminating every person who comes into the world (John 1:9). Civic institutions, societal relationships, the arts and sciences are at least vessels, which the new holy life can fill, and thus create a large circumference of life. The mature Christian perceives that piety is indeed the **source** from which all life is to be made fruitful, but not the only **object** of this life. So, as a result, mature Christians no longer direct their gaze so much at the outer extensions of piety, at

115

the limbs and branches, but at the **core,** to see whether it is healthy, whether there is life-giving sap in the **roots.**

As the limb is, so is the whole body. The church of the Lord on earth also had its childhood days, its milk-years, as did the individual disciples. The new spirit also came into the first Christian community like the wind of a storm, like an earthquake. Their hearts were so overflowing that, in the beginning, their activity was turned entirely to piety, although not merely to the kind of activity that **displays** piety, but mostly to that which **spreads** piety: they all became heralds and preachers who, like loud instruments of brass, proclaimed the joyful message to the world, and almost their entire lives were taken up with this activity. The entire life of the old world, containing what it did of truth as well as falsehood, lay before them like the land of Canaan. First of all, there was no ceasefire and no peace treaty, but rather: **Root out everything the Lord despises!** [Matt 15:13]. That was the battle cry with which the spiritual Israel invaded enemy territory. To be sure, that was also a narrow, exclusive Christianity. Yet, it was indeed necessary that all the activity springing from the new faith be concerned only with founding and fortifying the faith so that, right from the start, **the** power that consecrates all other talents and powers of life would truly be strengthened! Woe to the one who at that time would have poured waters of cool reflection on the joyous fires of enthusiasm! There, too, the morning dew was not to be wiped away by too hasty a hand. First the flower had to gain strength from the dew.

However, the sun rose higher, the Christian church soon reached maturity, and Christian life settled into all the forms that heathen life offered. Just as Israel appropriated Egyptian vessels for use in the service of the Lord, so too, says a Christian church father, the Christian church appropriated the forms and vessels in which heathen life had revealed itself and sanctified them with truth from God. There arose a Christian state, Christian learning, and Christian art.

Thus, wherever in the childhood years of God's children the heart and feelings overflow, bringing about an exclusive restriction to pious activity and an absolute rejection of everything that is not strictly Christian, no one should criticize and give derogatory names to what God himself has established in his wisdom. "When I was a child," says Paul, "I spoke like a child, understood like a child, and acted in childish ways" [1 Cor 13:11], but with these words he does not belittle himself because he had been a child. A person cannot begin to chide and find fault until childish ways **are carried over into adulthood.**

Yet we need to differentiate in yet another way. On the one hand, we find those who pay a great deal of attention to outer works and the outward activity of piety throughout their Christian life. Characteristic of them is much public prayer and church-going, much reading of Christian books, much Christian conversation, a particularly great deal of preaching and finding fault with the world, much judging, condemning, and excluding, while during all of this the life-giving power remains in the roots, rising to give life to the limbs and branches. On the other hand, we find those whose roots gradually dry up and whose outward works are grafted from elsewhere, and they trim here and there on the branches and twigs. It is of this group, the ones who either from the beginning had no roots with sap in them or whose roots gradually dried up, of whom we can say with certainty that piety, as the holy apostle expresses it, has turned into a **preoccupation.**

In regard to this kind of piety, is it not as if a person were learning how to make boots or doublets so that you could say to the trainee: "My dear friend, you'll need several weeks or months," or, "Friend, in two years you can be an apprentice." Here we see that dried-up formalists develop who, in arguing about the cradle and the baptismal certificate, forget the child. They are nervous pedants who seventy times avoid doing what is allowed in order to avoid just one time what is not allowed. They are people who, when things are going well, never make a mistake, but whose whole life is a mistake.

Moreover, in the end it is no longer easy to recognize the boundary between pietism and hypocrisy. If ultimately these people build a little tabernacle every twenty steps down their path, but there's no sacrament inside; if they ring the bells more than once a day, but no worship service is held; if they relegate the divinely ordained duties of civil and family life to last place in their lives, not having time for them since they are doing nothing but sacrifices to God (Mark 7:11–12); and if, while they are so negligent in carrying out their own responsibilities, they have plenty of time to judge unmercifully how their neighbors carry out theirs—that is what I mean by bad pietism.

The situation is totally different if **the heart is present** in all such outward works. Yet the force driving a person to search for blessing in these particular outward works of devoutness might be only a troubled conscience. This is the troubled conscience of those, for example, with whom Paul had to deal. They were unable to let go of the rules they had inherited from their fathers, and, in particular, wanted to eat no sacrificed meat out of fear they would be associated with the idols to which the meat had been brought. Wherever this situation arises, it is improper for us to rush in swinging a club, because persons who fear their conscience fear, in fact, nothing but God. Consequently, we should hold them in esteem, even if they commit gross blunders out of misunderstood anxieties. So it was that Paul himself became weak with those who were weak, and during his entire life preferred to abstain from meat in order not to create difficulties for someone with a troubled conscience (1 Cor 8:13).

Nevertheless, **where the Spirit of the Lord is, there is freedom!** Just as the angels once called out, "Why are you looking for the living among the dead?" [Luke 24:5], so it is here. Wherever the Spirit of the Lord is, it cannot be bound with outward rules, nor can it be held and contained in dead regulations. Luther says:

> Christ is not here or there, so neither does a Christian have to be **here.** Therefore no person can define Christ or a Christian with specific rules. We read: **he is not here.** He left the empty shell behind—secular justice, piety, wisdom, the law and whatever else remains. He simply left everything. You should not look for him in the things one finds on earth. You will not find him in your fasting, watching, or clothing. They are vain shells.[2]

So the primary fact is that the Spirit of the Lord is much too vast for us to grasp with any rules by which we might want to encompass all its actions.

As a result it is also totally impossible to find one uniform for all Christian soldiers. Let individuals have their own style of coat, helmet, and boots. Is it not enough that as soon as someone cries, **"The Philistines are upon you!"** (Judg 16:14–20), you see them run with **one** battle cry to **one** banner and all champion **one** person? Furthermore, it is written that the Spirit blows where it will, and the human being knows neither from whence it **comes** nor where it is **going;** that is to say, no one can construct any sort of barriers or set out stakes in order to direct the Spirit where it may or may not lead us [John 3:8].

What if a mean-spirited mob should come along and destroy all law and order? That, too, is taken care of, because we are also taught what the **fruit of the Spirit** is. The apostle writes, "But the fruit of the Spirit is love, joy, peace, patience, friendliness, kindness, faith, tenderness, modesty" (Gal 5:22); and, in truth, wherever no fruits are found, neither is the Spirit, even if people talk much about it. Again, wherever the beautiful, golden fruits of the Spirit are present, there, a Christian heart, without becoming a slave to one rule or another, has obeyed all the discipline, order, and rules that agree with God's Word. As Paul says, "Although I am free of everyone, **I have nevertheless made myself a servant of everyone,** so that I may win over many" (1 Cor 9:19). I have hands, feet, eyes, ears, and a tongue, which are appropriate for serving human affairs and morality, but my **heart**—it is free and belongs to no one else but my Lord Christ. Wherever I serve, I serve for no other reason and out of no other motivation than free faith and free love.

So it is with all good, devout practices and with the discipline of Christian life. I certainly want to continue going to worship and the table of the Lord and keep company with Christian friends in the faith. In the morning I want to pray the Lord's Prayer when I arise, give thanks at noon for my daily bread, and in the evening pray my evening prayers with my household. I sincerely want to turn away from secular society and its idle chatter, its worldly eating and drinking, and its attention to the stomach. Whenever necessary I would rather wear an apron than evening finery and would rather eat a little piece of bread and have a sip of water than enjoy wine and fancy foods. However, even though whenever necessary I genuinely want to do all this with my lips, hands, and feet, my **heart** shall remain free above all this and become a slave to no such outer work or practice, no matter how fine and praiseworthy. My heart shall stand in servitude to my Lord Christ alone. He alone binds my conscience, and he alone sets it free. **He** has given me the dispensation with which no pope and no teacher can interfere.

> Why should the moon deserve my praise
> When countered with the sun's warm rays?

Therefore nobody has a right to interfere if I feel like singing my little hymn under the dear blue heavens instead of in the dear house of God, if I feel like reading a comedy with the children of the world instead of the Bible with the pious, or if once in a while I feel like eating a rib roast instead of always eating cauliflower and beets. As Luther said so accurately against the hypocrites, "If God can create good, big oxen and pike, and good Rhine wine, then I can certainly **eat** and **drink** the same." It was not written in vain that our Lord Christ went to the wedding feast in Cana where they, too, did not drink just water and eat bread.

Meanwhile, since as you all know, "security is the greatest enemy of the human being," it is entirely proper and necessary to remind ourselves that while the devout apostle indeed counseled us, "Take care of the body," he also wisely added, "but at the same time not in excess" [1 Cor 9:24–27]. The apostle Peter counsels, "Live as free people, but not as if you had the freedom to cover up evil, but to **be servants of God**" (1 Pet 2:16). Even though I will not be subject to any outward things and practices, I must remain subject to God in my heart. Wherever I might notice that because of such freedom in outward works my heart diverges from God, there slavery again is present. Thus, as before under spiritual practice, so now under fleshly pleasure; as before under a "must," now under enjoyment. In any case, it is servitude and idolatry whether your little god is called Baal or Moloch, or Meüsim, for it is written, **"You shall serve only the Lord your God"** [Exod 20:3; Deut 13:4].

We should examine our hearts to see if, in the free enjoyment of life, we are maintaining clear consciences, so that at any time we could quietly pray the Lord's Prayer from the heart. If we cannot, then we should stay away from those things. For again it is written, "I indeed have all power, but it is not appropriate for everything" [1 Cor 6:12; 10:23]. You can put iron into a fire without harm, but not wax and blotting paper. I recall an extremely charming and instructive story told about the pious brother Nicholas von der Flüe, to whom a dandy in fancy clothing came and asked, "My devout brother, how do I look?" The brother answered, **"If your heart were good, then your clothing would be fine, too; however, if your heart were good, you probably wouldn't have put on such clothes."**[3]

Thus, I can only ask you, my dear Lord, to keep me in the freedom that you purchased for me with your precious blood, that I might know of no other justice than that which comes from your precious deed, and therefore will search for my salvation and justification in no outward activity of any kind but cling solely to you with a strong faith and take my strength and peace from you. All outward rules and practices and all pious activity, no matter how fine, are still not fine and noble enough that I should become their servant, since I am already **your** servant, my dear Lord and Savior. Since I am your servant, my dear Lord and Savior, I do want to be subject to all rules and good practices out of free love, and because you yourself did the same, I realize this is entirely in accordance with your heart.

Yet, if I should ever make use of my freedom so that I am no longer subject to you in my heart and bound to you in love, you should immediately place me under the discipline of your Holy Spirit so that I do not defame my precious gift of freedom, which you acquired for me, but at all times and in all ways live out worthily the name of a follower of Jesus Christ (Rom 14:16). Help me, through your mercy, to do just this. Amen.

In Christ Jesus
Neither Circumcision nor Uncircumcision
Is of Any Consequence,
but Faith Active Through Love

EDITORS' INTRODUCTION: This essay from Tholuck's book of edifying readings, *Hours of Christian Devotion*,[1] holds a key place in his writings because it bears in its title, and provides an explanation of, the seminal concept in the lives and careers of Tholuck, Fliedner, Bodelschwingh, Wichern, and all others who share the same motivation, that is, faith active through, or by means of, love.

Tholuck begins by defending the view that faith has power to direct one's actions, because people live according to what they believe. If that is true, to what does faith in the gospel direct a person? To love, says Tholuck, and he devotes the major portion of his sermon to a description of that love.

Unlike normal human love, this love forgets itself and avoids idolization because it loves God in the other person. While the desire of this love is to plant faith in the suffering soul, the means to this end are the same means Christ used: a life of service to assuage the concrete, urgent, physical needs of humanity.

You are not fond of faith at all.
It's like a waif to you.
Your faith indeed is poor and small.
Unlike **the** faith that's true.

"For in Christ Jesus neither circumcision nor uncircumcision is of any consequence, but rather faith that is active through love" (Gal 5:6).

O, how people have been able to dispute whether faith has power! Every day and every hour has made me more and more certain that what people believe, as well as do **not** believe, is the motivation for, as well as the restraint upon, their activities. If I **believe** what the word and the pale cheek of the messenger proclaim, that my death sentence has been pronounced and the next dawn will shine upon my scaffold; if I **believe** what the trustworthy builder assures me, that the load-bearing beam of my room will break in a few hours; if I **believe** the smooth tongue that says my friend is a scoundrel and my wife has been unfaithful: how can all of this not be an impetus, a driving force, a fresh wind in the luffing sails, a spur to the listless horse, a spicy drink after which your heartbeat quickens?

Yes, were faith merely a figment of the imagination, then all these situations would mean nothing more than placing many possibilities and beautiful phantoms before the inner eye. Indeed, you can get goose bumps just by picturing Mount Etna and Vesuvius in your wild imagination.

Faith is not mere illusion, something imagined. It is a piece of my own self, and what we believe travels on mysterious, inscrutable paths into the deepest depths of our being. Consequently, it cannot be otherwise: one lives what one believes. If you believe in no other truth than the transitory, fleeting structure that the four elements weave, then your life is nothing but a shadow of the elements. If you believe in the breath of another world, which enfolds here below what is otherwise only dull matter, then **this** breath will become the soul of your life, too.

Yes, I can truly shout to the world that faith in the gospel is an activating power; that it awakens a power of love in the person who possesses it. O, eternal love, be praised, for I can testify that when, through faith, your gospel enters into a person's heart day by day, it is truly like properly digested food, which combines with one's flesh and blood and renews the body day by day! It is the fresh fire from which the blood begins to pulsate. New energies emerge, and the person develops anew.

I do not know whether others possess a heart like mine once was, but I do know that when I looked deep inside myself, I found a heart so totally satisfied with itself, so much in love with itself, that I did not find it easy to love another person for any other reason than to the extent that this person contributed to the magnitude and richness of my own happiness. I could let all others go their way, for good or ill, as long as I was satisfied with myself. Still I imagined I loved others, but actually I loved only **myself** in them.

You, Sacred Love, instructed me in love, not because you were anxious about what was yours, although you were rich. No, you became poor so that we could become rich through your poverty (2 Cor 8:9). This is the love that faith teaches, and from then on, Crucified Love, you never pass by me without sowing, as a good sower, a few more seeds of love into my selfish heart [cf. Matt 13:23].

Most love that appears in life is actually a **sick** love, and only the love we know from Christ can be called **healthy.** The first reason why it can be called **healthy** is that in loving, this love really can **forget itself.** Yes, truly, what the Lord says about doing good is by no means unimportant. On the contrary, it is magnificent. He speaks of the left hand not knowing what the right hand is doing, and of the sole witness being the eye that **sees what is hidden** [Matt 6:3–4]. Probably few among us are so in love with themselves that they hang their good deeds in all their windows like gleaming, gold-embroidered brocade in order to collect the accolades of the passersby as though they were coins. However, how many do not desire at least one witness of their good work, the witness of their **own self?**

O, where are those noble souls who every morning go out into their sphere anew, like the sun, which rises in the heavens each day, spreading its gold to left and right on hills and valleys, yet unaware of it all? Where are the noble souls who out of an innate drive create anew in one place, bring beauty in another, heal, and in general spread blessings wherever they appear, like light that can do nothing but shine? There is only **One** in whom the image of such magnificent love has appeared to us in perfection, and it is only faith in Him that produces this love, which can totally **forget itself.**

> The souls of faith work hard,
> and any urge to rest they disregard;

but when they end the beauteous work they had begun,
then even they know not how it was done!

To be sure, there is also a **natural** love whose work is achieved in blessed forgetfulness of itself, for example, the love of a mother for her child. This is a love capable of forgetting itself because of the object to which it is devoted. Yet even then this love is not pure. Precisely because it is a natural love, it cannot escape forgetting not only itself, but also its God, because it turns the object of its love into an idol. In this regard, Dr. Luther even says that "when affairs have to do with God, a father should forget that his child is his own flesh and blood."[2] However, the love that comes from faith is a **wise** love, which neither loves nor wants to love the creature any differently than God loves it. Consequently, it does not love in human beings merely what blossoms today but is whisked away tomorrow by the storms of time. It loves what in all eternity cannot be destroyed: the inner treasure, the royal signature God has imprinted on the human spirit that is in his own image. The love that comes from faith also goes back to faith. It knows no higher good for itself and knows of nothing greater that it can bestow on others than faith.

There are, indeed, softhearted folks who would like to help people. They look all around to see if there is something good to give them. There are, of course, other souls who have a hard time seeing the tears of suffering in the eyes of strangers without having tears of sympathy come to their own. These are souls who—like reaching out one's hand instinctively when one sees something starting to fall—reach out their hand helpfully when they see others breaking down under their burdens. O, you tender souls, may you first recognize the heaviest burden humanity must bear, the one without which all other burdens would be as light as a feather! O, would that you could appreciate the need of a person whose heart is poor in faith! All the worry and care of such well-meaning folks to help their burdened neighbors get up again is no different than a person who expends great sweat and toil reefing the sails and plugging the leaks of a storm-tossed ship, not noticing that it has lost its **rudder!** And so it is said:

Though clear the weather,
though fair winds all the sails are filling,
though cheerful pennants fly,
if you have not provided for a **rudder**
the ship will founder by and by.

Faith is the rudder on the ship of the human soul, and as long as one fails to plant faith in the heart of suffering humanity, there is no real cure. The apostle says, "Godliness holds promise for this and the future life" (1 Tim 4:8). Can well-being in this temporal life prosper if godliness has not taught strength, discipline, modesty, contentment, and honesty? Therefore, the very first effect of faith active through love must of necessity be the longing to plant faith in the suffering soul.

Of course, it is necessary for you to be on your guard that merely by preaching you do not try to free yourself of the more trying duty of self-denying works of love. Many pious rogues would rather open their mouths with pious phrases than their hands with pious gifts. Many would rather assist at the bedside of the sick with a number of "Our Fathers" than with a number of night watches. Many, if someone broke a leg, would rather sing a psalm to the person than call and pay a surgeon. O, indeed, one forgets only too often that there is a sermon **without words,** as the apostle Peter writes regarding "those who, not believing the word, are to be won **without words** by the behavior of their wives" (1 Pet 3:1). Our testimony about Christ in the circle of our relatives and acquaintances, in case it is asked of us, should never be anything other than an explanation of our conduct. O, how those people err who think that by badgering the folks who have no faith they can awaken faith. If you do not have the right hammer, you will not get the right tone from the bell. Your shouting alone will not do it. But this is certainly the true hammer that strikes the right tone: it is the witness of the Spirit of God in your own life through your uncompromising integrity, unassuming humility, willing and joyful self-denial, and ever-ready, self-forgetful service.

This is what our Lord himself preached. O, example of all love, yes, you have left us an example of how we should preach your holy gospel! Your justice distributed the manna of heaven no differently

126

than your love-dried tears on earth. Seldom do we recognize how the story of the gospel shows us how a thoroughly self-denying love was part and parcel of the daily life of the Lord, how he was always surrounded by crowds in which he saw, along with spiritual afflictions, physical afflictions of every shape and kind. Around him were the blind, the lame, the maimed, the possessed, epileptics, and lepers. Indeed, sometimes he was so pressed by them all day long that he could not find time to eat (Mark 3:20), nor could he even find room on land and had to get into a boat (Mark 4:1). Wherever he went, people from the entire surrounding area brought the sick on beds and laid them down on the square so he could come and heal them (Mark 6:56).

Since he loved so much more deeply than any one of us, O how the spiritual misery must have been extremely painful to him. We read, for example: "And Jesus went out and saw a great crowd, and was moved with compassion because they were like sheep without a shepherd" [Matt 9:36]. Another time we read that he cried out, "O you faithless people, how long must I be with you? How long shall I suffer you?" (Mark 9:19). How seldom do we pour out tears over the sin of the world, and yet Jesus, the Son of God, wept—wept over the sin of his people (Luke 19:41). He even poured out tears about the thorns of affliction that naturally accompany our life on earth. For example, when he saw all the others crying at Lazarus's death he, too, began to weep (John 11:33). Thus did Jesus preach by his works, admonishing us throughout the holy scriptures to preach in the same way through works of love.

Christian love senses the spiritual need of one's neighbors before anything else, since all other needs arise out of this need, or are at least increased by it. If, however, those in spiritual need will not allow Christian love to plug up the wellspring, love can at least try to drain and dry out what flows from it. Such great value is placed in showing love toward those who are suffering outward needs! Here the scripture calls to us, "Do not forget to do good and to share, for such sacrifices are indeed pleasing to God" (Heb 13:16), and again, "It is God's will that by doing good you silence the ignorance of foolish people" (1 Pet 2:15). And again, "A pure and undefiled worship before God the Father is this, to visit the orphans and widows in their distress and keep oneself undefiled" (Jas 1:27). History books also tell how in the early years of Christianity nothing amazed non-Christians as much as how Christians had so much love for one another. One church father says they exclaimed, "See how they love one another!" During a great plague in the third century of Christianity, a bishop, Dionysius, writes:

> After we and they had been able to breathe easily for only a very short time, the epidemic hit us—a most frightful and horrible one for the unbelievers, but for us a special probing and testing of our faith. A great many of our people who out of deep love for their families and friends did not spare themselves, but looked out for each other, visiting the sick without caution, caring for them continually and serving them in Christ, joyfully giving up their lives with them. Many who had made others well through their care died in their place. In this way the best of our brothers and sisters departed from this world. Some were presbyters and deacons and proven men among the laity so that this kind of death, which resulted from their devotion and strong faith, does not appear to be any less than the death of martyrs. And those who closed the mouths and eyes of the dying Christians whom they bore away on their shoulders, whom they cleaned and wrapped in burial garments—they experienced the same fate soon thereafter. It was totally different for the unbelievers. They drove out those who began to get sick. They avoided their dearest ones, and threw those who were half-dead into the street, fearing the spread of death which, however, they were scarcely able to escape in spite of everything they did.[3]

O, my Lord Jesus, through faith I want to receive again and again the indescribable grace of God that I have received through you, in order that it bring forth the fruit of love. Grace has healed the wounds of my sin and will wipe all the tears of sorrow and earth's distress from my eyes. Therefore I want to walk in love and, wherever I can in the world, heal the wounds of sin and dry sorrow's tears!

Your holy example, Lord Jesus, I want to embrace. My joy shall be, as it was your joy, to walk in the places of suffering and misery. Make me wholly your own, then love will flow out of me like water from the spring! Give me the peaceful blessedness in the grace you obtained for me, opening my heart and making it compassionate toward all human misery. A heart softened by grace cannot remain hard toward any human tears. O, if I could become a branch on your vine, then I could not help but produce—though in all weakness—the fruit you produced. O, that I could let all other masters go and, with less and less distraction, look at you, my sole master. O, that I could increasingly turn my attention away from all other human activity and make **your** activity my single everlasting example!

Might I focus my attention
every day upon the question,
whether Jesus rules in me.
Am I toward the goal proceeding?
Do I follow willingly?

Do I fully live in Jesus?
Do I, like a branch that pleases,
draw my life from him, the vine?
Do I seek **his** heart for power
every time I reach the hour
when there is no strength in mine?

Am I never found neglectful,
unconcerned, yet unregretful?
Don't distractions catch my ear?
Do the daily wrongs committed
—not one day can be omitted—
cause in me regret sincere?

Do the sounds of earthly pleasure
never lure me from the treasure
found in quiet blessedness?
Do I yearn for Jesus wholly?
Am I struggling, striving solely
that he will my life possess?

Notes

INTRODUCTION

1. Karl Barth, *Protestant Theology in the Nineteenth Century: Its Background and History* (New York, 1959; reprinted Valley Forge, 1973), p. 509. See also Emmanuel Hirsch, *Geschichte der neueren evangelischen Theologie*, vol. 5 (Gütersloh, 1949), pp. 103–15.

2. Leopold Witte, *Das Leben D. Friedrich August Gottreu Tholuck's,* 2 vols. (Bielefeld and Leipzig, 1884, 1886), vol. 1, p. 4. Witte's two volumes are the most comprehensive source of biographical information on Tholuck, who, one notes, went by the name of August.

3. Ibid., vol. 1, p. 7.

4. Ibid., vol. 1, pp. 6, 26.

5. Ibid., vol. 1, p. 11.

6. *Exposition of St. Paul's Epistle to the Romans with Extracts from the Exegetical Works of the Fathers and Reformers* (Philadelphia, 1844), quoted in the preface by the translator, Robert Menzies, p. x.

7. Witte, *Das Leben*, vol. 1, p. 54. Witte cites Diez's birthdate as 1750.

8. The Community of Brothers, that is, the *Brüdergemeine*, was the movement organized by Zinzendorf in the years 1736–50. The Society for Christianity, that is, the *Christentumsgesellschaft*, was the pious group founded in Basel in 1780.

9. Peter Maser, *Hans Ernst von Kottwitz: Studien zur Erweckungsbewegung des frühen 19. Jahrhunderts in Schlesien und Berlin* (Göttingen, 1990), p. 132.

10. Maser, *Kottwitz*, p. 124.

11. "Erweckung/Erweckungsbewegungen," *Theologische Realenzyklopädie*, vol. 10, ed. Michael Wolter and Gertrud Freitag-Otto (Berlin, New York, 1982), p. 212.

12. *Zeitpredigten im akademischen Gottesdienste der Universität Halle* (Halle, 1847), in *Predigten über Hauptstücke des christlichen Glaubens und Lebens*, 2d ed., vol. 4 (Halle, 1847), p. 198.

13. *Gespräche über die vornehmsten Glaubensfragen der Zeit, zunächst für nachdenkende Laien, welche Verständigung suchen* (Halle, 1846), p. 60.

AUGUST THOLUCK

14. Felix Flückiger, "Die protestantische Theologie des 19. Jahrhunderts," in *Die Kirche in ihrer Geschichte*, ed. Bernd Moeller, vol. 4, installment P (Göttingen, 1975), p. 68.

15. *Gespräche*, pp. 55–56.

16. Ibid, p. 65.

17. Saint Augustine, *Exposition on St. Paul's Epistle to the Romans*, pp. vii–viii, quoted by Tholuck in *Gespräche*, p. 137.

18. *Zeitpredigten*, p. 150.

19. Ibid., p. 10.

20. Barth, *Protestant Theology*, p. 510.

21. Witte, *Das Leben*, vol. 2, p. 306.

22. *Realencyklopädie für protestantische Theologie und Kirche*, 3d ed., ed. Albert Hauck (Leipzig, 1907), vol. 19, p. 696.

23. Karl Heinrich Sack, *Geschichte der Predigt in der deutschen evangelischen Kirche von Mosheim bis auf die letzten Jahre von Schleiermacher und Menken*, 2d ed. (Heidelberg, 1866), p. 379.

24. Ibid., p. 378.

25. Horst Weigelt, *Erweckungsbewegung und konfessionelles Luthertum im 19. Jahrhundert, untersucht an Karl v. Raumer* (Stuttgart, 1968), p. 96.

THE LESSON LEARNED ABOUT SIN AND THE RECONCILER, OR THE TRUE CONSECRATION OF THE SKEPTIC

1. *Die Lehre von der Sünde und vom Versöhner oder: Die wahre Weihe des Zweiflers*, 7th ed. (Hamburg, 1851), pp. 1–11, 126–63.

2. Parmenides, Greek philosopher active in the mid-fifth century B.C., founded a school concerned with the phenomenon of change. Baruch Spinoza (1632–77), Dutch Jewish philosopher and thoroughgoing exponent of pantheism (whose influence was at its height in the nineteenth century), was also instrumental in establishing modern biblical criticism. Friedrich Schelling (1775–1854), German Idealist philosopher, in mid-career when Tholuck attended university, proposed the Absolute as the unity between mind and matter. Friedrich Schleiermacher (1768–1834), German theologian and preacher, was a pioneer of modern theology.

3. Veda, meaning "knowledge" in Sanskrit, is the designation applied to the oldest sacred literature of Hinduism. The Vedas, four collections of writings, are the most ancient religious texts in an Indo-European language.

131

4. Juno, in early Roman times the goddess and protector of women, was associated especially with fertility. Ixion, a cruel Thessalonian king, tried to seduce Juno. This angered Jupiter, who shaped a cloud to resemble the goddess, and Ixion made love to it.

5. In this paragraph Tholuck paraphrases several biblical passages, including, in order, Psalm 146:1; 107:14; 40:2; 103:15–16; Isaiah 42:3; 49:13; and Psalm 22:22.

6. Augustine, *City of God*, trans. Henry Bettenson (London, 1984), bk. 15, chap. 1, p. 596. Tholuck cites this quotation in the original Latin.

7. Augustine, *City of God*, bk. 17–18, p. 449.

8. Tholuck's own summary.

9. Saint John Chrysostom, *Opera omnia quae exstant*, vol. 9, in J.-P. Migne, *Patrologia Graeca*, 60:592. In the final sentence Tholuck gathers excerpts from a longer passage. When Chrysostom, ca. 347–407, became bishop of Constantinople, he earned his name, which means "Golden Tongue," from his preaching.

10. The sermons of Johann Tauler (ca. 1300–1360), popular German preacher and mystic, examined the "mystic way," especially one's abandonment to the will of God. Luther knew Tauler's work. Thomas à Kempis (ca. 1380–1471) was the probable author of the widely read *Imitation of Christ*, which counseled that one follow the example of Christ as a model for one's life.

11. Source unidentified.

12. Source unidentified.

13. According to Greek legend the lyre-playing Orpheus married Eurydice. When she died, he searched for her and found her in Hades. By charming the god Hades with his songs Orpheus was allowed to retrieve his wife, Eurydice, from Hades on the condition he would not look back at her. He did, however, and lost her.

14. Tholuck cites this verse in Greek.

15. Precise citation unidentified, but in Abraham Calovius, *Systema locorum theologicorum*, 12 vols. (1655–77). Calovius, or Calov (1612–86) occupied the chair of theology at Wittenberg, where he wrote the monumental work that Tholuck cites here. It became a standard of Lutheran orthodoxy.

16. Source unidentified; perhaps Calovius. Willigis (d. 1011), at birth probably of unfree status, rose to become archbishop of Mainz and archchancellor in the imperial German court.

17. *Vorrede auf die Epistel S. Pauli an die Römer,* in Weimar edition, vol. 7, pp. 10–11.

18. Weimar edition, vol. 40, p. 452.

19. Source unidentified.

20. Tholuck cites this phrase in Greek.

21. Count Nicholas von Zinzendorf (1700–1760) offered land on his estates near Dresden to a group of religious émigrés, Moravian Brethren, who settled there in 1722, founding the colony named Herrnhut (The Lord's Keeping/Protection), the original center of the modern Moravian church. The members of the community became known on the Continent as Herrnhuter.

22. A. H. Francke (1663–1727), the co-founder of Pietism along with P. J. Spener, was a professor at the University of Halle and founded in that city his famous institutes—orphanages, schools, and related ventures.

23. A. G. Spangenberg (1704–92), an associate of Zinzendorf, wrote *Idea Fidei Fratrum,* which was adopted by the Moravian Church as its declaration of faith. He became a founding bishop of this church in America.

24. Count Nicholas von Zinzendorf (1700–1760). See note 21.

THE BLESSING OF DARK HOURS IN THE CHRISTIAN LIFE: A MISSIONARY SERMON ON LUKE 22:31–32

1. *Der Segen der finstern Stunden im Christenleben: Eine Missionspredigt über Luc. 22, 31. 32,* in *Predigten über Hauptstücke des christlichen Glaubens und Lebens,* 2d ed. (Hamburg, 1838), vol. 1, no. 44, pp. 493–501.

2. The German rendition of Luke 22:31 to which Tholuck refers is: *Der Satan hat eurer begehret, dass er euch sichte.*

THE DRAWING OF THE FATHER TO THE SON

1. *Der Zug des Vaters zum Sohne* in *Predigten über Hauptstücke des christlichen Glaubens und Lebens,* 2d ed. (Hamburg, 1848), vol. 3, no. 20, pp. 221–33.

2. Augustine, *The Confessions,* pt. 1, vol. 1, in *The Works of St. Augustine* (Hyde Park, 1997), bk. 1, 1, p. 39.

THE SPIRITUALITY OF THE GERMAN AWAKENING

WHERE THE SPIRIT OF THE LORD IS, THERE IS FREEDOM

1. *Wo der Geist des Herrn ist, da ist Freiheit* in *Stunden christlicher Andacht: Ein Erbauungsbuch*, 2d ed. (Hamburg, 1841), no. 45, pp. 257–69.

2. *2. Predigt am ersten Osterfeiertage, Nachmittag*, in Weimar edition, vol. 32, p. 49.

3. St. Nicholas of Flüe (1417–78), patron saint of Switzerland. After serving as a soldier and a judge, he took up the life of a hermit in 1467, became known as Brother Klaus, and gained a wide reputation for his wise counsel.

IN CHRIST JESUS NEITHER CIRCUMCISION NOR UNCIRCUMCISION IS OF ANY CONSEQUENCE, BUT FAITH ACTIVE THROUGH LOVE

1. *In Christo Jesu gilt weder Beschneidung noch Vorhaut, sondern der Glaube, der durch die Liebe tätig ist* in *Stunden christlicher Andacht: Ein Erbauungsbuch*, 2d ed. (Hamburg, 1841), no. 49, pp. 293–300.

2. Source unidentified.

3. Eusebius, *Hist. Eccl.*, vii, 22. Tholuck is referring to Dionysius of Alexandria, called "The Great," bishop of Alexandria, who died in 264. Tholuck's mentor, Neander, included this same report by Dionysius in the first volume of his church history published in 1825, *Allgemeine Geschichte der christlichen Religion und Kirche* (Berlin, 1825–42), while Tholuck was still in Berlin. See also the translation by Henry John Rose, *The History of the Christian Religion and Church During the First Three Centuries* (Philadelphia, 1843), p. 158.

THEODOR FLIEDNER

Introduction

While many Christians, especially in the Catholic and Eastern churches, regard ministries devoted to contemplation or service as proper arms of the church, Protestants, beginning with Luther, generally repudiated all "orders" except the pastoral office of preaching and sacraments. In the nineteenth century, however, the dramatic impact of the Industrial Revolution made fresh ideas necessary, and Theodor Fliedner, extending the spirituality expressed by August Tholuck, pursued one of the freshest: a Protestant diaconate.

How Fliedner could overcome nearly three hundred years of tradition relates to his background and gifts. Anna Sticker, the biographer of Fliedner's first wife, credits him with a penetrating knowledge of many diverse areas from natural phenomena to human need, an extraordinary talent for organization, strong will power, and untiring energy.[1] To this we should add an ability to instill the boldness of his vision in others, male and female, high and low, at home and abroad. Above all, he possessed compassion, imagination, and a gift to inspire and influence women. His vision created new opportunities for women to develop and use their talents outside the home. Of course, Fliedner shared many of the chauvinistic attitudes of his generation, and his aim was not to liberate women as we might wish today. Yet he recognized—as few others did—the untapped resources of compassionate women. He was among the first to acknowledge their changing situation in an industrial society, especially those who were disadvantaged, extremely limited in options, and treated as second-class citizens.[2]

Fliedner emphasized one aspect of Tholuck's Awakened piety, the recognition of sin as the "need of all needs," but he also brought new elements to this piety. First, he stressed that Christ not only rescues from sin; he also comes to us as the merciful Samaritan who takes upon himself the misery of both body and soul. Hence, Fliedner drew a direct connection between serving Christ and serving the needy, since this service, or *diakonia*, pursued the complementary goals of physical and spiritual healing. Equipped with these insights, guided by the principle of faith active in love, and assisted by his gifted wife, Friedericke, Fliedner set out on a path that would change the course of nursing, aid the sick and needy, and above all create a female Protestant diaconate.

Fliedner was born almost as the new century began, on January 21, 1800, the third of twelve children. His father was a Lutheran pastor in Eppstein, a village near Wiesbaden, and in the devout home his mother used the evangelical hymnbook to teach him to read. His father gave him lessons in Latin when he was seven, and in Greek when he was eight. Theodor was barely in his teens when his father died of typhoid, probably carried by Russian soldiers quartered in the town. Years later Fliedner recalled how his father's example and the compassion of others for the fatherless family provided him with the high standards he wished to pursue.

> From the cradle you [God] gave me loving, tender parents who raised me in fear and obedience of the Lord, and who through teaching and example led me on the path of truth and life when it pleased the Lord to make me an orphan already in my thirteenth year, to take from my mother and us eleven uneducated children my father, who was also a loyal caretaker of souls for twenty years, who cared for and watched over the souls who were entrusted to him, and who found his death in fulfilling his duty as caretaker. O, at that time, when we wanted to fade away in our misery and when in our lack of courage we believed that everyone had abandoned us, you did not leave us. You awakened the hearts of many who reduced our need, strengthened our spirits, built up our hearts, and created for me the opportunity to make myself strong and capable of being a worker in your vineyard.[3]

Determined to enter the ministry, Fliedner began university studies in 1817, the tri-centennial of the Reformation. He attended Giessen, Göttingen, and Herborn, where he became acquainted with the works of Tholuck, August Neander, and the Krummachers, as well as Luther and the founders of Pietism—Spener, Francke, Zinzendorf, and the Herrnhuter (Moravian Brethren). He also admired the practitioners of Christian charity such as Johannes Falk and the orphanage at the University of Halle where he visited when he was nineteen.

We can trace his growth toward self-identity in these years by reading the searching and self-critical diary he kept from the age of sixteen. He called it his *Book of Self-Examination (Selbstprüfungsbuch)*.[4] This revealing document takes its place in a genre of reflective journals popular among the Pietists and adopted by many in the Awakening. It shows him coming to terms with the influence of his father's mildly Rationalist spirit in which the primary emphasis was on Christ as teacher and example of the moral life. Similarly, on January 1, 1819, shortly before his nineteenth birthday, Fliedner wrote two New Year's resolutions in a notebook of reflections *(Collektaneenbuch)*. First, he determined to advocate a practical ministry that, contrary to pastors who remain aloof and detached, would involve him in the daily life of his congregation. Second, and with equal enthusiasm, he expressed the conviction that ministers must preach sanctification, but a sanctification that turns outward in service to others.

> Examples in the entire history of theological conflict since the Reformation [demonstrate] how as soon as there is a blind clinging to dogmas and an over-estimation of them, practical Christianity (and the learned treatment of it, morality) is neglected, and all its noble commandments are tread upon; how the people remain coarse and immoral if one recommends to them dead faith in orthodox teachings as the main thing, and if the people are misled into the blindest, angriest party hatred with its learned leaders. Luther himself erred in this. Morality must remain the main thing, dogmatics the secondary thing, except for the belief in God, freedom, and immortality, etc.[5]

For the remainder of his life Fliedner embraced these youthful convictions—struggle, sanctification, and a willingness to become one with his people's needs—but within a few short years circumstances he could not control would put them to the test.

In January 1822 Fliedner accepted a call to a small evangelical parish in the predominately Catholic town of Kaiserswerth on the Rhine River, ten kilometers north of Düsseldorf. Of the approximately fourteen hundred inhabitants, 120 were Protestants. He arrived with a sister, who served as his housekeeper, and two younger brothers, who were still of school age. Within a month of his arrival the town's silk mill closed, and Fliedner was thrust into a crisis that changed his life. The closing of the mill, the last in a series of social and economic dislocations, brought added hardship to the parish because it threatened foreclosure on the church and parsonage and cut the pastor's already meager salary in half. Other than to withdraw in failure, Fliedner saw no alternative but to raise the necessary funds by personal appeal.

Thus, the man whom Philip Schaff, the great church historian raised among Württemberg Pietists, called "one of the greatest beggars in the service of Christ"[6] embarked on a "collecting tour" in the spring of 1822. He brought back twelve hundred talers by the end of a week. Spurred on by this success, he ventured further afield. He left for Holland in 1823, spent nine months there, and then sailed for England in February 1824. The first journeys abroad were, by his own account, a turning point not only for his congregation's financial stability but also in his own faith. He confessed to his congregation that a spirituality and a ministry based primarily on sanctification was inadequate:

> In the first years of my pastoral office, of course, I simply was not able to lead you into the entire depths of the Word of God because it pleased God not to give me the inner experiences that are necessary for that ability until I made the long collection trips to Holland and England. There I became acquainted with the rich life of faith of so many children of God, and I found so much generous love that also helped assure the outward existence of this congregation for the future.[7]

Gone now was the moralism of his earlier days in which Jesus served mainly as example and teacher, and in its place was an emphasis on the crucified Christ who conquers sin and empowers to service.

> Jesus Christ, the crucified, is the strongest bond in faith and in love, and through him the community of saints stands firm. See, this is the first lesson that I learned on the journey.[8]

In addition, he now had a clear goal for his career:

> I returned home in August 1824 with admiration and thanks for being permitted to see all these great miracles of love born of the evangelical faith. However, I also returned home with a deep sense of shame that *we in Germany* had let ourselves be surpassed in acts of Christian love, and specifically that up to now we had shown so little interest in prisons.[9]

Soon he put this declaration into practice by exploring the possibility of ministry in the closest prison to Kaiserswerth, located in nearby Düsseldorf. To Fliedner, prisoners represented "in-land heathen" who nonetheless deserved spiritual care as much as, or even more than, any other person. While the authorities denied his request that they lock him up with the prisoners for several weeks, they permitted him to conduct worship, give religious instruction, and offer pastoral counseling on a bi-weekly basis. Nothing like this had been done before. Beginning in October 1825, he made the eleven-kilometer walk every other Sunday afternoon, returning on foot to Kaiserswerth the next day. A year later he visited all the prisons in the Rhine region, and on June 18, 1826, organized the Rhenish-Westphalian Prison Society, the first of its kind in Germany, to provide chaplains and teachers, as well as to promote prison reform.

In 1828 Fliedner married Friederike Münster, who came from Awakened circles around Wetzlar and had served as a teacher in a shelter for homeless women. Fliedner's letter of proposal reveals that the future pioneer of Protestant diaconate for women still retained a large measure of paternalism.

> Most honorable Madame, in the final weeks of the year just ended it was my good fortune to become acquainted with you....When I hereby dare to ask whether I might hope for a response to my admiration, even though I do not have any reason for such a hope, you might make allowance for my boldness in my loneliness, which has so seldom granted me the joy of seeing you....One character of mine that cannot go untouched is namely that I am accustomed to asserting firmly the right of the man to be head of the house. This sounds repugnant, so I must explain myself a little. I also consider it the Christian duty of spouses to be accommodating, gentle, kind, and attentive to each other, and each should prefer to do the will of the other rather than one's own. However, in living closely together there can be situations—and there are such in each marriage—when, in disputes about earthly things, each spouse thinks he or she is right and has made the better decision, and yet only one of the differing wills can have its way. I believe that in such cases the man's will must, according to human and divine law, be given preference and the woman must give in—unless the statement that wives are to be subject to their husbands has some other meaning.[10]

Friederike soon responded:

> Most worthy Pastor,
> As unexpected as your correspondence of the fourteenth had to be to me, and as weighty as such a step can be, the manner of your inquiry left me with no misgivings and my soul felt at peace. Trustingly I can take your hand....I can agree with everything, except for not knowing whether I might be the assistant whom the Lord would like to prepare for you in his service. Here, too, I rely on him alone.[11]

Husband and wife worked together. Fliedner remained the consummate fund-raiser and the one who set goals and policy. Frederike cared for community life. Thus Fliedner could set off on another collection tour of England. This time he met Elizabeth Fry, the Quaker activist and prison reformer. Her work proved to him that women could serve legitimately in the church and be of great assistance, if they were properly prepared for their tasks. The Mennonite sisters in Holland and the positive features of the Roman Catholic Sisters of Mercy, with which he was familiar, may also have contributed to the formation of this emerging vision.

Thus, when a released prisoner, whom the Fliedners called "Minna," showed up on their doorstep in September 1833, they were ready for the challenge. They offered the cottage in their garden as a halfway house between prison and society. Although it was no more than a single room about ten feet square, with an attic above, it was to become the prototype of many Magdalene Houses that followed, and the beginning of the benevolent institutions that would establish the fame of Kaiserswerth. Within two years the Fliedners helped establish the first German nursery school on a model inspired by the English care for children in industrial cities. In time the related teacher-training institute became a large and influential college for women teachers not only for the Düsseldorf nursery, but also for public and vocational schools elsewhere.

Then, in May 1836, Fliedner finally took the step for which all this work had prepared him. With a group of associates he founded the Rhenish-Westphalian Deaconess Society, just in time for what turned out to be his greatest venture. With neither patients nor workers, he and Friederike purchased the largest house in town; on October 13 they dedicated it as a hospital and training institute for deaconesses and nurses, as well as kindergarten teachers, assistants to congregations, and "home administrators." The first patient was admitted three days later, and the first woman worker arrived within a week. She was Gertrud Reichardt, thereafter known simply as Sister Reichardt, the first Protestant deaconess in Germany.

Friederike died in 1842. In the following year Fliedner married Karoline Bertheau. The year after that they established a seminar for women teachers in primary and home economics schools, and in 1848, the year of the Revolution, the king granted the Fliedners funds to establish a home for the mentally ill. During the 1840s Fliedner also began to realize the power of the printed word. He built a press at Kaiserswerth from which flowed a steady stream of tracts, devotionals, psalm books, hymnals, and eventually the four volumes of *Das Buch der Märtyrer der evangelischen Kirche*, a Protestant book of martyrs. Among the most popular of his publications was the *Christian People's Almanac (Christlicher Volks-Kalender)*, a kind of religious *Readers' Digest* that reached a circulation of eighty thousand in Fliedner's lifetime. Both publications exemplify the continuing Awakened interest in instructional and edifying material. They also demonstrate Fliedner's interest in the world around him, as well as his ecumenical outlook, and contradict the notion that the Awakened were dour introverts.

During this entire time he not only kept up a schedule of counseling and correspondence, but he also preached on a regular basis. Today in the basement of the motherhouse one can find five boxes each containing ninety-nine handwritten sermons dating from 1821 to 1849. The demands on Fliedner's time increased at such a pace that in January 1849, twenty-three years to the month since his inaugural, he felt compelled to bid farewell to his beloved congregation and spend full time with the rapidly expanding work of the diaconate.

Fliedner was at the height of his prestige and influence. Once no more than a novice pastor of a poverty-stricken parish in a forgotten town, he was now the champion of compassionate care in church and society and the pioneer of a Protestant deaconess movement and its widespread institutions of mercy. A tone of confidence permeates his report on the first ten years of the diaconate, in which he also responds to his critics:

> The foundation on which the work is built, the spirit, and
> the uppermost guiding principle cannot be better charac-
> terized than with the verse:
>
> The rock of faith on which we stand
> Is Jesus and his costly blood.

The only goal toward which we've aimed
Is Jesus Christ, our highest good.
The only rule we understand
Is Jesus' living, mighty word.

Naturally people are again going to criticize this language as "the blood-theology style." That is how one critic, while praising the fruits of the institution, reproached the language of our annual report last year. We heard similar words from others: "The work of the institution is excellent; it's just too bad they pray so much!" But we take comfort in knowing that blood-theology language is the language of the apostles and of all Christians of faith in all centuries, of Luther, Spener, Francke, who with God did deeds of love.[12]

Towns and states sought out the sisters and teachers for their hospitals and schools. Friedrich Wilhelm IV of Prussia requested deaconesses to serve as nurses in the public hospital in Berlin. Motherhouses were established in Dresden, Berlin, Strasbourg, Paris, and elsewhere. Pilgrims of various ranks and walks of life visited Kaiserswerth. All these spread the fame of the institution and its founder and helped set the stage for the great surge in the women's missionary movement that lasted into the next century. One of these pilgrims was Florence Nightingale, who came to Kaiserswerth in July 1850. "There is my home," she exclaimed. "There are my brothers and sisters all at work; there is my heart."[13] From Kaiserswerth she went on to international fame during the Crimean War, beginning in 1853, when she used her experience at Kaiserswerth to help set the nursing profession on a new path.

Another visitor had considerable effect in the United States. William Alfred Passavant, a young American minister who had received his theological education at Gettysburg Lutheran Seminary, embarked on a promising career in Pittsburgh. However, by the time he attended a meeting of the Evangelical Alliance in London in 1846—a meeting also attended by Tholuck—he was exhausted by his labors and dissatisfied with the direction of his life. Before returning home he crossed the Channel.

> Again I am on the mystic Rhine at Kaiserswerth, an obscure village of two thousand inhabitants but celebrated all over Europe for the interesting institution of Protestant deaconesses which Pastor Fliedner, an unobtrusive Lutheran minister, has established there....Building after building goes up and, with nothing but faith for a capital, the necessary means are always at hand. Though the institution is only a few years old, it has already sent forth two hundred and sixty female teachers and a large number of nursing sisters who are scattered over Europe in hospitals, from St. Petersburg to Rome! It is interesting to see how the good and great from all lands made their pilgrimages to this obscure spot. Kings, queens, nobles, philanthropists, and others from all parts of Europe have seen, examined and approved of this institution.[14]

Passavant, too, found his mission in Kaiserswerth, and even before he set sail on the return voyage he shared his hopes with his congregation in Pittsburgh.

> In Frankfurt and many of the principal towns I visited, I found that the Protestant hospitals and charitable institutions of a similar nature were wholly given over to the care of these Kaiserswerth sisters and so great and happy had been the change for the better under their management that the city authorities could find no language sufficiently expressive of their approbation. When once fully admitted and set apart by prayer for this holy work, they enter upon it with a self-sacrifice truly astonishing and many of them never leave the hospitals till removed by death! They make no vows for life, but can return to their friends if so disposed. And yet very few ever use this privilege, but live and die in the service. Why cannot we find among us a devotion and self-sacrifice similar to that manifested by our

Lutheran sisters in France and Germany? Surely there is a
need equally as great in America for something of this kind
as in Europe where so many hospitals and other such institutions exist. Especially in our city, where no friendly asylum opens its mercy doors for the stranger and the
indigent sick, is such an order necessary.[15]

Within three years he was ready to open the Pittsburgh Infir-
mary. Later known as Passavant Hospital, it is the oldest Protestant
hospital in America. Fliedner himself attended the dedication on
July 22, 1849, stopping along the way to visit two kindred spirits:
Philip Schaff in Mercersburg and Samuel Simon Schmucker
(1799–1873), founder of Gettysburg Lutheran Seminary and Gettysburg College and "the eloquent advocate" of Awakening in the
new world. In his address Fliedner pointed out "how this house
could become a focus of mercy offered by women, a central institution of Christian acts of love for their America."[16]

Fliedner had brought four deaconesses with him, hoping to
establish a Protestant diaconate in America, but it never took root.
This remained for a German-born Philadelphia philanthropist,
John Dietrich Lankenau (1817–1901). Fliedner's deaconesses, however, spread to other countries; soon the number of stations outside
Germany reached eighty-three. Consequently, Fliedner invited
representatives to Kaiserswerth in 1861, a gathering from which
the Kaiserswerth General Conference was born. It had thirteen
affiliated motherhouses, and on its centennial in 1961, ninety-three
houses with thirty thousand deaconesses.

Fliedner's last years were concerned with ever-expanding
fields of service. With each journey abroad the distances covered
appeared to lengthen. In 1851 he visited Jerusalem to dedicate a
hospital and training school for nurses. The next year his deaconesses assumed direction of a hospital in Constantinople (Istan-
bul). Deaconess houses opened in Beirut, Bucharest, Florence, and
Alexandria. He made a triumphal return to Holland and Britain in
1853 and started out again for the Middle East in 1857, but poor
health finally caught up with him at Jaffa (the ancient Joppa), and he
could proceed no further. During these years Fliedner suffered

increasingly from lung disease and was rarely in robust health. He often spent his nights and even some of his days in a cow barn to breath the ammonia-rich air. Nevertheless, he continued to maintain a tireless schedule for another seven years, regularly putting in eighteen-hour days.

Fliedner died on October 4, 1864, succumbing perhaps to the unyielding application of a favorite motto: "We are lamps; we can light only so long as we are consumed." Today similar words welcome the visitor to the motherhouse at the center of the complex known as Diakoniewerk Kaiserswerth: "He must increase; I must decrease." From the motherhouse a large campus spreads out, including a deaconess center, church, press, psychiatric clinic, and schools. Further apart are the seminary, Stammhaus, and Florence Nightingale Hospital, which, with its eleven areas of specialty and over six hundred beds, is the second largest hospital in Düsseldorf. Beyond the campus is the broad network of deaconesses and their services. All perpetuate the widely influential legacy of a pastor who once came to the town simply to serve its struggling Protestant parish.[17]

The six items chosen from Fliedner's writings include two representative sermons and two dissimilar articles that span the years from 1834 to 1853—one an edifying commentary on the Apostles' Creed, the other an appeal for the Deaconess Institute at Kaiserswerth. The fifth selection is an excerpt from the *House Rules*, a document Fliedner penned to order deaconess life in community. The final reading consists of three hymn texts Fliedner wrote and that appeared year after year in numerous editions of the *Deaconess Hymnbook*. From the passion of his sermons to the biting argument of his commentary, from the details of the report to the poetry of the hymns, these selections sample the range of Fliedner's thought, the scope of his service, and the shape of his spirituality.

Sermons

Special Pastoral Care: A High Calling of Pastors and Elders— A Synodical Sermon on Acts 20:28

EDITORS' INTRODUCTION: In 1834 Theodor Fliedner seized a rare opportunity to promote the principles of his unusual ministry to a large audience of fellow pastors and elders. He had been invited to preach at the opening of a synodical meeting of the Evangelical Church near Düsseldorf. Fliedner did not hesitate to challenge his listeners to change dramatically their concept of pastoral responsibilities.

Fliedner begins by reviewing the apostle Paul's formidable charge to care for oneself and for the entire flock. At the heart of his sermon he proposes how the pastor, with the help of the church elders, can and must care for everyone. Pastors cannot wait for people to come to the church; they must go to the people. Above all, they must visit the spiritually, physically, or mentally weak and ill. Fliedner then counters three arguments pastors commonly raise against home visitation, and in doing so cites the benefits of this special kind of pastoral care.

Fliedner's exhortation to make home visits is, for its time, an extraordinary proposal. Apparently he was pleased with the sermon since he published it in the same year, as the title page explains, "for the benefit of the Evangelical Women's Halfway House for Released Prisoners at Kaiserswerth."[1] Given this purpose, Fliedner prefaces his sermon with a separate, firsthand account of the founding and first year's operation of the halfway house. An introduction, prayer, and New Testament text serve as transition to the sermon itself.

Preface

To Pastors, Heads of Congregations, and All Christians
Concerned About the Needs of Others

The purpose of publishing this sermon is to help promote an institution that seeks to lead desperately fallen and abandoned female souls back to the path of Christ, namely:

**The Evangelical Halfway House at Kaiserswerth
for Females Released from Prison**

All those who have been closely acquainted with the numbers and misery of these female prisoners who have lost their way have long felt the pressing need to open a shelter. The shelter would be established for those who during their imprisonment have shown hope for a thorough change of attitude but, upon their release, have been unable to find suitable accommodations right away. The shelter would be aimed at preventing such women from sinking into new sin, new incarceration, and as a result, ever-deeper decay due to a lack of work or activity.

In an attempt to satisfy this need, the **Rhenish-Westphalian Prison Society** for released female prisoners of the evangelical confession established the **Halfway House at Kaiserswerth** on September 17, 1833. Here, where a conveniently located building with a large yard has been leased and equipped for this purpose, women who are eager to be helped find accommodations for several months. They work at sewing, knitting, washing, and all the household and outdoor chores with which young women must be acquainted. They are under the constant supervision and direction of a Christian housemother from Braunfels, Katharina Göbel.[2] Out of love for the Lord she took on the care of these fallen ones for absolutely no pay. She is especially well suited for this difficult office because of her great patience, wisdom, firmness, as well as her knowledge of housekeeping.

The undersigned pastor, who, along with Baron von Hymnen auf Hain is in charge of the administration of the halfway house, attends to the spiritual needs of the women by giving them religious instruction three times a week. In addition, the previously mentioned supervisor not only leads them in daily morning and evening devotions but also reads the New Testament with them regularly, gives reading instruction to the illiterate, imposes Christian discipline, and with earnestness and love makes the women aware of their afflictions and of the Christian remedies.

If during their stay in the halfway house their conversion proves to be genuine, a job is found for them with a Christian family so that the women can benefit even longer from care of their souls, and they can strengthen themselves in their newly acquired attitude and way of life.

During the course of our first year, which ends today, fourteen women have been in our care. Three of them are there at present. Six of the eleven who have been discharged showed during their stay great hope for fundamental improvement, and they were placed as housekeepers with understanding people. Up until now their conduct has been to everyone's satisfaction. One woman ran away from the halfway house, and we had to send four back to the police authorities in the towns where they live because of their reluctance to improve. Nevertheless, we are happy that for three of these women the positive influences they received and the strict measures used with them in our institution bore fruit, because since their discharge they have at least outwardly conducted themselves honorably and remained industrious.

Thus, we have great cause to be thankful to the Archshepherd for the blessing he has given this work so far for the rescue of his lost sheep [Ezek 34:15–16; Luke 15:3–7], as well as for already causing many Christian hearts, particularly women, young and old, to be willing to support this institution with charitable gifts. Since, in fact, the Prison Society, because of its many other expenditures—in particular, for setting up a second halfway house for Catholics—can budget only 150 talers a year for our halfway house, our institution requires the additional, strong support of all noble hearts who are concerned about the needs of others.

Therefore, my distinguished brothers-in-office, my dear brother elders, and all you Christians who gladly bring offerings of thanks to the Lord for the mercy he has shown to your souls, please accept the sermon you find here before you! The sermon has been printed and is being distributed as widely as possible for the benefit of the institution for the rescue of your fallen sisters. This offering of love will be pleasing to him who was glad to show mercy to the penitent woman, Magdalene [Luke 8:2].

Theodor Fliedner
Secretary of the Rh.-Westph. Prison Society, Kaiserswerth
September 17, 1834

Introduction

The grace of our Lord Jesus Christ,
the love of God, and the communion of the
Holy Spirit be with you all. Amen!

Encourage one another and build up one another! In this way the apostle Paul exhorts the Christians at Thessalonica in his first letter, chapter 5:11, and at the same time praises them for actually fulfilling this duty by adding the words: **just as you are doing.**

We see that on the way to salvation these Christians were offering each other a hand as brothers and sisters. They were attempting to remind each other of their duties and warn one another of wrong paths. The apostle encourages them to continue in their work as a sacred duty of love and in particular holds before them the specific elements of that work: **admonish the ill-behaved, comfort the fainthearted, bear up the weak, be patient with everyone!** [1 Thess 5:14].

As we see, the apostle declares the sincere exhortation of one another to be important. It is expected of individual parishioners even though no special, official vocation binds them to it. Must not this activity then be even more important, be an even greater expectation of those, who like we—the assembled pastors and elders of the congregations in our synod—are solemnly called before God and our fellow human beings to watch over, and give account of, the souls of our brothers and sisters as though over our own?

Do we not, O so often, have to reproach ourselves for not working faithfully enough with our own souls? Do we not even more often have to accuse ourselves of the same sluggishness in caring for the souls in our parishes? Consequently, is it not useful and necessary for us in our preaching and teaching, in our watching and praying, in our warning and comforting to encourage one another and to promote mutual growth in greater earnestness? Yes, we consider this useful and necessary.

As a consequence, whenever we hold our synod assemblies in order to build Zion and seek the best for it, we precede our deliberations with a gathering in the house of the Lord. There, in the name of everyone present, we raise prayers to the triune God that he might sit in counsel with us and lead us according to his will. There, following the prayers, a pastor preaches from the Word of God in order to remind us of the one thing necessary and to stir up the holy fire in our hearts. There, before God and the assembled community, we then confess our sins together, and from his holy, uniting meal we take new grace and power for the work of the Lord.

Since for today's synod assembly I have been given the blessed assignment of preparing us for our deliberations by preaching the Word of God, what better thing can I do than encourage us—encourage us to carry out unwaveringly the office that preaches reconciliation! So, highly esteemed friends in the Lord, keep your eye not on the weakness of my address, but on the foundation upon which its admonition is built, on Jesus Christ! Keep your eye on the purpose of the address: to strengthen us in the care of immortal human souls, souls for which a purchase price has been paid that is more costly than the entire world can offer with all its treasures, the dear blood of Christ, the pure and innocent lamb [1 Pet 1:18–19]!

THE SPIRITUALITY OF THE GERMAN AWAKENING

Prayer

Dear Lord and Savior of our church, we wish to thank you for allowing us to gather again in your name in order to take from your Word new light and new power over our sinfulness and weakness, in order to encourage one another, and in order to build up our most holy faith. We thank you for continuing to reveal yourself as the almighty helper of all souls who are hungry for grace. We thank you for continuing to watch over all of your congregations on earth like a good shepherd, and also for leaving your witness, even until the present, in the congregations of our synod and fatherland.

We ask you to spread your high-priestly hands over us today, too, and from your fullness give us grace upon grace. Pour down on us in richer measure the rain of your Holy Spirit so that especially from us, the shepherds and leaders, streams of living water will flow, pouring out from us into the fields we are to cultivate, where so many plots still lie barren and desolate, and which we will sow with sighs! [John 7:35; Ps 126:4–6].

Yes, might you open yourself and be merciful to Zion, for now is the time for you to be gracious to her! Your servants wish so much that she might be strengthened.

O, send movement into these lifeless bones so that they come alive as those on your first Pentecost and welcome repentance to life! [Ezek 37:1–14; Acts 2]. Be close to us today, too, in our deliberations for the good of our parishes. Guide the officers. May you be our mouth and our hands!

Bless our dear king, the earthly protector and patron of our church! Be his sun and shield; give him grace and honor! Bless our dear crown prince and crown princess and the entire royal house! Bless our fatherland with all its communities and leaders! Bless also the community and leaders in whose midst we meet today through your grace. Reward them for the love with which they have received us.

And so, then, may you be kind to us all, fostering the work of our hands for your glory! Yes, help us, Lord, that our work might succeed. Amen. Our Father, (etc.).

THEODOR FLIEDNER

Text: Acts 20:28

Therefore, care for yourselves and for the entire flock in which the Holy Spirit has placed you as bishops, and tend the people of God, whom he has acquired with his own blood!

Sermon

In this text we hear the apostle Paul addressing the elders of Ephesus as he sorrowfully takes leave of them at Miletus. He is about to begin his journey to Jerusalem, where, as he knew, chains and afflictions awaited him (Acts 20:23). Both kinds of elders were present there: those who were preaching and teaching (1 Tim 5:17), whom we now call pastors or preachers, as well as other elders who were helping direct the congregation at Ephesus. They were present because the apostle had summoned all of them, as he reports in [Acts 20] verse seventeen. In connection with their office he wanted to review with them one more time the important duties with which they had been entrusted. One more time he wanted to impress upon them—down to the depths of their soul—the sacredness of their calling, so that they would not slacken in leading the souls entrusted to them on the way of life.

As a guideline for this pastoral care he points to his own example of how during the three years he was among them he preached repentance to God and faith in Jesus Christ, both publicly and "particularly," that is, going house to house, which the word "particularly" actually means in the original text. He tells how he did not slacken from admonishing each and every one with tears. Of that they were all witnesses [Acts 20:18–27].

And now, he calls to them in our text, **care for yourselves and for the entire flock** [Acts 20:28]. Here the apostle gives the elders of the congregation at Ephesus, and consequently the elders of every Christian congregation, instructions on practicing pastoral care, namely, **special pastoral care.** Hence, the duties that define this special pastoral care are important precisely for our gathering here today because the duties apply to both categories of elders: to our spiritual

155

leaders as well as to our other elder brothers. As a result these duties will **now be the object of our consideration.**

What, according to our text, belongs to special pastoral care?
  I. That we care for ourselves.
  II. That we care for the entire flock.

I. The shepherds of the flock must care for themselves.

If one does not provide for one's own soul, but lets it follow wrong paths toward destruction, will that person take better care of the community of God? We are to be lights for human beings in the night of error and sin! Yet, if the light within us is darkened, how can we illuminate others? Therefore, it is indescribably important that we pastors and elders present a pure life as well as pure doctrine so that the way we live throws light upon our teaching, and our teaching upon our living; so that—to use the words of Christ—we let our light shine before others so they see our good works and praise our Father in heaven [Matt 5:16]. What good is pure doctrine by itself, if an impure life gives the lie to it? O, then as a rule it no longer remains pure but is polluted by the unclean vessel.

And what do people like to follow the most, the teaching or the example? O, that we leaders would all constantly keep in mind how **one** impure desire that we do not resist draws a hundred weak parishioners into the same abyss and reinforces in their allegiance to sin a hundred others who are already mired in it. O, might we all keep in mind that if we allow ourselves to transgress indifferently **one** of the Ten Commandments, even in the slightest way, then a host of people will immediately think they now have permission to transgress all ten commandments. Yes, not one of the least of our parishioners who scarcely comprehends one out of ten of our sermons is so lacking in knowledge or intelligence not to comprehend what our lives preach.

Consequently, a special trick the devil has used from the very beginning has been to lay his snares and cast his nets especially for the shepherds and heads of God's church. The devil is sure that once he has caught one of them a great number of the sheep will follow into his trap. We see this in the case of the false prophets in Israel, through whom he misled such a great number of the people into his service. We see with sorrow in the case of **Peter,** and with horror in the case of **Judas,** how great the devil's skill is, even to enchant apostles.

That is why the Lord warns the apostles so emphatically not to cause any offense and pronounces woe on the person through whom offenses arise [Matt 18:7]. The warning applies to us, too, my brothers, because Satan yearns to sift us, too, like wheat [Luke 22:31]. The woe would fall on us, too, if in faith we did not resist his temptations. But have we resisted at all times? Have not all of us already fallen like Peter? And if so, have we, like Peter, always risen up again with bitter tears and drawn forgiveness and power from the Lord in order to tend his sheep and follow after him? [Mark 14:72; John 21:14–17].

O, how good it is that today we may again receive forgiveness at his meal of reconciliation! So wash us now, you precious blood of Jesus Christ, which today we can drink from the blessed chalice once again! Wash us clean of our sins, and cleanse us from all misdeeds! [Ps 51:2]. May your fresh, life-giving power flow in our veins so that we may bring forth new fruit from above and rouse our parishes to discipleship.

To the special pastoral care
belongs the responsibility…

II. that we elders take care to tend the entire flock.

Therefore, care for yourselves and for the entire flock, exhorts the apostle. Note carefully: the entire flock, that is, every single sheep, the sick as well as the healthy, the lost as well as those who have stayed with the flock!

What does the person do who has one hundred sheep of which ninety-nine have stayed with him in the good pasture and only one has gone astray? Because he loves each individual sheep he runs after the lost one, searches until he finds it, joyfully puts it on his shoulders and carries it by himself back to the others. You know who portrays himself with this imagery. It is the good shepherd, who already in Ezekiel 34:15–16 says of himself:

> **I shall tend my sheep myself and find a place for them to lie down, says the Lord God. I shall search for and find the lost, bring back those that have strayed, bind up the wounded and aid the weak, and I shall protect the sturdy and strong and care for them, as one should.**

In Paul we see a faithful copy of this portrait of a good shepherd that the Lord draws for us with his entire life, indeed, with his own blood. As we heard earlier, he is able to call upon all of the elders to witness that he did not neglect one member of the Christian community, that during the three years of work among them he taught them in public and from house to house, and did not let up from admonishing each and every one, day and night, with tears. That is why he can say: Follow my example, just as I follow Christ's! Care for the entire flock, just as I do!

The three categories of parishioners to whom we are to direct our special pastoral care are:

1. the sick;
2. the weak; and
3. the strong.

1. The sick, specifically
a. the physically sick

If even in times of good health a person sometimes needs words of encouragement, comfort, or warning, how much more necessary are such words in times of illness, when so often one's spirit suffers along with the body, when one's patience so easily wears thin, and when the light of faith often glows only dimly. If in this situation we approach the sickbed like a loving parent, offer the suffering person examples from the scriptures of suffering and patience, offer the richly comforting promises of the Lord, the one who gives mercy, and, with the patient, draw near to the throne of grace in humble prayer, O, then new oil is added to the lamp of faith, then the spring of living water thoroughly refreshes the languishing heart, which finds cooling under his palms of peace.

Just as the spirit suffers when the body is ill, so, too, the body rejoices when the spirit is refreshed. Even if, admittedly, we cannot remove human illness with the miraculous power of Christ and Paul, nevertheless, if we approach the bed of pain with their love, then the comfort to, and strengthening of, the soul will have a salutary effect on the body. The newly aroused penitence and revived trust in the fatherly heart of God will produce new obedience to the earthly physician, new moderation, new thankfulness toward caring friends, and a new earnestness about sanctification.

Of course, not all—indeed, not even most—sickbed promises and good intentions are kept after people recover. Of ten who get well, nine still act like the nine lepers whom the Lord healed. They forget about returning to the Lord and giving thanks [Luke 17:11–19]. Many an expression of repentance during illness is a false one, like that of Esau [Gen 25:29–34], and most conversions of patients who presume death is near are glaring self-deceptions or gross hypocrisy.

Are we, however, going to allow all these painful experiences—and the longer we are in office the more of them we have—to deter us from diligent, unsolicited visitation of the sick? Perhaps these experiences even justify us in visiting only those who do not call us until they are in great need—for example, to receive holy communion. May that not be the case! If of one hundred sick persons we visit, only **one** turns to the Lord, that is still reward enough for our efforts. After all, the value of **one** soul offsets the value of the entire world!

Also, it is our duty, my brothers, as interpreters of the divine will, to proclaim to each sick person the counsel of peace, which, by means of the illness, God offers the soul, and to impress upon the individual the gravity and nearness of eternity. The success of our visitation lies in God's hand; we are not responsible for it. The important thing is that the seed is sown, sown tirelessly on this field of pain that God's chastening hand has prepared as a field to be sown even by us! According to his promise the seed of his Word shall not return empty. Even though it may not sprout in many a sick person, in falling on others who are listening the seed frequently finds good soil without our knowing it [Matt 13:3–9]. As we alleviate spiritual distress we are able to reduce a great deal of physical distress at the same time, and such labor in love, such deeds in faith, deepen the trust of the Christian community in its pastor and open up new avenues for the pastor's work.

Yes, our congregations love the unflagging visitation of the sick—is it not so, brothers and elders?—and with justification they demand it as a sign of true pastoral care. And, thank God, frequently this sign of true pastoral care can still be found in the pastors in our country, much more frequently than in many other countries, and for that we can praise the Lord.

In addition there are a number of parishes in our country, especially larger ones, in which not merely devout members but the elders, in particular, help the pastor visit the sick. Certainly this work of love is not foreign to the office of the elders, as, indeed, our church rules indicate.[3] Certainly this work is of great importance, particularly in larger parishes where the pastor alone cannot visit adequately all of the sick.

May the participation in this work of love become increasingly the responsibility of the elders as well as of other devout members! It can bring only blessings to our congregations if it is done in love for the Lord's sake. And those who visit will not leave without blessings, either. Yes, the Word of the Lord applies to them, too: **I was sick, and you visited me** [Matt 25:36].

We elders are to care for
b. the spiritually sick

This is the most difficult part of the special pastoral care, and as a result it is the most neglected part. The Lord cites this as a sign of the unfaithful shepherd in Ezekiel 34:4:

You have not cared for the weak, you have not healed the sick, you have not bound up the injured, you

have not brought back the strayed, and you have not searched for the lost.

However, what really turns our attention to this part of pastoral care is the sad experience that a number of otherwise well-disposed pastors neglect this part of their office. They think their duty has to do with the unconverted and strayed, and with combating these people's doubts, unbelief, and immorality by means of public preaching. They do not consider it their responsibility to call on these spiritually sick persons individually in order to save them, as best they can, from the path of destruction. They leave that up to God. Just as they teach their healthier congregational members to flee from those sick individuals as from persons with the plague—and rightly so—they think they themselves should avoid them, too.

A sad confusion of duties! Why, then, have a physician of souls? What is more important to the physician's calling than visiting the sick souls who have been poisoned by the plague of false doctrine and vice, and offering them medicine? Who is to do this if the doctor does not? Judge for yourselves! If physicians for physical ailments wanted to give help only to the sick who still have the energy to come to their house, would they not be considered unkind? Rightly so! Is it not the same for the doctors of souls? The spiritually sick—and they need help the most—come neither to the pastor's house nor, at least for the most part, to God's house. Naturally they are not hindered, as a rule, by physical weakness but by the spiritual shackles that bind their souls. This is precisely the curse that arises from their slavery to sin, for the devil has blinded their senses through unbelief in such a way that they flee from their best friends who want to free them from slavery, their pastors, as if they were their enemies. Meanwhile they persevere on the path of the devil, the murderer of their souls, as though he were their best friend.

In this situation does not a deep sense of compassion drive every loving physician of souls to the sick who are tumbling toward eternal death, in order to rouse them from their dizzy fall by holding out to them the sweet light of heaven, by offering the healing medicine from the tree of life, and by beseeching them—for their eternal salvation—to open their eyes so they might turn from darkness to light, and from the power of Satan to God?

Meanwhile, people raise various objections to this duty of the pastor. Here we want to consider the three most important ones.

First Objection: "Preaching is our main office, and faith comes from preaching. We do not need to run after those who do not come to church to hear our sermons, and running after them would not help anyhow."

Where, however, is it written, that preaching, that the proclamation of the doctrine of salvation through Christ, is to occur only in churches or only in front of large gatherings? How often did the Lord, how often did the apostles, preach the gospel to only a few people, even to only one individual! Think of **Nicodemus,** think of the **Ethiopian chamberlain,** think of **the jailer at Philippi** [John 3:1–15; Acts 8:26–39; Acts 16:27–34]!

Second Objection: "Calling on the individuals in the parish who have strayed will take too much of the time and energy that would be spent better on our sermon preparation and in our other scholarly activities."

What, however, will yield better preparation for a fruitful sermon than investigating the condition of the souls of our parishioners from below the pulpit during the week? If we are not closely acquainted with the inner condition of our listeners, do we not run the risk of preaching over their heads and past their hearts, and will our sermons not have the feel of the study but not that of life? Even the most comprehensible preacher will discover frequently at such visits that some parishioners who have been the most ardent church-goers for years nevertheless, blinded by self-righteousness, do not yet know the way of life. The preacher will discover that one friendly explanation of the same, accompanied by listening to their remarks and questions, will bring them further than fifty previous sermons. Indeed, such a visit will finally make sermons beneficial to them for the first time.

To be sure, this faithful care of the individual, sick sheep requires a great deal of time and energy, but that is what we are for. Our best time and energy belong to our calling as caretakers of souls. As a rule, persons who make the most of their time will still have enough leisure for scholarly pursuits. However, one must give up learned or other hobbies if the office does not leave any time for them.

I certainly know well, dear brothers, that I, who have the smallest of the parishes in our district to tend, can practice the special pastoral care much more easily than my other brothers in office. Yet I struggle considerably with my own flesh and blood whenever my duty pushes me to attack individual unconverted and strayed parishioners with the weapons of Christ, and even I am easily inclined to make excuses for my slowness and sluggishness in this special pastoral care. Saying that, however, does not justify such sluggishness. This kind of pastoral care remains the duty of every single shepherd, and the Word of God warns of a curse on the one who performs carelessly the work of the Lord.

Consequently, the person who finds the special pastoral care too difficult because of the size of the parish must look around for assistance in this care wherever it can be found. The pastor always remains responsible for **all** the souls in the parish.

Or perhaps you say with Cain: **Am I supposed to be my brother's keeper?** [Gen 4:9]. Yes, you have been placed as the keeper over all of them, that you might warn them of the ways of the Lord, and if **one** godless person is lost from your parish without being warned by you, then the Lord will claim the blood from your hand [Ezek 3:16–18]. O, what a weighty, terribly weighty office is our office of the shepherd!

Third Objection: "By calling on the spiritually sick we will make enemies of many of them, primarily of respected parishioners, and in so doing we will rob ourselves of their support for causes of the church. Yes, most will rudely turn us away."

Well, as far as the rude rejection is concerned, the number of those in our country who would act toward us as pastors in such a way is still small. In fact, the beauty of our church here in our country—glory to the Lord for it—is that the pastors in all of our parishes are still recognized as the caretakers of souls who, as such, are obligated and justified to ask each parishioner: **How is your**

soul? Since we are able to bring integrity to our office through wisdom, love, and holy living, most people in our parishes will accept our questions about their spiritual life.

Yet, even if there are individuals everywhere who turn us away with disdain, what is unusual about that? This happened to the Master and his first disciples. Earlier we heard Paul proclaim, **Chains and affliction await me** [Acts 20:23]. Do we, the later ones who are to be the disciples' successors, wish to have it better?

If ridicule, hatred, and persecution are to follow, will we not of necessity be afraid?

> **Blessed are you, if people abuse and persecute you for my sake, says the Lord! But woe to you, if everyone speaks well of you! Whoever wants to be a friend of the world will be an enemy of God** [Matt 5:11; Luke 6:26; Jas 4:4].

Are we, for this price, to seek the friendship of worldly people in our parishes and not disturb them from their sleep in sin? O, if in exchange they were to build us the most splendid churches, parsonages, schools, and poorhouses, what would it help us? He on whom life and death, hell and salvation depend, would no longer regard us as his own. **If I were still pleasing to people, then I would no longer be Christ's servant,** the apostle proclaims [Gal 1:10].

But if Christ is for us, who can harm us? [Rom 8:31]. Even if the one who harms us is of very high rank, the one on our side is the king of all kings, the Lord of all Lords. In his service we stand. **We are to tend the community of God, which he has acquired with his blood** [Acts 20:28]. O listen, you who are timid, listen how our text gives us great comfort! The one whose sheep you tend is God, almighty God. Would you be fearful of human beings while being faithful to the commands of God?

Not in your own name do you exercise the office. **The Holy Spirit has appointed you bishops** and will be your comfort and power, and he will make your lips be fruitful [Acts 20:28]. Yes, if out of our seeds of tears only **one** piece of fruit grows forth and ripens for paradise, if we help only **one** soul from death, then what could all the sorrow that the unconverted might cause us matter in comparison with the joy to which even the angels of God add their voices and which will accompany us to the throne of his glory?

We elders are to care for
2. the weak

In every Christian community one can find among those who have turned to the Lord a number of souls who, to be sure, have been born again through a contrite faith in Christ. They have tasted his kindness, but, to speak with **Peter** in his first letter, 2:2, are still **"like newborn babes,"** still weak in faith, and still need to be given milk for their spiritual growth. Like all newborn babies they require a great deal of care because the world and the devil hunt after them in particular, and their own flesh and blood tries to stifle the divine beginnings of life in them. That is why the Archshepherd already said with the prophet: **I shall care for the weak** [Ezek 34:15–16; Acts 20:35], and for three years took care of the apostles. They were weak in faith, but he bore them with inexpressible patience until they were armed with power from on high, and wherever a crushed reed leaned on him he did not break it, and wherever a glowing wick rose up toward him he did not extinguish it [Isa 42:3].

Similarly, following his example, **Paul** said: **"For the weak I have become a weak person, so that I can win over the weak"** [1 Cor 9:22], **and in our chapter, verse 35: "I have shown you everything so that you would have to accept the weak."** Hence, just as we have to lead children into the community of the Lord, so, too, we must look after the weak—those who are children in their understanding and faith. We must view this as one of the most important tasks of our office. We must support these people in their frailty and stay by their side with spiritual counsel so that they develop strong hearts.

We elders are to care for
3. the strong

I will watch over what is sturdy and strong, says the Lord, setting an example for us [Ezek 34:16].

Those who have found recovery and salvation through Christ's blood, who are strong in faith, love, and patience, who walk in the power of the Lord, and who are active in good works still need to be on constant guard against the fiery arrows of the villain and need to struggle continuously for greater growth in faith and sanctification.

That is why the apostle exhorts the believers in Ephesus to wear the spiritual armament constantly [Eph 6], and he challenges the believers in Thessalonica—even though he calls them his joy, hope, and the crown of his glory—to become more complete so that his work with them will not be in vain. He asks the Lord to sanctify them through and through [1 Thess 4:5]. So, too, the apostle John exhorts: **Hold on to what you have, so that no one can take away your crown!** [Rev 3:11].

So, too, we must exhort the strong ones in our congregations to be increasingly diligent in fortifying their calling and their chosenness so that they do not go astray but rather persevere until the end and be saved. Certainly this is the most pleasant of the activities in the special pastoral care: rejoicing with members of our congregation in their living faith and encouraging them to remain in God's grace. Our faith is strengthened by theirs, our love by theirs, and the thirty-, sixty-, and hundredfold harvest we see in the field of their hearts and lives is a consolation for the futile spreading of the seed to others [Matt 13:3–8]. Yes, they are our glory, joy, and hope in the future of the Lord Jesus Christ!

Dear brothers, these then are the duties that constitute the special pastoral care. Certainly they are difficult and manifold, but the Lord who helps us fulfill them has prescribed them. Therefore we do not have the choice of asking whether we **want** to try to fulfill them. As faithful caretakers of souls we **must** try, and if we do not, we might as well lay down our office.

God calls us to this special pastoral care; human beings call us to it. Also, in the Church Order is a special stipulation—even referred to in most of the certificates we signed—that declares it a duty. The stipulation states that we are to hold annual **home visitations** in our parish.[4] The home visit is a beautiful, sacred practice that flows from the apostolic spirit, in which, according to Paul's example, we are to teach not merely in public but from house to house. It is a very beneficial practice that affords you, brother elders, new opportunities to carry out publicly your right and duty to care for the entire flock, and it gives us pastors the strength and aid of your support. Let us therefore hold firm, my brothers in the spiritual office; hold firm with all faithfulness to this sacred practice, and, along with our elders, engage in home visitation with Christian earnestness!

What if someone here or there complains that the custom has deteriorated into an empty formality? Whose fault is that? In and of itself any form is dead without a spirit to give it vitality. It is primarily up to us clergy to breathe life-giving spirit into the form of home visits and to maintain this spirit. Our comings and goings will bring blessings if we are hindered neither by the fear of others nor by the desire to please, if we enter each house simply in the name of Jesus Christ, and if we regard no laborer or maid too lowly, nor any lady or gentleman too noble for our visit.

However, whether or not home visitations are a blessing does not depend so much on us as it does on you, dear brother elders! Always carry out this helping office of pastoral care with the love and earnestness of Christ, without regard to the person. Support us with wise counsel. Help us to admonish the ill-behaved, to comfort the fainthearted, to support the weak, and to be patient toward everyone!

Your office that watches over souls is promised rich blessing, but it must give account of itself. May this be your motivation and your reassurance! [1 Tim 5:17–20]. So now, my dear brothers in the spiritual office and brother elders, may I close with this word of admonition in the name of the Lord; O, let me appeal with Paul just one more time:

Care for yourselves and for the entire flock, in which the Holy Spirit has placed you as bishops, and tend the

people of God, whom he has acquired with his own blood, so that you are sanctified, and those who hear you!

And you, too, **dear congregation in Urdenbach,** may you be sanctified! Obey your teachers and follow them, for they are watching over your souls as the ones who are to give account of them [Heb 13:17]. Walk worthily with them before God so that you, with them, yes, with all of us, will be offered entrance into the eternal kingdom of our Lord Jesus Christ, to whom, with the Father and the Holy Spirit, be glory forever!

Amen.

Sermon of Father Fliedner on the Fourth Sunday in Advent (December 24) 1843 on John 3:30

EDITORS' INTRODUCTION: Of Fliedner's numerous sermons this one stands out for its succinct exposition of the motto he chose for his life and work: "He must increase, but I must decrease."[1] Using this reference to John the Baptist's relationship to Jesus, Fliedner explains that the dedication of a young woman to diaconal service is nothing but the implementation of the call to decrease one's own life by elevating the lives of others, drawing strength from the ever-increasing presence of Christ in one's life.

The value of this sermon in illuminating Fliedner's life and work goes beyond the sermon itself, because attached to it are Fliedner's words of exhortation spoken to the new deaconesses at every consecration service, although it is not clear from the context whether a consecration actually took place on this Advent occasion.

Since Fliedner preached this sermon on December 24, one would expect some mention of Christmas Eve. However, in 1843 the twenty-fourth coincided with the Fourth Sunday in Advent, and Fliedner, who preaches in the morning, follows the ancient custom that Advent, a time of preparation, does not end until sundown.

One of the most beautiful expressions of John the Baptist in reference to Christ is John 1:19 [*sic*, 1:29]: "Behold, this is the Lamb of God that bears the sins of the world." With these few, simple words he describes the entire great work of reconciliation initiated for sinful humankind. However, in reference to the state of his own heart and his own attitude toward Christ, John the Baptist's most beautiful words are in today's text [: "He must increase, but I must decrease" {John 3:30}].

169

I. Under what conditions and in what sense does John speak these words?

II. How are we to speak them with John?

I. Who speaks these words? The man of whom Malachi prophesies: "Behold, I shall send my angel who is to prepare the way before me"; the man whose birth an angel of God announces; the man of whom Christ says he is a burning and shining light; the second Elijah, a prophet, indeed more than a prophet; among all who are born of women, no one [is]² greater than he [Mal 3:1; Luke 1:13; Matt 4:16; 11:7–14]. He is the man whom the Jewish people, even the highest-ranking ones, regarded as the Messiah, and, as a result, could have let himself be made king if he had wanted [Matt 21:26]. But no, he desires to be nothing but the voice of the preacher in the desert. There, like the poorest of the poor, he stands unpretentiously in his camel-hair clothing and leather belt: "Prepare the way for the Lord! Repent! I baptize only with water, but One [is coming after me] whose shoestrings I am unworthy to untie." [In this way he] points to Christ. Nevertheless Jesus lets himself be baptized by John [Matt 3:1–13]. This fills John's disciples with new hope for a great, marvelous future for their master, John. O, but just the opposite happens! Most of the people run after Jesus, who performs miracles and then baptizes. So, annoyed and angry, John's followers go running to John [John 3:25–26].

Consider how a morning star gleams in all its splendor as long as the darkness of night covers the earth. However, when the sun ascends in all its glory, not only do shadows disappear, but even the bright morning star fades in the presence of the sun's brightly beaming majesty. The star disappears from view and all its marvelous splendor is gone. So it was with John when Christ came.

Should that not cause John's heart to be filled with resentment toward Jesus? Jesus Christ was John's best friend. Yet we know what can happen with even the best of friends. If a friend's prestige, honor, power, and fame grow at our own expense, and, as a result, we lose prestige, honor, fame, and importance in the eyes of others, then touchiness, jealousy, and envy will develop, even if our friend is not at fault. The friendship will diminish. Coldness and bitterness will [replace] the former love, because our dear ego suffers too painfully. We are happy to see our friend get ahead, increase in honor, power, importance, and wealth, as long as we make the same gains or at least do not lose anything in the process.

But John is not like that, no: **He must increase; however, I, John, in contrast (verses 27–30), must decrease.** I do not view this relationship with sorrow, envy, pain, or bitterness. No, I, the friend of the bridegroom, rejoice that the bridegroom is taking his bride. I rejoice that sinful humanity is becoming his possession, his share. I rejoice that he is acquiring humanity through his holy work of reconciliation, delivering it from all misery, and sharing with it his happiness and glory.

I am full of sin and need to be baptized by him. I am of the earth and talk about the earth. He comes from heaven, is above everyone, and witnesses to the eternal truth. Yet no one accepts his witness [John 3:31–32]. [What a] deep look into the reconciling work of Christ! It is true that all the world runs after him, but very few come to him from the heart, and extremely few desire to believe in him, humble themselves, and, as he moves on, plead and beg for mercy.

Nevertheless, **he must increase.** His honor must and will expand and grow. The radiance of his reconciling work, even if seemingly darkened by his blood and wounds on the cross, will spread to the end of the earth. He is the Lamb of God that bears the sins of the world [John 1:29]. He received the spirit, not measured out, but without measure. Yes, the Father loves the Son, and has put everything in his hand. Whoever believes in the Son has eternal life. Whoever does not believe in the Son will not have eternal life. But I believe in him as my Savior, the bridegroom for my sins, and in him I have found eternal life, salvation, and blessedness [John 3:34–36].

O, look at this John, this baptizer. Is he not really, as the prophet Malachi says, an angel of God who is preparing the way for the Lord Jesus? [Mal 3:1].

II. What can we learn here from John the Baptizer? He must increase, but I must decrease. [We must], like John, speak this from the heart, believe this from the heart. He, the Lord Jesus, must grow. Naturally, people [are] happy to say this. Everyone likes the idea that he, our Savior, is to be a king of all kings and have all power and might in heaven and on earth. The more powerful our Lord is, the more secure we feel in him, and the more he can give us. We all like [the verse], "I was lying in heavy bonds; you come and set me free" [cf. Ps 116:16; Rom 6:17–18], because we relate this to our physical needs and lowliness, and expect we will grow, increase, and become greater with the Lord. We like the prospect of achieving grace, happiness, peace, and joy. Everyone will get in line for this.

But listen to this: if Christ is to increase, I must first decrease, must come down from where I am, must first encounter troubles and fear! [Well], in that case nobody is going to accept John's witness. First, I must let my honor be disgraced. I must take my seat alongside the other poor sinners. Before Christ can grow in me, my egotism, reputation, good heart, good works, good family, outward merits, money, and everything else must be silenced, must be transformed into heartfelt shame and into a timid, meek confession of my sins, which deserve only death and hell. Unless [we become] poor and lowly in spirit, the kingdom of heaven [will] not [come] to us [Matt 5:3].

[But no!] Preferably proud like Nebuchadnezzar! Or proud like the pharisee who, although he did thank God and gave God part of the honor, reserved a large part of the honor for himself! [Dan 4:28–30; Luke 18:11]. O, just ask yourselves—and I mean you dedicated church-goers, you who frequent the Lord's table, you zealous Bible readers, you friends of humanity who gladly help the needy—ask yourselves whether along with wanting to fulfill your duty and draw strength from it you are not doing these things for your own credit. Deep down is it not your wish to enhance yourselves, to elevate yourselves above the infrequent church-goers, infrequent communicants, uneager Bible readers, and those unwilling to be compassionate? Do you not look down on these people instead of remembering that only by grace was this love put in your heart, and that you were snatched, like a firebrand from the fire, from love of the world, love of the flesh, and death in sin? [Zech 3:2]. Do you not remember that nothing but unearned mercy changed you from children of hell into children of God, from heirs of damnation into heirs of eternal life? [Gal 4:1–7]. Who set you apart? What do you have that was not given to you? Yet, even if you have come on your own to acknowledge and confess your spiritual poverty, that is not enough. Our egos must shrink even more, because Christ is to grow in us.

One can be alarmed by one's sin, like a Governor Felix; one can cry, [like] Esau; or one can acknowledge oneself to be the greatest sinner, [like] Cain: "My sin is too great ever to be forgiven" [Acts 24:25; Gen 27:34; 4:13]. Yet, even [this is] not true repentance. It is only a momentary awakening of the conscience, which quickly [falls] asleep again, as in the case of Felix, or it is merely dismay at the bad temporal effects of the sin, as in the cases of Esau and Cain. It is by no means the deeply felt grief over sin as a harmful evil and wrong-doing in and of itself, as an ungrateful, despicable breaking away from God and his commandments. [We should] confess with David: "Against you alone have I sinned, and I have done wrong before you" [Ps 51:4]. We should be deeply displeased with ourselves and with our dear egos. We ought to suffer an extreme sadness that cuts to the marrow of our bones for thinking that we have maintained such pure hearts and led such good and well-behaved lives.

But do we always do this? O, I am afraid we often recognize our sin, cannot deny it, do not want to deny it, chide ourselves for it, but then we do just like Eli, the high priest, and do not even frown upon it. Whenever God's punishment threatens us we do not deny that it is justified. We say with Eli: "It is the Lord. He does what is pleasing to him!" But then we do not lift a finger to get rid of the sin, just as Eli did not remove his sons, [but] allowed them to go on managing things in their unjust ways, [thus] making himself a partner in their sin [1 Sam 1—4].

Yes, we do indeed profess that we would like to begin a new, different, more Christian life; we would like to serve Jesus, do his will, and in all things obey him instead of ourselves. However, when the Lord charges us to serve humankind, to follow in his stead in the vocation in which he has placed us, then we do not obey, but resist, following our own ambitions. We want to bow down before the Lord and humbly ask him for forgiveness, but when he charges us to bow down and humble ourselves before people whom he has placed around us, then, no! These people are not really any better than we are. We are able to point out their various deficiencies and weaknesses—which are surely greater in them than in us—and we do not obey.

Is this obedience to God? Is this serving the Lord Jesus? How else can we serve him, other than by serving our brothers and sisters? Unlike Mary and Martha we can no longer serve his own physical presence. We can no longer carry out Jesus' commands like the apostles, who heard them with their own ears. No, we must show our brothers and sisters the acts of loving service that we intend to show to our Lord. "If someone says, 'I love God,' and hates other people, that person is a liar. For how can persons who do not love those whom they see love God, whom they do not see?" (1 John 4:20). Which individuals among us, when holding the example of Christ before their eyes and being guided by it, will not find deficiencies of love toward their brothers and sisters, deficiencies in zealousness, flexibility, patience, and in a conciliatory spirit toward their neighbors? Yet, [because Christ] has left us an example, we must measure and guide ourselves by it.

O, you who are preparing yourselves to be companions at his table and taste his love, O, ask yourselves: must not you, too, place yourself under the same indictment? Does not your ego have to decrease even more? Does not the feeling of your unworthiness and sinfulness before God, of your lack of love toward your neighbor, have to grow much stronger? Above all, must not a greater sadness, a supreme sorrow penetrate your hearts, not merely because of the temporal, evil consequences of sin, but also because of the sins that have no concrete, evil results—sins of thought, sins of the tongue, and all the other transgressions of the commandments of God?

The obvious question is, how are you to arouse this supreme sorrow in yourselves? The Lord must do this through his divine omnipotence and according to his divine [love]. He must first increase in you. Yes, the Lord Jesus, the Lamb of God must first appear in your souls as the most compassionate, most loving friend and benefactor who loves you like a bridegroom his bride. O, picture him in the love in which he

174

lowers himself from the throne of divine glory and blessedness where all the angels serve him, giving up his divine form, letting himself be laid in a crib as a poor infant—**for your sake;** and how for thirty-three years he bears a life full of poverty, want, and persecution—**for your sake;** how he sweats bloody sweat in Gethsemane, bearing and suffering all the agony and punishment of hell—**for your sake;** how he is nailed to the cross through his hands and feet—**for your sake;** how he calls out, "Father, forgive them"—**for your sake;** how, when you were still his enemy, he moans, "My God, my God, why have you forsaken me!"—**for your sake;** how, as he is dying, he cries out the words of salvation, "It has been accomplished"—**for your benefit;** how, rising from the dead and ascending to heaven, he sends his Holy Spirit for ever and ever to all hungry souls who thirst for salvation, and refreshes them with the sweet waters of his saving grace; how he still invites you and me and everyone, all sinners on the entire face of the earth, "Come to me, all you who are weary and burdened, I will refresh you!" [Matt 11:28].

O, then the ice that encases your heart will melt, then the hardest thing on the face of the earth will not be too hard for you: to humble yourself, to despise yourself on account of your many sins, to turn your ego over to death, to deal the final blow to the serpent of ambition, to self-centeredness, to the Pharisee in your heart, and to come with nothing, naked, blind, poor, miserable, and weeping to your all-sufficient Savior, so that he might enlighten and clothe you, giving you riches, sight, and strength through the manifold spiritual blessings of heavenly riches and through the manifold expressions of his divine power that lead to life and godly living. Amen.[3]

(After this sermon, which, at the same time, was the call to confession, the holy supper was celebrated. The closing sentences of the sermon are reminiscent of **the preparation for celebrating the holy supper, found in our liturgy for consecrating new sisters.** It, too, was written by Fliedner.

After the congregation has knelt and prayed for the consecrated deaconesses, the sisters are called with the following words to participate in the sacrament:)

Thus, as servants of Christ, you have entered his holy vineyard! Thus, the blessed office has been entrusted to you to care for your Savior in his sick and weak members. So arise, dear sisters, arise, gird yourselves as wise virgins for his service. Behold, the bridegroom is coming! Go out to him, your lamps in your hands! [Matt 25:1–13; Luke 12:35]. He is standing outside the door, knocking, in the figure, of course, of a lowly laborer, in the poor and wretched around you. Let him in! Feed him in the hungry, clothe him in the naked, lift him up in the little child, visit him in the sick, and in the dying lead him to the final rest!

A blessed office, but also a difficult office! How soon your hands will want to rest and your knees will want to give in! But thank God! You will recognize the bridegroom of your soul as he comes to you in yet another form besides that of a lowly laborer: as the Lord of glory who anoints you with the ointment of joy in his Holy Spirit. That is why you have longed for this table of grace. You say, "I am weak! How can I think I am supposed to feed you, Lord! O, come and feed me!"

And behold, there he is, the king of glory, saying: "Come to me, you who are weary and burdened! I will refresh you" [Matt 11:28]. There he stands, the bridegroom, in heavenly majesty! He wants to adorn you with his wedding garment; wants to give you himself and his manifold divine power, together with his body and blood.

O, you have done well in coming. Everything is ready. So open your hands, your lips, and hearts, and take from his fullness grace upon grace! Yes, taste and see how loving the Lord is. How good it is for those who trust in him! [Ps 34:8].

Commentary on the Apostles' Creed

I Believe
in God the Father,
the Almighty Creator
of Heaven and Earth

EDITORS' INTRODUCTION: Fliedner's spirited and combative commentary on the First Article of the Apostles' Creed, representing his numerous edifying pieces, is one of a series on the Creed that appeared in his *Christian Almanac.*[1] In fact, the text presented here ends abruptly because Fliedner divided his long commentary and published the second half in the succeeding issue.

Fliedner, believing that the church's historical confessions have long been under attack, begins by defending their value and function. He uses the opening words of the Apostles' Creed, "I believe," to posit the underlying necessity of belief. From the confession that God is "Father" rather than an abstract principle flows the recognition that a person's relationship to him is one of intimacy and love established by faith as well as by reason.

Fliedner argues against three alternative views that for him represent the destructive rationalistic tendencies of his time. One is no belief in God; the second is a one-sided belief in only a good, undisciplining divinity; and the third is a Deistic belief that excludes the supernatural. Throughout, Fliedner clarifies his positions by contrasting them with the rationalistic counterparts he rejects, and, in keeping with the popular nature of the *Almanac,* he uses vivid images and colorful anecdotes.

1. First a Story About an Old Cathedral

I am acquainted with a village in our beloved Protestant Germany that probably has about sixteen hundred souls. It lies along the narrows of a rushing river that, however, cannot do much harm to the village, since for the most part the village is built on the heights. Once two churches stood in the village. The newer one is still standing. The other one was an old cathedral, constructed several centuries before Doctor Luther. It was a well-built, magnificent edifice, and it had two beautiful towers on its strong foundation. These towers were supposed to represent how, on the foundation of faith, love and hope are to rise confidently toward heaven. In addition, wonderful bells hung from the towers. When the bells started ringing early Sunday morning, the tones from the new church and the old cathedral spread over the village from both sides. Even if lazy church-goers were to creep down into their basements, they could still hear the bells. As long as the old and the new church reigned together, the village enjoyed good times.

However, next to the old cathedral lived a judicial officer who could not stand the bell-ringing. However, where there is a church, there is bell-ringing. I do not know why he could not stand it, because I was not acquainted with him, but even had I known him, I am sure he would not have told me the real, honest reason. Many people cannot stand church bells. The same is true about church air. Usually they blame it on their nerves. But it goes a lot deeper than nerves. For dance-hall air and concert music they have nerves of steel, but for church air and for the music of bells and organs they have nerves of fragile thread.

Anyhow, our old judicial officer could not bear the bells, so he began very carefully to bore and dig and work at the authorities so that the old cathedral would be torn down. He argued that it was enough to have one church in the village. He also prattled about needed repairs that would be expensive. And, like many authorities in the years from 1770 to 1800, they said yes.

The beautiful bells were thrown from the towers and sold, in part, to a button maker. And so the destruction proceeded. But just think, dear reader, the cathedral was built so well that they could not get the stones apart. The old master builder had had the stones set in mortar. Everything was bonded together as if the whole church were one great piece. The dismantlers worked and worked until they were worn and exhausted. They had to leave the main walls standing, and they still stand as a ruin.

However, the sound of bells no longer rings down from above, nor does one hear from within the confession of sin, profession of faith, the Lord's Prayer, or the interpretation of the Word. The old church has been turned into a lumber storage. Elderberry bushes are growing in the corners. Poor people gather the blossoms to make tea when they want to sweat. I can never go by the ruin without feeling very sad. This is a true story.

You Christian people of the Protestant confession—and if you of the Catholic confession want to be included, I have nothing against it—I know of a cathedral that is much older and much more sacred than the one in ruins. It is a cathedral built by the Lord Jesus Christ himself. But for the places where he did not finish the entire construction, he provided clear and precise plans so that his apostles and the early church fathers could easily add the finishing touches. Thus they completed the building—splendid, simple, and solid—of good, square stone blocks cut from the quarries at Bethlehem and Golgotha [Eph 2:19–22]. **This cathedral is the Apostles' Creed.**

For almost two thousand years the bells of faith have rung down from the creed. Their ringing has said, "repentance and faith, faith and repentance." Their ringing has reached into the cradle; their ringing has reached across the span of life; their ringing has reached into the grave, too, because their last reverberation is, "and life everlasting, amen." Yes, amen. With one another we all want to say "amen." If the sound of these bells of heaven did not reach into our lives, we would be the most miserable of people.

In our days a generation has arisen in the Evangelical and Catholic churches that cannot stand the sound that comes down from the bells in this cathedral. These people find it offensive when, into their happy lives, the bells of heaven ring "repentance and faith, faith and repentance." Faith interferes with arrogance, and repentance with pleasure. They do not want to be disturbed, particularly when their arrogance is built on the rubble of all kinds of self-deception and their pleasure on the manure pile of sin and shame.

Nowadays, to get rid of the offensive ringing once and for all, they are busy tearing down the old cathedral. In order for this to proceed more easily, they have damned up waters of newspapers and journals around the old edifice for many years. The waters are meant to soften up the structure. They have also sprinkled the stone with the acid of learning meant to eat away the stone. After these preparations they have tackled the job with crowbars, picks, and hammers. For a couple of years they have been hacking and picking so much that you can hear the sound throughout Germany.

Some of them began at the bottom, intending to undermine the foundation in hopes that the whole structure would collapse. Others wanted to knock out some of the stones first, thinking that if they just created some holes in the walls the rest would give way. However, between you and me—but it does not matter if they hear it, too—the first group are fools, and so is the second. When the first group gets to the bottom of the foundation, it will find that the foundation is set into rock. The others will discover they are certainly able to knock the human mortar from the stones, yet the stones themselves, as heavenly granite, can never be shattered and never dislodged.

These ravagers and robbers will never be able to steal the treasure from the Lord's congregation, but it could happen that these slick people are successful in loosening up the entire sacred structure, or some of its stones, in an individual's heart. Yet how distressing it would be if the edifice of grace in your soul stood there like the old ruin, without roof, towers, and bells. How distressing it would be if you were to scorn the medicine for your soul, if you regarded the balm of Gilead and the precious blood of Jesus Christ as nothing more than some rationalistic, or free-thinking, or neo-Catholic tea for what ails you. How distressing it would be if the holiest little chamber of your heart, the tabernacle of God in you, instead of being filled with mercy, faith, repentance, and forgiveness of sin, were nothing more than a lumberyard of secular thoughts and earthly interests.

Now and then little sayings torn carelessly from God's Word are still to be found in such hearts. But the only reason they hang on to these phrases is to deceive themselves so they can prattle about their right to do their destructive work. The most common ones are: "The law kills, the spirit gives life" (but which spirit?!); "Test everything and keep the best" (Does this also mean: test the Word of God with your cleverness and toss out whatever doesn't fit your own concoction?!); "Reconcile yourself with the times, for they are evil" (Does this mean: one must not swim against the tide; since so many others are falling away from the faith you, too, must fall away?!) [2 Cor 3:6; 1 Thess 5:21; Eph 5:15–16]. By using the divine Word in this way you are cloaking the devil in the robes of angels; you are decorating the raven with the feathers of a swan; you are laying palm branches over the wolf's den so that your soul will certainly fall in.

No, do not let it come to that. May God prevent it! Come, dear Christians, let us examine together honestly the old edifice of the Apostles' Creed. But first let us pray: Lord, enlighten my eyes so that I may see the wonders of your grace and wisdom! Let me feel and taste the rich mercifulness by which you have built up the old childhood faith into a beautiful whole! Let me become a child so that I might lie at the source of heavenly wisdom as a child at its mother's breast! May your spirit of mercy grasp my hand and lead me into the magnificent edifice! Amen.

2. The Door to the Cathedral of Grace

Every house must have a door. Even a prison must have a door. Otherwise how could the thieves, murderers, perjurers, and forgers be brought in? So, too, this cathedral of grace has a door. All three articles begin with the words: **"I believe."** This is the door into God's cathedral of grace, and this door is large and wide. Everyone can **believe**. The rich and the poor can **believe**. The old and the young can **believe**. The foolish and the wise can **believe**. The imprisoned and the free can **believe**. You can **believe** in the midst of life, and you can **believe** while dying. Praise be to God who has constructed for everyone such a wide gate into his dear, heavenly Jerusalem. We do not enter by means of great wisdom, for not everyone can achieve wisdom. We do not enter by means of great strength, for the weak, the disabled, and the distressed have no strength. We do not enter by means of great wealth, because many are poor. We enter by means of faith.

Not by works do we attain mercy, but by faith [Gal 2:15–16]. Take a look at the wretched persons lying in bed who cannot move their legs, whose arms are heavier than pieces of lumber are to a healthy person. They, too, want to partake in the riches of heaven. What kind of works can they accomplish? Take a look at the prisoners languishing in their chains, whose only comrades in prison are a few moths and flies, a little spider or mouse. They, too, want to partake in the riches of heaven. What kind of works can they accomplish? Faith is everyone's door.

If, however, it is said that faith is not for everyone, it means only that the proud do not feel like believing. They want to see the sun with their own eyes. They do not want to hold the darkened glass, as they say, before their eyes. It is their own fault that they are blinded as a result.

The Lord Christ likes to compare the treasures of faith to a magnificent meal set before us. Never has there been a more sumptuous or exquisite banquet. We are served the Father's heavenly love, salvation from sin and condemnation, adoption as the children of God, and, in addition, many more covered dishes whose covers the Lord of the meal will not remove until judgment day [Matt 22:2].

But what good is it for persons to sit at the most sumptuous of tables if they have no hands? They remain hungry even if the table were to collapse under the load. So it is with God's table of grace. We must have hands with which we can help ourselves. These hands are faith.

But can I not help myself with my insight and cleverness? Cannot my thinking become my hands? At this point we find ourselves among the philosophers or the wise of the world, that is, among those who do not want their salvation through **believing** but through **thinking.** Up to now they have not thought up much in particular. Indeed, they have not come any further than the heathen more than two thousand years ago. In fact, there are a few types who have become even more foolish than the old heathens. There is a great difference between the act of believing and the act of thinking. If a little bee comes flying along and finds a beautiful, open flower, the little creature crawls into the goblet-shaped blossom, sticks out its little tongue, and fills itself with the sweetest honey. But if a pharmacist's apprentice squeezes the same flower in his wooden press, then a juice runs out that can taste as bitter as gall. He cries out: "I don't taste any honey!" He also scolds the ignorant bee; what is it looking for in the flower? The same applies to the truths of salvation. They have been given to us for our faith, and they who sink into them with heartfelt faith will find honey. Those who put them into the press of unsanctified thinking will usually produce a useless juice. This is not the fault of God's flowers but of the bad press. Sink into them first of all in faith, and then think. In that way your thinking will be sanctified by faith, and, in your thinking, you will find blessed truth.

Then there is another type of individual, and, unfortunately, many of them are pastors. They have created a kind of crossbreed between believing and thinking. They wish to join their faith and thought in marriage. They do not want to believe anything that is not consistent with their good, that is, bad, sense. But it never occurs to them to say in regard to divine matters that they consider only those things sensible that are consistent with the evangelical faith. They prefer to measure faith by thinking, not thinking by faith. You can already see that in this marriage thinking is the man, and faith is the woman. She must obey. The lord of the house does with her what he wants.[2]

In German this mishmash is called "believing unbelief," or "unbelieving belief." In Latin: rationalism. If you want to be a pagan or a Jew, be one, and we will pray for you. If you want to be a Christian, be one, and we will pray with you. But do not mingle and patch unbelief and belief together. By doing so, unbelief does not become one whit better, and faith loses its essence, its power, and its beauty. Faith remains the door to the cathedral of grace. Faith remains the hand with which I seize the bounties of grace.

Do not imagine, however, that faith is easy. Those who have a good memory, who were among the best in school or even at the head of the class, who studied their lessons and Bible verses thoroughly and have not forgotten them, and who do not doubt what they learned, are still by no means believers merely on that basis. The devil, too, knows the scriptures by heart. He, too, believes.

"The devils believe, too, and tremble" (Jas 2:19). And yet the devil is no believer. With what can I compare faith? I would like to compare it to the "I do" of a bride. When she says "I do," she incorporates herself into the family of the groom, she takes his name, puts all her trust in him, is faithful, kind, and obedient to him until death; in a word, she gives herself to him completely. With faith—and faith begins in baptism, even if I do not see or comprehend it—I am incorporated into the holy nature of Jesus Christ. I receive his holy name, I put all my trust in him, I love him, I am true to him and obedient until death; in a word, I give myself to him completely.

To believe means to free with confidence the lines of the little ship of one's heart from the shore of human security and to let oneself be driven joyfully on the waves of divine grace and guidance. To believe means to love the Lord and Savior so much that he is more precious to us than father and mother, brother and sister, spouse and child. That is why faith of the tongue is no faith. The chaff of wheat and the pea and bean pods are not the wheat, peas, and beans, even though they enclose these fruits. The hulls are of value only if the good growth is within. So, too, with the confession of faith. It is of value only if the true life of faith is within.

So, my Christian, how deep does your faith go? When you say, "I believe," are these words merely coming from your lips as something memorized? You can easily tell. If they are merely memorized words your lips will clatter like mill wheels and your heart will not know anything about them. If, on the other hand, they arise from the source of your innermost life, then you will sense a surging within you like a holy sea because you have brought your most blessed possession, your greatest joy, and your one and only consolation to your lips. This you can do neither coldly nor halfheartedly.

3. Now Let Us Enter through the Doorway,

and immediately the word meets us that comprises the foundation and ground-plan of the entire structure:

I believe in God the Father almighty, maker of heaven and earth. O, lovely words: **I believe in God the Father.** They are the loveliest song of comfort and the loveliest melody that has ever been sung to humankind. God, one God; he has made all things. To him belongs the wide universe. Where the telescope searches out the farthest stars that appear like tiny, golden grains of sand, and where, behind them, there is a glow like a thin fog in which unknown stars are set, there he speaks: these are mine, I created all of them through my word. Where the microscope divides a little drop of water into twenty parts and then, in each one, you see tiny circular, spherical, or flower-shaped creatures chasing and catching one another like fish in a pond, there he speaks: these are mine, I made them. Where the sun floats in the firmament, hanging from invisible cords of his wisdom, and where a speck of dust weaves in a ray of sunlight that breaks through a gap in the roof, there he speaks: these are mine, I made them, and I let them weave and float according to my pleasure. Where a birth is celebrated in pain and joy, whether a little caterpillar being born from its egg on the twig of a plum tree, or an angel from a pale human body, there he speaks: you are mine; I brought you into existence. Where an emigrating people finds a new land covered with palms and breadfruit trees, rich in fertile soil to feed millions of hungering people, and where a wandering ant finds a seed of grain that it and its little sisters pick up and carry home, struggling as if they were carrying a bushel sack, there he speaks: I have prepared everything for you, because I thought of you. The heights where the eagle has its nest, where God sets loose the avalanches in springtime, are his. The depths of the sea, where creatures never seen by the human eye dwell, are his. And much higher heights and deeper depths are also his. To him belong the tempest and the placid sea, to him belong war and peace. Whoever is born falls into his hand, and whoever dies falls into his hand. No one can run away from him, whether by water, like the prophet Jonah, or by air, like the Englishman Green.[3]

Good and evil have no choice but to be in the service of God's glory. He is well pleased with obedience, but he also weaves into his plan the breaking of his commandments. His opponents must build up his honor [Rom 3:5–8]. The dear Lord God is a good general who puts a rebellious people under his forces. Yet he places them under only his loyal staff. Hence, they have to join the march and fight against their own plans.

185

The wolves help keep the herd very close to the shepherd, preventing anyone from getting lost [Acts 20: 29–30]. Naturally, one does not thank the wolves for this service. Nobody would say: Jacob's ten sons, who sold their brother Joseph into Egypt for twenty silver coins, saved the house of Jacob from starvation [Gen 37:12–28; 45:1–11]. Nobody would say: we owe our salvation to Caiaphas because he sent Christ to the cross [Matt 26:62–66]. In France the well-known mocker Voltaire set up his own printing works on his estate in order to publish his godless writings. Later the press was sold, set up in Geneva, and it served to print the Bible. An Englishman by the name of Gibbon, belonging more or less to the same riffraff, acquired with his writings an estate in Switzerland. After his death the property came into the hands of a man who turned the entire profit from it to the work of missions. We do not give credit to Voltaire or Gibbon.[4] The honor belongs to God, who knows how to direct human malice so that goodness must come out of it.

And this God is from himself and through himself, and because he is from himself he is from eternity. If you can comprehend this, fine, but the Babylonians were unable to build a tower to reach the heavens, and our wisdom is likewise unable to construct a ladder to reach the heights or a plumb to reach the depths of God. Such knowledge is too unusual and too great for me; I cannot comprehend it [Ps 139:6]. Once a king asked a wise person what God is. The wise person requested a day to ponder the answer. When the day was over the person asked for three more days, and when they were over, for nine more. Then the king said: "If this keeps up, I'll never get an answer." The wise person responded: "The more I ponder him, the greater he becomes and the less I am able to give you an answer."

Yes, mortal child, you are standing at the edge of an ocean whose waves are breaking at your feet and spraying all about you, but you do not know how wide and deep it is. Listen, and you will hear the sound coming across the ocean: **O, Child!** Someone emerges from the ocean whose figure is like that of a human. His eyes are clear and mild like the morning sun in springtime; then they flash like lightning. His garment is white like snow, and he walks with a godly bearing [Matt 17:2]. He says to you: "Call him **father.**" Hearing this, you feel at ease, the hesitations and questions in your heart are laid to rest.

> He, my father. I, his child.
> O, that sounds so dear and mild,
> like the organ's richest tone.
> This I learned from God's own Son.

Yes, now I, too, can believe. It is so difficult to believe in God. There is nothing about him I can take hold of. However, I am so happy to be able to believe in God the Father. Here love is the thing I can take hold of, for the Father and love belong together like the sun and light. **Yes, I believe in God the Father.** Therefore, since he is my Father and I am his child, he watches at my bedside when I sleep. When I am sick he provides the medicine, even if I am not aware of it. When I am hungry, he gives me bread. When I falter, he supports me; if I fall, he picks me up. Whatever I confuse, he puts in order. If I err, he straightens me out. When I am weak, he bears me on his arms, and his grace is the cloak he wraps around me [Luke 1:46–55].

Moreover, since he is a father, his omnipotence is not a hard, iron ring encircling the entire world. His justice and might are the hard bones inside his arm. So it is said: it is terrible to fall into the hands of the living God. Yet love is the flesh surrounding the bones, keeping them from crushing us. Baby birds sit in little nests, the outer part of which is made of hard grasses, brush and thorns, but the inside is lined with soft blades of grass, hair, and wool. And so it seems to me the word "God" sounds like the hard brush and thorns, but the added word "Father" is like the soft blades of grass, the hair, and the wool inside the nest. We are the fortunate ones, we are the little birds in the nest. He warms and feeds us, covers us with his wings when it rains and turns cold, and he protects us when predatory birds appear. **I believe in God the Father.**

4. Those Who Rebel Against God the Father

Have those who sought to tear down the cathedral left untouched the God and Creator of all things and the Father? Do not think it for a minute. These greenhorns are much too rapacious to want to leave anything standing. First of all, we must consider here **those who believe in neither a God nor a Father.** About three thousand years ago King David became acquainted with certain individuals whom he immortalized in the fourteenth psalm. The psalm begins with the words: "The fool says in his heart, there is no God" [Ps 53:1]. As you can see, at that time they spoke it only in their heart. But things have progressed; the fools, too. Now they say it right out in public in the postal coach, in the train, in guest houses, in newspapers, from the podium; and the free-thinkers and neo-Catholics speak it from the pulpit. If this bunch of people could wash off their baptism that was celebrated in the name of the triune God they would do it today. They are really ashamed of their old-fashioned parents, who carried out this odd practice with them, and they are not going to submit their children to the same old grind.

But, you might ask, whom do they think created the world and clever people like themselves, if they do not believe in a living God? I will tell you. The world's vast, immeasurable space, time, the sun, moon, and stars, the earth, the hamster, field mice, May-bugs and these great thinkers—everything has come from itself, yet only gradually over many millions of years. The earth has brought forth weeds and useful plants, along with animals, on its own initiative. The initial animals were still wild, dull, and stupid. It took a long time for them to progress gradually through numerous stages to greater perfection. Then at one point, with favorable food and weather, the dumbest human being arose from the most intelligent ape. From this dumb one have descended all the smart ones who do not believe in God. (We others descend from Adam and Eve, whom God created in the beginning from a clump of earth, and into whom he breathed the breath of life.) And so the process continues.

So, what will the smartest humans turn into with good food and weather? Angels? No, that leap is too small. What, then? They become God himself. Indeed, some of them already have. A type of intelligent individual now residing in many German universities teaches that we need first the human being—naturally, the primary ones are the professors themselves—before God can come into being. You might say these professors are, in fact, dear God's pineal gland or brainpower. **Since they consider themselves wise, they have become fools** [Rom 1:20–23].

Now we come to the second rebel sect. They desire to have only half a God, or put more accurately, they have thrown out God **and want to keep only the Father.** According to them the dear Lord God is always good—completely good. They can be as wicked as they want, but he is still good. They can break his commandments however they please, but he is still good. They do not even harbor the thought that he might punish. The dear Father is much too kind for that. Any bad weather that hits them does so in total innocence, or it is sent to test their devoutness. Suffering occurs only to test their virtue.

But where are the devoutness and virtue that are to be tested? They cannot be found with a lantern. Where is the sin that is to be punished? Actually it is here and there and everywhere. The heart is full of it, and if you take a look around, you will see it poking out everywhere. But they say the dear Father will never punish at all. He is pure love and goodness, he will always give and forgive, and his patience knows no bounds.

Would that just once people of this type would stop and think about their own father and their own youth! Certainly sunshine and friendliness did not always fill their fathers' faces. Rather, dark clouds covered their faces when their children acted in a way that caused the clouds. Sometimes lightning flashed from these clouds, striking now and then. If, as an honest, upright man your father gave you a thorough switching or thrashing because you had pulled something on him, did he say: "My dear son, I'm doing this to test your devoutness and virtue"? And if he made you go to bed hungry and you thought you would starve to death, did he say: "My dear son, I am doing this to prove your devoutness and virtue"? O, by no means. We know better. Perhaps your dear papa is still living. Ask him why he sometimes treated your backside and your stomach so roughly. Do you know what he will answer? "Where there is sin, there must be punishment." Wishy-washy fathers, the Eli-natures who always turn a blind eye to problems, never produce anything good in their children

189

[1 Sam 3:13]. The old Adam does not want to come out in response to goodness, so the father uses something bad to drive it out. The father was not able to accomplish anything with you, so the master had to step forth. So it is with God, too. Where God's love has worked in vain he must step in with a chastening hand. The Lord subdues those who do not want to listen to the Father.

Third and finally, we have one more very unusual group left. This group has turned the dear Lord God into a constitution. Thus it has **a constitutional God, but no longer a Father.** In a constitutional state the king, as monarch, can no longer determine or command anything new on his own initiative. Everything has to be done by the ministers according to the constitution. The king is not responsible for anything bad that happens, nor does anyone owe him thanks for the good that happens. What happens can be attributed only to the constitution. So, many clever people say: God has given his natural law. God can do nothing against it, otherwise it would be an act of coercion, like King Charles X is said to have committed in France with his ordinances.[5] Because everything happens according to strict laws of nature no miracles can occur. Any miracle would be a destruction of these laws. Nor can God hear prayers, because laws would have to be changed for that to be possible.

The gentlemen in this third group have either denied or given natural explanations for the miracles recounted in the Old and New Testaments. Would you perhaps like to have a few samples of their natural explanations? Listen! In the Christmas gospel we read about the shepherds: "And the angel of the Lord appeared to them and the glory of the Lord shone round about them" [Luke 2:9]. A very learned doctor of theology explains it in this way: When Mary was ready to give birth but was unable to find a midwife in Bethlehem, a sympathetic neighbor had to run across the fields at night in order to get one. Naturally she took along a lantern. As she ran past the shepherds' fences the poor, superstitious folk took the lantern for the glory of the heavens, for the radiance of the angels. When Christ was in the desert and, because they had nothing to eat, asked for bread, first a boy brought forth his seven barley loaves and two fish [Matt 14:15–21]. His example took effect. Everyone brought out his or her food and there turned out to be so much that Christ was able to satisfy everyone and still have food left over. (The fact that hereby they obviously make Christ a liar—see Mark 8:2—does not bother these gentlemen in the least.) In the Garden of Gethsemane, Christ asks his pursuers, "For whom are you looking?" Upon hearing the question they fall down as if dead [Matt 26:47–56]. What happened? We have always thought that the dignity and majesty of God's Son so struck these slaves of sin that they collapsed before him. But that is not how it is for the clever gentlemen who explain miracles. According to their opinion the pursuers were, to be sure, somewhat taken aback by Christ's question, they started to stumble and fell over the gnarled roots of the mulberry trees protruding from the ground. We are of the opinion that it is the clever folks who have stumbled and fallen, not over gnarled sycamore roots, but rather over their own gnarled arrogance.

These enemies of miracles have really worked overtime when it comes to Balaam's talking donkey [Num 22:28–30]. They have gone after this poor animal in such a way that it will be a long time before a second donkey opens its mouth if one of them wants to ride to Balak. And because they measure all the days that God in heaven allows with the same yardstick, the long day in Joshua 10 [:12–14] cannot be correct because, according to their yardstick, it is much too long.

Yet let us speak seriously with these people. It is true that God has given his laws. The stars run their courses, trees and flowers grow according to their kind, people and animals grow and die, water runs down the mountain, migratory birds fly south in the fall—God has written his laws into tree and plant, soil and rock, water and snow, people and animals, into heavenly bodies and soap bubbles [cf. Ps 104:5–30]. But do you know the laws? Can you say, "This and that is against God's law"? God's wisdom is an immeasurable sea. You have knelt on the sand at the shore and sipped the water out of your cupped hand. You have not once lapped like Gideon's three hundred and yet you want to explain the entire ocean? [Judg 6:4–7]. Shame on you! Look here, it is 859 $\frac{1}{2}$ miles to the center of the earth. This is pretty far. Miners have bored shafts up to two thousand feet deep, yet it would never occur to a sensible miner or a person knowledgeable about the earth to try to determine on the basis of these two thousand feet what exists further below and what it must look like down there. Likewise, have you not with your natural thought gone only about two thousand feet deep into the unfathomable and unspeakable depths of God? And yet you want to tell according to your powers of reason what God can and cannot do? Phooey, shame on you! Do you think you can already tell at a country's border whether the country is rich or poor and how much money the king has in his treasure chambers?

Let us assume for the sake of the argument that you did know all of God's laws (but don't get any strange ideas; this isn't true!). That would still be no reason for God to give his glory to someone else. **He** is himself everywhere. **He** is the sacred law. The world is not a wound-up watch that, if it does not stop, will run only two or three weeks. Some penitents asked a pastor in a little German duchy during a drought if he would pray in church for rain. He answered, "No prayers will help as long as the wind comes from the East." O, you fool; do you not know that the God to whom we pray is the same one who directs the wind according to his will? Is God supposed to sit behind his laws like an absentee father or an old man in deathlike inactivity, watching how everything goes its way without ever intervening? I can assure you that since God himself is the sacred law, you cannot determine that a particular day will be this way or that even after ten thousand years of experience. God dwells in a light that no one can approach. Nowhere has he signed a document that he will do things only one way and not another. The skeletons of gigantic animals dug out of the bowels of the earth are evidence that different laws were in force on the earth before the flood. According to today's laws of nature no elephants can live in Siberia, yet they are found frozen intact from prehistoric times in the banks of Siberian rivers.

I would like to give you a friendly piece of advice. This evening you can do nothing better than read Job 38 and 39. Test your wisdom there and see how far you get. Do not forget to read the last two verses of chapter 39! A constitutional God can be no

Father. Fatherly love cannot be captured in a constitution. A father does not make a contract with his children as to how he will love them. He reveals his love however and wherever he can. His love is always warm, is new every day [Lam 3:22–23]. His heart breaks for his children. A heart like this cannot be put in reins so that it can be led around, and least of all would it put reins on itself. Were it to do so, it would be surrendering its most sacred right, its very essence.

No, our God is the God above all law. He is the God who performs miracles. He is the God who hears prayers. Therefore all mortal beings come to him. He is the Father who accompanies his children in joy and sorrow with his love. He is the God who punishes and shows mercy. He is mighty above all might, full of love above all love. Just as the flood rose above all the mountains of arrogance, so the flood of his mercy flows down into the deepest depths of misery to refresh those who labor and are heavy laden [Matt 11:28].

Those who do not believe in God have no God. Those who believe in half a God have no God either, for theirs is a weak, self-made thing, and no God. Those who believe in a constitutional God have a dead law that knows nothing of grace. Then the life of the world and the life of the soul are mechanical. Under such a law—are you fully acquainted with it?—Gideon's pelt can, of course, not "become moist and dry out the earth all around," nor "become dry and moisten the earth all around" [Judg 6:36–40]. Nor under this law can any manna fall in the desert, nor does justice come out of mercy, and the forgiveness of sins remains foolishness forever [Exod 16:14–16; Rom 11:30–32; 1 Cor 1:23].

The Diaconate

Appeal of the Deaconess Institute at Kaiserswerth

*to all friends of the Kingdom of God, especially to the dear **brothers in the holy office,** to urge **Christian women** to consider whether they might want, and are able, to dedicate their lives to service of the Lord in*

the *office of deaconess.*

EDITORS' INTRODUCTION: This passionate appeal is a highly representative illustration of Fliedner's oft-repeated call for women to consecrate their lives to diaconal service.[1] By the time he wrote the appeal in January 1853, the Deaconess Institute was entering its seventeenth year.

In his typically clear style and organization Fliedner begins by tracing the history of the diaconate, starting with the apostolic church. A bonus for the reader is that Fliedner conveys the astounding success of his enterprise as he reviews its growth from 1836 to 1853.

Then Fliedner describes the pressing need for deaconesses, counters the most common objections, urges his fellow pastors to help dispel the objections, characterizes the kind of women who should apply, and cites the blessings awaiting those who enter the service.

Already in the **apostolic church,** as the apostle **Paul** reports about sister **Phoebe** in Cenchreae (Rom 16:1), and still many centuries later deaconesses have proved that to a certain extent they carry out Christian **diaconal service** in the most appropriate and beneficial way, practicing love in the service of the church to needy children, the sick, the poor, and the imprisoned. Thousands of young women and widows of every rank, even the highest, who are not bound by pressing family responsibilities have been compelled by thankfulness to their Savior to find in this practice of love the most wonderful vocation for their lives and have been an adornment of the church.

After the office of deaconess died out in the **Greek and Roman Church** during the Middle Ages only the **Waldensian Church** and the **Bohemian and Moravian Brethren** preserved it.[2] After the beginning of the blessed **Reformation** in the sixteenth century, when **Luther,** too, repeatedly expressed himself beautifully about the special vocation of women in practicing Christian love, the **Evangelical Church** in various countries tried to reintroduce the office of deaconess. This occurred in the Principality of **Sedan,** in **Wesel** on the lower Rhine, in **Holland,** and in **England,** to name only a few places. But due to unfavorable conditions at the time these attempts did not last very long. Only in the **Community of the Brethen** was the office reintroduced in 1745.[3]

The **Sisters of Mercy of the Roman Church** tried to fill the gap, and in their own way have accomplished, and are still doing, a great deal of good.[4] However, their constitution and structure, which are entirely or half cloister-like and contrary to scripture, made it incumbent upon our church to return to the original Evangelical Church.

The **deaconess office** was reintroduced to our Evangelical Church in 1836 in such a way that it was clearly authorized by the **Provincial Synods of the Rhine Province and Westphalia** and by our other highest church authorities.[5] Since then the deaconesses' Christian care and training of **children, the sick, the poor, the imprisoned, and the helpless and lost** of all kinds have been recognized as so beneficial that from year to year our **deaconess motherhouse here** has received more and more requests from congregations, from administrators of institutions, and from organizations and private parties to send deaconesses. The number of requests has grown steadily, even though in addition to our institution, and partially through its assistance, several similar institutions have been founded over the past eleven years in **France, Switzerland, Germany, Holland, Sweden,** and **North America.**

Our Deaconess Institute, the oldest of them, has been in existence since October 1836 and currently has 163 sisters. Of them 119 have been consecrated for the office of deaconess, and 109 work outside of the motherhouse, some in **private care of the sick,** some in **twenty-six hospitals,** others in **nine congregations, six orphanages, five homes for the elderly, three kindergartens, one teacher-training school, one secondary school, one halfway house** for released female prisoners, and **one Magdalene House.** These are in **Düsseldorf, Duisburg, Mülheim on the Ruhr, Cleve, Elberfeld, Barmen, Lennep, Dortmund, Hamm, Soest, Münster, Lippstadt, Cologne, Neuwied, Kreuznach, Saarbrücken, Worms, Wetzlar, Erbach, Frankfurt on the Main, Frankfurt on the Oder, Berlin, Stettin, Königsberg, Uetz near Potsdam, Breslau, Altdorf near Pless, London, Pittsburgh in North America, Constantinople, Jerusalem, and here.** Ten of these sisters are **teacher-deaconesses,** some of whom train and teach in kindergartens, some in elementary schools, and others in secondary schools. The rest are **deaconesses for the sick and poor,** but what a small number they are when so many are needed and the following places are now asking for sisters:

Hospitals at Bielefeld, Rheda, Frankfurt on the Oder, Neisse, Carolath, Sagan, Thorn, Danzig, Bonn, Remscheid, Lübeck, Rattei in Mecklenburg, Oberneuland near Bremen, Arolsen in Waldeck, Homburg and Schlitz in Hesse, Nieth and Mariaberg in Württemberg, Augsburg in Bavaria;

Prisons in **Brandenburg, Graudenz,** and **Wartenburg;**

Orphanages and **Women's Rescue Missions** in **Demmin, Cöslin, Craschnitz, Walk in Livland, Mitau in Curland;**

Congregations in **Ketwig, Wald, Solingen, Burgsteinfurt, Vörde, Großkrausche, Worfelde, Boizenburg, Reichau, Wiesbaden in Nassau, Osnabrück in Hannover, Rötha in Saxony;**

As well as **outside of Germany** in **Nijmegen** in the Netherlands, in **Paris** for the sixty thousand Protestant Germans, the majority of whom are languishing in terrible physical and spiritual distress, similarly in **London,** also in **Beirut,** Syria, where a Protestant hospital is to be founded, in **Smyrna,** where a Protestant school is to be founded, and in **Jerusalem,** to which we still need to send a teacher-deaconess. And so it goes. Almost every week we receive new requests.

Moreover, we constantly face the demand for ten to fifteen more sisters than we are able to send for **private care of the sick.**

O, my **dear sisters in Christ!** What a great field of work lies before you, the grain ready for harvest! [Matt 9:37]. And what a delightful field, rich in blessing, to serve the Lord in **congregations, institutions,** and **families** as **mothers of the poor and sick** by strengthening the weak, tending the sick, binding up the wounded, searching for what is lost, and bringing back what has strayed! [Ezek 34:16].

And what a delightful field, to do the same in **orphanages, rescue missions,** and **schools,** to shepherd the lambs on green meadows, to lead them to the fresh water of life, yes, into the arms of the Prince of Life, their Good Shepherd, so that he might bless them!

We cannot provide workers for even a **tenth** of this holy vineyard. Hundreds, thousands of bodies and souls are withering away without help. Yet they would not wither away, instead they would find help if all you dear sisters standing idly in the marketplace who are not required at home would come at the call of your God and Lord: **"Go, too, into the vineyard! I will give you what you need"** [Matt 20:3–4].

Why do you not come? Why do you stand idly about?

Most of you hold back for at least one of **three reasons.**

1) Many of you have no idea at all of the great physical and spiritual need around you. You would really like to serve the Savior out of thanks for his love, but you do not know how or where. In addition you feel weak and unprepared and are uninformed about the facilities for preparation and training that our Deaconess Institute and similar ones offer.

2) Others of you do indeed know all this and would like to come and help. However, you are worried that your passionate zeal for work might be a self-chosen path, not God's path. You think you have to wait for an outward call to place God's seal on your inward call.

3) Still others do not receive permission from their all-too-anxious parents—we, of course, find parental consent necessary according to the Word of God—or they let themselves be held back by relatives who are full of biases.

Therefore, **dear brothers in the ministry,** you can, with the aid of the Lord, help greatly to remove these hindrances. Whether from the pulpit, in Bible classes, missionary lessons, or confirmation instruction you can turn the attention of women to the burning need to send more women workers into the harvest. You can turn their attention to the rich blessing they can become for the church and to the blessed reward of grace from the Lord.

You can help if you make the women aware of how, according to their various talents and interests, they can receive instruction and guidance in our Deaconess Institute, either in care of the sick and poor or in the upbringing and teaching of the young, either as **nurse-deaconesses** or **teacher-deaconesses.** You can make the women aware of how in our motherhouse they will find a permanent refuge for the days when they are fatigued or sick and a worry-free home for old age.

You can help by making the women aware of how the office of evangelical deaconess is free of **nun's vows** and other **human statutes that go against the scriptures,** that the office stands in evangelical freedom, which, of course, does not allow one to make room for the flesh.

Thus, **dear brothers,** if you can help set a greater number of the available, energetic women to the task of building the kingdom of God, you will not only be doing a great service to our church in general but also to your own congregations. The blessings that your ministering daughters bring to other places will revert home. Yes, later if you need the women for work in your congregations, you can receive them in return, like an investment that has multiplied.

Do I need to prove to you how great the current need is in almost all large parishes and cities for such women helpers in the Christian diaconal service or inner mission?

The Roman Catholic priests know this, too, and make use of women's energies for their church to a far greater extent. To which hospitals, orphanages, homes for the poor, prisons, etc., especially in populations of mixed confession, do they not attempt to send their **Sisters of Mercy** in order that they can proselytize? Where do they not try to practice **private care of the sick** with the same aim? And O, how hundreds of sisters from the higher and even highest ranks answer their call!

But do women in our church also answer our call? O, that God might have mercy on us! How small the number is up to now! O, how some institutions and private parties, because they cannot get any sisters from us, must of necessity engage Roman sisters to provide care, and these are able to confuse the conscience of our sick! Is this not a disgrace for our church? Arise, therefore, dear friends and brothers, raise your voices in faith, call like a trumpet into our congregations and other circles: **"You daughters of Zion, come over and help! The Lord is in need of you"** [Matt 21:5; Acts 16:9]. Certainly not all of your voices will go unheeded. Many a wise virgin will respond to the bridegroom, even though he comes in the figure of a servant: **"Here am I. Send me!"** [Matt 25:1–13; Isa 6:8].

However, even though deaconess work is a **delightful** task, it is nevertheless **difficult** for flesh and blood. Therefore, these Christian women must be **energetic and strong**, not **physically ailing**, not **morose**, and not with **troubled souls**. Nor can they be **half-invalids** looking for **care and support**, like the ones who, unfortunately, are often sent to us out of a lack of judgment and with medical certifications that one could often call **falsifications. The Lord wants the best in sacrifice to his service. His service deserves nothing less.**

> Offer the vigorous, beautiful, blossoming flowers,
> Offer to him with thanksgiving your youth with its powers:
>   to Jesus your friend,
>   Jesus, whose care does not end,
> to him who great gifts on us showers!

The women need to have experienced for themselves their own sinfulness and that they deserve only to be condemned. Yet they also need to have experienced the mercy of Christ and in response must desire earnestly to do something for his glory and for the salvation of their neighbors, not through their own power, but only through the power of the Lord. They must find their honor and joy in being allowed as maidservants to serve him in his sick and helpless members.

Then they will see it is good to be in this service for him. They will see that because they renounce the paltry honors, joys, and goods of the world, he fills them with the abundant goods of his house, with his calm peace, his sweet love, and his joy in the Holy Spirit. The yoke that appears so rough to them becomes gentle, the heavy load, light, for **he** helps them bear the burden. He is in them, they in him. They are not deterred when thorns and thistles of the world harm them, when bitterness and hate, even from unsupport-ive relatives, often pursue them. As servants of eternal love they rejoice in being able to return love for hate, and where thorns were growing, to scatter imperishable seeds for eternity.

Thus, they do not desire to earn heaven on their own through their good works. They have already received eternal life through faith, through nothing but grace. Their lives are hidden with Christ in God [Col 3:3]. **"Blessed are the merciful"**—that is what they feel; **yes, they are indeed blessed** [Matt 5:7].

And when work is done and the evening bells call them home, even if early, then—O, never too early!—the **King of Glory** will approach:

> **I was hungry and you gave me to eat. I was naked and you clothed me. I was sick and in prison and you came to me. O, you devout and faithful maiden! You were faithful in a few things; I will set you over much. Enter into the joy of your Lord!** [Matt 25:35–36; Luke 16:10; 19:17].

If Christian women respond with interest about entering **dea-coness service,** we kindly request that you inform us. We will then send detailed information about the **conditions for acceptance into the probationary period.**

Kaiserswerth on the Rhine, January 26, 1853.

The Administration of the Deaconess Institute:
Fliedner, Pastor

THEODOR FLIEDNER

House Rules and Instructions for Service for the Deaconesses in the Deaconess Institute at Kaiserswerth

EDITORS' INTRODUCTION: Theodor Fliedner's *House Rules*[1] represents the culmination of his hope to re-create the diaconate on a Protestant basis. Among the many virtues of the document is Fliedner's concise introductory explanation of the rationale for diaconal life. The motivation for service, *diakonia*, is threefold. First, care for the sick and suffering is a grateful response to Jesus for bearing our sickness and suffering. Next, we serve others in emulation of Jesus' life. And, finally, we serve the poor and needy because in doing so we serve Jesus. Throughout the document we see that this *diakonia* is not ascetic withdrawal from, but direct engagement with, the world.

As is true of any great "rule," such as those of monastic orders in the Middle Ages, one cannot describe the high ideal of life in community without delineating the mundane responsibilities on which that life depends. Thus, Fliedner's attention ranges from lofty spiritual matters to practical details such as instructions on mail delivery.

Fliedner's original document went through many editions to which he added several appendices over the years. The following translation is of an early copy (1852) that belonged to a deaconess and is now in the Kaiserswerth archives. The text here presents key segments from six divisions of the much longer work, along with one of its appendices that explains the qualifications required of applicants for the office of deaconess, and at the same time conveys to the reader some insight into the deaconesses' daily life. While Fliedner quoted in full several extensive lists of supporting scripture passages, this translation provides only the references.

I. The Deaconess Vocation in General

§1.

In accordance with the apostolic rules for congregations, deaconesses have the vocation, like Phoebe in her service to the congregation at Cenchreae (Rom 16:1), of serving Christian parishes, doing this specifically through care of their needy children, their poor, sick, and imprisoned, thus being assistants, directly or indirectly, to the deacons.[2]

A. Deaconesses for the Poor and Sick
(This also includes the prison deaconesses.)

§2.

The first matter regarding **deaconesses for care of the poor and sick** is that if they desire to fulfill this vocation in the evangelical spirit they must take into consideration above all the necessity to care for the poor and sick as **servants,** which is also what the name of their office (deaconess) means, and specifically:

1) as **servants of the Lord Jesus,**
2) as **servants of the poor and sick for Jesus' sake,** and
3) as **servants of one another.**

§3.
1. Deaconesses as Servants of the Lord Jesus

Just as the love of Christ compels each true Christian henceforth to live no longer for self but for him who died and rose for us [2 Cor 5:15], so each deaconess must care for the poor and sick, not for the sake of an earthly reward or earthly honor, but out of grateful love to the one who also bore her sickness and took her sufferings unto himself. Hence, she must struggle to do everything in Jesus' name, for his sake, according to his example, and as a merciful Samaritan in his service.

202

Important Bible Passages as the Foundation for this:
1) 2 Corinthians 5:14–15
2) Colossians 3:12–17
3) Luke 10:36–37
4) Matthew 5:7
5) James 1:27
6) Romans 12:8–9
7) 1 Corinthians 13:4–7
8) 2 Thessalonians 3:5
9) 1 Thessalonians 5:14–24

§4.

However, in her service to the poor and sick the deaconess must regard herself not merely as a servant of the Lord Jesus, but also:

2. As a Servant of the Poor and Sick for Jesus' Sake,

according to Paul's example (2 Cor 4:5; 1 Cor 9:19). She must clothe herself in heartfelt pity, kindness, gentleness, and patience toward the poor and sick, and with such humility as though they were her masters. Yet she is to prove herself to be their maidservant **not for the sake of the poor and sick, but for Jesus' sake alone,** that is, not in order to gain praise from them (Rom 12:8–9; Gal 1:10), but rather out of love and humility toward the Lord, whose representatives she sees in them. Consequently, she is also never to serve them with such indulgence that she strengthens their stubbornness, pickiness, anger, envy, or other maliciousness. Rather, she is to serve them always with the intent of winning their souls for the Lord.
10) 2 Corinthians 4:5
11) 1 Corinthians 9:19

§5.

3. Deaconesses as Servants of One Another

In living and working together the deaconesses are to be **servants of one another** according to the example and commands of the Lord, who became our servant. They are to do nothing for vain-glory or with squabbling; rather, in mutual humility each one is to regard the other as higher than herself. The individual is not to focus on herself but on the others. Hence, she who would be great, even the noblest in the group, must be the servant of all [Mark 10:42–45; Phil 2:1–8].

In all of this the love of the sisters for one another is to be sin-cere. For the sake of God and their own conscience, in renunciation of their own will, and out of respect, they must obey their superiors [Rom 12:10]. They must strive hard to conduct themselves seriously and with dignity toward all others. However, in their efforts for the salvation of others they are not to neglect their own salvation. Along with the obligatory attention to their physical health they must care for their souls' growth in Christian understanding and godliness. To this end they must, in particular, keep up quiet companionship with the Lord, hold frequent self-examination, search diligently in God's Word, and gladly come to the Holy Supper.

If, at the same time, they seek to fulfill the daily tasks of their vocation in genuine humility of heart and for God's glory alone by repeatedly focusing their spirit on God, and by protecting their souls and all their senses from distraction, then peace and cheer will pour into their souls and upon everything they do. A power from high above will strengthen them for their most difficult tasks and tempta-tions, and protect them from the danger of sinking into the vain spirit of the world. Thus, in their quiet efforts for the well-being of their neighbors, they will lead a blessed life of peace and joy in God, and the Lord will be their shield and their very great reward [Gen 15:1].

Important Bible Passages as the Foundation
for Deaconesses Being Servants of One Another,
and for Denying Themselves

1. They are to deny their haughtiness,

a. through humility and sincere love of the sisters:
    12) Philippians 2:1–8
    13) Mark 10:42–45

14) Mark 8:34–37
15) Luke 14:33
16) Romans 12:10

Hymn (*Evangelical Hymnbook*, No. 478)
Melody: *Alle Menschen müssen sterben*

1. Your obedience I will treasure,
   finding joy in quietude;
   without speaking, yet with pleasure
   serving as your servant should;
   never boasting of my story,
   never seeking fame and glory.
   Grant this wisdom unto me,
   God of highest sovereignty.

2. And on unknown paths to venture,
   paths that only your eyes know,
   everyone I see, a stranger,
   still in patient calm to go:
   teach me so to live, O Teacher,
   Jesus Christ, the source and giver
   of the truly humble heart.
   Help me yearn to do my part!

3. God of all the still and lowly,
   who avoid the limelight's glare,
   and, devout, seek thy will only,
   lonely in life's work and care:
   let me not complain, O Father,
   if my load is heavy labor;
   let me rather turn within,
   humbly look to you alone!

4. God, you are my God, I kneel
   deeply humble at your feet.
   You grant everyone renewal,

and you grant me grace complete.
You support my quiet striving
more in you to shape my living,
less to trust in my own skill,
building firmly on your will.

Verse 7 from Hymn 539 in the *Evangelical Hymnbook:*
"Come, Christians, Let Us Go"
Melody: *Aus meines Herzens Grunde*

So may the stronger neighbors
support the weak who fall,
ease everybody's labors,
bring peace and love to all!
Join hands with us today!
In meekness be the surest,
and gladly be the purest
along our pilgrim way.

b. By giving up all falsehood, all envy, quarreling, and backtalk:
    17) 1 Peter 2:1
    18) James 3:13–18

c. By giving up vanity in one's clothing and other outward things:
    19) 1 Timothy 2:9–10
    20) 1 Peter 3:3–4

d. By obedience to one's superiors:
    21) 1 Thessalonians 5:12–13

2. They are to deny their desires of the flesh:
    22) 1 John 2:15–17
    23) Galatians 5:16–24

3. They are to deny the desires of the eye:
    24) 1 Timothy 6:6–12
    25) Deuteronomy 10:9

Blessings of Such Love and Self-Denial:

26) Psalm 41:2–4
27) Isaiah 58:7–11
28) Mark 9:36
29) Mark 10:28–30
30) Philippians 4:4–7
31) Matthew 25:34–46
32) James 1:12
33) Revelations 2:10

Such Blessing is the Reward of Grace Alone:

34) Luke 17:10

[....]

IV. Special Duties of the Deaconesses
in Regard to Care of the Sick

[....]

§21.

In caring for the poor and the sick—those afflicted in the body as well as those in the spirit—the deaconesses are to remember constantly that they are to care for them as:

Servants of the Lord Jesus, and as: Servants of the Poor and Sick for Jesus' Sake.

(See §3, 4)

In her spiritual care of the sick, the deaconess's love must be guided constantly by the holy love of the Lord in which he smites the sick but also binds up (Job 5:17–18), in which he allows suffering in the flesh so that they cease from sin (1 Pet 4:1), in which he makes well so that, from then on, they sin no more (John 5:14), and thereby the works of God are made manifest in them (John 9:1–3). Therefore she must constantly treat her wards as people who, through their own cross, have been placed in the school of the Lord in order to learn with their hearts his vision of peace. As his co-worker she must teach them to understand this peace. She must endeavor continually to show them great kindness (Prov 15:13, 30) and patience.

However, she cannot comfort everyone all the time and encourage them to trust in God's grace. When it is necessary, she must, in loving earnestness, warn against self-assurance and admonish them to perceive in their sickness the wakening voice from above: "Those whom I love, I reprove and chasten. So be zealous and repent!" (Rev 3:19). In particular, she must seek to promote in the sick a Christlike submission to and rest in God's will, so that they do not agonize about their physical recovery or about other earthly cares but rather throw all their cares on the Lord, following the admonition of the apostle: "Do not worry about anything, but in all things make your requests known to God in prayer and supplication and with thanksgiving!" (Phil 4:6).

The goal is that the sick, just as the apostles, worry about the One Thing only—that they might be pleasing to the Lord, so that whether they live or die, they are of the Lord (Rom 14:8; 2 Cor 5:9). To that end the deaconess is to share with them—in addition to instruction and comfort from the Word of God—sound devotional writings, Christian hymns, and edifying stories from the bedsides of the sick and dying. Therefore it is incumbent upon the deaconesses to divert the sick from talking a great deal about worldly and earthly things; nor should the deaconesses themselves engage much in such topics. Nor should they allow relatives who visit the sick to converse much about them; in fact, deaconesses should not allow the relatives to visit long or frequently at all.

Even about spiritual matters the deaconesses are not to speak often or at length with the sick, in order not to interfere with their private reflection and quiet communion with the Lord. This will be of no less benefit for the deaconesses. They are not to let themselves get drawn into disputes with the sick about spiritual matters or to permit such disputes among the sick. In regard to the conduct of the sick and keeping order, the deaconesses are to operate according to the *Nursing Rules for Male and Female Patients.*[3]...They are to see that these are posted in all of the patients' rooms and are to make the patients aware of them when they arrive.

§22.

One of the methods of arousing in the sick a patient and God-pleasing attitude of heart is for the deaconess to engage the sufficiently healthy patients in some light and pleasant physical activity. In this manner one eliminates boredom—the mother of much impatience and other harm. However, the work of the patients is to be done for the good of the institution, not for the good of individual sisters, even if a patient should volunteer the latter kind of help. [....]

VI. Relationship of the Deaconesses to One Another

All of the deaconesses in the Institute form **one** family, in which, united in the bond of love, they live as sisters for the **one** great purpose of their presence here. Everything that promotes unity of spirit—gentleness, love, intercession, modesty, readiness to serve—is, at all times, to be the adornment of this circle of sisters bound together in the Lord. Everything that threatens to weaken or destroy unity is to be banished from this closely knit group. To this end, may they, in their life and work together, constantly endeavor to be **"servants of one another,"** as paragraph five is entitled. Therefore, if two deaconesses are doing **one** task together, whether caring for one or more of the sick or carrying out some other responsibility, they are not to try to gain honor, one before the other, from the sick or from others. Rather, each one should secure and promote the honor of the other one before her own (Gal 6:12) and, like Paul, recognize that neither the one who plants nor the one who waters is anything, but only God, who gives the growth (1 Cor 3:7). If, in doing a task together, one sister is subordinated to another, then the subordinate must follow the other sister willingly and meticulously, as she would the head deaconess. Within her special area of work each deaconess should try to set an example for the others of the most faithful performance of one's duty without encroaching on the special areas of the others. Any unnecessary running back and forth and any useless conversation should be avoided.

§27.

If one sister has a complaint against another, she is obligated according to the law of Christ (Matt 18:15), instead of getting angry—whether keeping it inside or expressing it openly—or closing her heart to the other sister, to go to her immediately and, in a spirit of kindness, explain in person the actual or supposed wrongdoing. She must not let the sun go down on her anger or unhappiness before having done this [Eph 4:26]. If she does not do this, then each sister who knows the situation is obligated to admonish both parties in sisterly earnestness and faithful love to reconcile themselves as Christ's redeemed and to extend to one another the hand of peace.

If one or the other party does not want to settle the matter humbly but instead holds a grudge, then the head deaconess must be informed. If the efforts of the head deaconess, too, are fruitless, then she reports the situation to the inspector, who calls in both parties and seeks reconciliation in the spirit of love. If this is of no avail, then one must proceed according to the scriptural principle that it is impossible for the stubbornly unreconciled person to be a servant of Christ and a loving nurse to those who are suffering (1 John 4:20; 2 Tim 3:3–5; Matt 5:23–26; 18:15–17).

VII. Public and Private Edification of the Deaconesses and of All Other Members of the Institution

§28.

Christian women who have willingly devoted themselves to the service of the Lord simply should not have to be admonished to hear the Word of the Lord diligently and devoutly in his house on Sundays or to use his day primarily for the edification of the soul. However, housekeeping and the care of the sick cannot suffer because deaconesses attend public worship. If necessary, deaconesses must take turns going to the morning and afternoon church services.

Deaconesses must also try to make every Sunday as important and edifying as possible for the sick. They can recount some of the sermon to evangelical patients whose conditions permit this, but who are unable to go to church, or, particularly during the public worship service, they can read them a short, clear sermon or other edifying piece, sing a hymn with them, and so forth. If the time of the public worship service is not suitable for patients to have private worship, then, as far as their conditions allow, the sister on duty should make use of the time for her own edification.

§29.

During the public worship service no sister may accept visitors who have come to see her, the sick, or the institution in general. Should visitors of the sick or the institution arrive before the beginning of worship, then, when the service is about to begin, they must be requested either to attend worship or to leave, and, if necessary, to return after the service.

§30.

It is up to each sister to come to the Lord's table as often as she desires and according to the needs of her heart. She informs the inspector beforehand. If, however, her care of the sick or her other duties do not allow her to go, she is to request the head deaconess to have another sister who is not going to the Lord's supper to take her place if possible. If deaconesses who are being sent out to distant locations of service wish to celebrate the Lord's supper before their departure, then other sisters who feel the need may celebrate with them. However, they need to inform the inspector beforehand.

§31.

Every morning before breakfast and every evening before going to bed, the sisters, along with all healthy, evangelical, female companions in the house, assemble for devotions with prayer and lessons. The lessons are read in the morning from the sacred scriptures and in the evening from a book of devotions. The reader is the head deaconess or one whom she chooses. If time permits, they also sing. It is self-evident that each individual's private devotions, with prayer and reading from the sacred scriptures, are not, as a result, to be neglected, but to be practiced as time permits. Nevertheless, neither the common nor private devotions may be allowed to interfere with the care of the sick or with other pressing duties. On the contrary, a sister must, when necessary, break off in the middle of singing, in the middle of the most passionate prayer or the most zealous reading of the sacred scriptures, in order to hurry to a sick person or to another pressing duty of her calling. Such carrying out of one's duty is also worship of God, and naturally during the work one can keep one's soul in a prayerful attitude, which, after all, is what matters (Jas 1:27; Matt 12:1–3; Hos 6:6). [....]

APPENDIX II

Conditions for Admission into the Office of Deaconess in the Deaconess Institute at Kaiserswerth

1) Christian women who wish to assume the office of deaconess for the sick and poor must possess a **rather well developed understanding of Christianity.**

A mere religiosity, mere attendance at Christian gatherings, and reading of Christian devotional literature is not sufficient. A love of reading God's Word, along with diligent application of it, must have been present for some time, as well as acquaintance with the more important narratives in the Old and New Testaments. Furthermore, recognition of the sinful heart—based on personal experience—as well as experience of Christ's grace must be present, for they indicate that the individual has learned to despair of herself and, in her weakness, find consolation in Christ's power alone.

2) A **Christian life** must have adorned such Christian women for some time.

Thus, the women cannot simply have a good reputation, which is necessary, of course, and which the apostle requires of the deacons; and they cannot simply be individuals who were never fallen women [1 Tim 3:8–13]. Rather, they have to have put their conversion into practice through their good works; through a gentle and peaceful spirit, which is a delight to God; through humility and childlike obedience to parents, rulers, and other superiors; through industriousness, good-naturedness, and self-denying love for the good of the neighbor as far as their situation affords the opportunity; and by earnestly struggling to walk in simplicity and purity before God and humankind. As a result, they are to submit with their application

a **character reference**

from their pastor.

In addition, they must not possess a tendency to be gloomy or melancholy but must have developed a friendly, gracious, and loving personality.

In listing such qualities as the condition for acceptance, we obviously are not speaking about perfection, but, in part, **only** about an earnest, evangelical struggling toward further growth in them, and, in part, about one's predisposition. In regard to friendliness, for example, one's natural temperament is either a significant help or hindrance. The tendency toward melancholy can lie so deep in one's temperament that no matter how hard one fights against it one does not achieve the friendliness necessary for the care of the sick and poor, although one may nevertheless be a very good Christian.

3) **Being in good physical condition** is necessary, whereby not merely a large, robust physical frame is required, but it is even more necessary that the individual does not have weak or sensitive nerves, respiratory problems, physical frailties, scrofula, or any other similar harbingers or signs of sickliness. Therefore, whoever comes here as a trainee must beforehand submit

a **certificate of health**

issued by the applicant's local doctor or nearest health official.

4) Regarding **age,** the applicant must, as a rule, be over eighteen and under forty. Under special circumstances exceptions can be made.

5) Applicants must **be knowledgeable about, and have practice in, common domestic activities,** such as knitting, sewing, washing, cleaning, and so on, and, in general, possess the skills for all kinds of work. To be sure, the tasks of a deaconess for the sick and poor do

not consist of merely caring for the sick in their rooms and of visiting the poor, but also of cooking and housekeeping for the sick as well as the healthy, of seeing after their clean clothing and linens, and so forth. This does not mean, however, that the deaconess is expected to be a master at these tasks, because the most important thing is that she be a sincerely willing worker in order, for the sake of Christ, to attack with confidence whatever jobs arise, no matter how unfamiliar or difficult, and, as a humble pupil, to learn as much as possible. Naturally, when work assignments are made, proper consideration is always given to the person's physical strength and other characteristics.

6) Applicants must be able to **speak, read, and write German well, and do arithmetic well.**
In their application for acceptance they must submit a

short **autobiography**

written by themselves about their outward and inward development, the main goal being a simple, honest portrait that flows from the heart and hand and is composed or corrected by no one else, even if it contains errors.

7) **Applicants must successfully complete an unpaid probation and training period of at least six months** during which only room and board are free. If, at the end of the half-year's probation, they are judged not to be qualified yet for permanent engagement in the office of deaconess, although there is reason to believe that after longer preparation they will be suited for the office, then the probationary period is extended. Meanwhile, they receive an annual compensation of twenty-five talers beginning at the end of the first six months' probation. During the probationary period they receive free of charge from the institution the caps, collars, and skirts that they are required to wear. In regard to their clothing they are to bring several simple, dark-colored dresses for work and at least one dark-colored, simple Sunday dress, along with an adequate supply of undergarments. They are also to bring their Bible and hymnbook.

8) Applicants are to **cover their own travel expenses to come here as well as expenses to return home** if they withdraw voluntarily or if they are found not to be suited for service as deaconess.

If, after completing the probationary period, they are found to be suited for the office of deaconess **they must obligate themselves to the office for at least five years.**

Then they receive an annual salary of twenty-five talers and, at no charge, the garb worn by deaconesses, that is, the blue blouse for workdays, the blue skirt, white cap, and white collar. If a deaconess, during faithful exercise of her office, becomes sick or incapable of working and has no means of support, then the administration will assist in providing for her needs in the motherhouse or in some other way.

Kaiserswerth on the Rhine
The Administration of the Deaconess Institute
Fliedner, Pastor

APPENDIX III

Rules for the Probationary Nurses

1. Immediately after her entrance into the institution the sister must turn over her papers of identification, such as her passport, to the **supervisor of training** in order to receive another passport from the local mayor's office for future travels. If the papers she has brought are inadequate, she must write home immediately in this regard.

2. The sister will be made familiar with the **House Rules.** Later the sister must demonstrate to the supervisor of training through questions and answers that she knows the main content.

3. During the first few days the supervisor of training will look through all of the sister's clothing. The sister must leave in her trunk whatever is found to be too colorful or inappropriate.

4. All articles of clothing the sister will use are to be clearly identified.

5. As much as possible the undergarments of the sister must also be dark in order to save laundry. Therefore she may not wear

any white slips or nightgowns, and, as a rule, she may put only one pair of white stockings in the wash every two weeks.

6. When acquiring new pieces of clothing she is to ask the supervisor of training for advice.

7. She must put together for herself a little booklet in which she lists the dark wash she turns in. The wash is turned in at a specific time.

8. She must draw up a list of all the items she has brought to the institution and take it to the place stipulated by the supervisor of training. She may not keep any clothing, whether dirty or clean, on her bed or on her night table.

9. She must pick up her clean laundry at a certain time and look carefully for her own mark.

10. She is to comply with the instructions of the supervisor of training in regard to dressing and undressing, washing, brushing the teeth, cleaning combs and shoes, and so forth.

11. She must always keep her articles of clothing clean and orderly; wear the caps, skirts, and collars given to her; and never take them off in any season of the year or at any task. She is to carry a purse containing a handkerchief, small notebook, and pencil.

12. She must record her income and expenditures in a separate little book.

13. If a sister runs out of money, she may not borrow from other sisters, and she is particularly forbidden from borrowing from the sick or others in the institution. She is to inform the head deaconess instead.

14. Nothing may be purchased from or sold to the sick. If a sister wants to sell something to or buy something from another sister or seminarian, she must ask the head deaconess for permission.

15. She may not arbitrarily use the various implements meant for one place at another place. If, however, she does so with the permission of the division supervisor, she must bring the implements back to their proper place after using them.

16. She may not go to the men's station as long as she has not been assigned work there. If she thinks it is necessary for her to do

something there, she must ask the supervisor of training to arrange it for her.

17. If she wants to go out, she must ask the supervisor of training, unless she is going to the director or head deaconess. She must also tell where she wishes to go.

18. She is allowed to go to church as often as possible, but first she must ask the sister who is next in authority above her.

19. Every two weeks she must write out one of the sermons she has heard, and she must tell the supervisor of training if she is prevented from doing this.

20. Just as she receives her mail from the doorkeeper, so also she is to give her the letters she wants to mail.

21. She must keep the door to the room where she dresses and undresses during the day locked. At night, however, the doors to all the rooms in the institution remain unlocked.

22. She is to be punctual about using the hours the supervisor of training allots her for taking walks.

23. She is to attend classes regularly according to the instructions of the supervisor of training.

24. She may use the library of the Deaconess Institute and is encouraged to do so. She is to check with the librarian and follow instructions in regard to the books.

25. The director and the head deaconess of the institution, Pastor Fliedner and his wife, are the chief authorities over each sister; each sister owes them obedience and trust. However, each must also obey the division supervisor, the supervisor of training, and all other superiors.

26. A sister's wishes, comments, and complaints will, if expressed humbly and in good faith, be heard at any time by her superiors, who will take them into consideration to the best of their ability. Each sister is asked sincerely to report to her superiors deficiencies she notices and things that are wrong, without going into needless discussions about them.

27. The administration will, to the best of its ability, give the opportunity to every sister during her training period to learn as much as possible about everything she will need later for her vocation. At the

same time, the administration counts on each sister's desire to learn and expects each one to be devoted to making good use of her time and instruction. Each sister is also free to tell the administration what she thinks is still necessary for her, in particular, to learn, and to request the opportunity to learn it.

Kaiserswerth
The Administration of the Deaconess Institute

Three Hymns

EDITORS' INTRODUCTION: In addition to all his other memorable accomplishments, Fliedner composed verses to fill the need for hymns related directly to diaconal service. Included here are three of his best known, all of which appeared in the *Deaconess Hymnbook.*[1] The prominence of this hymnbook can be seen in the fact that by the time the Deaconess Institute was thirty years old, the hymnal was already in its seventh edition.

The distinctiveness of the first hymn, reflected by its placement at the head of the hymnbook, derives from its use as a greeting sung at the worship service that welcomed new sisters into the community. The hymn also contains the key motif of Fliedner's spirituality, choosing "the one thing needful." The second hymn, which stirs the new deaconesses to go forth in service, focuses on how they should live if their work is to be fruitful. The verses close with the biblical quote Fliedner had chosen for his own life's motto: "He must increase; I must decrease." The simple, direct style of the third hymn lends beauty to its description of the deaconess's calling, which is to feed, clothe, and care for Jesus in those who are needy.

Welcome Greeting to Probationary Sisters
Melody: *Was Gott thut, das ist wohlgethan*[2]

1. O welcome, maiden of the Lord,
    to join us in our station!
    Your heart we joyfully escort
    upon the path to Zion.
       Our harmony
       brings victory,
    relief, and blessings many
    upon our pilgrim journey.

2. How good, like Mary to embrace
   the one thing that is needful,
   and find at Jesus' feet your place
   to serve the cross's people.
       Working as one,
       fearing no scorn,
   to bow in humble living
   in witness to his giving.

3. Then happily you'll ease the ache
   and pain of those who suffer,
   will overcome for Jesus' sake
   impatience of endeavor.
       Gladly you'll bring
       children to him,
   will train them through his power
   on earth for him to flower.

4. So come, step forth assuredly,
   though steep your path may wander!
   If weak be your ability,
   God's aid will be the stronger.
       You serve him who
       likewise serves you.
   He calls you and prepares you;
   with tender love he bears you.

O Widespread Fields!
Melody: *Jerusalem, du hochgebaute Stadt*[3]

1. O widespread fields! O see them, sisters dear?
   To scatter heaven's seed,
   that is your task! A wondrous harvest year
   shall follow from your deed.
   And though from many a kernel
   you see no sprouts arise,

the Lord knows what's internal,
what's hidden from your eyes.

2. But not alone—that's not the path for you;
   together strength's assured!
   So like the twelve—he sent them two by two—
   he treats you, sisterhood.
   Come, join your hearts in labor,
   in discipline and prayer,
   then sacred flames will favor
   your efforts everywhere!

3. So venture forth! Yet fight the holy fight
   in pureness, for your part!
   Give vanity and other self-delight
   no room within your heart!
   For when your work has ended,
   your glory and true worth
   will be the flock you've tended
   upon the fields of earth!

4. The work is his! Give him the love and praise!
   He is your help and might.
   The tasks you do are but reflecting rays
   of his redeeming light.
   So aim for, without ceasing,
   this goal your whole life through:
   each day to be decreasing,
   that he may grow in you.

Deepest Source of Joys from Heaven

1. Deepest source of joys from heaven,
   Jesus, who enflames my heart,
   you to feed, to clothe, to strengthen
   is, O Lord, my grateful part.

2. If in love so thankful-hearted
   burdens of the sick we bear,
   then, "O come to me, you blessed!"
   is the call that we shall hear.

3. They who love the little children,
   they who soothe the poor and sad,
   they who comfort those in prison—
   you are their reward and shield.

4. Spread, O Lord, the flames of heaven
   brighter, warmer in our breast.
   You to tend is our deep passion.
   May we grow in love obsessed.

Notes

INTRODUCTION

1. Anna Sticker, *Theodor Fliedner,* 2d ed. (Kaiserswerth, 1959), p. 32.

2. Ibid., pp. 15, 25.

3. Theodor Fliedner, *Antrittspredigt am 27. Januar 1822,* in *Der Armen- und Krankenfreund* (Kaiserswerth, 1928), vol. 80, pp. 191–92.

4. Excerpts published by his son, Georg Fliedner, *Theodor Fliedner: Sein Leben und sein Wirken* (Kaiserswerth, 1903), vol. 1, republished in *Der Armen- und Krankenfreund* (Kaiserswerth, 1933), vol. 85, pp. 119–42. See also Martin Gerhardt, *Theodor Fliedner,* 2 vol. (Kaiserswerth, 1933), vol. 1, p. 95.

5. Gerhardt, *Theodor Fliedner,* vol. 1, p. 51.

6. Philip Schaff, "Fliedner, Theodor," in *The New Schaff-Herzog Religious Encyclopedia* (New York, 1909), vol. 4, p. 333.

7. Theodor Fliedner, *Abschiedspredigt...am 28. Januar 1849,* in *Der Armen- und Krankenfreund* (Kaiserswerth, 1928), vol. 80, p. 197.

8. Sticker, *Theodor Fliedner,* pp. 28–29.

9. Gerhardt, *Theodor Fliedner,* vol. 1, p. 146.

10. Anna Sticker, *"...und doch möchte ich nur meinem Sinn folgen...":* *Friederike Fliedner, Stifterin der Kaiserswerther Diakonissenanstalt* (Offenbach/Main, 1986), pp. 7–8.

11. Ibid., pp. 8–9.

12. Theodor Fliedner, *Das erste Jahr-Zehnt der Diakonissen-Anstalt zu Kaiserswerth am Rhein vom Oktober 1836 bis Januar 1847...* (Kaiserswerth, 1847), p. 7.

13. Anna Sticker, *Florence Nightingale, Curriculum Vitae, with Information about Florence Nightingale and Kaiserswerth* (Düsseldorf-Kaiserswerth, 1965), p. 10.

14. G. H. Gerberding, *Life and Letters of W. A. Passavant, D.D.* (Greenville, 1906), p. 145.

15. Ibid., p. 154.

16. Gerhardt, *Theodor Fliedner,* vol. 2, p. 456. The tribute to Schmucker is by Martin Schmidt, *Pietismus,* 2d ed. (Stuttgart, 1978), p. 154.

17. The German website for the *Kaiserswerther Diakonie* offers a concise description of all its branches of service, as well as of the archives, museum, bookstore, and other topics. It includes photos and a detailed map of the campus (see http://www.kaiserswerther-diakonie.de).

SPECIAL PASTORAL CARE: A HIGH CALLING OF PASTORS AND ELDERS—A SYNODICAL SERMON ON ACTS 20:28

1. Theodor Fliedner, *Die besondere Seelsorge: Eine hohe Pflicht der Pfarrer u. Aeltesten, eine Synodalpredigt über Ap. G. 20, 28 gehalten zu Urdenbach, den 20. August 1834 vor der versammelten Düsseldorfer Kreissynode* (Crefeld, 1834).

2. Katharina Göbel was the first woman employed by the Fliedners. This was prior to their founding of the diaconate in Kaiserswerth.

3. Fliedner notes here: "Church Order of Jülich-Berg, Section 58: 'The duty of the elders, along with the pastor, is to watch over the entire flock, to exercise diligent supervision of the teaching and lives of both those who preach and those who listen, to tend to whatever is necessary for the growth of the church, **to visit the sick, poor, widows, and orphans,** to comfort the fainthearted and the troubled, to discipline those who lead an evil life, etc.' See also the Church Order of Cleve-Mark, Section 56."

4. Fliedner's note here refers the reader to his previous note.

SERMON OF FATHER FLIEDNER ON THE FOURTH SUNDAY IN ADVENT (DECEMBER 24) 1843 ON JOHN 3:30

1. Theodor Fliedner, *Predigt Vater Fliedners am 4. Advent (24. Dez.) 1843 über Joh. 3, 30* (Düsseldorf-Kaiserswerth, Fachbücherei für Frauendiakonie, n.d.), document no. FL IIa 27.

2. The editor of the German edition of this sermon notes: "All words appearing in brackets have been inserted into the original manuscript." Such brackets around words are retained in this translation. Brackets around scripture references indicate, as throughout this volume, references inserted by the editors of this volume.

3. Here the editor of the German edition, in making the transition to the remaining paragraphs, inserts the short explanation that follows in the text. The editors of this volume have set it off with parentheses.

THEODOR FLIEDNER

I BELIEVE IN GOD THE FATHER, THE ALMIGHTY CREATOR OF HEAVEN AND EARTH

1. Theodor Fliedner, *Ich glaube an Gott Vater, den allmächtigen Schöpfer Himmels und der Erden*, in *Jahrbuch für christliche Unterhaltung* (Kaiserswerth, 1849), pp. 54–68. Originally published in the *Christlicher Volkskalender*, 1848.

2. Fliedner notes here: "The Word of God teaches us quite differently about this. See, for example, 2 Cor 10:5."

3. This paragraph represents a general exegesis of Psalm 107 plus themes in Exodus 3:8, Psalm 8, Romans 8:39, Matthew 8:23–27, and Jonah 1:1–3. The Englishman Green is Charles Green (1785–1870), one of the most renowned balloonists of the nineteenth century. He is credited with many famous flights and is said to have made over one thousand balloon ascents.

4. Voltaire (1694–1778)—writer, author, and philosopher—represents to many scholars the quintessential representative of the French Enlightenment. Edward Gibbon (1737–94) wrote his monumental *The Decline and Fall of the Roman Empire* in part to dispute the traditional claim that the Christian church was the culmination of Roman civilization.

5. Following the French Revolution Charles X (1757–1836) led the ultra-royalist opposition and became king of France in 1824. His government attempted to reestablish the pre-revolutionary order by means of measures, such as rigid control of the press, that ran counter to the constitution.

APPEAL OF THE DEACONESS INSTITUTE AT KAISERSWERTH

1. Theodor Fliedner, "Aufruf der Diakonissenanstalt zu Kaiserswerth," *Der Armen- und Krankenfreund: Eine Monatsschrift für die Diakonie der evangelischen Kirche* (1853), vol. 4, pp. 10–15.

2. The Waldensians, or Vaudois , arose in southern France in the twelfth century under the leadership of Peter Waldo and survived into the Reformation especially in the Piedmont region of Italy. The Bohemian and Moravian Brethren were formed in 1467 out of elements of the Hussite movement and later reorganized in Germany under Count von Zinzendorf as the Moravian Church.

3. Fliedner notes here: "For the respective places in Luther's works and the other historical data see the *Armen- und Krankenfreund*, vol. 4 (1849), pp. 9–17."

4. A Roman Catholic order founded in Dublin in 1827.

5. The reintroduction of the deaconess office to which Fliedner refers is his own founding of the Institute at Kaiserswerth.

HOUSE RULES AND INSTRUCTIONS FOR SERVICE FOR THE DEACONESSES IN THE DEACONESS INSTITUTE AT KAISERSWERTH

1. Theodor Fliedner, *Haus-Ordnung und Dienst-Anweisung für die Diakonissen in der Diakonissen-Anstalt zu Kaiserswerth,* unnumbered ed. (Kaiserswerth, 1852).

2. Fliedner notes here: "The office of deacon is established in Acts 6:1–6 and referred to in 1 Timothy 3:8–13. The office of deaconess is referred to in Romans 16:1, 1 Timothy 5:9–10, and Titus 2:3–5. The activity, in general, of Christian women serving the Lord through works of love is mentioned in Luke 8:1–3; Acts 9:36–39; Romans 16:3–4, 6, 12–13; Philippians 4:2–3. Yet public preaching and teaching by women in gatherings of the worship community is prohibited: 1 Corinthians 14:34–35; 1 Timothy 2:11–14."

3. Fliedner's note here directs the reader to Appendices VI and VII, not included in this translation.

THREE HYMNS

1. *Diakonissen-Liederbuch,* 7th ed., ed. Julius Disselhoff (Kaiserswerth, 1866), "Willkomm-Gruß an eintretende Probe-Schwestern," pp. 75–76; "O weites Feld," pp. 136–37; "Urquell sel'ger Himmelsfreude," pp. 75–76.

2. Tune attributed to Severus Gastorius (c. 1675). J. S. Bach also set the tune in Cantata 100 for the 15th Sunday after Trinity. The tune is still found in hymnbooks today, e.g., *Lutheran Book of Worship* (1978), no. 446.

3. Tune attributed to Melchior Frank (c. 1573–1639). It is still found in hymnbooks today, e.g., *Lutheran Book of Worship* (1978), no. 348.

JOHANN HINRICH WICHERN

Introduction

Friedrich Naumann, a one-time protégé, described Johann Hinrich Wichern as "the Saint Francis of the Hamburg underground," and William O. Shanahan, a Roman Catholic interpreter of evangelical responses to social issues, ranks Wichern behind only Hegel and Schleiermacher as shaping forces in early nineteenth-century Protestantism. Had Wichern limited his efforts to the Rough House, the home he founded near Hamburg for orphaned and destitute boys, he would still deserve attention, according to Helmut Rünger, as "the father and precursor of all modern education in homes for youth."[1] For all this, however, Wichern is not much better known outside Germany than Tholuck.

The fact that Wichern's small institution served only as the starting point and foundation of a much larger venture sets him apart from other Awakened activists. Wichern knew many of them and their works, including Johannes Falk's Society of Friends in Need *(Gesellschaft der Freunde in der Not)* in Weimar for those ravaged by the Napoleonic Wars; Amalie Sieveking's ministrations during the cholera epidemic in Hamburg; Baron von Kottwitz's work program for the poor in Berlin; and above all, Fliedner's Kaiserswerth institutions and Wilhelm Löhe's center for the diaconate at Neuendettelsau.

Wichern believed, however, that these achievements, though significant, were nevertheless circumscribed. In speeches and publications he called the attention of friends and donors to the environment out of which the destitute children came; to the solutions offered by socialism, liberalism, and communism; and especially to the kind of society to which his charges would return. Wichern was not the first to ask these questions, but when he turned to the problem of the individual's relation to three fundamental structures—those long before identified by his hero, Martin Luther, as family, state, and church—he opened a new vista for Awakened spirituality. Between the founding of the Rough House in 1833 and the adoption of the Inner Mission by the Wittenberg *Kirchentag* (church confer-ence) in 1848, Wichern consciously and steadily led the Protestant Church to address the "social question"—a euphemism for the widespread tensions and degradations caused by industrialism—with a comprehensive social-action program.

Wichern was born in Hamburg in 1808, just two years after the Battle of Jena, when Prussia suffered a humiliation it had not known since the Thirty Years' War. The experience left a bitter taste among many, including Johann's father, a Hamburg notary. Taking his wife and children with him, he fled to the village of Kulau in 1813. The indignity of living on the margins became acute when the elder Wichern died in 1823, while Johann was still in *Gymnasium*, leaving the support of six children to the fifteen year old and his mother. Johann did his part by tutoring other students, and he never forgot the "experience of redemption" through his mother, who kept her hope and always encouraged him.

We possess a youthful and enlightening journal for some of these years, 1826 to 1828 and again for 1831, from which we can garner a feeling for his developing spirituality. At the start of his education learning came slowly because he lacked a sense of clarity and direction. But then, he writes:

> The breakthrough occurred when God's spirit began to give me a new birth. The light of the gospel also illumi-nated the branches of knowledge for me, and since that time—I dare to confess this without arrogance or self-conceit—I have made progress in everything. [W]ithout knowing it, I began again from the beginning.[2]

An Awakened dedication to church and tradition manifests itself in these pages. Wichern knew his Luther and quoted him freely, attended worship regularly, and by the end of his *Gymnasium* years had decided upon a career in the ministry. With financial help from the social activist Amalie Sieveking and a circle of friends in Ham-burg, he began his theological studies at Göttingen.

Then Wichern transferred to Berlin, a momentous step in his young career, for here he came under the influence of a great teacher, the mediating theologian and church historian August Neander. To be sure, Hegel and Schleiermacher were dominant figures on the university faculty at the time, but Neander made the greater impression, not only because of his humanity but also because of his love for history and the church. He emphasized the priesthood of all believers and set forth an image of the kingdom of God as the "gradual entry of the Christian spirit into the whole domain of life" that served as the link between God and humanity, church and society, reason and revelation. Neander also introduced Wichern to Baron Hans von Kottwitz, and although Wichern's relationship with the baron was not as close as Tholuck's, it brought the impressionable young student of humble birth and limited means into contact with the influential members of the Kottwitz circle. These included, besides Tholuck, the theologian E. W. Hengstenberg, the jurist F. J. Stahl, the Gerlach brothers, and even the crown prince himself, the future Frederich Wilhelm IV.

After Wichern had completed his examinations with honors at Berlin, he returned to Hamburg to work with Pastor Rautenberg of St. Georg's Church. Rautenberg had instituted a parish visitation program, an initiative largely unheard of until Theodor Fliedner warmly recommended it. Rautenberg had also organized a Sunday School, a concept first introduced by Robert Raikes in London in 1780. Wichern became superintendent in 1832 and took his role as parish visitor seriously, with far-reaching consequences.

The Hamburg in which Wichern began his ministry had taken on the characteristics of a massive metropolis, with rising crime rates, poverty, prostitution, disease, and class conflict. While the number of those belonging to parishes was increasing enormously, church attendance was plummeting. Wichern set to work in the city's poor quarter, keeping notes from 1831 to 1833 on the conditions he found during his visits. His entries, such as the following, describe the impoverished families:

Gerhard Family (named Doctor)....I went to the family October 10. The place has a hallway and small room. In the room a wooden chest of drawers, a chair, a thing that is supposed to be a table, a tattered easy chair. In the corner a pile of straw, on it a sack of straw and rags, under the rags a seventy-three-year-old man with a horrible chest illness so that he could hardly talk, no underwear, no pillow—a picture of wretchedness and heartrending misery. The wife (thirty-nine years old), wearing only a cotton blouse and skirt, and simply nothing else on her body—without any undergarments. Even the cotton things she was wearing were ragged so that you could see her skin. The same for a grown-up girl, Marie (thirteen years), and a big guy (Louis, twenty-three years) and two boys, Heinrich, eight years old, and August, ten years old, and a girl, Naucke, five years old. All without underwear, pale figures, chattering from hunger and cold. They were all talking at once, their lips overflowing with complaints about their misery. Marie, the thirteen year old, was sitting on the floor peeling a grass-green apple with a piece of glass, and set it down for the sick father in front of his bed. They hadn't had a fire in the fireplace for a long time.

Here it was a question of rescuing and helping without being a respecter of persons, but how?[3]

The "sad and rotten" state of Hamburg's poor convinced Wichern that he could help children only by separating them from their environment. On September 12, 1833, at the tender age of twenty-five, Wichern founded the Rough House *(Das Rauhe Haus)* in Horn, a suburb of Hamburg, for neglected children from the city's squalid quarters. He used a small farmhouse and plot of land made available by Karl Sieveking, a Hamburg syndic and relative of Amalie Sieveking. The intriguing name, Rough House, stems from the Ruges, the owners of the house and surrounding farm in the seventeenth century. Over time, the designation *Ruges Hus* became in High German *Rauhes Haus*. Consequently, though in translation *rauh* means "rough, raw, harsh," the word refers neither to the appearance of the house nor to the character of the children.

In his inaugural address Wichern described his plan for a "redemption home," referring to the similar work of Daniel Kopf in Berlin and Johannes Falk in Weimar. Taking his audience on a Dickensian journey through Hamburg's back alleys, he declared:

> Whoever ventures into this circle of people, in spite of any displeasure and disgust, and experiences with the senses what is happening here, or whoever believes those who have such experiences daily, will no longer care to question the necessity of an institution for the rescue of the coming generation.[4]

Wichern asserted that the family is "the natural, moral circle in which the good in the human spirit is situated, and in which it ought to be tended and protected."[5] Yet children of the slums, rather than being embraced by loving families, are surrounded by alcoholism, prostitution, illegitimacy, poverty, despair, and suicide.

Repulsed by these horrors and the inhumane conditions of the old asylum system, Wichern proposed that the house adopt the cottage system where small groups of boys, twelve at a time, could learn, pray, and share chores. This system would permit the house to offer a substitute family structure and avoid the barracks atmosphere prominent in many orphanages. Living in small groups would also make the boys more susceptible to conversion and infuse them with the spirit that had been missing from their environment.

> This is the spirit of faith in Christ that proves to be active, effective, and assiduous in love, and because of this spirit a person neither wants to nor is able to quit believing or loving....Wherever this spirit dwells, hearts beat without falsehood and hypocrisy; truth, wisdom, and justice are revealed; and free, happy, healthy, patient, and humble hearts and minds thrive....Our institution intends to approach each child at once with this spirit and with the love that is as warm as it is earnest, and which promises salvation. How can it do this more powerfully than with the joyful and liberating words: "My child, you are forgiven of everything!"[6]

Wichern believed that by separating destitute youth from their squalor they could discover their own identity and above all their worth, learn Christian piety, and acquire the experience needed to establish responsible families of their own.

To grow in this way the boys had to learn a trade, because through one's occupation one enters into society and contributes to community life. Once they completed their stay, the Rough House placed the "graduates" in the hands of craftsmen for employment. Wichern himself remained in fatherly contact with his former students and on occasion reunited them. Thus, while Wichern established his mission on a traditional Lutheran interpretation of vocation, one's calling in life, his understanding of this doctrine reflected a view of Christian society structured on occupations, estates, and government influenced by the Christian conservative thought of his day.

Late in October 1833 the new superintendent moved into the old house, and in November he took in the first three boys. By the end of the year twelve boys were in residence, the youngest one five years old. Most were delinquents from broken homes. Eight were illegitimate, and one had a record of ninety-two thefts. Wichern soon enlisted his mother and sister to assist him, as well as a housemother, Amanda Böhme, who later became Wichern's wife.

Yet he needed even more help, especially if he wished to tackle wider challenges in German society. His solution was to institute the Brothers of the Rough House, a program that began when he called Joseph Baumgärtner in May 1834. Each brother would serve as housefather for a "family" of children. Soon Wichern began to encourage young men, usually with a modest education, to share a wider, more ambitious task to serve city missions; seamen's missions; and missions to the poor, sick, and addicted; as well as to establish folk schools. In 1843 he established the Institute for Brothers to coordinate their efforts. Aware that some clergy still resisted the idea of a Protestant office other than the pastoral ministry of word and sacraments, Wichern never used the title "deacons" for his brothers, although they were clearly the male form of Fliedner's deaconesses at Kaiserswerth.

Like Fliedner before him and Bodelschwingh afterward, he quickly discovered the power of the printed word as a means to assuage the skepticism of reluctant clergy and to support and increase the work of the brothers, instituting his own publishing company in 1841. His popular newspaper, *Flying Leaves (Fliegende Blätter)*, helped make the Rough House the most influential charitable institution of its day in Germany and brought increasing fame to its founder. It also gave him the opportunity to express himself on the burning issues of the day, on the merits of a people's church *(Volkskirche)* over a state church, and on the obligation of the church to take up the social question. Central to his approach is the concept of community and its related forms.

> God's people, God's congregation, is the household and family of God, in which the Lord preserves the fountain of loving care that brims over on all sides to awaken, maintain, and preserve the intimately connected spiritual and physical life....This model is reflected among humans to the extent that individual families and families of nations accept the kingdom of God and let the divine powers of God's family do their healing, disciplining, caring, and transforming work in them.[7]

By now Wichern was moving beyond the limits of charitable work among a handful of boys. Through the brothers and the *Flying Leaves* he began to issue a call for a comprehensive program to promote the spiritual and bodily welfare of an entire nation, especially the thousands nominally within the church. In 1836 he used the expression "inland mission" to describe the work, while in 1841, writing to his wife, he changed this term to "Inner Mission." Two years later the phrase appeared in print for the first time in a report on the work of the brothers, but only with a second report, *The Inner Mission and the Crises of the Protestant Church*, did the idea finally take on form and purpose.

Wichern laid before his readers the notion of a national organization ready to meet the tidal wave of those suffering from bodily ill or the ruin of unbelief. Parishes, he declared, must come alive as vital communities, overcoming barriers between rich and poor, and between a suspect church and a needy society. To bridge the gap, the Inner Mission would offer "deeds of love that flow from faith," yet not through individual works of charity alone. The Inner Mission, as the servant of parishes and the whole church, would both promote concern for human suffering and coordinate the diverse services of the charities under its umbrella.[8]

Wichern's plan reflected the central importance of the priesthood of all believers in his thought. While this was not uncommon among Awakened activists, his conviction that charity involved more than individuals and demanded more than scattered good works sets him apart as the prophet of a unified social action agency. To bring about his plan he traveled constantly, speaking, raising funds, and setting up new missions. Friedrich Wilhelm IV showed his favor with monetary gifts, and the monarch's call to mobilize charitable resources to combat pauperism among his subjects virtually gave royal sanction to the Inner Mission.

The revolution that broke out in Berlin in March 1848, together with the publication of the *Communist Manifesto*, stunned the emerging leadership of the Evangelical Church nearly as much as it did Friedrich Wilhelm IV. Hengstenberg, Stahl, and other former members of the Kottwitz circle rallied the counterrevolutionary forces in the church, which eventually emerged from the whole affair more closely identified with the monarchy than before. Wichern, while sympathetic, nevertheless stands apart not only in his compassion for those who suffered but also in his perception that the crisis provided proof of his earlier predictions. The Inner Mission, he wrote in *Flying Leaves*,

> has for a long time pointed to the newly opened chasm, has called out, prayed, pleaded, warned, advised, and shown in advance ways to help...; it has exhorted people to get ready to build fortresses of saving, preserving love among the small and the great, the high and the lowly, those near and far, in cities and in the country, using church and state resources, and, above all, the resources of voluntary and powerful Christian organizations in

236

order to wrest the field from the enemy who dwells in the hearts of our people in state and church....[But] in part people have not wished to engage in this peaceful war of redemption, they have had neither the time nor courage for it, so the unholy war of destruction has broken out in the midst of the people, and who can prophesy where it will end?...For all that has happened since February 24, 1848, the Inner Mission has won something incalculable. Since this event has laid Europe bare, thousands of facts dictate the necessity of the Inner Mission. Who now could dispute its necessity or justification?[9]

In spite of Wichern's passionate pleas, some leaders, including confessional Lutherans such as August Vilmar, Claus Harms, and Theodor Kliefoth resisted the Inner Mission, and many more remained indifferent.

When the first *Kirchentag* of Evangelical Churches met at Wittenberg in September 1848, an admirer, Moritz von Bethmann-Hollweg, helped to get the Inner Mission on the agenda. Perhaps out of impatience, but also because he had a keen sense of time and place, Wichern delivered three impassioned speeches. According to Shanahan:

It was the great moment of Wichern's life. It was also a great moment in Protestant history: the force of Wichern's remarks compared in dramatic intensity with those of the young Luther before the Diet of Worms. On both occasions, the future of German Protestantism hung in the balance.[10]

Almost by dint of his rhetoric alone, Wichern succeeded in obtaining a mandate to form the Central Committee for the Inner Mission. Hardly had he returned to Berlin when he assembled the group and completed the task of writing his magnum opus, the *Memorandum*, which offers the rationale for the Inner Mission and outlines its tasks.

At last Wichern had the vehicle for reform and redemption about which he had so long dreamed. Now he could turn to unfinished tasks: reform of the Prussian prison system in 1857; creation in 1858 of an institution at Spandau near Berlin on the model of the Rough House; the initiation of a field service *(Felddiakonie)* by the brothers in the wars of 1864, 1866, and 1870–71; and the coordination of numerous charitable works around the country.

In his long career associated with the wide-ranging activities of the Inner Mission, Wichern, who retreated to his beloved Rough House in 1872 and died in 1881, remained the foremost exponent in the Awakening of the principle "faith active in love," expressed in the broadest terms. It is a phrase he used over and over. At its root was Wichern's belief that people throughout Germany were living in misery and sin and that the remedy was to attack the problem with the "faith-filled, saving work of the church," because "love for those who are lost or in distress was in the nature of the Evangelical Church from the very beginning."[11] The church engages in *diaconia* because "Christ's incarnation is the full revelation of diaconal work. He summarizes the reason for his coming with one word, that he came to 'serve.'"[12] Wichern added his own emphasis to a common theme in the spirituality of the authors in this volume when he declared that "deeds and revelations of faith and love" are "the one thing necessary" for the church to be the church. Belief alone is not the one thing necessary, but sets the stage for it. In Wichern's words: "Saving love must become the great implement by which the church demonstrates the fact of its faith."[13]

Thus, concrete acts of love constitute the work of salvation, as among the women who "are working at the great task of salvation." Wichern cites Amalie Sieveking as a leading example.[14] When using phrases such as "rescuing people" and "saving love," he did not differentiate between a physical and nonphysical rescuing or saving. All these activities belong under the umbrella of the Inner Mission, through which "the people must be filled anew with the divine Word and its spirit of new life."[15] The people to whom Wichern refers are not the destitute alone. He argued that regeneration is needed in the hearts of those who serve as well as those who are served. All people must be filled with the life-giving breath from God, with the divine Word, and with the spirit of new life. As a consequence, the Inner Mission would be able to redeem not only the poor and needy, but also the Evangelical Church.

When Wichern spoke of the church he drew an important but controversial distinction between the community of the faithful and the state church. He was not sanguine about the latter's capacity to carry out programs of serving love, since a state institution is inhibited from being the serving community. He wished that the state church would become a people's church *(Volkskirche)*, but he did not reject the existing structure, nor did he propose an alternative. Rather, he advocated that a regenerated state church should embrace the Inner Mission.

Wichern discovered the building blocks of this approach to society—the estates of family, church, and government—not only in Luther but also through a tradition reaching back to the "house of Israel" in scripture. This house is the family, the people, of God from which his love pours forth to awaken, support, and maintain both spiritual and physical life. Community, defined as relationship, is the critical factor.

On the other hand, Wichern's inclination to identify societal structures with crown and conservatism tended to blunt his critical faculty both toward a paternalistic state and the causes of poverty. He detested communism and revolution, viewing these as the result of moral decay that could be eradicated only by spiritual regeneration. At the same time, his knowledge of social problems was massive, perhaps unsurpassed in his day, and he was broadly ecumenical. Erich Beyreuther has observed that Wichern was the best of his century in grasping the suffering of humanity and the need for a total vision of relief, but less able to see that the cry of the masses was neither anti-Christian nor anti-church, but a cry for justice.[16] Nevertheless, the issues Wichern raised still remain acute in the twenty-first century, even after we have witnessed the irony that voluntary associations working within traditional structures could outlive Marx's more radical alternatives.

239

Today in Hamburg the Rough House continues to provide its historic children and youth welfare service along with three additional branches: help for those with disabilities, social psychiatry, and geriatric care. Related programs include the Wichern School, which serves over thirteen hundred students from elementary through high school; the Deaconess Institute (for men and women); the Evangelical Institute for Social Work; the Institute for Geriatrics; the Institute for Social Practice; and the Publishing House. Altogether, a staff of eight hundred serves approximately three thousand individuals at over one hundred sites throughout the greater Hamburg area, putting into practice the institution's motto "in the midst of life."[17] Beyond the Rough House, Wichern's visionary leadership of the Inner Mission inspired the development of the Protestant social-welfare institution that is now a vital part of the church in Germany and the United States, where it has contributed significantly to the development of a modern social-welfare program with emphasis on aging, adoption, refugee placement, home health care, counseling, and public advocacy.

On the following pages we illuminate important dimensions of this influential figure by presenting four of his works. One is an early essay in which Wichern grapples with the nature of the true community. Another is his informative explanation of the fundamental principle of diaconal service. The other two pieces are essential reading because of their historic importance: his presentations at the Wittenberg *Kirchentag* and his monumental *Memorandum*, in which he defines and explains the Inner Mission.

Essay on Community

The True Community of the Lord

EDITORS' INTRODUCTION: Is the state church the true church? A debate about this issue in Hamburg throughout 1839 spurred Wichern to write his own definition of the essence of the true church.[1] He read the essay to a circle of friends on October 10, 1839, probably at the Rough House. Tellingly, Wichern, whose thoughts frequently turned to the priesthood of all believers and to the role of the church in society, focused on the "true community" rather than on the "true Christian" or the "true church," because for him the feature that distinguishes the church from the rest of the world is the kind of community it creates.

Wichern's essay contains three distinct parts. He begins with a three-point theological exposition: the true church is founded in freedom; this freedom produces truth; out of this truth grows the true community of believers whose aim is to carry out the vision of what Christ meant the community to be. Then, in order to illustrate his thesis, Wichern provides an extended exegesis of chapters 13 to 17 of the Gospel of John. He finds the prototype of the true community in the Johannine portrayal of the relationship between Christ and his disciples.

By "community" Wichern means a real, physical entity—a body where small groups of like-minded Christians meet regularly for activities such as Bible study, and where spiritual growth is a product of the individual's active participation. Acutely aware that the Christian community, so defined, is not the same as the state church, Wichern closes by explaining in six detailed points the relationship between the state church and the small-group Christian community.

Wichern did not give his paper a title. Peter Meinhold, the editor of his works, chose it on the basis of entries in Wichern's diaries. The title is indeed warranted, because no concept remained closer to Wichern's heart than "the true community." Thus, the occasionally dense prose should not hinder us from appreciating the significance of the text. It reveals the fertile, highly organized mind of a young theologian coming to terms with a complex question that, particularly because of massive societal changes in the early nineteenth century, he could not disregard.

The peculiar **essence of the Christian church** presents itself in the **freedom, truth,** and **community** of the believers—characteristics that flow **from Christ.** I would like to explain briefly each of these facets of life.

In regard to **freedom** it is necessary to distinguish between its negative and positive expressions. To a certain extent the Christian church is predicated on **negative** freedom, without which the church would have no room to exist. As a result, the church usurps negative freedom even when it is withheld. Negative freedom refers to keeping life's restrictions at a distance. Life, particularly life in its ideal expression—the Christian life—desires and recognizes no limitations. This life wants to do **everything,** penetrate everything, conquer everything, and its only limits and barriers are self-imposed.

Nevertheless, restrictions confront life in the world, and the world, having once succumbed to sin, places limitations on itself through the law. This phenomenon has a providential basis, for only through it can the false course that has taken hold of life in this world be checked, lest our present life be completely destroyed. The entire sum of law confronts the totally unrestricted, true life in the **state** as an organized **power.** The state, as the agent that creates and upholds the law, cannot accept or be a partner to things it cannot legitimize with its stamp of approval. Consequently, anything vital and living that is taken into the state's structure must harden immediately into law and, in order to maintain itself as such, must try to win support from powers and forces outside itself. In this manner even that which was a product of **life** will *eo ipso* become an opponent of "life" through its assimilation into the state.

According to the declaration of its founder, the Christian church is the proprietor of eternal life. Hence the state and church will always be in conflict, or the conflict between the two must arise again and again, even if the state is, or wants to be, a Christian one. Indeed, to the extent that the church, with its authorities and structures, is, or becomes, a kingdom of this world, or to the extent that it adjusts to the state, becoming, for example, a part of the state's economic structure, it will shift toward the letter of the law the more it merges with the state. Then, when the opportunity arises, this church will oppose the invisible, eternal power of life that, as the inexhaustible source of life, resides in the true church.

Because the fatherhood of the true church is not of this world, but rather the church lives because life has been **given** to it, and because the church cannot leave this life or its own life, it has no reason to go to the state or to the state church to inquire about its existence. Were the church to do this, it would be denied life. In addition, the church must struggle with the world to secure its right to live, and through its spiritual strength compel acceptance. Thus, as a constant reaction of life, the church entered the world, and in this manner it has persisted until now, of necessity defining itself again and again in contradistinction to the state and the state church.

Hence, this freedom is a prerequisite for the true community, and the struggle for recognition of this freedom is an essential characteristic of the community's life, even though it can live without this recognition because it possesses life. The church will never be totally free in this sense, or it will be free only temporarily, for the servant is not above the lord. The law of the state and of the state church kills the Lord of the church.

* * *

The positive freedom of the Christian church. This freedom is nothing outside of the church. It is an innate part of the church. The church itself is born with it. This freedom remains the eternal, maternal, elemental soil from which and in which alone all life from God prospers. Of necessity this freedom is also bound to a negation of life's restrictions. However, the restriction negated here is entirely an **inner** one; it is the **world** in the sense in which the Savior speaks of the world. It is the power of life born of the flesh and dwelling in every person. Positive freedom springs forth only where in faith and in personal union with the Son of God the individual or community **has** overcome the world. Human life means freedom to the extent that through the power of faith life is in fact rooted in the Savior like an oak to the earth: "Whomever the Son has made free is truly free" (John 8:[36]). Without the mediation of God's Son we would have no such freedom.

On the one hand, this freedom is the **counterbalance** to acquiring and securing negative freedom. On the other hand, it is the very **power** whose claim encourages one to strive for this outward freedom with inward legitimacy. Similarly, outward freedom, or rather the desired fruit of its development and perfection, is the source from which negative freedom acquires its real value. The mature fruit of positive freedom, its final masterpiece, is the thorough embodiment of the kingdom of God in the redeemed human race. Accordingly, positive freedom is always the initial, essential factor, and negative freedom the second, coincidental factor. Thus, the first can never be sacrificed for the sake of the second.

Participation in, and possession of, this freedom is the guarantee that the Christian church, because of its principles, can never be associated with the striving and struggling of the world for negative freedom, which the world lays claim to as its most precious treasure. The world desires this freedom only in order to live its life, to maintain itself, and to raise to autocracy the subjectivity it has torn free from divine objectivity. The Christian church struggles for this freedom, too, but only in order to bring about the kingdom of God.

Thus, both the world and the church strive for the same good but in different spirits and for different purposes, and for that reason with different perceptions of the One Good. Only inadvertently or providentially—not because it is in its nature—will the world use its freedom in order to promote the Christian kingdom. The world, with the freedom it has attained, will do nothing but oppose the church with the intent—no matter how conscious it is of this intent—of ruining it. The Christian church, on the other hand, is able to use this freedom purely to overcome sin and separation from God in the world, in this way winning the world for eternal life and permeating the world with the fullness of divine love.

The fact that the Christian church operates the same everywhere is its law. This does not mean that positive freedom is without law, but that the law is the product of its common life. This law within it never exerts pressure and never wants to be the **basis** of its life (the basis is the spirit of Christ), but rather the ever renewed and re-engendered result of life. Therefore the stability of the law is foreign to the church. The church's law is absolutely elastic in its progression through the stages of development toward life's greatest need for freedom. Freedom is its law.

* * *

The two heavenly products that arise naturally from positive Christian freedom are the truth found in the Christian church and the perfected community of believers. Untruth and the isolation of the individual are freedom's sworn enemies forever. Both truth and community are rays of freedom's light that break through everything. They are the intertwined and intimately connected forms in which the nature of freedom appears.

Truth, in Christ's sense, is a practical concept that means that the manifestation of life corresponds completely with the divine vision of life. In every moment of inner or outer activity the Christian who is living in divine truth manifests, or is supposed to manifest, this divine vision in word and deed. At the core of each Christian life is the original image that Christian living is to reflect or reproduce. This original image of Christian life is the Word become flesh, Christ, in whom as a human being the vision of the perfect human life was fully realized. Therefore, in his manifestation as a person, Christ is, according to his own words, the **truth.** He is the incarnate truth of life. In turn, those who are free in Christ are also to make the truth of **his** life become reality.

If positive freedom is removed, then *eo ipso* untruth enters. This happens whenever worldly goals supersede the heavenly, or when the latter are abandoned completely in order to achieve the former. The state in the broadest sense, as the proprietor of all secular property and as the regulatory agent and official judge regarding the material means by which secular property is transformed into personal property, is, with all its temptations, the greatest seducer of the

Christian church. It entices the church to sacrifice its heavenly riches for earthly ones, or to adorn itself with the appearance of truth rather than with truth itself. The state offers the promise of all worldly goods by extending and bestowing civil recognition, honors, and awards, thereby promoting secular achievements covering the broadest range of practical and intellectual endeavor.

The state church, with its offices and legal structures, portrays itself in its public pronouncements as the mediator between Christian and civil interests. The state turns to the church and relies on it to steer the truth of Christian life between these two cliffs. Since the state church has borrowed this function from the state, it cannot protect the truth because it has the responsibility of carrying out the demands of the state. Therefore, the church often becomes, against its will, the protector, indeed even instigator, of inner falsehood in order to satisfy the laws of the state. This is the case, for example, with confirmation, with the granting of church offices, with the consecration of marriages, and with anything where the church accepts supposedly free pledges from members of the parish, since secular benefits promised by the state are connected with fulfilling these pledges.

The forgoing does not mean that falsehood must necessarily be present in the situations mentioned. Rather, truth **can** exist in all of these cases because the **truly free** also belong to the state church. Though the truth will always be an exception, members of the true community will be compelled fully by their love of, and esteem for, the truth to insist that **falsehood** be the **exception** and truth be the rule, to insist that the possibility of the lie be reduced to a minimum in the Christian church, and to work seriously toward the goal of fully emancipating the church from the claims and promises of the state.

The true church, as the true church, must not strive to be regarded as such by the state or the state church but, quite the contrary, must strive to permeate completely the state and **its** church. The true church must try to do the best it can for this institution, namely the state, and must value the importance of the state's highest honors and awards. Nevertheless, if the lot so falls, then the true church must gladly bear disgrace, persecution, and being forgotten as natural consequences of its higher origins. The church's task remains that of making the truth of life a reality by emulating the master, by doing, praising, and loving everything except the lie, because it harbors the death of the church's freedom. The church's greatest virtue is not the law but the spirit that suffers injustice with equanimity and thus perfects itself. Here, too, the servant is not above the master whom the world has rejected, because the world is not of the truth.

* * *

Presenting the truth is not the task of the individual Christian, as such, but of the individual as a member of the **community** of those who, likewise, are inwardly free. This does not mean that an individual member of the Christian church is not required to practice a life of truth, but that an individual can practice it only in community with those who are like-minded. Only this sort of community, one that corresponds to the divine vision, can produce, as a community, the life of the **full** truth. One individual is only one radius; only the entire whole can produce the full circle of rays that shine from the one light and core of life. Truth appears in and from each individual only incompletely. It needs to be augmented in a multitude of ways. Being in community with all other believers in the truth complements each individual believer.

Individual life in truth exhibits itself in two ways: in meeting the needs of the community's life and in meeting the needs of family or private life. Both areas are connected by thin but strong threads and should promote each other's peace and contentment. If this is achieved in the individual, then this person's role in the community's life will be determined inwardly and outwardly by the natural **gift,** the spiritual talent, of this individual.

The irrepressible urge to bring forth the desired life is found, of necessity, in one's awareness of one's gift or talent. The gifts or talents in the community of believers are as diverse as the needs of the community itself. When the gifts appear, so too will the diverse needs. One person will ask for assistance, and the other will offer it. The overflowing power of this give-and-take, or more precisely, this harmony, will pour into the community. Both sides, stimulated by the vitality of the community, will also become the agents through which this vitality with its continually rejuvenating power can be transmitted to the community.

I want to point out a few of these gifts. They include the gift of exhortation, of comforting, and of the discursive as well as the contemplative understanding of Christian truths; also the gift of prayer, of trust, of inner watchfulness; the gift of teaching, the gift of differentiating between spirits and gifts, the gift of understanding and examining the heart, the gift of awakening and stimulating Christian life, and, in great contrast, the gift of guiding the life that has begun; in addition, the gift of steadfastness, gifts in reference to the various cultural ranks or age groups within society, namely in reference to Christian youth, and so on. Other groups of gifts are those necessary for the administration, governance, and representation of community affairs in smaller as well as larger circles, both in relationship to and within the civic and academic worlds.

The kind of community in which the truth of eternal life is to be realized must be an **organic** community. The heart of the organism is the one spirit that is the same in **everyone** and **everything** in the community. This spirit governs all the gifts or talents in the community, and at various times it has called forth from the particular gifts of the individuals the type by which it desires to spread itself and demonstrate its power to **overcome the world.** One member, by carrying out various tasks of Christian life with these gifts in the one, sacred spirit, assimilates all the other members, and the community becomes what it is supposed to be, one body, a life-filled organism to which the promise has been given that it will one day transfigure **humanity,** filling it with divine life.

Permeating and conquering the entire world with this divine breath of life is the one great task given to the Christian church to pursue outside its own body. Out of the awareness of this task all, or in a narrower sense, most of the so-called works of love have arisen in all ages, including the present. These works, which can be categorized as to whether the people to be won are found outside of Christianity or within Christian countries, constitute foreign and home missions in particular, and taken together, mission in general.[2] It should be noted that these endeavors have been created and developed independently of the state and state church. They have arisen from the bosom of voluntary, Christian associations. These have, by the power of the democratic character of Christ's community, assigned the works to their chosen representatives in these organizations.

The more the community's spirit has proven itself in the context of mission, the further behind it has slipped in vigorously developing and forming the community's own life. It took up its work on the outside first. The task of the community in reference to itself is none other than increasing the positive freedom explained above, removing the hindrances to it within the community, and constantly unfolding more and more of its richness in the hearts of the community members. The more the spirit of the congregation overcomes what remains of the world, the freer it becomes. This freedom increases to the extent that the community works as an organic whole. The magnitude of its work will stand in direct relationship to the amount of truth present in the community. As the power of this truth develops down through the ages, it will also gain negative freedom from the state. Furthermore, the more the state permits this new kingdom of truth, the more the state will be borne upon this **eternal** foundation.

In the foregoing I have indicated the way in which freedom, truth, and community constitute the real essence of the Christian church. Freedom is the eternal foundation upon which and out of which the structure of truth and community of necessity arises. Correspondingly, the genuine Christian church is the association of people freed for truth.

* * *

At this point I cannot avoid drawing our attention to the speeches of the Lord of the church that are contained in chapters 13 to 17 of the Gospel of John. My purpose in the following is:

> First, on the basis of these words to define the concept of the Christian church more precisely, or to make what I have said even more understandable; and then to develop in more detail the unique relationship between the true church and the state church.

For both of these I can provide only a brief sketch.

John 13—17

It is apparent that the Savior reserved these, his final speeches (which he gave in the intimate circle of his disciples, after the departure of Judas, at the evening meal, and in the night when he was arrested), to lay out for his disciples the basic principles uniting the "believers," as he calls them here. A careful analysis of these earnest and, in a way, most sacred words of Christ leads one to the conclusion that the essential thing, the focal point at which all other words of the Lord converge, is the unity of the disciples with one another [John 17:6–26]. The Lord calls this sense of community among his people **"their love for one another"** (John 13:34–35), ἀγάπη εἰς ἀλλήλους.

The unique character of this love is, first of all, that as **mutual love it is conceivable and feasible only within the closed circle of Christ's disciples.** Because of its unique nature it stands apart from love of one's neighbor as well as love of one's enemy, yet in such a way that only this circle of disciples can carry out both of these forms of love in full accordance with God's will. Thus, it follows that love for one another, or brotherly love, as Paul, Peter, and James call it in their writings, is the most intimate circle of love. This circle contains the potential and aim of eventually becoming the all-encompassing love through which all those who originally stood outside the circle—neighbors or enemies—are conquered by the power of love that dwells in it. God's kingdom comes when this love is fully victorious. Brotherly love is to transfigure all merely natural associations of love.

In order to define more precisely the essence of the community of love and life he established, the Lord adds that the prototype of this mutual love is found in **his** love for them, his disciples. "Love one another, **as I have loved you**" (John 13:34). With these words the sense of community among the disciples is illuminated most clearly. The Lord presumes that in each individual who possesses this kind of love the love of Christ is made known. Consequently, whoever is not conscious of this love of Christ cannot be a part of this community. Only the personal relationship to Christ as the one

250

who loved us enables us to enter into this association "with one another." It is the fellowship of the reborn.

Careful reporting by the evangelists puts us in a position to identify precisely the essence of the love Christ had in mind when he gave his command. According to the context the Lord's words are connected directly with the foot washing with which the sacred conversation began that evening (John 13:1–17). The point of this extraordinary action, which Jesus carried out in awareness "that the father had put everything into his hand" (v. 3), emerges clearest when one compares verses 10–11 with verses 14–15 (see also v. 7). What the Lord wanted to symbolize with the foot washing was nothing other than the effect of his love, whereby he cleanses the last vestiges of sin from those whom he loves after he has granted them general forgiveness. In this way, through foot washing, he cleansed Peter of the remaining subtle self-interest that had made it impossible for Peter to surrender totally to Christ's love.

Referring to this demonstration of his love, the Savior adds, **"as I have loved you"** when he establishes the new commandment to love one another. Thus, the immediate aim he sets before his disciples for their association with one another is to cleanse each other of the sin, impurity, and weaknesses that still cling even to the reborn. Or, as we have said above, the true community's task for itself is to work more and more by means of its fellowship to remove whatever hampers each individual's life in God. Or, stated positively, the task is to work so that **true freedom** in the community gains its exclusive place through ever-growing strength and ever-increasing energy. In the light of all this, the concept of love in the community of believers is very specific, thoroughly concrete, and, if one stays with the Word, impossible to disregard.

However, in John's portrayal of the community the phenomenon we have described is only the introductory element, which, of necessity, is joined immediately by other elements, and these bring greater clarity to the vision of community. Indeed, the concept of Christ's love is by no means exhausted by that single, symbolic demonstration of foot washing. The portrayal of Christ's love and glory progresses through the course of the evening conversation until Christ reveals the love and glory in their final perfection. **Along with** the step-by-step unfolding of Christ's love and glory comes the parallel unfolding of love for one another, the unfolding of the vision of the Christian community.

This progression is already indicated by the connection between verse 34 in chapter 13 and the preceding verses. Christ has just spoken about his transfiguration in God and God's transfiguration in him, and he connects the commandment about community directly to the transfiguration. Out of this connection arises the concept that "the love his disciples have for each other" is to be a genuine substitute for his presence. In **their mutual love** they are to keep him, the Savior, among themselves. In their love and life together they will reveal **his** love and **his** life (see 14:16–20, 21). The community of Christ's disciples in love is, according to his promise, to be a **new** ἐνσάρχωσις [embodiment][3] of the Son of God in the world that continuously occurs anew.

Chapter 14 sheds even more light on this process as a result of the questions by Thomas, Philip, and Judas (vv. 5, 8, 22). Through the personal union of the Savior with believers the transfigured Savior will accomplish through them **even greater works for his glorification** than he himself did in the days of his flesh (v. 12). The love of the believers for Christ will manifest itself in keeping his commandments, which are summed up in holding firm to, and bringing to reality, fellowship with one other in Christ (v. 15).

However, insofar as he himself is **"the truth"** (v. 6), and insofar as he fulfills these promises given to the community of his own people only through the "spirit of **truth**" (v. 17), the life that is revealed in the community is nothing other than **the life of truth.** This life will, of necessity, be manifested in the community that is sanctified and freed by Christ.

The revelation continues in chapter 15. After Christ again indicates, as in chapter 14, how prayer is the means by which personal communion with him can be maintained, he presents the relationship of love between himself and his Father as the archetype of the mutual relationship among those who are his own. The love of the heavenly Father for his only begotten Son is reflected in the love of the only begotten Son for the community, and his love for the Father is to serve as the measure of the community's love for the Son (vv. 8–11). If the community makes this love a reality, then the joy of the community will be perfected by Christ's joy in the community (v. 11).

How does the community demonstrate its love for the Son? Verse 12 says explicitly that this occurs only in the familial relationship with him, in the ἀγάπη εἰς ἀλλήλους [love for one another]. However, in identifying **his** love of the **redeemed** as the measure of familial love (v. 9), he places his love on a much higher level than at the beginning of his speeches and, in doing so, sets a much higher goal for familial love. In verses 13–16 he calls these lofty revelations that he did not want to withhold from them the sign of his "friendship" (φιλία). He chose them for this friendship with the aim that they "produce fruit" specifically in familial love (v. 17). This explains why (in vv. 1–8) the community in Christ (as branches of the vine) is to develop within itself his life in ever-greater purity. It is to do this with love, prayer, and parental care.

The κρίσις [literally a "separating," "putting apart," hence "distinction," "differentiation"] that is the basis for all the thoughts in John about the **community** comes most clearly into focus in verses 18–25. Since the life of Christ recurs in the community, the nature of the world must reveal itself to the community in the same way that it revealed itself to the Lord. The world without Christ and the community in Christ are placed next to each other in sharpest contrast. The **community** of believers, which through Christ is being transfigured into the image of God, is surrounded by the hate and enmity of the world. Indeed, the community will, like its master, partially become a victim of the world. From verse 26 to chapter 16, verse 11, the community is promised victory over the world and its conversion to the truth. The community of the Lord will be successful in this through the testimony of Christ given to the world in the power of the divine Spirit. In the conversation from verse 13 to the end of the chapter, Christ speaks further about the effect of the Holy Spirit in the community. The Spirit will transfigure Christ in the community and place the believers in the closest relationship to the **Father.**

Chapter 17. What the Lord says about the relationship of his people to himself and to each other reaches its high point in the closing prayer. The unity and fellowship of all believers is the reflection of the glory of divine love itself. God's love lives in the coming together of believers, and they live in God. In many ways these words look back on what Christ has developed up to this point. At the same time, they complete the image of the community to the extent that the Savior sees his own transfiguration and the transfiguration of his Father both in the community and in the eternal glory of his Father, and he connects these in his prayer.

Here I would like merely to mention how, in many ways, the above points correspond greatly to the explanations of the apostles Paul, Peter, and John and to the Letter to the Hebrews, even though none of these reaches the high level we have seen in the foregoing.

* * *

It is not at all difficult to see that the vision Christ has of his community is totally different from the one we normally find in the Christian world. Moreover, it is just as easy to see that according to God's simple yet great words, which we have reviewed, the Savior has in no way relegated the implementation of his community to some who-knows-when distant eternity. On the contrary, he intends that his community become, and be, the type he presents here so clearly, which does not exclude its **perfection** and greater glory in another world.

One cannot deny that the life of the faithful is far from the ideal. Their life is so far from it one would think they have become virtually unaware of it, or they are at such a distance from the ideal one can hardly tell whether they are actually striving for the goal. As a result, the question naturally arises whether the nature and life of Christians corresponded more closely to the prototype at some other time and place. If, remembering the nature of the community in the first three centuries, we answer in the affirmative, then it does not seem very difficult to answer the question about the change in the community and the causes of its decline.

Ever since the appearance of a state church at the time of Constantine, the church has ceased to be for most people an organization of freedom in the Christian sense. The life of the world gradually gains a foothold in the church because it satisfies the requirements of church law. The world stops hating the church, and the community stops offering the world the testimony of salvation through its united ranks and eternal freedom. The church, which has changed from being persecuted to being a powerful ruler and even an upholder of the princes, ceases to guard the true freedom within. This is the freedom that had developed in truth and fellowship most dynamically when under the harshest yoke, when all those in the community had united against the lie of the world. But instead of seeking freedom, the church seeks legal recognition, and with that, its **rights.** It gains both but loses its own special beauty and dignity to such an extent that little can be found of the legacy of him who went ahead of the church bearing the cross.

However, the earlier struggle appears in a new form. It is soon apparent that the response of the life once practiced by the community of truth has not died out. As I already indicated in the first pages, the role of the law has simply been taken over by other persons; the state has found a partner in the state church. With and often for the state, the church forms the opposition to the ineradicable life of the true community. Just as the state has a constitution, so the state church has acquired its constitution in creeds and ecclesiastical regulations.

Against this structure the waves of life pound as soon as life's innermost depths have been seized and inspired by **the Spirit.** The Savior compares the Spirit to the wind about which no one knows where it comes from or where it is going. The state church is not always able to fend off this salutary and invigorating assault of the Spirit but at times accepts its breath of life. However, the only terms on which the state can recognize the Spirit's power and effect completely is to transform its vital form into the deadly form of law, against which, after a certain length of time, the struggle is again repeated.

In short, since the introduction and organization of state and national churches the true essence of the Christian church—its freedom, its truth, and its fellowship in Christ—has become less and less visible and increasingly something only to be hoped for and only to be realized in the next world.

In order to clarify our view of the relationship between the state church and the true community of Christ we must dispel a myth that we have possibly let slip by until now. We are convinced that our following assertion will cause the truth to stand out even more clearly. We consider neither the state nor the state church to be totally the product of lies and errors. In no way do we consider them to be diabolical institutions, even though this might have appeared to be our view. We protest against this. On the contrary, the state as well as **its** church are institutions of divine governance in the world. Yet we do not believe that the state church's purpose is to make a reality of the divine vision of the Christian community. Rather, its calling is to prepare for and, to the extent that it can, protect the formation of this community that comes from elsewhere, and then, through this means of blessing and during its preparatory stage, to share more and more in the true community of life. Both the state and the state church share the office of Moses and have taken over different aspects of the same. Both discipline the people who need **their** discipline, the state primarily in connection with material interests, and the state church more in connection with moral concerns. Consequently the two cannot be separated entirely from each other, although the state church, given the truth that lives within it, strives for separation if at all possible.

It is also right and proper that the civil servants of the state church in a certain sense be servants of the state as in fact they are, to a greater or lesser degree. The church has police just like the state has police, because there are church laws that can be broken, just as there are state laws that can be broken. For example, the state church must see that public sermons befit the oath given by the servant of the church, the preacher. It must use its power to punish any violations. On the other hand, in cooperation with the state the state church is responsible to see that this vow does not impinge upon the conscience of the civil servants.

Since our main concern here is the relationship of the **true community** of the Lord to the state church, we would like to define that relationship in more detail.

1. We believe that the community in which we hold firm to the principles developed above is thoroughly independent of the state and national churches and confessions. Just as there is no religion at all for the North American state since, as the state, it is neutral to **all** religions and favors no particular one, so for this true community there are, first of all, no confessions or state churches. The true community breaks through all of these boundaries on every side wherever a path for truth remains, particularly since the confessions are not totally exclusive of each other. **All** church communities recognize the **ecclesia catholica** through their acceptance of the apostolic creed that is accorded the same validity and is a requirement for baptism in all of them.

2. We believe that members of the true community are present in all confessions. All churches in Christendom believe this, as well. Thus, we find ourselves in agreement with the view generally held by Christians. However, we add that what had to be taught and extolled out of sight should step forth now from invisibility into visibility. The members of the community **should,** because they can, step forth from invisibility by the power of the freedom dwelling within them, that is, by God's power of life. The community lays claim to this power so that it can become the truth. The more consciously this life is led, that is, the more truthful through the community, the freer it becomes, and the freer it becomes, the more powerful it is in spirit.

3. We believe it is not necessary for members of the true, free community to leave the fellowship of the state church, unless the state church were to demand that they leave. **That would cause the greatest danger for the true church,** and therefore clearly should be avoided. The state church has concluded that its peculiar possession until now has been to administer the sacraments of baptism and the Lord's supper. The community of the Lord can certainly participate in these sacraments, even though in many ways it might feel hurt and offended. The Lord's supper, according to Christ's institution, is

supposed to fill an entirely different role in the life of the community than it now does. The true community is not concerned about the existing differences over the Lord's supper, since the Lord's supper is the Lord's supper wherever it is, insofar as the person and office of the administrant have no influence on the sacrament.

It should be stressed here that civil servants of the state church can, indeed, be full members of the true community, and, in the event they share the spirit of the community, they certainly are. However, if they indeed share the spirit, then they ought not appear in the community of truth as civil servants of the state church, since the community could probably confer its offices on others who are more gifted. The participation of the community in those institutions retained by the state church guarantees that the life of freedom, in its power that overcomes the world, will be manifested increasingly in the community. To the extent that members of Christ's community actually participate in the institutions of the state church, they do it in the spirit of freedom and hence with a clear conscience.

4. The dual stance of the "believers" (as I like to call members of the genuine community)—being both in the state church and in the true church—is, strictly speaking, not a dual one, and therefore not dishonest. We believe that each confession contains in its special nature a particular piece of the truth that expresses itself in one place in doctrine, in another in administration, discipline, organization, and so forth. If this is indeed true, then the believer can, with the power of freedom, transfigure the truth that is in the character of the confession and thus perfect this character. Therefore the characteristically developed differences will not become a gulf separating one believer from the believers in other confessions. Rather, the great variety in the natures of the confessions will become the product of the **one** spirit of freedom, and the **richer** presence of the great variety will, instead of promoting separation, promote and perfect unity in the spirit of freedom. The bond of the various natures in one Spirit will become an element in the presentation of truth (see above). In this way the **hostile** differences between confessions can be removed by the **truth** in their natures, and ultimately the various churches will come together as one church.

5. It follows that the relationship of the believing community to the state church by no means can be a passive one, nor can the impact of the community on the state church be a matter of chance. Through the fellowship of altar and baptism as well as through many other connections, for example, the consecration of marriages, believers already have a reciprocal relationship with the state church. Surely they know that they have been given the promise that they are the salt of the earth, the light of the world (Matt 5:[13–14]). To know this is not to be presumptuous, for it is the natural result of their true community with the Lord and one another. Therefore, working in all humility and in the freedom that they have obtained, their goal should be to halt the decay that the state church causes and the decay to which they might fall victim, and to penetrate the state church with the leaven of divine life.

a) Unusual circumstances in the state church will call forth **unusual** actions of this kind, although it must be left up to the freedom and conscience of individuals whether they want to participate. The community as such cannot be compelled to act. Only a few need step forth from its midst. The community is not to act as a *corpus* because the state church should not recognize the community as a *corpus*.[4]

b) Arising out of the above-mentioned general goal is a system of individual, practical goals. The community must incorporate them into its organic circle of life, must aim to achieve them through the gathered energies of volunteers from its midst and from the state church in order to spread its life and thereby tie the state church ever more closely to the highest ideal of truth. The formation of Christian associations for compassionate aims belongs here.

We will add one more example. Faith-filled preachers, that is, those who belong to the true community, can select assistants for pastoral care in the broadest sense of the word from the faith-filled members of the parishes assigned to them by the state. In this way the pastors can help make a reality of the spiritual, royal priesthood of believers in ever-widening circles. The community will have to keep its eye on those practices in particular of the state church in which the dependence of the state church on the state (which we can hardly expect to be eliminated entirely) proves to be the cause of a variety of errors, such as in the current practice of **confirmation.**

6. Regarding the **organization** of the believing community the following comments will have to suffice. Two principles must dominate:

(a) individualization; and

(b) unification of the individual communities into one great whole according to organic laws.

In other words, the community's life unfolds in concentric circles.

Basic characteristics of an organism that might develop in this way are found in the following points, a–g.

a. It stands to reason that the beginning of a common life of this sort is found in the desire of those who are of the same mind and spirit. They should unite **to foster** individual and common life through an exchange of what the life in freedom can promote directly and **for companionship** with the Lord who granted us the opportunity for this companionship in the legacy of the sacred documents given to the church. Nowhere else than in these holy scriptures is found the pure, unmistakable vehicle of his messages to the community. To keep company with the scriptures in the spirit of Christ is to keep company with him. His own Word preserved there is the revelation and bearer of his spirit and of his love, which gives freedom and fullness. Without a connection to the Word of Christ that has been preserved by the Christian church it is impossible for believers to have a lasting bond for the above-named purpose. Consequently, it is logical that in the gatherings of believers they will read and discuss the holy scriptures. (Uniting like this around the holy scriptures is nothing totally new. It is already practiced in many places, or is the quiet wish of those who feel this higher need.)

b. Those who gather together, united in his Word, believe the Lord is present in his Word as the one who, by sharing **his** life and spirit, personally inspires them to share their life from him with one another. A vibrant gathering like this—certainly there are some exceptions—can take no other form than that of a conversation. The stimulation of the intellect as well as the emotions will find its fulfillment, or at least seek it, in the Word. Given the present state of the church it would be hard to estimate how many fruitless sermons are preached, yet it would be even more difficult to estimate how many of the seeds of life produced by a sermon are then stifled at their first sign of growth and robbed of their life by the sermon itself. Yet, for now, nothing can be done to change this. Hence, the gatherings we have in mind must from the very start avoid becoming hours of edification through sermons.

If, on the other hand, the interchange of ideas through conversation, through talking about and talking through issues, is to be possible, then above all else it is necessary for the number of participants to be as small as possible. In the Gospel of John, chapters 13—16, we have a prototype of this kind of Christian gathering. Likewise, the earliest gatherings of the apostolic Christians (Acts 2) serve as examples of small meetings in homes and family circles.

c. If the above is true, then with the growing number of community members one would have to form more and more small circles, one after the other. That which belongs together would soon join together and crystallize around the spiritual center of truth. The **closeness** within these circles would cause the members to stay far away from any elements not related to the community and, in contrast, to form an all the more genuine and intimate bond with those who belong.

A further result of these relationships would, of necessity, be the sanctification of family bonds. As a result, the blessing would be passed on to the younger generation and wider family circle of relatives and members of the household. The reintroduction of family devotions would follow naturally. Consequently, public worship services would gradually become more full of a purer truth, meaning that over time a reformation in preaching would become inevitable.

d. It follows that all of the small circles would become aware that they are all bound together. Hence, people would see the necessity for some gatherings of everyone and for some meetings of representatives of the individual groups.

e. Through the awareness and growth of the expanded, higher community and through its increasing vitality a powerful urge would also develop to spread the blessing beyond one's own borders. Consequently, the outward-directed, practical aims of the Christian association that were indicated above would appear in an ever-greater variety.

f. The representatives (mentioned in section d above) of what we might appropriately call **house-churches** would have a twofold focus. The **first** would be to care for the inner, spiritual needs of the individual house-churches. The **second** would be to look after carrying out the practical aims, which all can be summarized with the one concept of **mission** (in the broadest sense of the word).

(The practical execution of the tasks that emerge would necessarily make a claim on the talents in the community; see above. With the liberation of the community and genuine fellowship in spirit and life, the talents and gifts of the spirit would blossom. This flowering, necessary for active life and pure love, would lead by means of a rich variety of gradations and combinations toward the achievement of the virtuosity of Christian life in all members of the free community. Since the officers within the free church would be members of the house-church—in which the priesthood of house fathers would have to regenerate itself in patriarchal dignity and simplicity—the spirit of the entire community and the interest of the Christian fellowship in life would be imparted to the house-churches. Thus, reciprocally, the life of the **entire** body imparts power to every individual, down to the very last person.)

g. Let me draw attention once more to the fact that the differences in confessions and in state church districts, as well as all politics, would be excluded from the community's life. As a result, the organization of the free community would crisscross and cut through all existing churches with its faith, its hope, and its love. Therefore, the community of truth, with an endorsement to be granted by history, could become the spiritual base for the state church without being dependent on it. The communion of saints, as the apostolic word and the creed of the apostolic church call this community, would then be the priestess of blessing and the spiritual queen of humanity.

h. I would like to add only one more thing to points a–g. The efficacy of the organizing principle must arise through the Christian δῆμος [people as a corporate body], because in this people lies the promise as well as the power of monarchy, though only insofar as Christ gave his life for it. Christ's will is monarchical and reliable, reliable in and of itself as well as because of the knowledge we gain through his own spirit entrusted to us in the Word. He carries out his will through his people, and each person is bound to him, the king, in a direct relationship and through him is to grow in the recognition and discharging of his will. The aristocracy, or monarchy, or anarchy that exists in the state church is only a way point, a signal or signpost showing the community the way it actually needs to go in order to reach maturity and truth in its life. It must prove itself worthy of the responsibility, and then he will declare it mature and reveal his promised glory in it. This is his last word in the circle of the apostles about his community: "I have made the Father's name known to them and will make it known to them so that the love with which the Father loves me will be in them and I in them" (John 17:26).

In closing I will allow myself a historical reference in connection with the foregoing.[5] The history of the Christian church following the personal activity of the apostles can be divided into three periods of development. The so-called apostolic period covers the founding and initial development of the life of the Christian community. Christ's influence in fashioning Christian life was most direct and therefore purest at that time. Just as the intensive fullness of life is always greatest at its inception, so it was then. The beginnings of the roots and the normal state of all future development of the inner and outer affairs of the community are present in the apostolic period. The historical document for all of this is the New Testament alone— hence the exceptional dignity and canonicity of the same.[6]

a) The first epoch [extends from] after the apostolic period until the first appearance of a state church. Rome and Carthage, Antioch and Alexandria become the types of the future form of the church. The primary interest is in the administration and constitution of the church under the influence of the organization of God's people found in the Old Testament. In the East the dogma [is] primarily under the influence of Johannine concepts and Greek philosophy. The nature of paganism is combated.

b) Since the formation of the state church, the churches in the East and West diverge more and more. The power of the Christian spirit is concentrated in the West, with an unintentional exclusion of the Johannine influence. In Augustine the power of the Pauline fashioning of the spirit arises, and it continues to have a quiet effect without **true** public recognition.

Addresses at Wittenberg

Wichern's Explanation, Address, and Speech at the Wittenberg Kirchentag, *1848*

EDITORS' INTRODUCTION: An invitation to the first *Kirchentag* of the Evangelical churches in Germany urged clergy and laity to attend a voluntary, provisional gathering at the Castle Church in Wittenberg from September 21 to 23, 1848. The goal was to discuss the church situation in Germany, a topic made especially urgent by the upheavals of the revolution earlier that year. What Wichern called "the social question" was, however, not on the agenda. Nevertheless, he was determined to have his say, and his challenge to the *Kirchentag*—the three-part message included here[1]—represents one of the remarkable moments in modern church history.

Wichern's successful initiative came neither without difficulty nor all at once. When the *Kirchentag* opened on Thursday, September 21, the first item of business was to establish a federation of Lutheran, Reformed, Union, Moravian, and Bohemian Brethren Churches. Despite this, Wichern took the floor to explain why the "practical question" ought to be inserted early in the agenda. This brief request is the "Explanation," the first of Wichern's three turns at the podium. On the recommendation of the chairman, Moritz August von Bethmann-Hollweg, the delegates granted Wichern time to present his motion on the following day. Because other agenda items intervened, Wichern could not take the floor until the afternoon. He used only a few minutes to advance his proposal that the new church federation should vote to make the Inner Mission its own responsibility, and he closed by expressing the desire to speak later in detail.

Unexpectedly, the assembly asked Wichern to continue then and there, so the young director of the Rough House began a stirring message that lasted another 75 minutes. This long "Address" is an extemporaneous tour de force in which Wichern displayed his broad knowledge of church history, his extensive experience with inner mission activities, his careful theological reflection, and his deep faith. He elaborated and defended his motion that the confederated churches initiate a programmatic response to the growing moral decay, suffering, and needs of the people. This response, which he identified as "saving love," and calls "Inner Mission," is the one thing necessary for the church to be the church. Led by the warm thanks of Bethmann-Hollweg, the delegates responded with enthusiasm and voted unanimously to approve the chair's motion "to promote Christian social goals, associations, and institutions, especially the Inner Mission."[2]

The modern reader of the printed "Explanation," "Address," and "Speech" may well have difficulty recapturing the dynamism of Wichern's oratory. Audience response, however, testified to his considerable charisma and the power of his message. Delegates in Wittenberg apparently saw for the first time what few had perceived until then: first, the revelation that vast numbers of European Christians were estranged from the church, with thousands of them living in misery; and second, the stunning solution that called for a new initiative to evangelize Germans as if they were "heathen." This "inner" mission must parallel "outer" missions to foreign lands. It must attack unemployment and squalor; advance prison reform and the education of children; offer care for orphans, seamen, and prostitutes; help journeymen and blue-collar workers; attend to the German diaspora; and assist poor parishes, Bible societies, temperance groups, and women's organizations. To all these the Inner Mission must bring "saving love," which means more than preaching and almsgiving. Wichern believed that the 1848 Revolution was a turning point in German history, and, if the *Kirchentag* would adopt the Inner Mission, the year could become a turning point for the church as well.

That evening, from his room in the old Augustinian Cloister in Wittenberg, across the courtyard from where Luther once lived as a monk, Wichern wrote to his wife about the electrifying events of that afternoon. He estimated that about five hundred delegates from Bavaria, Hesse, Rhineland, and all the Prussian provinces filled the huge nave of the Castle Church, while spectators crammed the galleries.[3]

Wichern observed "great excitement" when he rose to describe conditions in Europe. Although required to speak extemporaneously, he assured his wife that "the Lord heard my prayers," and reported that, being thoroughly familiar with the subject, "I could speak in a manner I enjoy, because I do not lose sight of the ones for whom I am speaking."[4] He could still feel the drama of the event:

> I am sure the moment was decisive for the future of the most important matter to be dealt with by the Evangelical churches....I almost feel as though my life's vocation has been completed. Now the opponents must keep still....It is the greatest celebration the Inner Mission has ever had.[5]

Finally, he saw great promise in the possibility that a Central Committee will take up and coordinate all the activities necessary for renewal in church and society.

> The regeneration of our church will follow from this....All the hope that seemed to have been dashed with the Revolution appears to have come to life again many times over.[6]

Having a pragmatic as well as theoretical mind, Wichern took the floor on Saturday to call for the formation of a committee to establish a central coordinating agency of the church for the disparate activities of the Inner Mission. This "Speech" constituted the final part of Wichern's presentation.

The assembly approved Wichern's proposal, and that evening Wichern once again wrote to his wife, this time to articulate his vision:

> With this [development] the Protestant Church becomes what it has not yet been: a true people's church. With this

development the church, for the first time, makes a reality of the doctrine of the priesthood of all believers.[7]

In a final reflection Wichern expressed his satisfaction with the place in which the *Kirchentag* was held:

> One more thing! The deliberations were conducted right next to Luther's and Melanchthon's graves, and from the old lectern of the University of Wittenberg from which both men once taught and proclaimed the Word of God....Who can reflect on this without being struck by the situation and by the power of the history of God![8]

He closed on a lighter, more personal note:

> Greet our little Hans, and tell him that I am sending him happy birthday wishes from Luther's grave and lectern, and that after finishing the *Kirchentag* work yesterday we drank a toast to him with some good German wine in the old Augustinian monastery.[9]

Wichern was impressed by the masterful way in which the conference was led and noted that four secretaries were used in order to keep pace with the proceedings.[10] The text that follows consists of Wichern's three presentations as a secretary recorded them. At some points it is unclear whether the secretary is quoting Wichern directly or paraphrasing what he said. The following translation attempts to distinguish as accurately as possible between the two.

Wichern's Explanation on Thursday, September 21, 1848

"The condition for my acceptance of the invitation was that the church's praxis[11] should take precedence as a great issue of the church—the proposition that the church, as the church, needs to pay a great debt regarding its praxis and then begin anew. In this regard, a thorough study of church history, an obligation that scholars have yet to fulfill, will make clear what a great deficiency the year 1848 revealed in the church. The turning point in world history at which we currently find ourselves must become a turning point in the history of the Christian church as well, particularly of the German Evangelical Church, given that this church must enter into a new relationship with the people. For some time these ideas, wishes, and hopes have been circulating in our church. During the last decade they have grown into an ever-stronger current within groups of those genuinely and deeply concerned about the salvation of our people.

"However, the difficulties and obstacles standing in the way of fulfilling the hopes appeared to be as insurmountable as they were diverse. Then came February, with its horrors for our neighbors to the West, followed by March, with its disastrous events in our fatherland.[12] The humiliation and misery, and the power of sin that came to light, cut deeply, and are still cutting into people's hearts. Yet the eye of faith was able to see what was hidden: the dawn of a day of promise for the rejuvenation of the faith-filled, saving work of the church. It is a day whose nearness we can greet only with jubilation and living hope. With these recent events a day of God has dawned before our eyes, a day of salvation for our church in our dear fatherland. One cannot help but see that our Evangelical Church can and must become a **people's church**[13] by renewing the people through the gospel. The church must do this in new ways and with new power, filling the people with new life-giving breath from God. The actual beginnings of this process are already in place, no matter how unfamiliar they might be to many.

"I welcome today's *Kirchentag* as a great step forward. We have long been pleading for it. It is a great step on the path that will turn our Evangelical Church into a true **people's church,** in spite of the impression that the church might lose something as a result. Yet if deliberations are to lead to this progress, if implementation is not to be delayed but the hopes of a great many church members fulfilled by having the practical issues worked through carefully, clearly, and thoroughly in their important relationship to this morning's questions, if what hundreds and thousands can expect from the Wittenberg *Kirchentag* is to emerge, then the practical issue must be moved to the foreground—also in terms of **time**—with its meaning and scope to be developed later. May the practical issue, as one belonging essentially to the Church Federation, be taken up early tomorrow morning when the committee is named."

Wichern's Address on Friday, September 22, 1848[14]

[Secretary]

He [Wichern] has been extremely familiar with this subject[15] for a long time. There are few places in Germany where any significant activity of this kind could have been developed, and few individuals who could have achieved anything new or noteworthy in the field about which he would not have heard through his many personal contacts. Some who supposedly have a strong interest in the cause occupy high offices in church and state. They would like to see the subject treated from a more comprehensive, statesmanlike perspective. He has fought many a battle quietly and otherwise because people view the activity of the inner mission as something that works against the church and even strives to undermine it. For this reason people of the church, even those who confess their faith freely, openly, and gloriously, have gone so far as to warn against activities of the inner mission. Therefore one could well be surprised at the suggestion that the Church Federation ought to enter into a relationship with these activities.

[Wichern]

"In any case,…my conviction about the relationship of the church to inner mission has never been any different from what it is today. From the very beginning I have held firm to the conviction expressed here that the church must take ownership of the inner mission. Currently people are carrying out the work to some extent with troubled hearts because individuals who represent the church do not consider the activity legitimate. Mistrust of inner mission has developed, and it cannot be removed even with the sincerest protestation that the inner mission desires only to serve the church and the other divine institution, the state.

"If this gathering were to announce that the Church Federation will **promote** and **protect** the activity, that it will make the inner mission a part of itself without detriment to its necessary freedom, then this work would be imprinted with a seal from which God's blessings certainly would flow. Indeed, this step is absolutely necessary if the inner mission is to develop its activities everywhere. In many ways the inner mission cannot establish an organic connection as long as the Church Federation does not declare that it will act as the spiritual center. Moreover, I think it is highly necessary for the Church Federation to declare the cause to be its own if the church desires to be the source of all Christian life in our people. For these reasons I support the proposal that the inner mission be included on the agenda, and I reserve the opportunity to speak about it in more detail at another hour."

[Secretary]

However, the gathering expressed the wish that the speaker do this immediately. The speaker's entire presentation was extemporaneous. The liveliness of the address, which contained many individual facts, figures, and names, made it all the more difficult to transcribe in its original form. On the other hand, **Wichern** has been requested to treat the subject in a special, short article, and he has promised to comply with the request. He continues:

In identifying the sphere of the inner mission it is first of all a great mistake to think that the inner mission is concerned only about rescuing the poor and uneducated. It is just as concerned about rescuing the rich, the richest, and the most highly educated. The boundaries of the inner mission's sphere are set by baptism, whose great worth the inner mission fully recognizes.

[Wichern]

"I recognize baptism in the Lutheran sense. This statement itself will make those who think the inner mission rejects baptism to feel obliged to give up or reexamine their doubts. The question is whether in the midst of Christianity a fundamental attitude and way of life is becoming more and more like paganism. Proof of this development can be cited. Yet as recently as a year ago this view was contradicted and, logically, the inner mission was condemned at a large German pastoral conference. Many of those who at the time opposed the inner mission have already admitted they were deceiving themselves about the state of affairs. Meanwhile, the revolution that has broken out—ours in Germany more than that of the French—offers proof of the justification and necessity for the inner mission.

"Inner mission can be practiced within **individual, separate parishes.** In such cases it is primarily the initiative of practical-minded pastors. It is often connected with the church's care of the poor, which, of course, cannot solve the problem by itself.

"The inner mission goes beyond individual parishes. We Germans are not a people simply with permanent residences, but a nomadic people, by the hundreds of thousands. One need only think of the **traveling journeymen** who every year wander through our fatherland in vast numbers. As wandering journeymen they have no other home than their overnight lodging in workers' hostels and, until most recently, no other fellowship than with their colleagues.

"I have already described in writing what it is like in a workers' hostel. Things happen there that one must call—to use the word of the apostle—unspeakable. The only place where one could talk about them at all would be in a small circle of men who are on very familiar terms. Whoever knows about the orgies of the pagans still has no idea of what has gone on and still goes on there. Since the time of Charles V laws are in place against these things, and up until now the police keep fighting the evil, but they will never win. In these hostels the essential nature of our modern, revolutionary clubs was modeled in secret, and the path that this preparation followed stretches across centuries.

"How is one to go about satisfying the religious needs of these hundreds of thousands? Whose calling and responsibility is it to look after these people? Who has worked with God's Word among them? To which church or parish do these multitudes belong? It is undeniable that no one has worried about them up to now.

"Added to this is a second, related realm of the inner mission: **the Germans outside of Germany, first of all in Europe.** (The emigration to North America is a chapter in itself.) The German diaspora in Europe also consists chiefly of journeymen and can be found in the large European capitals, especially Paris, Marseilles, Lyons, London, St. Petersburg, and so forth. What is the Evangelical Church here in their fatherland doing for them? As recently as two years ago those who spoke seriously about the dangers of **communism** among Germans in Paris and London, for example, were disturbed because people would merely frown at them or quickly turn away. But circumstances were to teach a different lesson. Those who understood the state of affairs saw the threatening monster approach. Then the storm of communist revolution unleashed itself. Journeymen played a greater role than even some of the most sober thinkers have been willing to admit. Many had been trained methodically right in Paris for their acts of barbarism. The police had known about many of these circumstances for a long time, but did not believe they ought to speak about them openly; they thought they could eliminate the danger on their own.

"Those unfamiliar with the situation can scarcely imagine the cleverness and timing of the attacks by the journeymen. The radically atheistic communist party in French Switzerland set up one of the nearest training schools. The primary means for achieving their goals was **atheism,** which, of course, was often disguised. In a notorious book that appeared about two years ago (it was not banned, and therefore, unfortunately, it was not read, either) the author, **W. Marr,**[16] as a traitor to his party, recounts in detail his activities and those of his like-minded companions. He states as his fundamental principle, 'People must be turned into personal enemies of God.' He boasts of having prepared, step by step, thousands of German journeymen for the cause. To be accepted into the brotherhood one had to respond with a decisive 'no' to the question, 'Do you believe in a god?'

"In 1845 **Marr** gave the sign for lighting the bonfire on Signal Peak near Lausanne. The flames that rose up were the signal for the outbreak of the revolution in the entire canton. His friend **Druey,**[17] in order to get rid of him, instructed him to continue his propaganda in **Germany.** Marr visited **von Itzstein, Hecker, R. Blum,**[18] and others, trying to spread propaganda wherever he went. Then his book with the title *Young Germany*[19] appeared.

"The home of all recent revolutionary endeavors with their damnable, satanic agitation is the journeymen clubs, whose secret intentions were recognized by very few people, not even by some of their own directors. The clubs were organized without any fanfare, frequently supported by many law-abiding people who, often in spite of warnings, meekly let themselves be duped. The associations are usually guided by covert leadership and try to break up any other organization of journeymen that shows any kind of initiative. I hope that one verse of a song sung in Hamburg at a meeting of skilled laborers just a short time ago can serve as an example of the spirit prevailing among many of the workers. After cursing kings and the wealthy, the song continues:

> A curse on the god without sight, without hearing,
> to whom we prayed vainly though we were god-fearing,
> upon whom we waited with unfulfilled hopes!
> He made us the fools, and we are the dopes.

"In spite of all this I, as a Lutheran, recognize even such people, including a **Marr** and his companions, as **baptized** Christians, and therefore objects of the inner mission, which demands and has the courage to attack Satan's work with the almighty Word of God."

[Secretary]

Then the speaker turned to other areas, for example **the railroad workers,** of whom thousands are accustomed to living in shacks like nomads. Who has worried about their needs? Who caught the sound of their individual cries for help that faded away without a trace? No one thinks of satisfying the religious needs of the railroad workers. Isolated attempts, such as that of trying to meet the religious needs of crossing guards in the vicinity of Magdeburg, do not warrant our attention at this point. But nothing can compare with the terrible situation of the proletariat in the **large cities** of our fatherland.

Moreover, out in the countryside we also come across miles of territory full of people who neglect the church. Yet they all belong to us. All who are in the church are members of the one body. What is said here might not be applicable to this or that particular village, small town, or larger city with more resources.

[Wichern]

"Yesterday people raised objections to my friend **Kuntze**,[20] when he spoke about the 99 percent. His reference was not meant to be as all-embracing as people in the meeting took it to be. He had in mind his own parish or a similar one. **Kuntze** is a pastor in Voigtland in Berlin. This district and similar ones, such as St. Pauli, which is the seamen's quarter in Hamburg, or St. Antoine, St. Martin, and St. Denis in Paris, and certain districts in almost all the large cities of Germany, are such that Kuntze's words apply to them in many ways.

"Based on my experience during fifteen to sixteen years of almost exclusive involvement with this issue, and based on convictions I have gained from reading the literature, from personally listening to hundreds of people, and from personal investigation in various parts of our fatherland, I can attest that **Kuntze's** words contain a great deal of truth. There are sections of the cities where it is physically impossible for the clergy to go about their work. It is impossible for them to worry about all those who are living out their lives in complete isolation from the church. As a result, these people live without any care from the church. Their children are baptized, and it **could be** that they have been married, but that is the extent of their connection with the church.

"The views that came out of the latest philosophical developments in **Feuerbach**,[21] etc., along with their moral consequences, have been known and practiced by our lowest level of rabble for a long time, and this explains the revolution. Communist views, which go against all sound political and moral, to say nothing of Christian, principles, are attached to the pseudo-philosophy that has been adopted by the so-called leaders of the people, and promptly the masses who have risen in revolt accept these views as the rationale for revolution.

"Several factors created the condition that helps explain how revolutionary events were able to spring forth suddenly, as if out of soil that had been prepared for a long time. One factor was the difficulty of counteracting the propaganda with an antidote, because the traveling journeymen, with passport in hand and protection from the authorities, carried the propaganda to the four winds. Another cause was the organizing talent and sharp minds in these circles. We must note among other contributing factors the far-advanced de-Christianizing in all classes of people. One can only marvel and praise God's mercy that a people so poisoned and undermined down to its deepest roots has been able to stand firm, especially since the pernicious principles did not stay within the proletariat but rose to the heights of the intellectuals and often even to those in power."

[Secretary]

What can be done? While this situation was spreading like a huge web over all of Europe, we were sending emissaries to the non-Christian world in ever-increasing numbers. Naturally it was not difficult to deduce that we could carry on missionary activity right at home in our own backyard. That is how the name **inner mission** came about, originating in the group of those who were regularly involved with carrying out the work of the foreign, or outer, mission.

However, the required help will remain incomplete as long as the vision of the effort does not broaden to include national and political life. The work is as necessary for the nation as it is for the church. The strongest moral foundations upon which the nation's life rests have been shaken, and, in part, they already appear to have sunk into an abyss. Hence, the revolution and threatening anarchy!

The issue of **crime** is also a part of this. Unfortunately, within the circle of those associated with the church little is known about what has been planned, aimed for, and accomplished most recently, or about what has become absolutely necessary in order to improve the situation of crime and prisons. Ever since Constantine linked the church and the state, the power of paganism that is still present in Christendom has maintained an influence in this sphere. We were unable to begin breaking down this influence until about fifty years ago. One need only hear the laments voiced by so many prison chaplains and directors!

The speaker cited a number of cases, noting among others the city of **Glückstadt.** The prison there always has about eight hundred inmates. The need of individual prisoners for God's help is so great that two felons needing salvation made a pact of friendship with each other in order to find a little consolation, since they felt themselves totally abandoned and lost. Soon they felt that there must be help **beyond** mortal beings. Not knowing **God,** they created for themselves a supernatural being—an angel or a spirit—with whom they spoke and to whom they prayed. So it is that pure idolatry arises in the midst of Christianity. These conditions exist even now.

The prisons annually release hundreds of criminals who are worse than when they were incarcerated. Those who are released look for refuge in the world outside and become criminals again. In prison Carsten **Hinz** learned how to pray to the devil and when released committed a double murder, but before he was beheaded he made the memorable confession of a converted Christian. I have eaten at my table with such released prisoners who are looking for help. I am acquainted with their needs and know how little compassion they receive on **earth.** Thousands of them are becoming a plague on our fatherland, against which many have recently armed themselves.

Indisputably the Christian church is called to help in these and all other related situations, primarily through developing the activity of the **inner mission.** The nature of the work depends on the **respective need.** Above all, we must recognize and acknowledge, "The sharp eye of love can see everything." It is deplorable how, in general, people **know so little** about what is already happening within our church in Germany alone. A great network of initiatives has spread throughout our entire fatherland in order to rescue the lost.

[Wichern]

"It is primarily **women** who are working at the great task of salvation. Once they were the first to see the risen Lord, and they were the ones who, after a new day of faith in love had dawned in our Evangelical Church, laid their hands with determination to the task of inner mission. In our fatherland this love in their hearts was born in the blood and pain of the Wars of Liberation and lives on today in numerous voluntary associations. As it is in Germany, so it is in all the countries of evangelical Europe. We have seen Christian women working with us in this field of endeavor in a manner that the Christian church probably has never experienced before.

"Elisabeth **Fry** and Amalie **Sieveking** deserve mention in this connection.[22] The fountain of life in the souls of these and other women like them sprang forth without measure. In New York[23] Elisabeth **Fry** introduced a new world among prisoners who, even though they were in chains, would not be approached by the guards unless the guards were armed. A new Easter of love for the imprisoned went out from her, crossed France, Switzerland, Italy, and Russia and spread its blessing even in Germany. Amalie **Sieveking's** Christian care of the poor and sick gained public attention in 1830, the first year of cholera in Hamburg. In self-sacrificing devotion she spared no effort on the work she had begun quietly. Even though she did not seek emulation, her example was followed in all major cities. These initiatives are branching out and bearing fruit in Denmark, Sweden, Russia, Holland, France, and Switzerland. In other places poor, young housemaids have taken up the cause and in this way have laid the foundation for an extensive organization. One example is in Nuremberg.

"In the same way, rescue homes are helping **young people.** Ever since Johannes **Falk,** Count von der **Recke,** and **Zeller** the work to rescue young people has progressed across our fatherland.[24] In fact, it has spread not only across Germany but also far beyond our borders, and everywhere it appears it does so in a Christian spirit. Christian faith is its foundation, and profession of that faith is its divine adornment. All the workers participate with the same Christian zeal and with sincere loyalty to the church to which they belong.

"In addition, attempts are being made to combat widespread vices such as drunkenness; to regenerate entire classes of people, such as the traveling journeymen; and to spread many kinds of materials, such as popular periodicals and similar diversions, all of which serve the one purpose of renewing the kingdom of God among those who are estranged. At this point we will mention only in passing the various endeavors to meet the religious needs of those who have emigrated to North America."

[Secretary]

The speech illustrates the crisis in North America and indicates how at the borders of the United States, German blood is intermingling with pagan blood. Having given an impression of what is already being done to alleviate the needs, he continues.

Thus, as we have seen, bountiful, invisible assets of love have been brought down from heaven through faith and placed in our church. On that faith a hope is built that cannot be destroyed. Nevertheless, all this is only a **mustard seed**. It is **nothing** in comparison to the need. The **success** of the revolutionary movement alone is enough to show that all the work up to now has had no effect on the whole. If people had had the will to grapple with all of these ideas much earlier, if the Protestant Church, as a people's church, had developed its ethical dimension, then an invincible power would have been created against the violent revolt. Look at London! In May, at the anniversary celebration of the great **city mission, Lord Ashley**[25] said it was his firm conviction that the London City Mission, as well as other associations of this type, had contributed greatly to averting the dangers and confusion of the revolution threatening to break out at that time and maintained peace.

However, we can also learn from England what is larger than a mustard seed. On Sundays in London one can see from the post office tower for the radius of a mile a crowd of many thousands of lost and abandoned children gathering in Sunday Schools. The point here is not to highlight the needs of the children but rather the wealth of voluntary, efficacious love that is the outgrowth of the evangelical principle. Almost ten thousand men and women from all levels of society serve these children every Sunday with the word of life. Still other examples from London can be added. According to the excellent news from **C.-R. von Gerlach,**[26] in ten to eleven years fifty churches, along with the necessary facilities for the pastor and school at each, have been built in the London parish of **Bethnel-Green** at the urging of the bishop. Each cost seven thousand pounds sterling, almost all of which came from private sources. The extent of moral decay in that metropolis and the misery that goes along with it are, of course, nearly incomprehensible to us. English bishops gave remarkable accounts at the large meetings held frequently last year as a result of the school question.

[Wichern]
"The bishops themselves testified that in many parts of the capital city total paganism is rampant among the lowest classes. In England such observations serve all the more to awaken and develop Christlike, saving, voluntary agents of love in great abundance. Studies showed that in London over 100,000 children were growing up without school or church. In three London districts alone thirty-six thousand such children were wandering about. Beginning in 1844 **Ragged Schools** were founded in order to combat the emergency. After only three years of existence 450 teachers, of whom 400 are volunteers and only 50 are paid, were teaching almost five thousand unfortunate children daily. Lord **Ashley,** who directs these schools, said at last year's anniversary celebration that he would consider it an honor to be allowed to put the title below his name, 'President of the Schools for Beggar Children,' if, at the same time, he should lose the two flattering and influential letters **M.P. (Member of Parliament).**

"One of the greatest ventures of Christian love is the **city mission,** operating for twelve years in England—in London, in particular. Lords and clergy have joined together here with the most diverse collection of volunteers. Clergy have laid down their offices in order to devote all of their energies to this mission on the Thames. Last year two hundred missionaries were working in London. Year in and year out they make their way into the hidden recesses of depravity with the Word of God and celebrate great victories for the Lord.

"May it suffice that I have held up this mirror before the German Evangelical Church. I could describe equivalent examples in Holland, France, Switzerland, and other countries. These activities, too, are expressions of the rejuvenated life of love born in Christ, fully matching the spirit of those in England. However, I can only allude to them, as well as to the internal, unmistakable progress of these initiatives. The progress can be seen in the quiet ways—not yet registered by history—by which various countries, still unaware of what was born in them, are beginning to learn and profit from each other. This interrelationship is causing the work of the inner mission, the rescue of the nations' peoples, to penetrate ever deeper and in an ever-greater variety of ways into the life of our people. Thus the inner mission is led toward its great fulfillment in the future—and who knows what that will be!

"We now return to our own homeland, to the German Evangelical Church, where help is needed for the complete unfolding of the inner mission for the salvation of the people! The inner mission, hand in hand with the truth that has been won and preserved by the Evangelical Church, must become the power of our church. The inner mission was given life within our church in order to give life to the world.

"Love for those who are lost or in distress has been a tenet of the Evangelical Church from the very beginning. Yet to awaken this love in its full abundance belonged to a later, perhaps current, stage in the development of the spirit of our church. Two of our church's most gifted men of God, **Spener** and **A. H. Francke,**[27] were the foremost contributors, so it appears, to what was to come: Spener by proclaiming the general priesthood, and Francke through his well-known work of mercy in Halle. Unfortunately, at that time the activity of saving love was, and up to the very present is, directed primarily at the poor and the young. However, we cannot think one-sidedly of only these groups. The church's thinking must also turn in all earnestness to adults, families, households, to **all** ranks in the entire public domain, to the poor and the rich, the lowly and the great. We need a **reformation** or even more a **regeneration of the condition deepest within our hearts.** The church is called to work toward this new birth through new and renewed deeds and revelations of faith and love.

"It is indisputable and plain for everyone to see that sin and injustice have seized and infiltrated the life of the people, spreading in all directions like a plague, breaking forth in the widest variety of forms in **political, social,** and **religious** life itself. In the work of the inner mission the church, armed with God's power and authority, must rise up against this massive corruption. The inner mission, as a well-knit, well-designed organism of the saving, freely gathered, genuinely grass-roots people who are essentially one with the church, must look this corruption in the eye, in all of its sinful configurations. Then with these people the church must take up the victorious battle or, where the battle has already begun, continue the fight."

[Secretary]

The speaker indicated briefly the tasks and activities of the inner mission in reference to the three spheres he mentioned above. In regard to **political** life he said, among other things:

[Wichern]

"The inner mission absolutely must be involved in politics, and if it does not work within this framework, then the church, along with the state, will perish. Clearly it is not the task of the inner mission to make judgments about political structures and to decide between political parties as such. However, beginning today, one of its most fervent concerns must be that citizens be filled with the Christian spirit, no matter what the political structure."

[Secretary]

In connection with **social** issues the speaker again gave only a brief sketch. He mentioned, among other things, that what Thiers said recently in the French National Assembly about the social problem of our day is accurate, though mostly negative, because the state is incapable of producing the entire solution of the problems on its own, even though indirectly it has paved the way by granting the important right of freedom to form associations.[28] If, in this regard, the church becomes conscious of its great calling to work with the people and makes use of the right of association to the fullest extent, that is, if the church acknowledges, cherishes, and employs this right in order to fill it with Christian spirit and make it develop in the direction of the inner mission for the good of the people, then the church will be blessed as the savior of the community as a whole. In following this path the door is open for the church into the hearts of all people, into all categories and ranks of public and private life from the family to the community, from the cradle to the grave.

The church must give new shape within itself to what has already begun. The beginnings, embryonic forms exist in many inner mission endeavors that up to now have been isolated, that is, in the numerous Christian associations. In this context Wichern cited the conditions in one area of **Upper Silesia** as an example of the problems that must be solved. Wichern had just come from there. He had had the opportunity to get acquainted closely with the needs of the almost four thousand orphans and a great portion of the populace.

In any case, whatever is done and however it is carried out, one thing must manifest itself in all endeavors: the people must be filled anew with the divine Word and its spirit of new life. Hence, the church must keep a sharp eye on that facet of the inner mission that works most directly **toward this end,** namely, the facet that focuses on the real crisis in the **church itself.** Here we are confronted above all with the fact that hundreds of thousands, particularly in the larger cities and metropolises, live out their lives without ever hearing God's Word. The church must set itself the task through the inner mission of not resting until **everyone** hears again the proclamation of the Son of the living God. The following declaration, as one of the fundamental principles, must be at the head of the list: If the people do not come to the church, then the church must go to the people. That is how our Lord Christ did it. He came to us. He did not wait until we had come to him.

It will be difficult to achieve this goal other than through a freely formed association, because this will make possible what was impossible, given the approach used up to now. **We must have street-preachers,** chiefly in the large cities. The street corners must become pulpits, and the gospel will again penetrate the people. England is ahead of us in this respect, too.

This new institution can be modified in manifold ways and does not need to come forth and grow only according to the English model. Among us it ought to develop in a genuinely German

manner. We should not worry about the initial results of the under-
taking but rather, with humility and courage, keep our eyes on, and
keep in our prayers, the salutary effects on a people estranged from
the Word of God.

The resulting imperative is **to apply ourselves with new zeal
to all the existing efforts of this sort as individual branches of
the inner mission.** In many cases what is required has more to do
with expansion and organizing than with creating something new.
What is required is a new, more all-embracing concept of the
church. This will become possible more quickly the sooner people
stop viewing these endeavors as activities of dilettantes and as
merely philanthropic initiatives. The endeavors must be regarded
as the sacred tasks of the Evangelical Church and, as such, brought
into the life of the people with new earnestness. Henceforth they
should be proclaimed from the pulpits.

As an example of what ought to be given new life and how,
Wichern cited the **Bible societies.** "The spirit of the Bible must
descend on the Bible societies." The only person in Germany to be
mentioned at this time is **Feldner,**[29] who understood the work of
the Bible societies in this spirit. Yet Feldner was by no means alone.
The light of a rich, unique model in this field shines in England.
The speaker reported about what had been inspired at first by sea-
side tourists in Liverpool and Manchester, and in what numbers
bibles had been distributed to factory workers and Sunday School
children, at first without any assistance—that is, of the clergy, who
joined in later on. The same localities had similar experiences with
the journeymen. Through courageous proclaimers of God's Word
fit for the task not a small number of communist journeymen clubs
have been transformed into Christian gathering places in which the
gospel is now loved and fostered.

[Wichern]
"All these and the related work of a living faith still face us as
tasks to be done, and in their future lies the future of our Evangelical
Church. In revealing and radiating the heart of God through these
activities the church will reach its fulfillment as the true people's

church, and then it will see the people who belong to it transformed into the people of God.

"I greeted the news of this assembly in Wittenberg with a bright and joyful spirit and have placed great hopes in it for our people and our fatherland. It is in God's hands whether my hopes will be fulfilled.

"My friends, one thing is **necessary,** that the Evangelical Church as a whole acknowledge, 'The work of the inner mission is mine!' and that it set one great seal on the sum of this work: **love, as well as faith, belongs to me.** Saving love must become the great implement by which the church demonstrates the fact of its faith. This love must burn in the church like God's bright torch, revealing that Christ has taken shape in his people. Just as Christ reveals his entire self in the living **Word** of God, so, too, he must preach himself in the **deeds** of God, and the highest and purest of these deeds, and the one closest to the church's purpose is saving love. If the message about the inner mission is accepted in this sense, then the first day of a new future will dawn in our church.

"First the evangelical preachers must gather with their brothers in the office and do penance for everything that has been neglected in this field, and through their penance move all the congregations to penance. Who could and should avoid such penance? Let us all humble ourselves before the Lord! The accumulated guilt is not that of certain individuals, but of everyone, a guilt not merely of this generation, but an inherited one, passed on from century to century, a guilt that is to be expiated in the new age that is dawning in the world.

"Such penance would be the dividing line between the old and new age in our church, and the new age and its fruits would be more magnificent than the old age as it comes to an end. Those who go forth out of penance will be resurrected in faith for the great work of saving the people from misery and sin through Christ's power and glory.

"The entire church must acknowledge such work. Then the heart and treasure of the Evangelical Church, the general priesthood, which we treated more as a duty than a right, which has its focus and protection in the office ordained by God, will cause the mustard seed of the inner mission to keep growing. Then, like a tree that spreads its shade over everything, the inner mission will proclaim the saving power of the Lord to our entire people.

"This is how I view the inner mission. This is the basis for my motion, which essentially proposes **that the inner mission will be one of the matters to be addressed by the confederated church.** Motions dealing with specifics can be saved until later."

Wichern's Speech on Saturday, September 23, 1848

"The most important task is to create the opportunity so that the conviction to which people came yesterday on behalf of the inner mission might become life-giving power. The concept of inner mission, like the light that transforms the crystal, must prove to be the power that transforms reality. The totality of the means by which the inner mission works is manifold and diverse, as are the needs themselves. The task is to develop at each particular place the amount of energy necessary to meet the need. First one must identify the tasks necessary at each place. In a large city the inner mission has different problems to solve than where its activity is not bound to one locale.

"Those who are well-informed know that the beginnings of almost all the programs of the inner mission are already in place. The total number of its initiatives in Germany is in a class by itself. The inner mission naturally has much to learn from France, England, and from the Roman Catholic Church as well—though not from its orders; the principle of orders is not evangelical. However, the Roman Catholic Church has produced a great number of activities having a Christian spirit and a great number of rich organizations that can be instructive to us. In carrying out this work churches in dispute about their specific doctrines come into contact with each other, and the work in Christ paves the way to a unity that goes above and beyond knowledge.

"For a number of years the ever more pressing need in our church, as well as in the Roman Catholic, has been to form **living, spirit-filled centers** for the diverse activities that often intersect in a confusing manner. Germany has been very weak in this regard, although it has taken the first steps here and there. As far as I know, England has never made an attempt to form a coordinating organization. France offers the greatest promise in this regard. Last year on the occasion of the second great Penitentiary Conference in Brussels men from almost all of Europe (not without German influence) came together in order to discuss the idea of **one great alliance of saving love all across Europe.**[30] Today we would already be celebrating the implementation of this idea if the **revolution** had not intervened. Vicomte de **Melun** from Paris was the main figure.[31] Paris was to serve as the center. The greatest statesmen of France also participated. Notables in Germany, Norway, Denmark, England, Spain, Italy, and France were ready to help and had offered their collective moral and material support. The revolution appears to have terminated the plans.

"Meanwhile the same idea, independent of the one in France, has been alive in Germany, and it is Germany's responsibility to seize the initiative vigorously, intensively, with fresh enthusiasm. For fifteen years I have been inspired by the ever clearer and ever more intense hope and idea: whether it might be possible for our fatherland, this heart of Europe, to bring forth for the kingdom of God an **alliance of faith and love.** This alliance would offer itself in service and sacrifice to nation and church in order to save generations who have fallen away from God. It would be armed with the power of learning, the wisdom of statesmen, the strength of the ecclesiastical structure, and the spirit of God's eternal grace, from which alone the peoples of the nations can receive salvation and blessing. The hope was so distant, the plea seemingly unheard, and wherever the idea was expressed, most people regarded it as a fantasy.

"Then it appeared as though France would offer help; but look, it has fallen! In Germany, given its condition, the seed could not sprout. The blindfold had to be removed from everyone's eyes, but by God's miraculous hand it happened. The abyss has been exposed; the field has been plowed and prepared for the glorious sprouting of God's new seed that is the saving love that reigns in one's faith. The day of planting appears to have dawned over **Wittenberg.** Might not the **Evangelical Church Federation** be called to begin carrying out the work, thereby revealing itself to the entire evangelical people as an alliance of salvation in which something new has begun? I consider it possible, given the existing, earnest spirit of determination rooted in God. I consider it not only possible, but also easy, as long as people hold fast to a sense of earnestness about the cause.

"Hence, the question now is **whether from the bosom of this church body, and in awareness of the great evangelical-catholic community, a committee will proceed that will begin dealing with this great responsibility, molding what God desires out of the resources gathered from our abundant, but as yet hidden, inheritance.** My proposal aims at having such a **Committee for the Inner Mission** linked to the future executive body of this organization. Committee members should include one or two members from this assembly's elected executive committee; perhaps one member from a German university; in addition, individuals who are already familiar with the operation of the inner mission as a whole, or who are already familiar, or would like to become familiar, with particular aspects of it and can appreciate the difficulties that can arise. The number of those who form this Central Committee should not exceed twelve, and they should live as close as possible to each other and hold their meetings at various places. In addition, something like subcommittees would have to be created at the various main centers. These details still need to be examined more thoroughly.

"**Such a committee would have several tasks.** One would be to take initial steps in evangelical, Christian love to provide the necessary religious, moral, and often physical help for Germans living in Europe but outside of Germany. A second would be to focus attention on emigration as it relates to the church—an immense need. Third, the committee would provide the link for meeting the various needs of our fatherland's church in city and countryside by identifying and mobilizing the inner mission's remedies at the various locations. Furthermore, the committee would see to the spread of the inner mission concept in general through written material, speeches, activities, meetings, and involvement with the people. Another task would be to work toward establishing branch centers, along with initiating a truly vital organization of the various activities already present and still to be created. Above all, however, the committee would try as hard as possible to engage individuals in the work of the inner mission who bring devotion, wisdom, and skill. Naturally, linked to this would be the task of creating opportunities through which individuals and talents can be engaged and trained for the work. As a result, individuals who can inspire and lead—of whom the church has an abundance—will blossom. These individuals and the office of the church will draw ever closer together, as the apostolic order requires. This is a great need at present, and the free realm of the inner mission offers the best vehicle to accomplish this task with the most certain guarantee of success.

"For such purposes various associations could be formed here and there independent of a coordinating committee. The committee's role is not to dominate but to serve and to help, even where people might not want its help. It is to ensure that all of the work with, and alongside, one another advances the cause, that one endeavor does not disrupt another, but rather that everything thrives in a joyful, vital relationship. The committee, in ways to be determined, would inform members of this assembly of its activities, would discuss its work in print, and would provide the next assembly with a full report.

"If we take these actions, suddenly the German church will have gained an immense amount of capital for its deeply sacred work. It will have discovered a true treasure of life. To cite just one example, we do not know how the relationship between church and schools will look, but if the church were to pledge itself to the endeavors of saving love, then it would find itself in close alliance with a great number of institutions and organizations all over the fatherland. The way would be paved for bringing into the church almost a hundred rescue homes that carry out work in the evangelical spirit to save young people.

"These would be the natural training ground for energetic, believing teachers. At the teacher-training colleges faithful professors admit that even under Christian teachers it is not unusual, though obviously not always the case, for unbelief to grow. Only an unfettered approach and an unfettered relationship of love and life can provide a sure guarantee of a generation of believing teachers. A number of the already existing rescue homes could be developed into training institutions. It is not necessary to go into more detail how, through this kind of purposeful, organized activity, the church will enter deeply into the life of the people and, building from within and creating what is new, will bring blessing and salvation.

"**Progress** on one of the most promising paths for rebirth of the evangelical life of the people will be guaranteed by the proposed determination to implement an organic program of activity. However, it will take a year of work before we can say with some assurance which of our hopes we can or cannot fulfill.

"May I be permitted to add a few words of explanation to my motion: **that this assembly create a Committee for the Inner Mission.** Such a committee would have both an organizing and an operating function. Accordingly, the committee would try to bring about the voluntary, internal unification of existing inner mission activities. This organizing side should be emphasized first, because out of a life-filled organic structure the power to create something new will emerge on its own, out of an inner drive.

"There is such confusion and lack of coordination in the efforts of the inner mission in Germany that the resulting disadvantages for the cause are plain to see. Berlin can be cited as an example. If you ask the preachers there, they will tell you about their great problems with splintered and splintering organizations. It all goes back to one fact: there is no active, organized hub from which the whole structure can radiate. And so it is with minor exceptions in our entire fatherland. In one city in northern Germany an agency was organized to meet the spiritual and religious needs of those who were emigrating, and it asked for help. Instead, a number of other agencies were immediately organized independent of it and of each other. The first association endured, while the others either led short, unsuccessful lives, or remain weaklings. These agencies undermined, even though unintentionally, some of the original group's power and had the negative effect of preventing other sources of help from developing. Had there been a common center for these activities, then the nature of their success would have been entirely different.

"At a number of universities students organized for the same cause. Authorities at two universities completely stamped out these efforts of love, in effect choking in its infancy the life of benevolent love that was gaining strength and courage among young people. At a third and fourth university the cause died for lack of support. If a committee like the one proposed were to take the matter into its hands and develop a program that represents the entire national church, then the authorities could scarcely act as they did, and individuals would not have to stand by so helplessly.

"I receive hundreds of visits and letters in which, among other things, people inquire about this and that regarding the inner mission. How often must I tell the inquirers, 'What you are seeking you have in your own town or province,' yet up to then they had never heard of it. Many of the agencies in question operate for the most part without knowing that similar institutions and societies exist, and they are even less aware of the abundance of life they could create together through an active, organized association. So it is that many a sound effort of saving love is crippled from the beginning, and many an initiative goes to its grave of shameful inactivity soon after birth. Had these initiatives been supported by the whole, and had they come to feel and know they were members of one body, then they would have had sufficient vitality to fulfill their very blessed calling.

"I can emphasize how salutary this unity would be by referring again to the example of the rescue homes. If an effectively organized team effort were to come into being among these homes, what could they not do! How many more immortal souls could be saved if, for example, in certain cases an exchange of youngsters among several homes were possible. Instead of fifty, perhaps one hundred could be saved. O, how the power of faith would grow in the housefathers of such institutions because of the link with the entire Evangelical Church! Mutual prayer, mutual intercession, and helping hands reaching out in every direction cannot be considered impossible.

"Let me give one more example, which is right before us today. Descriptions of a new church association in Berlin and a newly established evangelical association in Elberfeld have been distributed here. It is true that by doing this both organizations are directing their attention more or less to the whole church. However, my point is not simply to raise the question of how many members of the Evangelical Church in Germany will find out about their efforts. I am far more interested in emphasizing how much the strength of each association would increase if through good organization, and not merely happenstance, a path would be prepared where the message and goal would stand like a series of gateways through which hundreds of church groups could enter—groups which would rejoice in getting involved and would keep these endeavors in their hearts. How much better it would be if these and related organizations could reach out their hands, energizing and supporting each other in their work.

"All these conditions, whether present or not, explain why in more than one place the longing has developed for a more heartfelt, invigorating, organized fellowship and cooperation in the activities of the inner mission. Out of this deep desire arose, for example, the general meetings of the temperance associations; other analogous groups have the strong wish to gather together. This has not happened yet.

"However, even if people do gather together, they will not produce the desired results until they raise their vision above and beyond their separate programs in the field and learn to see and love their individual endeavors as part of a great and manifold whole. The desired results will be produced when the church has become fully aware that it must put into practice the principle that lies at the base of all the various, separate initiatives. Putting that principle into practice will lead the Evangelical Church into, and bring it alive in, the hearts of all the people who belong to it. Then, through fellowship in the activities and linked with the ordained office—that is, preaching, administration of the sacraments, and pastoral care—the well-being of the people will blossom forth. Then the increasing, ever more visible blessings will become a fountain of new life-giving power for the closely related family of activities.

"Yet all of this requires a focal point, a beginning, an instrument born in the freedom of love that knows its purpose is to serve the church. This organ will raise the banner around which will gather **those** who, united with all like-minded brothers and sisters who are related to us through their action, cannot rest from the labor and sacrifice of life until our evangelical people are permeated by the revealed word of truth and filled with the fruit of faith that makes us righteous before God.

"And so I come back to the motion I made, that this church assembly bring forth out of its bosom an effectively organized and organizing focal point for the activities of the inner mission in the Evangelical Church, and as a sign of the deep seriousness with which this assembly takes the cause of the inner mission it set up a committee to create such a body. The intention is **not** that such a committee strive to become some kind of general administrative authority in the field. To want this would be not only extremely foolish but also self-condemning evidence that people do not yet understand at all the essence of the activities in question. The freedom and independence of the individual societies and institutions, given their common right of existence, are inviolable and the prerequisite for their existence.

"Instead, what is necessary is to bring forth a similarly free and independent locus that gives itself in **service** to the totality of the work. Its inner freedom and independence would be made manifest precisely in this willingness and dedication to serve everyone. By virtue of its connection with the princes of life who are rescuing human beings it would struggle to become a fountain of life. It would be a fountain to which all could, and would want to, turn in love without reservation, in order that through this unity the many small streams could swell into one great river of light and life filling the

Evangelical Church. The task of the committee would be to knit a sacred network of love whose individual threads are already spun but await being tied together in one well-designed, beautifully organized whole. Through the communications of such a committee it would be possible for all to learn from one another, to give and receive, so that the life-blood of love would circulate though all their veins.

"Were the Lord to bless this alliance, and were the established body to bring about the active coordination of the main participants in all their evangelical works of love of the inner mission, then the wisdom gained from the wealth of experience and the illuminating, igniting flashes of love that rescues people would proceed from the established center. A great academy of evangelical love would rise at the site. From it a powerful stimulus for new work, advice, and encouragement would emanate, and it would also have to exert a creative influence. Since I addressed these functions earlier, I will not go into more detail about them now.

"In closing I would like to comment briefly on statements made by a few gentlemen who preceded me. I cannot reject **Dr. Schmieder's** reservation.[32] What is necessary for forming an organization such as the one projected is an **inner** calling. However, if only those who name themselves become members of the committee, then many who have perhaps the greatest calling for it would be left out. In addition, many have already gone home, and many outside of these circles have both the outer and inner calling. It can only be our wish that they, too, have the chance to become involved.

"I doubt, as another dear friend suggested, that there will be a lack of financial support. In the beginning the committee will need relatively few means, and to some extent, none at all to carry out a number of important tasks. So in this regard the speaker did not need to have any reservations. However, when the committee does need financial support, including larger amounts—and that can certainly be the case—the means will be there. This concern belongs to the abundant God who is a God of the wealthy and who, through the poor, can also bring forth riches. One should not doubt but, without testing God, believe, and the results will thoroughly justify one's trust. The help one needs is always near.

"Probably never have people done so much for the cause of the Lord as they have since the outbreak of the revolution this year. Great sums have been given in recent months, and the greater our confidence, the more joyfully and abundantly earthly goods will be offered. This correlation rests on an eradicable law of the divine world order. Therefore, we have little to worry about in this regard if we simply make sure we have the right spirit and do not go against the divine order. The one who helps in all need lives, and the greater the need, the more gloriously he is revealed. If this is true, then why hesitate! **Today,** I say, **is the time to put our hands to the task.** It is still day; who knows how soon the night will come when we can work no more!" (John 9:4)

Reports on Inner Mission

The Inner Mission of the German Evangelical Church: A Memorandum to the German Nation on Request of the Central Committee for Inner Mission

EDITORS' INTRODUCTION: Following Wichern's request at the Wittenberg *Kirchentag* on September 21–23, 1848, that the delegates appoint a steering committee to form a coherent structure for the Inner Mission, less than two months elapsed before an ad hoc group gathered in Berlin. During its meetings on November 11 and 12 the participants took two important steps. They appointed a provisional Central Committee for the Inner Mission, and they asked Wichern to write its charter.

Wichern had already written a draft of such a document for the meeting in Berlin, so early in 1849 he set about the task of expanding it. The result, finished on April 21, was far more than a brief charter, and it bore the auspicious title "The Inner Mission of the German Evangelical Church: A Memorandum to the German Nation on Request of the Central Committee for Inner Mission."[1] The first printing sold out in a few weeks. Wichern had obviously reached the audience he aimed for—not just a committee, but also the entire "German Nation." The *Memorandum* turned out to be Wichern's magnum opus, and, in the judgment of Peter Meinhold, "belongs to the classical works of the Evangelical Church."[2]

Wichern impressed readers by demonstrating his mastery of the issues in a clear and thorough presentation. He organized the document into three parts: a definition and explanation of Inner Mission; a review of its geographical locations and range of activities; and an administrative plan. The most appealing part for today's readers, and the one presented here, is part one, "General Description of the Inner Mission." Its appeal lies in the candid observations on conditions in Germany; in the explanation of the Inner Mission in relation to family, state, economic classes, and, above all, church; and in the characterization of the program's ecumenical breadth.

The foundation for Wichern's argument consists of two key points: Europe is in a moral and social crisis; and the church, by its very nature, is to practice loving service. From this foundation it is a short distance to the conclusion that the nation needs a concrete incarnation of loving service to meet the crisis. That incarnation is the Inner Mission. With the *Memorandum* Wichern hopes to promote the activities of love and compassion that "manifest Christ and rescue people for him," and he concludes with a stirring vision of the great work to be accomplished.

Part One:
General Description of the Inner Mission

For those who build their lives on the life of the Redeemer and follow the course of world events in his light it is axiomatic that life proceeds from death, resurrection from decay. This truth is anchored in the reality of Christ's incarnation and woven into the new Christian world order. The end of the old is the more glorious beginning of the new, just as spring, the herald of a fruitful summer, emerges from the hard winter and its wild storms. The gentle signs and stirrings of new life in the midst of the old, dying life escape most everyone's eyes. Some people are hindered by the activities and pressures of everyday work from paying attention to what is unpretentious and inconspicuous, while others are too little practiced in the one skill that would enable them to perceive the germ of the future in the aging present.

In many places where evangelical Christianity is found, these thoughts, along with the hopes and prayers produced by them, have been accompanied by the deep anguish and painful wounds that the past year has brought to our fatherland and its church. When the wild hurricane and volcanic tremors began to shake Europe, and Germany, too, plunged into the sea of revolution, with pestilence, revolt, and war proclaiming the judgment of God, then those who were waiting and watching saw in these events the birth pangs of a new and better age in the kingdom of God.

Even though deep moral decay, profound alienation, and widespread falling away from the gospel had manifested themselves in a variety of horrible forms, few people recognized the actual enemy who for decades had been undermining the solid foundation. However, at the heart of a very firmly anchored segment of Christianity a force had been developing for a long time that recognized the source of the spreading disaster and had already put the axe to its roots. These roots had sent their tendrils into all areas of life—public and private, church and state, work and leisure—to men and women of every rank. Nevertheless, the hand that offered healing followed the twists and turns of the roots wherever they went, even though the pernicious power had had a tremendous head start. For a number of decades the active proclamation of Christ and salvation through him alone had found its way into the hearts of many people. This proclamation of the Word had reached their hearts despite, or precisely because of, both the disgrace the Word brought and the ever-bolder contempt people showed for it.

Through the spirit of this miraculous Word and out of the depths of faith that emerged from it a love sprang forth, often without the proclaimers knowing or hearing about it, indeed, in places they had never really intended. This love, coming to life with a clear vision, began to move out from itself in order to discover what its presence could offer, for it alone can save and preserve individual people as well as entire states.

In this context we do not fail to appreciate what Christian scholarship and Christian skills have accomplished, how they have renewed the Christian way of life here and there, and how, in terms of actual religious education, they have brought such good things to the people. But that which was new, special, and had not previously appeared as it did now, was found in the stirrings and expressions of a **love** that was powerful in faith and active for **Christ**. This love, weary of and gradually freeing itself from mawkishness and feebleness, desired to manifest **Christ** and **rescue** people for **him.**

Not by chance, but by logical necessity, this love adopted from **society** a form of organization that had become an increasingly effective way of meeting most other human needs. That is, in response to the widespread decay, and according to the need of those in distress, it formed a great number of free, Christian fellowships. These fellowships are all one in their foundation and one in their goal. Their foundation is their faith in Christ as the savior of the lost. Their goal is, by means of Christ's Word and the helping hand of brotherly love, to free the people from the crises that have arisen from sin and its consequences. All of these gradually developed and little-known Christian efforts to rescue people constitute for us the **Inner Mission.**

When in the memorable spring of 1848 we experienced the turning point in world history whose consequences we will not be able to comprehend for a long time, it appeared for a moment as though these already present, quiet Inner Mission activities for peace would be buried under the massive ruins. Only a small number of people continued to think of the efforts in a kindly way, while others turned away from what had become "inconsequential," away from these "trivial things." Such things, people thought, would have to give way to "bigger things" and die out. People gave little thought to the fact that in the midst of the instability that had developed, these structures, because they were founded directly on the Redeemer, because of their internal and external freedom, and because of their relative independence from all other institutions, had a firmer foundation than could have been achieved by any other means.

Many people believe that God has reserved for the future a great calling for the Inner Mission. This **Memorandum** will take up the issues of where God has led the Inner Mission up to now; what immediate tasks he has placed before it; what connections it has already established with the other most sacred relationships in the lives of the people; and, as of now, what hopes are blossoming with it after the overturning of the old ways of life. Throughout the exposition, the **Memorandum** will pay special attention to the role of the Central Committee.[3] This presentation makes no claim to be complete. It speaks of many things for the first time, and for that

299

reason hopes all the more that people will understand. Above all, it does not want to cause conflict with its brothers and sisters but rather work with them toward unifying effectively against the common enemy who has turned against all of us and has been working hard to woo the masses of people who up to now have been left to their own devices.

The **Memorandum** seeks to open the door for a word of Christian compassion to the miserable and dejected people of our nation. Naturally, it seeks support of this goal from those first and foremost who welcome the Inner Mission as a conquering weapon blessed by God for the salvation of the people. Yet this **Memorandum** also hopes to serve as a willing, reliable, and unselfish friend and guide to those who are unfamiliar with these endeavors of Christian love.

We consider the Inner Mission to be not this or that **individual** activity but the **entire** work of love born of faith in Christ. This work desires to renew, within and without, the **masses of people in Christendom** who have fallen prey to the manifold expressions of inward and outward corruption that, directly or indirectly, have sprung from the power and domination of sin and who have not been reached by the ordained Christian offices, as would be necessary for their Christian renewal. Neither any inner nor outward crisis that can be met by the work of Christian, saving love lies outside the bounds of the Inner Mission. Furthermore, the Inner Mission has at its command the most abundant wealth of aid, for its work is rooted in Christ, whose heart is moved by every need and in whose heart is found help for all misery.

Since the founding of his kingdom, a Christian atmosphere has gradually spread to all areas of life, both for individuals and nations, whether they are aware of it or not, and whether they accept it or oppose it. Within this Christian atmosphere the Inner Mission arises freely and creatively in a multitude of forms, in order, by reproaching sin and by healing, serving, and transfiguring life, to bestow **new** life. The Inner Mission takes advantage of the indestructible unity of life gained through Christ in state and church, in nation and family, and in all segments of Christian society, so that it can apply its saving powers of life to each respective need, wherever it is, and even before those in need call out for help.

With strength in its freedom the Inner Mission has already become an **international** and **interconfessional** institution. Christian nations, which otherwise often rebuff or even combat one another, and the church confessions and parties that otherwise often contradict or isolate themselves from each other while they go on handling their spiritual and material interests, have learned to help and serve each other. They have learned this through the work of the Inner Mission, which is theirs in common.

England has already helped France, Germany, and Switzerland—which in this context is inseparably connected with Germany—as well as all other Christian nations; Germany has helped France, Denmark, Sweden, and Russia; and France and Switzerland have done no less in already sharing with other nations the best they have learned from their practice of love. Likewise, the various confessions in these countries have begun to exchange their best gifts of helping love. If we are not greatly mistaken, this exchange must of logical necessity continue and increase. Even in the midst of the tension that seems to be developing at present in nations and confessions, this offer of a helping hand will, by and large, not cease, but rather increase.

This mutual help will increase because it is unperturbed by all existing hindrances and conflicts. The Inner Mission is not susceptible to them since they are totally foreign to its nature. In its sphere of activity the Inner Mission brings out the power of that most holy campaign whose goal is the one salvation of Christians from the clutches of the common enemy, whose well-defined presence has appeared in its atheistic and anti-Christian form with all its unholy, practical consequences. Even in the strangely twisted and distorted circumstances of the present age, in the face of which people become frightened, authorities grow powerless, and churches fall silent, the Inner Mission discerns the pleading of the people for **its** saving work. Trusting in grace and in the divine promise, it hopes for a salvation of society through which both state and church will rise again to new life and acquire a new form in Christ. The closer we come to this goal, the closer we come to the end of the work of the Inner Mission, since it views itself as nothing but a servant who, when the work is done, will withdraw from the scene.

For the successful development of the effectiveness of the Inner Mission it is imperative that its service be directed to those places where, within the existing structures of Christian life, it properly should serve. From the very start the Inner Mission has always been on friendly terms with its circle of opponents in spite of their opposition. Their doubts and misgivings arise as a result of the relative newness of the cause, and certainly any of these opponents can be won over through the place that the Inner Mission takes. As long as the opponents do not dispute the gospel, one can, through discussion, at least build a basis for understanding.

On the other hand, it is equally necessary for the friends and supporters of the Inner Mission to come to an agreement about certain principles of practice in order to move forward with a sure step and be certain they are on the right path. Above all, it is of practical importance in this context that the Inner Mission have a clear understanding of its relationship to family, state, and church, and that it make this relationship clear.

The **family, state,** and **church**—with the essential offices that are implicit in them—are the three focal points around which the activity of the Inner Mission is gathered. The Inner Mission regards all three unquestionably as divine institutions having a vital interrelationship, considers them sacred, and aligns itself with them in order to help them attain their highest goals. The Inner Mission does this because a spirit that, in comparison to them, is obviously **far more** aware of its goal, is working hard to overthrow these three. For a long time this spirit has been seeking and finding access to the masses so that, if possible, it can stamp out the belief that these three institutions are from God's hand, thereby completing the overthrow of everything that is precious and holy. Hence, the calling of the Inner Mission is clear: by the power and deeds of the Christian spirit to preserve these sacred institutions, the offices serving within them, and the means belonging to them; to reopen in them the springs of truth and salvation; and to bring the masses of people alienated from **Christ** to recognize him again as the common Lord and foundation, the common bond and center of the threefold order.

In our view the real starting point for any discussion about the so-called **social** questions is the **family.** As a result of the power and implications of the conviction that the family is a divinely ordained institution, the Inner Mission will be shaped and guided not merely by its fight against socialist initiatives, but, in many ways, by its positive efforts to prevent aberrations and to discover the right ways in which to exert a positive influence. One of the main tasks of the Inner Mission—one to which this **Memorandum** will have to return frequently and in more detail—is to reestablish Christian families and households in all respects and to bring about the renewal and rebirth of all directly related affairs of education, property, and work, as well as the classes determined by work.

In reference to the **state** the Inner Mission is able to distinguish its responsibilities from the particular responsibilities of the state's political and economic systems. The Inner Mission is not predisposed to represent any one specific political view about constitutions and their design. It participates in politics only to the extent that politics coincides with **this** Word of God held fast by the Inner Mission: "Every person should be subject to the authority that has power over that person, for there is no authority that does not come from God, and wherever there is authority, it is established by God. Whoever resists authority resists God's order" [Rom 13:1–2]. The individual and general falling away from this truth within the mass of people is a summons to the Inner Mission to put its salutary powers into action. The purpose of this action is to get people to recognize once again that authority is divinely instituted and lawful, and that their freedom is rooted in it.

To be sure, the Inner Mission carries out this action with the weapons of the spirit, since force and compulsion are foreign to it. Its realm is that of freedom and love. Accordingly—that is, without relinquishing this freedom—it will be ready to serve the state in any situation, whenever and wherever in its territory the state requests deeds of Christian mercy, wisdom, and power. Yes, it will be the task

303

of the Inner Mission, through its totally unselfish service and voluntary sacrifices of goods and life, to bring the state to admit that, given its embarrassments, needs, and dangers, it too finds its ultimate source of life in Christ and nowhere else. Initially the Inner Mission expects nothing from the state but the granting of the right to free association for its purposes, without which it cannot reach its full potential, as well as the right to pursue its voluntary service, service that is obviously spurned by the state or so little of which can be pressed from the state in comparison to the amount required of the Inner Mission.

We must go into greater detail regarding the role of the Inner Mission within the **church.** Wherever the church is, its opponents and those indifferent to it turn away from the activity of the Inner Mission, while friends of the church take a very different position. That is, some of them bless the Inner Mission as a genuine friend and servant of congregations, while others view it with mistrust as a force allegedly destructive of the church. They are afraid of it and would be inclined even to attack it. The widest variety of interests intersects at this point, where they encounter this worker of peace on whose behalf we now speak. However, the Inner Mission is absolutely sure that its favor and love cannot be denied those who understand its hopes and the spirit of its work.

The Inner Mission is neither an organism outside of, nor alongside, the church, nor, as people fear, does it want to be the church, either now or in the future. Rather, it wants to reveal one side of the church's life, namely, the life of the spirit of faith-filled love that looks for the lost, abandoned, and neglected masses until it finds them. The Inner Mission acknowledges the boundaries placed on it by foreign missions, by confessions, and by the ordained office.

The Inner Mission is neither mother nor daughter of foreign missions, but rather its twin, and, like it, a daughter of the one spirit. The Inner Mission hopes for growth of, and rejoices in, the success of foreign missions without wanting to mingle its own work with that of its sister. The Inner Mission does not convert the unbaptized, neither Jews nor heathen, but works within the church in the realm of the **baptized.** It never regards the baptized as heathen, for the special worth of baptism, as a highly sacred sacrament, is its irrevocability. Consequently, the Inner Mission never forgets that it is working with people to whom the Lord already bestowed himself personally in the sacrament.

In this connection, one special facet of the role of the Inner Mission will not emerge until the anti-Christian element in the spirit of the age and the related Satanism—this already exists in strength and cannot be called anything else—have taken over more territory in people's hearts. It seems to be beyond doubt that we will have a generation of those who are neither Jews, nor pagans, nor Christians. Will the battle against this development and the **bringing back** to the church of those who have fallen away become the task of the **Inner** Mission? It appears to us that only those who do not recognize the facts pointing to this development—and they are manifold and widespread—can dispute that such a future is quickly closing in on us. With many initiatives the Inner Mission already stands at the brink of the fateful **new** day, and up to the present has been carrying out the battle at that frontier with those who have been baptized.

Confession is another boundary to the activity of the Inner Mission. The Inner Mission does not get involved in the arguments of confessional bodies. It recognizes true religious expression of doctrine in one's devotion and in what comes from the heart. Wherever the Inner Mission steps forth to work in a teaching capacity it works as a daughter of the church in its confessional sphere. In regard to doctrine, its task within the scope of the church is to transform doctrine into spirit and life for the masses who are not acquainted with it, or for whom it has become dead words, while not changing the content of the doctrine itself.

Yet even more central to the Inner Mission than doctrine is the helping, serving deed. The Inner Mission carries out its deeds purely as acts of compassion, without asking who is being served. Rather, true to the example offered by the great Samaritan, it has already served before it is asked.

Until now the Inner Mission has encountered no hindrances to its activity of love due to differences between the confessions within the Protestant Church. In word and deed the confessions have expressed their unity in relation to this work of compassion. We know of no conflict caused by the Inner Mission in the Evangelical Church. Such conflicts are also to be avoided with the Roman Catholic Church, and this will be even more the case on the evangelical side, as long as any tendency of the Evangelical Inner Mission to draw believers over from the other side is rejected. Not only is there no justification for doing this, but also if one did, then one could not deny the other confession the right to do the same. If we proceeded to do this anyhow, we would forget how much work still needs to be done in our own house, and what a far higher goal we ought to aim for by mutually encouraging love in both church communities. Both Western churches not only can learn from each other about this love, but also indeed have learned already. Naturally, the preservation of the rights of each confession does not rule out extending, either mutually or singly, the hand of love in the service of those in need. Nor does it rule out any less the common struggle, organized according to the respective camps, against the common, anti-Christian enemy who deems all Christian church communities, indeed, every religion and form of worship, without distinction, worthy of extermination.

In general I wish to refrain from presenting my convictions of a more personal nature. However, were this *Memorandum* an appropriate forum for such expression, then this would be the place to present the Inner Mission as the great practical-catholic force that is beginning to penetrate and deeply unify the various **churches** and **Christian nationalities.** The Inner Mission, born in God's Spirit, is the reality of Christianity's love and compassion that are rooted in and rule in Christ. The Inner Mission is the self-transfiguration of the God-man—the one who saves everything that is lost—in his community.

Meanwhile, having reached this point in our argument it is no longer necessary to delay an issue mentioned earlier, namely, the relationship of the Inner Mission to the church's **ordained** office, in particular the ordained office in the **parish.** We will examine this issue to the extent that it relates to our concerns. By parish office we mean not merely the office of preaching with its service of Word and sacraments, along with pastoral care in the parish. Rather, we also mean all other ordained offices in the church, namely, in the presbytery and in the permanently ordained diaconate, the latter of which is in many ways related to the Inner Mission. The Inner Mission places at the head of its activity the full recognition of these and all other offices as orders established and sanctified by God. Any intentional disruption or hampering of the church's offices caused by a supposed Inner Mission activity would become an object of concern for the true Inner Mission.

On the other hand, the Inner Mission can rightfully expect no less recognition of its rights from the ordained office. It can expect this recognition since the practice of saving love is the duty of the church, and the church, by means of its office, wants to arouse the practice of this duty. If not, it will inhibit the amelioration of the most dangerous crises.

A look at the dreadful condition of the church will offer us indispensable help in determining precisely the demarcation between the Inner Mission's field of work and that of the office of the congregation. In addition, this determination will help us identify the particular task and form of the Inner Mission's activity within the parish and in the church in general.

Sin and moral decay have brought about a crisis today. The relevance of this situation for our discussion is that the nature of sin and moral decay in the church and, for the most part, in individual congregations, has become twofold. On the one hand, it is more of an individual, personal nature, making its appearance in people one by one. On the other hand, it is more of a societal, general nature, encompassing the whole of society, affecting **masses** of people. Likewise, some manifestations of sin and their respective crises are limited **locally** to specific parishes, while others go beyond the purview of the parish unit, having spread through the whole church or at least a great number of the individual parishes. These are the crises that belong to the **church** as a whole, to the church as the connecting and uniting bond of all the individual congregations.

We see a parallel phenomenon in the ailing condition in the material life of the people. Here, too, we can differentiate between the impoverishment of the individual and that of the masses. The impoverishment of individuals in a community is something that can be accounted for and treated quite differently than the impoverishment of an entire community or of a large complex of communities. While in the first case the normal office for assistance of the poor is capable of meeting or eliminating the need, in the second case—that is, in the face of a need of epidemic proportions, of pauperism as impoverishment on a national scale—the help offered by offices for the poor in the individual communities will only fail. The **state,** whose means to attack the problem are the most extensive and encompassing, must make the crisis its own responsibility. The office of the church and the Inner Mission relate to the distinctly religious crisis in the same way. Both of them will have to identify and delegate tasks, based on whether the crisis in a parish is localized, broader in scope, or extends even beyond the parishes as an issue of the **church.**

The scattered, grotesque manifestations of sin within parishes—for example, the individual who despises the divine Word, the instance of an unchristian household, the drunkard here or there—are the responsibility of the church's ordained spiritual office and come under the care of the pastor or the diaconate, who in individual cases cross over into the realm of the Inner Mission. The same is true for a parish's care of the poor, as long as that care is within the church's purview.

However, the situation is entirely different when sin and corruption are on a huge, epidemic scale and have become characteristic of the entire people; when a non-church, anti-church, anti-Christian spirit and lawlessness have penetrated and taken hold of the parish in general, or parts of it, affecting everyone or certain circles and classes; when sin, vice, and the misery proceeding from them become an inundating flood indifferent to the individual parish, beyond its control, and transcending local parish boundaries.

Particularly in large cities, where the actual ecclesiastical framework and organization often have crumbled or were never present in the first place, the agents of the church stand forlorn in the chaotic confusion, without any firm organizational footing.

They are neither authorized nor officially obliged—at least never strongly enough—to grasp hold of the moral, social, and religious decay and bring it to a halt, to say nothing of forcing it to retreat. And how altogether difficult or impossible it is to help where collegial difficulties in the parish come into play!

Just think of the alienation from God and the indifference to the church; of the dependence on mammon and the chasing after money, honor, and pleasure; of the inner strife in the middle classes; of the vice of alcohol and sexual offenses; of the widespread ruin of family lives in the upper and lower levels of society; of the manifold corruption and waywardness of youth who have run wild; and of the increasing degeneration of the household, which is due to and accompanies impoverishment. Just think of the nomadic streams of traveling manual laborers, of the throngs of day laborers and railroad workers, of conditions for seamen in the port cities, and of the criminals who are released by the thousands every year. We need only remind ourselves of these circumstances in order to be certain we agree that they constitute a yet unfulfilled responsibility of the **church.** Or who would deny that in the face of these circumstances the **church** needs to develop new powers of rescue born of faith, new, comprehensive initiatives through which the Christian populace, in all its groups and classes in state and church, must be helped! Just as the state has to get to the bottom of and counteract material pauperism in all of its causes and effects by summoning up entirely new strength and applying such **far-**reaching measures that **all** citizens will feel them and will have to contribute to them either directly or indirectly, so too the church, in its own way, must combat the inner pauperism that is its responsibility, that is, the manifestations throughout the populace of **massive** moral and Christian degeneration.

While the state and those who carry out its responsibilities are still searching in vain for means to remedy material pauperism and are at a loss to know what to do, the church, in contrast, already possesses the help it needs. The source of this help lies entirely in the unfolding power of the Inner Mission. Its task, and that of the ordained office freely associated with it, is to reduce the **massive moral decay** in the Christian populace. In the Inner Mission the church has new ways and means it can use and new resources it can offer to investigate, combat, and finally conquer this evil. These are ways, means, and resources that should affect equally **all** sound members of the church, and to which **everyone** must contribute by working and sacrificing in free love, just as in the other domain they cannot refrain from acting similarly by helping the state.

Yes, the true members of the church will have to work and sacrifice **doubly** since the needs of the state **and** church affect them and call out to them for help. Without a doubt it will become unmistakably clear to them that pauperism and the crisis in the masses which the state is to combat are, with **few** exceptions, intimately connected with the inner crisis whose relief is the task of the church. So, too, it will become clear that the various remedies for the crises in both domains are intimately connected. In fact, whether the life of the people is to be improved from the ground up depends precisely on recognizing this **connection** and organizing the means of assistance **according to it.**

Likewise, given this viewpoint, one cannot speak of any conflict between the office of the church and the activity of the Inner Mission. The true spirit of compassion and inner liberation that keeps the ultimate goal before one's eyes will recognize with ever-increasing clarity the inner unity but at the same time the necessity of dividing up the work. This spirit will also freely acknowledge that with the Inner Mission a new force for salvation has been born in the church and should continue to grow. This new momentum for salvation will seek and find its place in every **true parish,** bringing to fruition there, far more than in the Inner Mission, all the fullness of love, wisdom, and gifts that Christ has given to his community called to do the work of salvation. There one will see revealed in an irrefutable way that the Christian life itself is an **office** given up only at death, an office of emulation. It is emulation of the one who is preached to the congregation in the Word, and given in the sacrament, as he who showed compassion to all, yet first to "tax collectors and sinners" [Matt 11:19; Luke 7:34; 15:2], and who desires to have this compassion activated in the parish and in the church as its Inner Mission.

In what has already been said we have an indication of what **form** Inner Mission activity will have to take. First of all, for example, its form does not grant each spiritually sound individual in the parish the **right,** but rather it addresses each person's conscience primarily in terms of **duty,** to work in the spirit of the Inner Mission where one is. In their congregations the clergy are to be children of this spirit for the households and parish members who are in need of saving activity. Likewise, in their households fathers and mothers are to be children of the same spirit with their children and servants, relatives and friends; so, too, the master craftsman with his apprentices and trainees, and, in turn, the servants, apprentices, and day laborers with their circle. The schoolteacher is to be of the same spirit in school to the extent that it is required, as well as the businessman in his occupation, the lord of the estate, the judge, the statesman, the professor, salesman, soldier, sailor, city folk, farmers, and everyone else, wherever God has placed them. The true power and glory of the Christian community will be revealed wherever this life of saving, helping love blossoms forth in many individuals in the church. Their activity makes a reality of the **general priesthood** (the laity principle) in which the church achieves fulfillment in itself, and, of course, in Christ who transfigures himself in the individuals as the saving Redeemer.

All citizens are affected by the need and suffering brought on by the massive deterioration of material life, so the help of the state is invoked. The state calls upon everyone for assistance, sometimes even for compulsory contributions or work. So, too, it should be for the church and its crisis, although for its work the church would far rather enlist voluntary sacrifices and the voluntary activation of love from all vital members of the body of the Lord. It desires to see them rise like one priestly people offering its brothers and sisters blessings, prayer, and work, helping through word and deed in spirit and power so that everyone is helped. This is what we mean when we say the Inner Mission is based on the concept of the general priesthood. The general priesthood neither interferes with nor restricts the ordained office in the congregation but rather allows this office, as the agent that administers the divine Word and the sacrament, to be recognized properly as the head and organic center of the congregation. By helping in this way, by bringing together around the Word those who are dead and those who have fallen away, the life-filled and vitalizing members of the congregation unite in a new, truly evangelical way around the office.

At the same time, the foregoing discussion suggests that in view of the **massive amount of sin and need,** the life-filled members cannot forge ahead chaotically, en masse, but must form ranks in a systematic way, joining together in saving phalanxes. The purpose of this arrangement can be none other than to confront the general corruption that has overgrown the parish or pervades the entire church with a similarly far-reaching, organized resurrection and raising up of the church to be the free community of **God,** bringing the message and gift of salvation wherever and however it is needed.

A unique feature of this arrangement is the freedom in which the ranks are formed, not the freedom that is capricious and simply defies constraints, but which is of a higher order based on the gifts of the Holy Spirit and cannot help but follow the urgings of love. If there is one way in which the inadequacy of the church's statutes come to light, it is that they provide no guarantee that the gifts and the office will coincide, no matter how much the Spirit that forms the congregations from above desires precisely this confluence [1 Cor 12:1–13]. How can we meet this apostolic demand on the life of the congregation? At present scarcely any other solution seems possible than the free, more or less fluid formation of groups within the church and congregations, such as really exist in the realm of the Inner Mission. Yet the groups are not aimed at the office, nor are they organized for that purpose. They are not based on laws and orders of the church hierarchy. Rather, they emerge freely, full of vitality and effectiveness, at the heart of many congregations that have achieved a truly apostolic power through them.

Out of these circles have come forth many hundreds of institutes and voluntary workers—come forth in a way never before seen in the church. All of these voluntary, Christian structures will have a bright future once they are generally and genuinely recognized and supported by the church as resources serving to build the church. Through the unity of the two elements—the strictly established office, on the one hand, and the more fluid Inner Mission, on the other—the order of things will come about all the sooner whereby the office increases and the Inner Mission decreases.

Through this unity the selfless tendency of the true Inner Mission will appear with ever more clarity. The clarity will increase the more it serves others and produces fruit, and the more it desires and works toward its own dissolution. As a result, the church and its individual parishes can move more confidently toward a future in which they will have become rich enough to take care of the needs of their own ordained offices and, due to the new spirit flowing into the church, will have unfolded a new wealth of offices—offices for which the Inner Mission offers models today. This future remains, of course, far off, but we should not linger a moment before setting out to reach it.

Details about how the Inner Mission activity of the various associations can be unified with the church office and hence with the parish itself will be taken up later in this document.[4]

At this point, in order to avoid any misunderstandings from the start, I would like to reject specifically the opinion that the Inner Mission is nothing but a work of charity carried out in a Christian context, hence a renewed Christian care of, support of, or work for the poor. On this fundamental misjudgment the view is based that the entire work of the Inner Mission is the same thing as what people have called the church's care of the poor. The otherwise splendid negotiations in the Swiss Synod during the final months of 1848 proceeded entirely from similar assumptions.[5] It is, of course, fully correct that in many cases the Inner Mission is involved with the poorer classes, but this is in part only because so many of those who lack the gospel are among the needy, and in part because the Inner Mission has not achieved sufficient clarity about what it should and wants to do, namely, to bring Christian life and the riches and treasures of peace and rebirth to the places where they are missing. One can think of the most munificent activity of the Inner Mission—and such does exist—which does not require a single act of material assistance. It is possible to think of a parish in which the rich and educated constitute the only field the Inner Mission can select because they are poor in God, while the poor, because they are rich in him, could be its supporters.

The Inner Mission works independently of all societal classes, standing at the center of a people composed of all classes. In every class the Inner Mission has representatives who work for it. In every class it has particular tasks that it must perform. The more freely the Inner Mission proclaims and explains itself in this sense; the more straightforwardly, in this spirit, it rebukes sin, attacks godlessness, pursues immorality, and breaks down pride without regard to the person; the more fearlessly it works for justice in **all** classes; and the more precisely it follows its spiritual compass; then the more gratefully the hearts of all those—high or low—who understand the people will open up to the Inner Mission; then the more readily they will find access into hovels and palaces. From the rich, the poor, and the middle classes who share its spirit the Inner Mission must enlist workers, though not in a calculated way, but because it can be no other way, because their lives bring about this forming and mixing of members.

In this way the various classes of citizens—in actuality, the whole people—are united in Christ under the umbrella and the blessing hand of the church, and salvation goes forth in all directions. In the power of this community—thus as an action of the whole people—and, in this spirit, renovating the church into a people's church, the Inner Mission will become a sermon to the poor. It will search out those multitudes of miserable, hungry, naked, and impoverished people who are feared by the one, despised by another, and misused by the third. It will establish works of mercy among them, foster existing works, and connect the dissociated ones. In this way the poor will see who really has them in their heart, and the rich will discover how they can give their hearts—and their gifts from the heart—to those whom Christ has left in his place so that we can love him in them.

Yet even where such offerings might no longer be needed, the Inner Mission would have to keep working until nothing were any longer opposed or inaccessible to the spiritual order of the parish.

The charity that is also practiced by the Inner Mission in the name of the Lord is, as often as not, an interim stage in its work, frequently, yet only coincidentally, connected with its work, and in no case its actual purpose.

The full significance and lofty ecclesiastical justification of the Inner Mission, as well as the deep obligation to it, can be appreciated only by knowing its history. However, we still await the historian.[6]...[I]f the history [of the Inner Mission] is ever written, then the German Christians will discover in this story what a wealth of God's grace and wonderful love has been preserved in them and directs their lives, and in how many hidden places faith, prayer, patience, and hope have done their work. They will discover how the beginnings of that which is greatest, upon which many now place their hope for salvation, are found in the hearts of the least. They will discover how in Christ both rich and poor, high and low, those of all ages and both genders have put their hands to the task. They will discover how God's treasure chambers were, and still are, open to the poorest, and how love for the church and awareness of the one fellowship in it, even if deeply hidden, had not died out among us. They will discover how in this field an abundance of talents and character strengths developed just when they were needed in order to lay the foundation for a lasting work.

The highly diverse activities are found at hundreds of scattered locations, yet they are united in Christ, and through their collective effort the history of the Inner Mission's work has, after thirty or forty years, reached a new stage. Now, in the midst of these stormy times, the Inner Mission can step into the wider circle of all the friends of the people and of the church, believing it can offer its hand to the evangelical people for their salvation and to the church for its service.

Report About Diaconal Service and the Diaconate

EDITORS' INTRODUCTION: Wichern's *Report*[1] is much more than a report. It is also a clarion call for diaconal service. In the judgment of Wichern's biographer, Peter Meinhold, the *Report*, together with the *Memorandum*, "is the decisive document for the renewal of the Evangelical Church of the nineteenth century."[2] In no other document does Wichern identify more succinctly the roots of Christian service, and in so doing, reveal the origins of his own spirituality, vocation, and vision for the church.

The term Wichern uses in the title and throughout, *die Diakonie*, is the German equivalent of the Greek *diakonia*, referring to the concept or practice of ministering to or serving someone. Since Wichern consistently uses the word in reference to the work that is done, we have translated it here as "diaconal service." Less clear is Wichern's differentiation between *Diakonie* and *Innere Mission*. On the surface Inner Mission ought to be a broader concept, because Wichern begins the *Report* by asserting that diaconal service is aimed at the poor, while Inner Mission, according to what Wichern says elsewhere, covers a broader spectrum of needs. However, the more he explains diaconal service, the more comprehensive or perhaps fundamental this activity appears.

Wichern begins by explaining that state, church, and private individuals can practice diaconal service. Yet the church has completely neglected it. Lest the void be filled by the state, the church must reenter the field by reviving the office of the diaconate. In defense of this ministry Wichern points to the historic precedent of diaconal service in God's care for the people of Israel.

Wichern then traces the history of God's care into the New Testament, concluding with the assertion that "Christ's incarnation is the full revelation of diaconal service. He summarizes the reason for his coming with one word, that he came to serve." Serving love, the distinguishing feature of Christ's life, is to be the mark of those who follow him.

Wichern highlights two facets of this love. First, it simultaneously serves a person's mysteriously but intimately connected spiritual and physical life. Second, serving love becomes concrete only in sharing with another. Consequently, since the Christlike life is inseparable from family, household, and community, diaconal service affects not only individual but also communal life. With the end of this discussion Wichern brings to a close the first section of the *Report*. The remainder of the document, not included in this volume, presents a historical review of diaconal service in the West, beginning with the Roman Empire.

General Survey of the Content

We want to indicate briefly the viewpoint from which the issue of diaconal service and the diaconate is treated in the following report.

Diaconal service is loving care turned toward the poor. In the pagan world before Christ and during Christ's lifetime there was no diaconal service. It is the signature of Christianity. Because of its nature there is only one diaconal service, like the revealed love of God himself, from which it derives. When this service appears, however, it is broken up as in a prism. Its tasks, starting with the simplest, have proliferated into the richest variety. The original form in which diaconal service appeared in Christianity is the norm, insofar as it contains the basic principle. However, under the changing conditions of history this form takes on a variety of chief configurations within which the original form is either retained or, if it has diminished or weakened, can and must be restored anew.

Looking at these chief configurations we can distinguish between three kinds of diaconal work: the church, the civil, and the private. These three are as different as the corresponding societal spheres of church, civil, and private life, and likewise should be kept separate from each other as a matter of principle. Not differentiating these three kinds of diaconal service has been the source of deep, harmful confusion. Mixing them together, or neglecting or elevating one in relation to the others, ultimately ruins even the favored one.

So it was that in the Middle Ages the church's care of the poor, which along with the church had become incapable of effectively countering the state, ruined the civil care of the poor immediately after it had begun, and brought about its own end, which the whole world could see at the time of the Reformation. In turn, civil care of the poor likewise ruined the beginnings of the newly intended church care, as the latter, along with the church, lost the power of the divine Word. Today the civil form has again reached a severe crisis and lost the people's confidence.

These shifting circumstances produce dangers not only for the well-being of the poor but, at the same time, for all the people. If, for example, the civil care of the poor takes over the entire sphere of diaconal service, then, in principle, the state is gradually compelled to become a socialist system. In the end, only the appearance of true diaconal service remains. It becomes mere philanthropy or administration. It becomes a caricature of itself, and the conscience of the people is ruined to the core.

Therefore, we see that our task is to categorize diaconal service properly and connect organically the various parts from the lowest to the highest levels. A portion of this task will be to reorganize the rather deteriorated main forms and conserve or purify those forms of diaconal service that do exist. According to our view, for example, no church care of the poor exists at all today. Whatever is inadvertently given that name is essentially free diaconal service or a lifeless shadow of the truth.

In contrast, civil care of the poor has taken over the entire field. As the proper antidote to this destructive excess, free diaconal service has again come into its own in the dual form of individuals and associations putting Christian love into action. Yet here, too, new dangers have arisen, even if only sporadically—namely, in the associations—by their tendency toward separatism or creating utopian Christian worlds.

However, this path in the history of diaconal service in the life of our evangelical people appears to us to be a providential one, as well. Given the current state of affairs the call has gone out for diaconal service to arise in the church again. However, the true, full awakening of the church's diaconal service is dependent on the renewal of the apostolic diaconate. This diaconate is an independent office of the church and is to be an organ and member of the ecclesiastical order of offices. As such, it manifests the grandeur and fullness of love to the poor in its intended role as an integral part of parish and church. Diaconal service perceived in this way, viewed not in opposition to but in harmony with civil and private service, appears to us to be the only possible mediator for the entire field of loving care in state, church, and private life.

Our intention in the following is to pursue these thoughts in a little more detail. The limited room for this report, which, moreover, might have to be appended to an already existing presentation—the *Memorandum*[3]—allows only a fragmentary analysis. Nevertheless, the discussion will, for the time being, provide ample support of the views presented, both in regard to basic principles and, in particular, in regard to prevailing, practical circumstances. From what has been said already, one can see that in the end our attention is directed to the diaconate. Earlier and recent literature on the subject and relevant historical documentation are not cited specifically, but have been taken into account as much as possible throughout this report.

I. Diaconal Service in the History of God's Revelation

First we will recall with a few broad strokes how diaconal service developed in the world as a product of divinely revealed love and remind ourselves of the further development and fulfillment promised by the Word of God. This discussion of the foundations provides, if only to a limited extent, the scriptural support for the value, significance, and justification of the very existence of diaconal service.

The richly compassionate love of God that helps, saves, disciplines, supports, cares for, and reaches down to the misery and needs of sinful humanity is the radiant light shining through the entire pre-history of Christian revelation. In this love God chooses and sanctifies in Abraham one **family** out of which he transforms a people into God's family. Israel, the people, is in the deepest sense of the word, a "house." Jehovah is the head of the house, and from his hands the people as a whole, and each individual member, receives everything necessary for body and soul. This people is a people of the poor, who are all cared for and maintained by Jehovah, as the *diaconus*, deacon of the people. He promises and gives the people a land blessed with vineyards, he sends rain early and late, and he alone looks after their life and limb. Therefore, he alone is due the honor in this house.

Yet whenever the people give him the honor and bring him their offerings of thanks and praise, the Lord gathers the family anew around his table in the temple and nourishes it with holy meals that are referred to as "being joyful before the Lord" [Deut 27:7]. This love manifests itself to the people no less in miracles and signs. In miraculous ways, for example, he offers the people manna in the desert, opens springs of water in the rock, and heals them from the bite of fiery serpents [Exod 16:11 ff.; 17:1 ff.; Num 21:4 ff.]. The veiling of this love during the age of the judges, as under Ahab [1 Kgs 16:28], is the incentive for its all the more glorious revelation through the words and deeds of an Elijah and Elisha [e.g., 1 Kgs 17:17 ff.; 2 Kgs 2:8; 4:8 ff.].

The Lord calls upon the members of his household to imitate the love of God by loving one another. In the basic law of the people he places the genuinely poor in the merciful care of those who live from nothing but his divine mercy. The revelation of Jehovah in the laws of Sinai breathes a spirit of love toward the needy, debtors, orphans, widows, and strangers, to whom later, as in Amos,[4] prisoners are added [cf. Isa 61:1; Luke 4:18]. No trace of this spirit exists outside the land of revelation, in Greece or Rome, for example. The depth to which this spirit of helping love penetrates the hearts of faithful Israelites is documented by the constant flow of testimonies from the prophets—Amos, Isaiah, and others—by the prayers of David with their promises for the poor, by Solomon's proverbs, as well as by the sacrificial deeds of Nehemiah. Serving, merciful love toward the poor runs through all of these like a golden thread that we continue to trace until the one appears in whom this love finds its fulfillment as the love of the God-man.

Christ's incarnation is the full revelation of diaconal service. He summarizes the reason for his coming with one word, that he came to "serve" (ἦλθε—διακονῆσαι [he came—to serve/minister],[5] Matt 20:28). He becomes the true *diaconus*, deacon of his people (διάκονος περιτομῆς [deacon/minister to the circumcised], Rom 15:8). The light of his compassion radiates like the sun in its full splendor. In this compassion he wondrously connects the spiritual and the physical so that his apostle and evangelist is justified in interpreting the prophetic word about the suffering servant of the Lord in terms of this diaconal service, though its meaning might have seemed to point in a quite different direction (Matt 8:16–17).

The healing rays of this love flow into the hearts of the sick and into the confused cries of the mentally ill. To all of them he offers spiritual riches in earthly gifts. The conquering power of this love woos the poor, crippled, lame, blind, and those gathered from the highways and byways (Luke 14:21) and makes them models of those who are to surround him as kings and priests. He feeds thousands with but little bread and then proclaims **himself** the true bread of heaven. The exemplary story of the poor man before the rich man's door [Luke 16:20–21], the self-denying love of the compassionate Samaritan [Luke 10:30–35], the immeasurably meaningful words and parables offered from his sacred lips to the poor, needy, worried, and suffering for their comfort and renewal, and, in the end, his sacrificial deed, which he himself calls his greatest διακονεῖν [literally "to serve/minister," hence "diaconal service"] (Matt 20:28), complete in an inexhaustible way the archetypal model of diaconal service.

Yet there is more! He is not merely the subject of diaconal service; his love reaches its fulfillment when at the same time he becomes the object of that love. We see him as such in the fisherman's house at Capernaum (Matt 8:15), at the table of the sisters in Bethany [Luke 10:38], in the circle of his friends who give him lodging, with his disciples who feed him (John 4) and give him a place to sleep (Mark 4:38), and in the circle of the "many" women who follow him and give him of what they have (διηκόνουν αὐτῷ [they ministered to/served him], Luke 8:3). As the object of serving love he allows himself to be anointed by Mary [John 12:3], allows himself to be buried and adorned in the grave, and after his resurrection allows himself to be refreshed with fish and honey [Luke 24:42].

So it is that he teaches them to understand his words: "You always have the poor with you" [Matt 26:11], and "What you have done to one of the least of these, you have done to me" [Matt 25:40–45; 26:11; Mark 14:7; John 12:8]. Obviously his **entire** earthly life was borne by this love for his people. It was one love that he gave, and one love that he received, or wanted to receive, until his death.

What are his disciples to do when he sends them out but combine the proclamation of the kingdom of heaven with the demonstration of compassion like his. To this end he shares with them the power of his own glory. With his power, and as witnesses to his glory, they are to bring comfort, healing, and recovery to the suffering and outcast (Matt 10:1–8). Those who accept his gospel and believe in him will manifest their faith through their love by offering the disciples hospitality (Matt 10:11 ff.); whoever accepts one of his disciples accepts him (v. 40) and receives a great promise (v. 42). The experience of his love that bestows salvation is to ignite the "mutual love" of those desiring their salvation in him alone and is to perfect this love in the self-denial that derives from faith in his forgiveness. The fact that he has become the "deacon of the people" (Rom 15:8) is to cause the faithful to serve and receive one another (Rom 15:7), and in this way his love will be manifested in them.

This is the love that he made the distinguishing feature and mark of identity of those who are his own (John 13), and which he commanded that his apostles preach and practice when they went out in his name to win the multitudes of the nations for him (Matt 28). The ultimate goal ("ἵνα [the conjunction "that," as in, "the goal is

322

namely that you…"], John 13:34) of all his love for his people was to create this love in them, a reflection of the original love and fellowship that lives in the triune God as eternal life (John 13—17).

It could not be otherwise. The Son of Man, after completing his work on earth and pouring out his spirit, likewise became—since he is the inexhaustible divine fountain of love—the source and destination of a loving care that poured forth from him over everything that became his own in faith and returned to him again. His πνεῦμα ἅγιον [holy spirit] could only cause the κοινωνία [literally, "being together," that is, "community"] and διακονία [diaconal service] in his people. Thus, the new Christian community becomes the true Israel, the true house of God, the genuine family of God. In it, as in a new miracle of creation, dead humanity comes to life in love, and the love turns into loving care.

The practice of love is the pouring out, the living out, the embodiment of the love that lives and grows deeper only through giving, and it can give only by having become poor through the Holy Spirit and by having received everything from the Lord in faith. Into this practice of love flows the entire life of the newborn in Jerusalem; in it the entire life of the community becomes one life in **service to God.** The focus for both is the nourishment of the community with his body and blood, which comes from the Lord alone. His people's songs of thanks and praise gather around this food. In the presence of the eternal ruler who has sanctified everything, he alone remains rich, and all the rich become poor, and all the poor rich, so that no ones lacks anything, but rather everyone has enough, not only spiritually, but also physically (Acts 2:45; 4:32). One food that is **both earthly** and heavenly nourishes them all. Everyone has sacrificed everything to the Lord, and whatever anyone needs one gets back from the Lord.

Thus, the love of Christ produces the true "being joyful before the Lord," which under the old covenant was celebrated only in the temple and with infrequent thank-offerings when all the guests were at the table of the king of Israel [Deut 27:2]. Now, in this κοινωνία [community] each house becomes a temple and at the daily noon and evening meals the people remain the house and table companions of the eternal king. Thus, all life is born anew at the table of the Lord, which is the table of the house and at the same time the table of the great, new family of God. This was the κοινωνία [community] in which the general διακονία [diaconial service] came true, for who could belong to the community who did not, in giving or taking, participate in diaconal service? Through it a new plan of mercy is born in each house. Wherever the message of his salvation is carried, and wherever his holy supper is served, this new order of life, born in the Lord, also appears. It is the visible, aromatic, refreshing fruit that cannot help but grow to maturity wherever the word of life goes.

To the same extent that the community, as his body, keeps growing, so too this love shall and will grow until the end of time. One of the clearest prophetic words from Christ's lips connects diaconal service of the faithful directly with the end of this world and with the beginning of the fulfillment of God's kingdom (Matt 25). Going into specifics, the Lord calls to mind the respective personal needs of the poor, naked, hungry, thirsty, sick, imprisoned, and the pilgrims. He does this for the sake of the love that, in serving them, serves him (Matt 25:31 ff.). These words of the Lord contain no metaphoric language but are the presentation of the most concrete circumstances of everyday life that he wants to see saturated with love from his people, circumstances into which he wants to see his people immersed, and in which he wants them to search for **none other than himself. He** wants to remain the object of their diaconal service, which acts in extremely concrete forms, **until the end,** in order finally to reveal himself as the **Archshepherd,** who is, at the same time, the **Archdeacon,** who has "seen" his community "in that which is hidden," that is, in that which is most sacred (Matt 6:6).

Those whom he leads to fulfillment and eternal glory are, in turn, to share at last in his eternal, most holy diaconal service. They are to eat and drink at his table in his kingdom (Luke 22:29). He will "tie back his garment, show them to their places, and go about serving them" (Luke 12:37) in that great supper in whose unmistakable image the concept of diaconal service finds its highest expression in the complete, sacred family of God. This is how the great concept of diaconal service reaches its fulfillment in the scriptures.

In view of our task we would like to bring out just one point from everything that has been said up to now, and that is how important in this context the concepts of **house** and **family** become. The people of God, the community of God, is the house and family of God in which the Lord is the effervescent spring of caring love that brims over on all sides to awaken, maintain, and preserve the intimately connected spiritual and physical life. The Lord builds up and disciplines his house, he gives food and drink to his household companions, he gathers them around his table where they are guests and household companions, and he serves them with his gifts. One trivializes the real content that comes to light in the rich and manifold application of this concept if all of this is understood only metaphorically. Rather, in this language we recognize a ἀληθινόν [a true thing/truth] or καλόν [noble/beautiful thing] in the Gospel of John: in this family of God, and in the διακονεῖν [diaconal service] of the Lord that is devoted to it, we are given the actual archetypal image of the **family.** This model is reflected among humans to the extent that individual families and families of nations accept the kingdom of God and let the divine powers of God's family do their healing, disciplining, caring, and transfiguring work in them.

From this it is clear how the concept of diaconal service could not help but intervene in a deeply transforming and incomparably promising way in the entire personal and communal, private and public life in state and church when it proclaimed itself to the world in the person of Christ, full of glory and truth, and applied the plan of salvation to the full range of societal conditions.

Notes

INTRODUCTION

1. Helmut Rünger, *Heimerziehungslehre*, 2d ed. (Witten, 1964), p. 7, quoted in Erich Wittenborn, *Johann Hinrich Wichern als Sozialpädagoge, dargestellt an seiner Rettungshauserziehung* (Wuppertal, 1982), p. 261.

2. Martin Gerhardt, *Johann Hinrich Wichern: Ein Lebensbild*, 2 vols. (Hamburg, 1927), vol. 1, p. 30. For the entire diary, see *Der junge Wichern: Jugendtagebücher Johann Hinrich Wicherns*, ed. Martin Gerhardt (Hamburg, 1925).

3. Johann Hinrich Wichern, *Hamburgs wahres und geheimes Volksleben*, in *Johann Hinrich Wichern: Sämtliche Werke*, ed. Peter Meinhold (Berlin and Hamburg, 1958–80), vol. 4, part 1, *Schriften zur Sozialpädagogik: Rauhes Haus und Johannesstift* (Berlin, 1958), p. 42.

4. Johann Hinrich Wichern, *Wicherns Ansprache auf der Gründungsversammlung des Rauhen Hauses vom 12. September 1833 in Hamburg*, in *Schriften*, vol. 4, part 1, p. 101.

5. Ibid., p. 102.

6. Ibid., pp. 107–8. On the shape and goals of the cottage-home system in contrast to the old asylums, see Leroy Ashby, *Saving the Waifs: Reformers and Dependent Children, 1890–1917* (Philadelphia, 1984), pp. 6–7, 30–31.

7. Johann Hinrich Wichern, *Gutachten über die Diakonie und den Diakonat*, in *Johann Hinrich Wichern: Sämtliche Werke*, ed. Peter Meinhold (Berlin and Hamburg, 1958–80), vol. 3, part 1, *Die Kirche und ihr soziales Handeln: Grundsätzliches, Allgemeines, Praktisches* (Berlin and Hamburg, 1968), p. 134.

8. Johann Hinrich Wichern, *Notstände der protestantischen Kirche und die innere Mission*, in *Sämtliche Werke*, vol. 4, part 1, pp. 235–36.

9. Johann Hinrich Wichern, *Die Revolution und die innere Mission*, in *Johann Hinrich Wichern: Sämtliche Werke*, ed. Peter Meinhold (Berlin and Hamburg, 1958–80), vol. 1, *Die Kirche und ihr soziales Handeln: Grundsätzliches und Allgemeines* (Berlin and Hamburg, 1962), p. 129.

10. William O. Shanahan, *German Protestants Face the Social Question*, vol. 1, *The Conservative Phase: 1815–1871* (Notre Dame, 1954), p. 208.

11. Johann Hinrich Wichern, *Erklärung, Rede und Vortrag Wicherns auf dem Wittenberger Kirchentag, 1848*, in *Sämtliche Werke*, vol. 1, pp. 155, 162.

12. Wichern, *Gutachten*, p. 132.

13. Wichern, *Erklärung, Rede und Vortrag,* pp. 163, 165.
14. Ibid., p. 160.
15. Ibid., pp. 163–64.
16. Erich Beyreuther, *Geschichte der Diakonie und Inneren Mission in der Neuzeit,* 3d ed. (Berlin, 1983), pp. 88–89, 109–10.
17. The German website for *Das Rauhe Haus* provides a brief history of the institution and an up-to-date description of its many services (see http://www.rauheshaus.de).

THE TRUE COMMUNITY OF THE LORD

1. Johann Hinrich Wichern, *Die wahre Gemeinde des Herrn,* in *Johann Hinrich Wichern: Sämtliche Werke,* ed. Peter Meinhold (Berlin and Hamburg, 1958–80), vol. 1, *Die Kirche und ihr soziales Handeln: Grundsätzliches und Allgemeines* (Berlin and Hamburg, 1962), pp. 57–72.
2. This is an early, if not the first, distinction Wichern makes between mission fields. He uses the terms *heidnisch* and *inländisch,* literally "heathen" and "in-country," for which "foreign" and "home" are the commonly used English equivalents.
3. Where Wichern did not translate the Greek, we have bracketed translations of the terms in the text.
4. Wichern notes here: "Would it not thereby become a province of the state church? Or what is the relationship?"
5. Wichern's editor notes here: "The closing remarks appear on a sheet separate from Wichern's final manuscript. He did not expand them and incorporate them into his final copy."
6. Wichern's editor notes here: "Wichern adds in the margin: 'The circles of influence of James and Peter, Paul and John intersect from all directions. The taciturn, deeply thoughtful John is the last to leave the scene.'"

WICHERN'S EXPLANATION, ADDRESS, AND SPEECH AT THE WITTENBERG *KIRCHENTAG,* 1848

1. Johann Hinrich Wichern, *Erklärung, Rede und Vortrag Wicherns auf dem Wittenberger Kirchentag, 1848,* in *Johann Hinrich Wichern: Sämtliche Werke,* ed. Peter Meinhold (Berlin and Hamburg, 1958–80), vol. 1, *Die Kirche und ihr soziales Handeln: Grundsätzliches und Allgemeines* (Berlin and Hamburg, 1962), pp. 155–71.
2. From Meinhold's afterword, *Die Kirche,* vol. 1, p. 403.

3. Johann Hinrich Wichern, *Briefe und Tagebuchblätter des Johann Hinrich Wicherns 1826–1848*, in *Gesammelte Schriften des Johann Hinrich Wicherns*, ed. D. J. Wichern (Hamburg, 1901), vol. 1, p. 452.

4. Ibid., p. 453.

5. Ibid.

6. Ibid., p. 454.

7. Ibid., p. 455.

8. Ibid.

9. Ibid., pp. 455–56. Hans, who turned three years old, was Wichern's third son.

10. Ibid., p. 453.

11. *Praxis* refers to the practical application of principles, in contrast to theory.

12. In February 1848 rebellion broke out in Paris, and in March in Berlin.

13. Wichern draws a distinction here between *Volkskirche* (people's church) and *Staatskirche* (state church).

14. Wichern gave this address at the beginning of the afternoon session.

15. Wichern picks up on the immediately preceding remarks of Moritz August von Bethmann-Hollweg, chair of the conference, who had recommended the subject of the afternoon deliberations be "advancement in society of Christian aims, organizations, and institutions, in particular, the inner mission."

16. Wilhelm Marr, *Das junge Deutschland in der Schweiz: Ein Beitrag zur Geschichte der geheimen Verbindungen unserer Tage* (Leipzig, 1846).

17. Henri Druey (1799–1855), member and leader of the Waadtland Canton Government; 1850, president of the Swiss Confederation.

18. Johann Adam von Itzstein (1775–1855), after 1822 leader of the radical opposition in the Baden Parliament; in the Constitutional Convention in Frankfurt a member of those farthest to the left. Friedrich Hecker (1811–81), a representative of radical liberalism in Baden, fled to the United States. Robert Blum (1804–48), Leipzig city councilman; representative at the Constitutional Convention in Frankfurt; sentenced and shot to death for participating in the October 1848 uprising in Vienna.

19. Marr, *Das junge Deutschland in der Schweiz*, appeared in 1846.

20. Eduard Kuntze, a pastor from Berlin, who had spoken at the first session the day before.

21. Wichern was particularly critical of the piece *The Religion of the Future* (1843) by Friedrich Feuerbach (1806–80), not to be confused with the better-known Ludwig Feuerbach.

22. Elisabeth Fry (1780–1845); Amalie Sieveking (1794–1859).

23. A mistaken reference; the city is Newgate, England.

24. Johannes Daniel Falk (1768–1826), precursor of Wichern in exemplary work for neglected children, founded in Weimar the Society of Friends in Need; Adalbert Graf von der Recke-Volmerstein (1791–1878), pioneer in care for needy children, established the influential institute at Düsselthal in 1822; Christian Heinrich Zeller (1779–1860), organizer of work for neglected children, led from 1820 the Institute for Teachers of Poor Children in Beuggen.

25. A member of parliament who actively supported service to poor children.

26. Reference unidentified.

27. Philipp Jacob Spener (1635–1705) and August Hermann Francke (1663–1727), chief figures of German Pietism.

28. Adolphe Thiers, speaking on September 13, 1848, said the state could not improve the proletariat's situation except by means of "the greatest industrial freedom. Completely unfettered competition improves the situation of the workers" (quoted in *Priviligierte wöchentliche gemein-nützige Nachrichten von und für Hamburg*, no. 222 [September 16, 1848]).

29. Pastor Ludwig Feldner (1805–1890), minister at Elberfeld, was active in the Bible Society of Königsberg in Neumark. Under the influence of Thomas Chalmers in Scotland he was also active in reorganizing the care of the poor.

30. The Penitentiary Conference was held in Brussels, September 20–23, 1847.

31. The Vicomte de Melun was president of the *Société d'économie charitable* in Paris.

32. Dr. Heinrich Eduard Schmieder (1794–1893), member of the committee that established the Evangelical Church Federation and later the Central Committee of the Inner Mission, was opposed to the strategy of electing a Central Committee. He favored having interested individuals volunteer.

THE SPIRITUALITY OF THE GERMAN AWAKENING

THE INNER MISSION OF THE GERMAN EVANGELICAL CHURCH: A MEMORANDUM TO THE GERMAN NATION ON REQUEST OF THE CENTRAL COMMITTEE FOR INNER MISSION

1. Johann Hinrich Wichern, *Die innere Mission der deutschen evangelischen Kirche: Eine Denkschrift an die deutsche Nation, im Auftrage des Centralausschusses für die innere Mission*, in *Johann Hinrich Wichern: Sämtliche Werke*, ed. Peter Meinhold (Berlin and Hamburg, 1958–80), vol. 1, *Die Kirche und ihr soziales Handeln: Grundsätzliches und Allgemeines* (Berlin and Hamburg, 1962), pp. 179–90, 196–97.

2. In his introduction to the *Memorandum*, ibid., p. 411.

3. The chief coordinating body of the Inner Mission.

4. Wichern is referring to part 2, no. 2, not included in this volume.

5. The synod was held August 1–2, 1848, at Chur.

6. This translation omits Wichern's short excursus here on the history of the inner mission in the Christian church.

REPORT ABOUT DIACONAL SERVICE AND THE DIACONATE

1. Johann Hinrich Wichern, *Gutachten über die Diakonie und den Diakonat*, in *Johann Hinrich Wichern: Sämtliche Werke*, ed. Peter Meinhold (Berlin and Hamburg 1958–80), vol. 3, part 1, *Die Kirche und ihr soziales Handeln: Grundsätzliches, Allgemeines, Praktisches* (Berlin and Hamburg, 1968), pp. 130–35.

2. In Meinhold's afterword, ibid., p. 280.

3. Wichern is referring not to his own *Memorandum* of April 21, 1849, but to a short report by Aemilius Ludwig Richter (1808–64).

4. Perhaps he means Isaiah, e.g., Isaiah 61:11 (cf. Luke 4:17–18), since the book of Amos contains no references to prisoners.

5. We have bracketed translations of Greek terms in the text.

FRIEDRICH VON BODELSCHWINGH

Introduction

Friedrich von Bodelschwingh was a man of action. Called in 1872 by the Inner Mission in Rhineland-Westphalia to become director in Bielefeld of a fledgling home for epileptics and of a small, affiliated deaconess house that had opened in 1869, he multiplied these two initiatives in less than forty years into the largest care-giving institution in the German Protestant Church. His work continues today as the largest church-related charitable institution in Europe.

One is awed by the sheer magnitude of the program. It serves approximately ten thousand individuals annually and utilizes the talents of about eleven thousand co-workers. The collected activities, officially called The Bodelschwinghian Institutions of Bethel, or Bethel, for short, focus on seven areas of care: the aged; the young; those with physical or mental disabilities; the homeless; psychiatric care; urgent care hospitals; and the historic concern at Bethel, epilepsy. Bodelschwingh himself became a pioneer in the care of epilepsy, paving the way for Bethel's international renown in the research and treatment of the disease.

Bethel, with its main campus covering a mile-and-a-half square in Bielefeld, delivers its services in a broad range of facilities, including clinics, living units, job sites, and even a special, fully handicapped-accessible hotel. It also operates kindergartens, schools, and a theological seminary. Moreover, it maintains a variety of national and international exchanges, partnerships, and cooperative programs reaching from Tanzania to Cleveland.[1]

Seeds for Bodelschwingh's compassionate social action can be found in his earliest years, for he was born in 1831 into a devout family associated with public life. His father held posts of increasing rank in the Prussian government and served in Berlin from 1842 to 1848, first as minister of finance and then as minister of the interior.[2] During these Berlin years one of Friedrich's playmates was Crown Prince Friedrich Wilhelm.[3]

333

Young Bodelschwingh trained in farm management, and in 1852 he took his first managerial position. He was disturbed by the miserable conditions of his farm workers and already as a twenty-one year old tried to assist them. Out of concern for the children who worked for him clearing the sugar-beet fields, he distributed children's religious tracts—these a product of the Awakening in Strasbourg, Stuttgart, and Basel.

Then came an event that changed Bodelschwingh's life: one Sunday in mid-1854 he happened to read one of the tracts himself. Bodelschwingh recounts the event. The story in the tract was about "Tschin, the Poor Chinese Boy," who had been orphaned during the Opium War between England and China and then brought to England, where he became a Christian. Soon thereafter Tschin contracted a fatal illness and died. Bodelschwingh continues:

> However, the whole time he longed for only one thing, and that was to tell his countrymen about the Savior whom he himself had found. One time he expressed it with utmost seriousness: "What can I ever say on judgment day if my brothers ask me why I, even though I knew the way of salvation, did not tell them anything about it?"
>
> As soon as I heard these simple words, it was as if my eyes had been opened, and I saw my life's calling.[4]

Intending to become a missionary, Bodelschwingh went to Basel so that he could combine the study of theology at the university with informal learning from the circle of Pietistic, ecumenical, missions-oriented Christians in that city.

While in Basel, Bodelschwingh had the occasion to write a summary of what he considered to be the heart of the Bible and the Christian faith. His biographer, Martin Gerhardt, summarizes a portion of the document:

> He proceeds from the premise that God is love and, in a personal testimony, emphasizes the joyful experience of this love in one's own heart. In this connection the motto

for his life, 2 Corinthians 4:1, appears for the first time. He renders it this way: "Since we have experienced mercy, let us not become weary." He cites individuals led by the spirit of sacrifice, such as August Hermann Francke, Oberlin, Wilberforce, Elisabeth Fry, people "who sit at deathbeds, who crawl into prisons, who pick orphans from the street—in short, people whose entire lives are really the breath of love instead of empty words."[5]

Bodelschwingh never went to China, but he did begin his career in a type of missionary service in Paris. There he became assistant pastor to the approximately eighty thousand destitute German émigrés, many of whom had run out of resources on their intended journey to America.

Bodelschwingh's six Paris years, 1858–1864, proved to be rich in experiences that shaped the rest of his life: he married Ida von Bodelschwingh (a cousin); he learned to treasure Luther and the Lutheran Confessions along with a commitment to compassion above doctrine; he developed a masterful talent at inspiring people to contribute resources to his work; he began publishing his first monthly journal; he became a brother to the poor, sick, and suffering; and, having witnessed that people struggling with poverty are ill-suited to be concerned about the Christian faith, he committed himself to a strategy of social engagement.

The now well-prepared young pastor returned to Germany to serve a parish near Dortmund in the rural town of Dellwig from 1864 to 1871. Less than a year after arriving he began publishing *The Westphalian Family Friend (Westfälischer Hausfreund)*, a Sunday magazine that offered a variety of articles, including his own views on current issues and events. In effect, he was continuing an activity he had begun during his last year in Paris, when he introduced the monthly *Christ's Little Ship in Paris (Das Schifflein Christi in Paris)*. When Bodelschwingh eventually moved to Bielefeld he continued to publish *The Westphalian Family Friend* for an additional fifteen years.

Bodelschwingh's articles about events of the day demonstrate his opposition to liberal positions in politics and theology. He believed the workers needed to turn to God rather than to "the liberal, enlightened social politicians" of the period.[6] He recognized that industrialization was the catalyst for much impoverishment. Yet he believed the prior problem was moral and spiritual poverty, and he judged that the motivation for the workers' movements was selfish gain. Believing that the state was a divine institution resting on Christian values, he drew a connection between faith in God and loyalty to the nation and respect for those in authority.

Factors that influenced Bodelschwingh's views were his upper-class family background and the sudden jolt to this background when the outbreak of the 1848 Revolution in Berlin caused his father to resign his post in the Prussian government and leave the city.[7] Bodelschwingh remained sympathetic to Prussian authority because it was led by an overtly Christian monarchy whose social policy, in comparison to other governments, was quite benign. In the 1880s Bismarck described his own social policies as "practical Christianity."[8] The historian H. W. Koch notes:

> One tends to forget that enlightened absolutism brought benefits to its subjects which were the envy of many contemporaries abroad, and even a hundred years later Richard Cobden considered Prussia as a highly efficient, well-administered state which did more for its population than any other. Where is the need for revolution from below when reform is carried out from above?[9]

Hence, for Bodelschwingh, the commitment to faith active in love would not be practiced by opposing existing political structures but by alleviating existing suffering.

During the Dellwig years one experience overshadowed all others for Friedrich and Ida von Bodelschwingh: the tragic death of their four children. In grim succession all four succumbed to pneumonia within a two-week period in January of 1869: Karl, one year old; Friedrich, two; Elisabeth, four; and Ernst, six. Because of the great outpouring of public concern and interest, Bodelschwingh included an account of the fourfold sorrow in his *Westphalian Family Friend*.[10] The moving narrative met with such demand that it was reprinted in booklet form and published in edition after edition.

The heartbreaking experience was another turning point in Bodelschwingh's life. Later, when consoling a grieving father, Bodelschwingh explained how the tragedy had affected him:

> It was when our four children died that I realized for the first time how hard God can be toward humans, and since then I have become merciful toward others.[11]

Later the Bodelschwinghs had four more children, including Gustav, author of a biography of his father, and Friedrich, or Fritz, who succeeded his father as director of Bethel from 1910 to 1946. Pastor Fritz, though sympathetic with some goals of National Socialism, is recognized for his determined refusal to cooperate with the Nazi program of euthanasia, whereby he prevented authorities from removing a single person with a mental or physical disability from Bethel.

The call to Bethel in Bielefeld offered Bodelschwingh the promising opportunity to follow his heart and develop concrete programs of mercy. Indeed, the watchword over Bodelschwingh's many years of work was *Barmherzigkeit*, "mercy," and Bethel gained the title the City of Mercy. Year by year Father Bodelschwingh, as he came to be called, extended the umbrella of care to the sick, the orphaned, the disabled, the mentally ill, the homeless, and the unemployed.

At the heart of Bodelschwingh's vision was his conviction that the disabling condition from which all the individuals suffered, regardless of what brought them to Bethel, was their dislocation— dislocation from family, home, work, society, and the Christian faith. His aim was to treat the soul as well as the body, and engender a sense of belonging. Believing in the importance of the family for a person's well-being, he housed those receiving care in living groups. Believing in the dignity and therapeutic power of work, he created employment opportunities for the residents, including shops such as a brick factory and a bookbindery. Recognizing the need of the chronically unemployed for reintegration not only into the work force but also into an ordered life, he introduced the first workers' colony in Germany. It was a farm community, called Wilhelmsdorf, where men were provided accommodations and placed under strict discipline for three to six months of training.

Parallel to Bodelschwingh's expansion of services at Bethel was his expansion of the deaconess program, and he came to be recognized as a national leader in the movement. Though no less able than Fliedner to escape the chauvinistic culture of his day, Bodelschwingh also recognized the value of the vocation for women and the importance of the service for those in need. As he told a group of women being consecrated as deaconesses:

> For a feminine person to be given a specific life's vocation is a great deed in and of itself. How many lives of unfortunate women and girls go to waste just because they have no calling! How great, however, is your good fortune to have found just such a life's vocation!...As called and ordained assistants of the clerical office, you are working on building up the kingdom of Jesus. Of course, one does not hear your voices from the pulpit nor in large gatherings; the quiet way of life without words, serving love, is indeed the weapon with which you fight. Yet your mouths are not closed. Softly, softly, while you bind the wounds, you tell the wounded of the true balsam that heals all wounds. Softly, softly, while you wipe the sweat of death from cold foreheads, you point to the Prince of life. Softly, softly, while you bring refreshment and help into the huts of the impoverished, you remind them of the One who sends you and is the true friend of the poor.[12]

Bodelschwingh's well-known work and his voice in social issues made him a highly visible public figure, and his numerous followers convinced him to stand for a seat in the Prussian Diet in 1903. He was elected and served from 1904 to 1909, but his heart remained in Bethel. Nevertheless, he is known for taking a leading role in persuading the Diet to enact a law in 1907 that would provide homes for factory workers. He believed that one of the leading causes in the breakdown of families was the lack of appropriate housing. His longstanding conviction—which ran counter to general opinion—was that employees had a right to their own homes, and that credit institutions and employers, whom he said before parliament were "as concerned as fish," were obligated to help make them available.[13]

From the start, Bodelschwingh rooted his exemplary work at Bethel firmly in the tradition of Theodor Fliedner, Johann Wichern, and Wilhelm Löhe. He explained in 1883:

> I know that I am one with all my co-workers in the field of carrying out acts of Christian love. We *all* want one faith that is *active in love* and that is not satisfied with propositions that are learned by rote memory. We *all* want a Christianity that does not consist of words, but deeds. Above all, we do not want a Christianity that judges, condemns, embitters, and thrusts away others who are not of our faith, but one that wins over *precisely these people* through special kindness and sincere love....That is what Wichern and Fliedner wanted, nothing more, and we all sit at *their feet*.[14]

The source of this conviction was the simple, yet profound principle that Bodelschwingh found expressed in the New Testament verse that was the motto of the first motherhouse at Bethel: "By this we know love, that he laid down his life for us; and we ought to lay down our lives for the brethren" (1 John 3:16). In Bodelschwingh's own words:

> All diaconate is based on the service that the Lord Jesus has given us and still gives us richly and daily. It is service and sacrifice in thankful love returned to him who first served and loved us.[15]

Bodelschwingh's most widely known legacy is in the institutions and programs of Bethel, but his writings offer us a means whereby we can have a firsthand look at the spirituality of this last great exponent of the Awakening in late-nineteenth-century German Protestantism. The selections that follow were written between 1864 and 1878, during Bodelschwingh's years in Dellwig and Bielefeld. Three are sermons, three are articles from the monthly he published, and one is the short pledge that all of his deaconesses solemnly spoke. The final selection, Bodelschwingh's speech to a general conference of deaconess houses in Germany, takes us back to the beginning. By the time it was delivered in 1878, Bodelschwingh had assumed the mantles of both Fliedner and Wichern. He had become the national leader of the diaconate and the Inner Mission movement, two of the remarkable legacies of the German Awakening.

Sermons

Come Out, Joachim, the Savior Is Here!

EDITORS' INTRODUCTION: The curious title of this engaging sermon[1] derives from Martin Luther, who, in illustrating the spirit of charity, referred to a German silver coin by its popular name, the Joachim taler, a practice similar to that of calling the one-cent coin an Indian-head penny. Luther wrote:

> When he [the Christian] sees a man who has no coat, he says to his money, "Come out [of my pocket], Joachim. There is a poor, naked man who has no coat; you must serve him. Over there lies a sick man who has no nourishment. Come forth, Sir Taler! You must be on your way! Go and help him."[2]

Bodelschwingh prepared this text for the Christmas season of 1867 and, with the nativity in mind, begins with the premise that the effect of God's gift upon us is our desire to give to others. Bodelschwingh explains that the function of those in need is to provide the grateful person with the opportunity to implement the desire to give. To what end? The giver needs the activity at least as much as the recipient, because giving and serving are necessary antidotes to greed and self-centeredness. The discussion illustrates Bodelschwingh's characteristic emphasis on the inseparable connection between one's response to God and to human beings.

This piece, published December 22, 1867, in Bodelschwingh's popular Sunday magazine, *The Westphalian Family Friend*, demonstrates his clear, inclusive perception of human need, not only in his own region of Westphalia but around the world, and his unshakable belief in the necessity, virtue, and efficacy of serving love.

"Come out, Joachim, the Savior is here," Dr. Martin Luther once said to himself after a poor man had knocked on his door, and Luther was pulling the last Joachim taler out of his pocket. The exhortation, "Come out, Joachim, the Savior is here," serves as an excellent lesson for a meaningful Christmas celebration and expresses approximately the same thing as Paul's message: "Make your gentleness known to all people; the Lord is near" [Phil 4:5]. We cannot overlook this instruction by the apostle if we do not want the joy of Christmas to be diminished.

Naturally, we know quite well that our own works of love are by no means the source of our joy. Rather, we sing at Christmas time with Paul Gerhardt:

Joy and comfort without measure
are, Lord Jesus Christ, in you,
and your gladness is the pasture
where our happiness is true.[3]

Yet, whoever is truly serious about this confession will experience what the ancient doctor of the church, Jerome, experienced, who made his dwelling in Bethlehem at the place where Christ's crib had stood, and who wrote in his old age:

As often as I look at this place my heart has a conversation with the child Jesus. I say, "O, Lord Jesus, on what a hard place you must lie for the sake of my salvation. How can I ever repay you?" Then I hear the little child answer, "I desire nothing. Sing 'Glory to God in the highest,' and that is enough. I am going to become much thirstier on the Mount of Olives and on the sacred cross." I then say, "O, you dear child, I really must give you something or I'll feel so bad I could die. I will give you all my money." The little child replies, "Heaven and earth are already mine, silver and gold are already mine, I need nothing. Give it to the poor. That I will accept as if it were given to me." Etc.[4]

FRIEDRICH VON BODELSCHWINGH

It cannot be otherwise. People experience in their hearts the kindness and openness of our God and Savior who appeared at Bethlehem, and these cause in them a drive, a pressure, an inclination, and a compulsion to show their thanks for the over-abundant amount of love and mercy they have experienced. They would feel terribly deprived if they had no opportunity at all to show their genuine thanks. The blessed Conrad Heinrich Rieger wrote, when assuming a very strenuous task with which he hoped to serve others:

> If I were to express fully how my heart feels and what the secret and innermost driving force is behind my undertaking, it is this: the one at the right hand of God who indeed rendered far too great a service for me. I, in turn, would very much like to do something for his service and honor.[5]

In this sense, then, the charge "Make your gentleness known to all people" is a real necessity—particularly at Christmas time—for all those who know that they have been treated with compassion. Since we, unlike Mary, cannot wash the Lord's feet ourselves, he, with his words "You will always have the poor with you," has solemnly promised us that to the end we will never lack the opportunity to practice toward others what he did for us [John 12:3–8].

It is fundamentally false to think that the poor, sick, naked, hungry, and wretched are a bothersome burden for the rich and healthy. It is, of course, correct that poverty, illness, and need are a result, above all, of sin and are an evil. But the thistles and thorns of the field, the sweat of the brow with which a man must earn his bread, and the pains of a woman are also, above all, results of sin and are an evil [Gen 3:16–19]. Yet, at the same time they are a powerful antidote to sin because they keep alive the sighing for salvation and are laid on the scales as a heavy counterweight to the rampant proliferation of sin. Hence, all the needs, all the tears that appear before our eyes here on earth, all the sighs we hear are healing medicine for the primary sin in our hearts, for self-centeredness.

"Those who live for themselves" and "those who no longer live for themselves" but for the One who died and rose for us—that is how Paul divides human beings into the unhappy and the happy

[Rom 14:7–9]. Those who live for themselves are the unhappy ones who actually have no truly joyful hours. Those who no longer live for themselves are the happy ones who lead a very cheerful, joyful, and comfort-filled life.

During the past year a great number of complaints have come to my ear that the matter of fund-raising has become simply unbearable. The offering collections at church and at home never stop. First there were the institutions for the blind, deaf, mentally disabled, and lepers. Then came the asylums for prisoners and the institution for epileptics. In addition, there are home and foreign missions, the deacon and deaconess homes, homes for orphans, halfway houses, church and school buildings, Gustavus Adolphus Societies, Jerusalem Societies, societies for the care of prisoners, societies for Israel, and so on. Above and beyond all that come misfortunes from fires, the suffering of hunger, and cholera with its effects. It has become simply unbearable!

Granted, the matter of offerings is a delicate issue that has to be approached with chaste hands, both in regard to the collection as well as the disbursement of the contributions. Yet, I would like to ask: what would become of our present generation if all these thousands of needs did not surround us, and all these cries of help did not press upon our ears? Would it not drown completely in materialism, love of money, and the addiction to pleasure?

Of course, even to see an offering collector far off is enough to make some people feel sick and hide. There are also those who turn their eyes away quickly whenever they see a call for help in any newsletter, and they carefully avoid any situation in which they might come close to another person's misery. But are these folks happy? Are they not like that oriental lord who had three walls built around his magnificent palace and marvelous gardens and would not tolerate ever hearing a sound of complaint within the walls, but only happy music and the noise of jubilation, while outside hunger, pestilence, and wars raged among his poor people? In spite of that, he himself was never happy. He became more and more gloomy and miserable until finally, half mad, he had the gates of his palace torn open and let the wretched, with all their sounds of misery, stream in to his throne. Finally, in the midst of the misery of these people and the songs they sang, he became truly happy for the first time.

No, the life of the Christian does not consist of pursuing enjoyment but in practicing love—practicing a self-denying, serving love. The poor and wretched are not an oppressive burden that Christians push away as best they can but are aids to their joy. They are dear friends whom Christians search out in order, through them, to quiet the longing of their own hearts.

The poor are not only aids to their joy because they give them the opportunity to practice love, but they are also aids to them in the battle against flesh and blood and against the self-centeredness of their own hearts. What a help they are, for example, against greed, the root of all evil, by which Christians, too, are tempted so fiercely, because the thousandfold cries of spiritual and physical need, combined with Christ's promise, "What you have done for the least of these you have done for me," work against the heaping up of mammon [Matt 25:40]. What a help it is against slavery to fashion, against vanity and arrogance, when I see so many naked people who need to be clothed. What a help it is against luxurious living and lavish eating and drinking when I see so many hungry people who need to be fed.

I have often thought, if just once a week a conscientious offering collector would go through our towns and cities, one who knew how to present in a vivid way any one of the thousands of wounds of a sighing humanity and knew how to ask for help, what a healing medicine that would be for the voracious ills of our time. Nowadays people will spend more at one shooting-match festival or at a single carnival than they spend in ten years for the kingdom of God or for the needs of their brothers and sisters. This also explains why the parishes that give generously to the kingdom of God are generally more well off than those that do not—those where, instead, shooting festivals and so forth rule the day, for it is much less expensive to serve the poor and the kingdom of God than to serve the world.

Serving love must be learned by practice. It is curious that the farther away and the less the need, the harder and stiffer the hearts. The latest report of the Basel Missionary Society[6] includes the strange fact that during the last year of the war those countries that were most closely touched by the war and had to pay the highest war taxes went forward with their gifts, while the countries lying further away and not touched by the war at all have remained behind. I hear from many collectors, as if from one voice, that during the war last year collecting was much easier and the proceeds much greater than in this year of peace, when higher grain prices should make giving easier, at least in the countryside. Thus, need—one's own as well as that of others—is an aid against the hardness of one's own heart.

Of course, it is certainly more pleasant if one's heart is softened by God's goodness rather than by his judgment. How relatively well we in our land of Westphalia, especially the farmers, are doing this year! While news reaches us from so many states in the east, west, and north of people suffering from hunger, our barns are fully stocked with grain and feed. In addition, war and pestilence mercifully have passed us by.

Yet, may this time not become a trap to people so that they only save money and close their hearts against their suffering brothers and sisters who are living in want. Christmas is not at all the time for putting away one's cold, hard cash. Now is the time to look around for those who increase our joy—for the hungry with whom we break our bread; the naked, whom we clothe; the wretched, whom we can guide to our house; all the poor and sick, all those wasting away in body and soul; yes, Jews, Turks, and others must now be our aids in joy.

However, in this season of Jesus the little child, it is above all the little children for whom we search and to whom we reach out our helping hand. No one can be at a loss as to where to find them. I will name only our Westphalian redemption homes at Schildesche, Börde, Zoppenbrück, the Walpurgis Institute at Soest, our Hellweg Educational House at Rausingen, and the orphanages and confirmand institutes in Hamm and Höxter. For those who would like to reach their saving hands across the borders of our fatherland I will name the thousands of poor German children in Paris, namely, the poor children of the street sweepers in Batignolles and on the Green

Hill, and the orphans of Bon Secours. I will also name the hundreds of millions of children in foreign lands who someday would like to be as happy in the radiance of the Christmas sun as our children.

O, no, whoever desires to offer thanks to the little child in the manger lacks no opportunity. Therefore, as the blessed Luther writes: "Do not fumble around a long time looking for nickels and dimes, but reach in cheerfully: 'Come out, Joachim, the Savior is here!'"

At the Consecration
of Seventeen Westphalian Deaconesses

EDITORS' INTRODUCTION: This sermon[1] contains in one sentence a summary of the conviction that motivated many in the German Awakening to a life of service. It is the foundation for their spirituality and the lens through which they see society:

> Your blessed, lovely, easy calling is to serve the Lord Jesus in his wretched ones in humility, obedience, and faithfulness as a thank-offering for the humble, obedient, and faithful love with which he loved and served you unto death, and continues to love and serve you daily.

Preaching at a consecration service in the winter of 1875–76, three years after arriving in Bethel, Bodelschwingh directs his words to seventeen women pledging their lives to the diaconate. He applies to their lives the analogy of the Israelites who had been captives in Babylon. Just as the imprisoned Israelites knew suffering, so, too, the women have had their afflictions. As the Lord freed the Israelites, so, too, he frees the women from their sin. As the Israelites responded joyfully, so, too, the women can respond with a lifetime of great joy. As out of thankfulness the Israelites rebuilt Jerusalem, so, too, out of thankfulness the women can rebuild lives with the mortar of serving love.

Of the variety of tasks required for this reconstruction the women have the best job, which is to practice quiet, reconciling love where it is best employed—with the poor and lowly. Furthermore, this work elevates the status of women by making them trained professionals in a full-time vocation.

Should the women place great demands upon themselves as they pledge their lives to the diaconate? All that is required is the conviction that they are poor sinners and, in response to Christ's love, their humble obedience.

"The Lord has done great things for us; we rejoice because of it," Psalm 126:3.² That was the confession of the pilgrims who were returning home to Zion from Babylon. Onlookers stood along the path, amazed as the pilgrim train of Zion's prisoners, whose prison the Lord had opened, drew homeward through the desert toward Canaan. The wonderfully miraculous deliverance that had come to them after seventy years of imprisonment compelled the onlookers to confess: "The Lord has done great things for them." The pilgrims thought they were dreaming! Their good fortune was almost too great for them to believe. Their voices were full of laughter, their tongues full of praise, and the confession of the onlookers found a resounding, joyous echo in their hearts: "Yes, the Lord has done great things for us; we rejoice because of it."

O, you little group gathered here today at the altars of the Lord Sabaoth! We look at you, too, in wonder and amazement, in fact almost in envy, and cannot help but declare: "The Lord has done great things for you." I am also convinced that when you look back on all the wondrous paths on which the Lord has led you up to the present, on all his love and suffering, on his innocent humiliations and loving deeds of comfort, then you, too, can do nothing else but join thankfully and joyfully with heart, voice, and lips in our declaration: "Yes, it is true, the Lord has done great things for us, and we rejoice because of it."

O, how many more reasons for such a thank-offering from heart and lips do you have than did that original group which preceded you in singing the song of thanks! Their experience was that only of precursors compared to what has been bestowed upon you in blessed fulfillment, in deed and truth. You, too, know of the hard chains of slavery that Babylon tries to put on the daughters of Zion. You, too, have sung your tearful songs at the waters of Babylon in foreign countries [Ps 137:1]. Not a few of you have tasted the bitterness of great physical affliction along with needs of the soul and have walked through more than one dark valley. However, he who breaks open all bonds has thrown open your prison, shattered the mighty bolts and iron gates, led you out of life's dark valleys, and cast the light of his loving countenance upon you.

You are no longer prisoners of Zion, but the redeemed of the Lord who, clothed in salvation and adorned with justice, approach Zion with exultation! Though still living in the flesh, you know the glorious freedom of the children of God. You are able to join in the hymn of praise sung by the joyous apostle Paul—though delivered, yet in chains—who writes to the Colossians from his prison in Rome:

> Give thanks to the Father, who has made us worthy to be heirs of the saints in light, who rescued us from the rulers of darkness and transferred us to the kingdom of his dear Son, from whom we have salvation through his blood, the forgiveness of sins! [Col 1:12–14].

You have just come from the table that the bountiful, gentle host has prepared for you in the presence of all your enemies [Ps 23:5]. He called to you, "This is my body, this is my blood, given for you, shed for you for the forgiveness of sins" [Matt 26:26–28]. In the light of the new bond of fellowship you spoke your words of thanks, "Praise the Lord, my soul, and what is in me his holy name! Praise him who forgives all your sin and heals all your infirmities!" [Ps 103:1, 3]. What further proof do we need? Yes, the Lord has done great things for us.

However, the exulting prisoners of Zion did not merely go home. Rather, having arrived home, a task was awaiting them, a joyful task through which they could demonstrate their thankfulness for their deliverance. They could rebuild the destroyed Temple, dwellings, and walls of Jerusalem. Of course, their enemies did not want to allow this, so the workers had to hold a trowel in one hand and a sword in the other [Neh 4:16–23]. The same Lord who led them home from Babylon was now helping them build Zion. "May the Lord rebuke you, Satan, may the Lord rebuke you! Is this one not a firebrand snatched out of the fire?" Thus, he drives the Adversary away from his children saved by grace (Zech 3:2), and, turning to the latter, says, "I shall be a fiery wall around you." "Whoever touches you touches the apple of my eye." "Behold, I am coming and want to dwell with you" (Zech 2:5, 8, 10). With loving and comforting words like this he encouraged them in their joyful work.

Yes, you redeemed of the Lord, in addition to the great things the Lord has done for you in forgiving all your sins and healing all your infirmities, there is another great thing: he gives you the opportunity to thank him for his great deeds your whole life long. Naturally, you cannot thank him only with your lips and with words, but also with deeds and the truth. You can help build Zion. In working on the destroyed Zion, the church militant, you can help do the jobs of the simple laborers—the happiest, most blessed jobs that arise during the reconstruction of Zion. You do not have to be architects or construction supervisors who draw up the plans, nor business managers who have to worry about whether the budgeted figure will cover the debts, nor stone masons and brick layers who must prepare the heavy building blocks and put them in place. You do not need to stand on the walls and towers as supervisors or foremen who drive the sluggish workers on with loud voices. As simple laborers you need to look after only the mortar, and this mortar that holds the joints together consists of the quiet work of serving love.

Thus, your lot has fallen upon something delightful. You do not come to the construction of Zion's walls in order to preach, teach, or supervise, but to practice serving love. Furthermore, you are allowed to practice this love where it is most easily and lovingly practiced: among those in misery, among the poor, the sick, the lowly, the orphaned, the lost, and the strayed. In fact, by gathering together these crumbled, scattered, and despised little chips and chunks of stone and working them into the mortar, you create good masonry. By means of them you are able to fill in many a crack or crevice in the walls, drawing the poor to the rich, the high to the lowly, the healthy to the sick.

In addition, you are able to practice such joyfully thankful service not just on the side, in addition to your daily activities—as is the duty of every Christian—but as your actual life's vocation. For a feminine person to be given a specific life's vocation is a great deed in and of itself. How many lives of unfortunate women and girls go to waste just because they have no calling! How great, however, is your good fortune to have found just such a life's vocation!

We do not hear of a single woman during our Lord Jesus' earthly life who was hostile to him. While he had to suffer such a vast amount of hostility from the men, every one of the women, even up to Pilate's wife, stood by him. It is understandable, too, because the feminine gender, above all, owes the Savior especially deep thanks. Out of what imprisonment, out of what undignified bonds did he raise women and make them equal to the male gender as co-heirs of the mercy of life! [Gal 3:28]. Not only did he bestow on women as well as men the same mercy of salvation, but also the same share in giving thanks for and in spreading salvation. Already, along with the disciples, women accompany the Savior in service upon his pilgrim path, offering what they can of their possessions, and he is pleased to accept alms from these first deaconesses [Luke 8:1–3]. Though weak vessels, they, before anyone else, even before the disciples, are allowed to be witnesses of his crucifixion, burial, and resurrection [Matt 27:55–61; 28:1]. And immediately we find them as helpers of the messengers of peace, active in an ordered, ecclesiastical office as servants of mercy in the congregations [Rom 16:1–6]. This is how high the Lord Jesus placed women; they were found worthy of such a service.

Your office, dear sisters, to which we call you today, has an apostolic basis, is founded in God's Word and in the ancient Orders of the church. As called and ordained assistants of the clerical office, you are working on building up the kingdom of Jesus. Of course, one does not hear your voices from the pulpit or in large gatherings; the quiet way of life without words, serving love, is indeed the weapon with which you fight. Yet your mouths are not closed. Softly, softly, while you bind the wounds, you tell the wounded of the true healing balsam that heals all wounds. Softly, softly, while you wipe the sweat of death from cold foreheads, you point to the Prince of life. Softly, softly, while you bring refreshment and help into the huts of the impoverished, you remind them of the One who sends you and is the true friend of the poor. Softly, softly, while you gather the little children around you, you invite them to the One who gathers the little lambs into his arms [Isa 40:11].

See how great, how rich, and how blessed your calling is! As a result, not only should you say, "The Lord has done great things for us," but you should provide the evidence: "We rejoice because of it." Your joy, your abundantly joyful heart should be reflected in your life and work. To be sure, the homeward bound pilgrims of Zion still speak about the seeds of tears. As we know, they are returning initially not to their heavenly but to their earthly Jerusalem, and they will not bring in the sheaves without tears until they are above. Yet that does not prevent them from singing the song of joy: "The Lord has done great things for us; we rejoice because of it." Joy remains the master. You, too, beloved, do not yet carry out your vocation in triumphant Zion, but initially in militant Zion; you, too, must think first of all not about the harvest but about sowing the seed, and the period of sowing is also the period of tears [Ps 126:5–6]. Nor is it said of the tender, good hearts that have accepted these seeds of the divine word: "They bear fruit with joy," but rather, "they bear fruit in patience" [Luke 8:15].

Nor will you lack in fears or enemies who seek to dampen your joy and hinder you in building Zion. Yet, just remain very calm. The Lord himself will fight for you and rebuke your enemies. He will be a fiery wall about you. "Whoever touches you, touches the apple of my eye," he says. And again: "I shall come and dwell with you." Wherever he makes his dwelling, we hear, in spite of all the raging of the enemies, "Nevertheless the city of God with its streams will remain joyful, for the sacred dwellings of the most high are there" [Ps 46:4]. Therefore, be joyful, very joyful, dear sisters! An exceedingly joyful heart belongs to your service in order that the world can see how blessed it is to serve in his vineyard, and in order that others will be attracted to it. A most joyful heart belongs to your service in order that you can bring joy into all the dark valleys of suffering, poverty, fear, sin, and death, not the transitory joy of this world but the joy of the Lord, the master of joy. Yes, may this joy in the Lord be your strength! May it help you win victory after victory!

Be joyful, be joyful, dear sisters, and respond with a joyful "yes" to the call, which we now direct to you!

You hear the call, for nothing more is demanded of you than was already included in your baptismal pledge. No great deeds! No meritorious good works! You can only be and remain poor sinners who, through grace, are made worthy to serve the Lord Jesus, serving him who himself served in poverty and lowliness. This is the humility of the deaconess. With David you can say: "I want to become even less than I was, and want to become lowly in my own eyes" [cf. Ps 131:1]. Then obedience will not be difficult for you but will be a blessed exercise of love for Jesus, the sweet, blessed freedom of the children of God acquired through the perfect obedience of the Son of God. Out of this humble obedience will flow faithfulness and an enduring love that regards the lowly as great, that never tires but persists to the end, and to which the reward of life is promised.

Your blessed, lovely, easy calling is to serve the Lord Jesus in his wretched ones in humility, obedience, and faithfulness as a thank-offering for the humble, obedient, and faithful love with which he loved and served you unto death, and continues to love and serve you daily. And to reiterate: in order to say "yes" and assume such a vocation today you need nothing but the conviction that you are and will remain poor sinners and can do nothing without him. Then his strength will be mighty in you who are weak [2 Cor 12:9]. Consequently you may, you can, give a cheerful, peaceful, complete "yes."

May the God of grace who has called you to his blessed service prepare you, strengthen you, and give you a firm foundation in the same! May he enable you to recognize his will more clearly every day and become more obedient to it, so that you are a delight to his heart in faithful, genuine love expressed in a life dedicated to him. May his grace comfort you to the end in your firm belief in his precious gospel!

May his undeserved, faithful mercy foster the work of your weak hands! Yet to him alone be the glory, now and forever! Amen.

FRIEDRICH VON BODELSCHWINGH

Sermon on the Anniversary of Bethel

EDITORS' INTRODUCTION: Under Bodelschwingh's leadership the home for epileptics that he had taken over in 1872 developed into an entire complex of facilities serving a range of human needs. Bodelschwingh's anniversary sermon of 1893[1] provides a picture of the institution's success and communicates his own motivation rooted in God's enduring love.

As Bodelschwingh delivered his message before patients and others in Zion Church, the focal structure in Bethel, he was keenly aware of the pain and sorrow that a year represents. He offers poignant illustrations of the distress and death of children and the accompanying anguish of their parents. Given this reality, Bodelschwingh addresses the perplexing question of whether there is truth in Jeremiah's assurance that God has loved each person forever. Bodelschwingh affirms that illness and suffering are a means by which God in his love draws the helpless and poor to himself. Bodelschwingh draws an analogy between these individuals who receive God's care and the biblical example of Mephiboseth, Jonathan's lame son, who was treated kindly by David.

As Bodelschwingh reviews the year he finds further evidence of the Lord's love in the record of the institution—in the amount of care provided, in the growth of the facilities, and in the financial and material contributions. For all of this he concludes with confidence that the Lord "has done great things for us."

> I have loved you forever and ever;
> therefore I have drawn you to me out of pure goodness.
> (Jer 31:3)

Is this really true, my dear friends? Do you all agree with the words, "The Lord has loved me forever and ever"? Is it really true? Is it really love that he shows to us poor people here? It is not always easy to recognize this love. When a mother, a widow, loses all five of her healthy children one after another and has only one left, and that child has epilepsy, is this really love? Just ask the widow if it was love and she will tell you, "For a long time I didn't realize that it was love. Nevertheless, it was nothing but love, because through the disciplining he drew my son Heinrich and me to his heart." Among the many joyful hours granted to me in Bethel, a special one occurred when I entered the small room where this mother had closed the eyes of her epileptic Heinrich. I really could not tell who looked happier, she or the son who had died.

Recently a father and mother traveled here from far across the ocean. Three of their children were epileptic. Is it really love that the three children sit here in church today, even though the parents returned to South Africa, having to leave their dear, sick children behind? Is this love? Yes, this, too. For even if the parents' hearts could break, a ladder to heaven has been raised in far-off South Africa on which they can climb to God. Where such separations have occurred, he has something particularly good in mind. Of course, it is not easy to understand what God intends, and so we sometimes ask, "Is this really love?"

Many a father and mother ask, "Tell me, is it really love that you have taken my child so far away from me?" Many poor people have to wait five, six, or seven years until they can see their ailing children again. Or when the fathers and mothers of epileptic children die, and neither the brother nor sister is able nor wants to keep them, should they not feel very sad and say, "Is this really love?"

How often our dear black Johannes Ali said sorrowfully, "I no longer have a father or a mother," but added quickly, "Now you, Jesus, are my mother and father." Johannes recognized that God had loved him forever and ever, even at the time that the Arabs raided the little hut on Lake Tanganyika, apparently murdered his parents, and dragged him off through the desert. When he was first brought to us he often felt very homesick; yet homesickness is a

356

good thing. Whenever we get little children who do not feel home-sick at all I become concerned that something is wrong. In order to eliminate homesickness in the right way, the poor, sick soul has to become acquainted with the father's house above. The message must be clear: "You have drawn me to you out of pure goodness."

My dear sick ones! He has drawn all of us to himself out of pure goodness. Our King David in heaven has called to himself us poor, fallen people and helpless Mephiboseths [2 Sam 4:4, 9:6–13], and all of us are allowed to eat at the king's table. His table is always ready so that we will never hunger and weaken again. He has left the door to his Father's house wide, wide open for everyone who is homesick. Yes, blessed are those who are homesick, for they shall come home.

Out of our community of Bethel alone sixty-six have been car-ried home this year, and out of the community of Zion perhaps three times as many. In addition, three of our dear confirmands went to their home. It is always a day of great joy when a group of confirmands sits here. Elsewhere people shout to them, "Go away, leave the school! Go away, leave the church! We can't use you. You are always having seizures!" Forty-three of them sat here on Miseri-cordia Sunday.[2] Tears of joy are shed every time the Good Shepherd robes such a flock of Mephiboseth-children in his wedding gown and they are incorporated into the blessed, joyous community of King David in heaven.

At the same time we did not need to mourn any of the three children who were missing. The first of them to go home, the poor, little, crippled August, had fought valiantly. Suffering greatly, he called out a few hours before his death, "Is the Savior here now?" He was a genuine Mephiboseth. Katherine Schmidt, his fellow sufferer, had to be confirmed in the chapel on her sickbed. Her verse was, "I have loved you forever and ever. Therefore I have drawn you to me out of pure goodness." From that time on she felt intensely home-sick, though no longer for her father and mother who lived far, far across the ocean, but for her eternal home. She was so anxious to cel-ebrate the Lord's Supper one more time, but she wanted to wait until the Savior was near. Pastor Schmidt administered communion half an hour before her death. She was indescribably content when she passed away, and whoever saw her contentment knows that in the short period of her difficult pilgrimage she was granted God's pure love and pure goodness.

Johannes Ali also had to be carried into the church, even for his baptism. His verse was, "I rejoice in the Lord." O, yes, he was so happy, and Elisabeth said, "From now on it won't be difficult for him when he has to die." His final prayer was, "Jesus accepts sinners." After that he went home in the comforting, joyous awareness that he, too, would be received by God's love and goodness. Was it really love when the Arabs drove him through the desert with whips and ropes? Yes, nothing but love, nothing but the love of the Father in heaven.

Now, all you dear people, there are some among you—and I could name you by name—who came to me and said, "I didn't understand for a long time, but now I understand that everything God has done to me is love, nothing but love."

Once there was an obedient son who had never caused his father any distress. Yet his father tested him to the maximum degree. In a garden called Gethsemane he was pleading on his knees because his father intended to give him a bitter, bitter cup from which to drink. So he prayed three times, "Father, if it is possible, take this cup from me!" But he had to drink the cup and he had to hang on the cross [Matt 26:36–46]. Was this really love? Yes, a love, a mercifulness about which people now preach in all the world's languages. O, if the Lord does not do what you humbly request of him—"Take me back to my father and mother!"—then do not forget to think about the man who prayed in Gethsemane!

You also know about a man who had a thorn in his flesh. The early church fathers were of the opinion that it was epilepsy. He, too, prayed three times in deep humility that the burden be taken from him. Even so the Lord did not do it. He said simply, "Be satisfied with my grace because my power is mighty in the weak" [2 Cor 12:7–9]. No, such wishes do not work, for then you are on the point of becoming arrogant. It is far better to be sick than haughty. If he makes you wait, it is nothing but pure mercy and love.

In our cemetery sleeps a little boy, and he, too, was terribly homesick. One day a little lad arrived from Ratibor in far-away Silesia with a big note pinned to him. Written in large letters were the words, "Please help this sick child get to the institution of Bethel at Bielefeld," and he arrived here without trouble. During the trip he had learned thankfulness, because he could not forget how the conductors had always carried him in their arms and taken care of him with such kindness. Later he always wanted to become a railroad conductor. To this little chap we also owe the opportunity that we are able to travel by train so inexpensively. Three times I had requested of the officials that the sick and their nurses be able to travel at reduced rates. Three times I was turned down. Then I sent him the cardboard note the boy had been wearing, and, do you know, the answer I wanted came back immediately.

Every time our little Ida from Korbach had been home for two weeks she became homesick for Bethel because she could not go to church here. As a result, she also aroused in her parents homesickness for the eternal home. Many a father and mother have said to me, "Where would I be if this poor, sick child had not taught me to pray."

The Lord has loved us forever and ever; the Lord is in the midst of us. We have been able to see this again this year. "It is a magnificent thing to thank the Lord and sing praises to your name, you most high" [Ps 92:1]. Yet it is also fine when one thanks the people, all of our dear friends. Also, I want to cite a few numbers for those who always criticize.

In the preceding year we housed and fed in our community 1,563 sick persons in 444,604 days of care. We admitted 278 sick persons. Only sixty-six died during the past year. Twenty-four were healed and went home—a large number. The doctors have recorded this number on their official certificates; whether they are actually healed only God knows. We have 113 epileptic children in our schools. Forty-three were confirmed. 125,423 epileptic fits were counted. Of those who died, fifty-one were under forty years of age; only four lived to be over sixty. We die young here. Here you can say, "The span of human life is thirty years, or at most forty" [Ps 90:10].

Last year we were able to move into our dear Little Bethel and put the water system into operation. We now have a flow of one hundred forty liters of good water per minute. We were also able to open New Tabor. In Alpine Meadow we made room for fifty more epileptic men, after the Wittekind Home at Volmerdingsen took those with severe mental disorders. In addition, we received a "Wilhelm's Cottage." Moreover, we laid the cornerstone for Moriah since we had to send away so many epileptics who had become mentally ill, and this situation was too difficult for us. In the future we want to extend our facilities again and lay the cornerstone for a building for those who, along with epilepsy, have other illnesses, such as typhoid fever, diphtheria, and throat diseases.

Last year thankful parents contributed 43,390 marks to us for Little Bethel. More than 30,000 marks came from the penny collection. On their deathbed loving individuals gave us 28,905 marks. The reason we have had higher debts than last year is because we had to buy a piece of property for which, however, the Lord clearly pointed the way. By August 1 we will be able to pay the entire sum—280,000 marks. Although this sounds like a tremendous amount, we certainly have not acted carelessly, because when our Savior sends us poor, ailing people, we have to care for them. We owe the Lord Jesus even more.

A worker in a spinning mill who sent me two marks from his modest earnings writes, "I am shocked at your high debts, but such debts drive one to prayer. Consequently, the debts bring a hidden blessing." His letter continues:

> All you sorrowful people in Zion, may God give you joy! If it is already so glorious here below at your anniversary celebration, how wonderful it will be in the heavenly kingdom. Since the Lord has blessed me with six very healthy children, I am sending you some coins of thanks. May the Lord bless all those who serve him at your place, including the dear teachers.

A poor seamstress writes, "I am sending you one mark for your building. It is the result of my pledge that I will give a tenth from all my work. This is the first contribution." Also a student at a poly-technic institute donated ten marks from a grant of forty marks, and he is already looking forward to donating more when he is earning his own money.

God certainly turns little children into a genuine power. The pupil August Fricke, who collects the album pages we send out, laments that his little page has become dirty. He promises to keep the sheet clean if we send him a new one. He writes in closing:

> My papa and mama always try to do as much good for others as they can, and I want to learn to do the same. Mrs. Thomson gave me a piggy-bank, and now I am going to start saving.

Since July of last year we have earned 29,000 marks from the used articles sent to us. 6,000 cartons arrived. Eighty people worked on them. Many Christians find great joy in collecting items for us.

In closing I must read a beautiful letter to you. A teacher writes to me first of all regarding a poor, miserable orphan who has been beaten by his stepfather and whom we must admit in a few days. The letter continues:

> Our daughter Christine, the sunshine of our home, just passed away at sixteen years of age. An hour before her death she asked us to show her the picture of the Good Shepherd above her bed. After she had looked at it for a long time she said, "Mother dear, the little lamb that the Savior has in his arms—that's me," and in this blessed faith she fell asleep.

We do not need to fear that the Savior will abandon us. To you dear farmers, in particular, I say thanks for your gifts of love—the fruits of the field. I cannot enumerate all of them because the list is too long. If something should happen that you do not like, please tell us face to face. We do not want to stop making requests of you. We also do not want to miss out on even your smallest donations.

We have a rich God who is greater than David in mercifulness, and we are fortunate Mephiboseths in that we can sit down at his table. When the Lord eventually releases the prisoners of Zion we will be like those who dream, and with joyful lips we will praise him:

"The Lord has done great things for us [Ps 126:1, 3]. Glory to God in the highest!" [Luke 2:14].

Amen.

Essays on Current Issues

One Thing Is Necessary

EDITORS' INTRODUCTION: Near the end of his six years in Paris as an assistant pastor to thousands of impoverished German émigrés, Friedrich von Bodelschwingh began publishing a newsletter called *Christ's Little Ship in Paris (Das Schifflein Christi in Paris)*. The magazine was to be a common bond for the diaspora and a vehicle to inform readers in Germany of the ministry as well as to encourage their support. The newsletter's logo depicted a sailing vessel bearing a banner with the word *Augustana*—Latin for "Augsburg"— referring to the Augsburg Confession of 1530.

The logo soon drew criticism for directing attention to a Confession instead of to Christ, "the one thing necessary." The text presented here is Bodelschwingh's response to his critics.[1] He argues that the word *Augustana* indeed turns our attention to Christ, for this was the goal of the reformers in Augsburg. Yet, he continues, why is a confession of faith necessary at all? Bodelschwingh explains that God's Word is his revelation to us; the confession is our indispensable response to him.

He then differentiates between the confession of faith by an individual and by the church. The historic Confessions of the church are necessary in order for the church to define its doctrine, defend the faith against attack, and preach a consistent message rooted in the whole body rather than an idiosyncratic version devised by one individual. Bodelschwingh notes that the church uses confessions to focus not on Luther or Lutheranism but on the one thing necessary—salvation through Christ.

In the course of his argument Bodelschwingh underscores the integrity of his position by recounting his own personal struggle. Six years earlier he himself had subscribed to the view that the church's Confessions were unimportant, until, as a pastor of the diaspora parish in Paris, he was compelled to clarify and articulate his own faith. Thus, besides a defense of a confessional faith this essay documents Bodelschwingh's personal spiritual development.

Our little ship, having scarcely set sail for the high seas, has already had to face a variety of challenges. Some friends think the ship is sailing along too proudly and upright, while others take exception to the Latin inscription on the side. What seems to be most irritating, however, is the handsome banner. We do not complain about these gusts of wind. They are good for our ship, because it must prove itself in stormy seas. In any case we are deeply thankful to all our friends for their kind hints, and we take them to heart. While we cannot please everyone, we can, once again, ask the Savior to set the rudder of our little ship according to his pleasure. For this time we would ask only that people allow us a word of explanation.

First of all, as far as the basic design of the little ship is concerned, events went like this. Your author asked a kindhearted artist to draw a very poor little ship that is being battered by a storm, and the viewer should be able to see from the crew that the cry on their lips is: "Lord, help us, we are ruined!" However, the dear artist simply could not get a little ship to turn out like that. He produced one sketch after another. Finally, when there was no more time to lose, I asked a friend to go and not leave the artist's side until the little ship was finished. It was then that he produced the little drawing that now appears at the head of our newsletter.

I accepted it confidently as a sign from above, that since Jesus, in his state of elevation at the right hand of his Father, is at the helm, the ship of his church really should not be allowed to look very fragile, like the one he boarded during his state of humiliation on the Sea of Galilee [Mark 4:35–41]. Also, it seemed even less proper now than it did then for his disciples to be apprehensive in a storm. They should much rather be able to sit quietly and confidently at his feet at all times and say: "My soul is quiet before God, who helps me. The protector of Israel neither slumbers nor sleeps" [Ps 62:1; 121:4].

The explanation for the Latin inscription on the side of the ship is as follows. Whoever has been in Paris knows that the city's coat of arms is a proud, three-masted sailing vessel. A person might not have noticed, however, that the coat of arms bears the inscription *Fluctuat nec mergitur*, which means, "It rolls but does not sink." A friend once commented that in the long run these words would have to prove untrue for the proud international city, when, like ancient Babel, it meets its demise through the judgment of God [Gen 11:8–9]. My friend suggested, however, that the words could well be transferred to Christ's church, of which we know that even the gates of hell cannot prevail against it [Matt 16:18]. Yet, in no way do we want to lay claim to this view in regard to our poor little newsletter, of which we said right away in the first issue that we would not mind seeing it come to an end if only something better takes its place.

But now regarding the flag with the inscription *Augustana*. One letter-writer asks: "Why does your ship bear such a proud name? Take care that your eyes are not drawn toward the waving flag and away from the Savior, who stands beneath it. Christ must be the center of attention. In our times, more than ever, one thing is necessary! Wherever he is not the beginning, middle, and end, he cannot give his blessing, and the vessel, along with the crew, will go under. There the spirit of the age will beat the mast and rip the proud sails."

We agree with all our heart, one thing is necessary, that sinners be saved, and salvation occurs only through Christ and his blood! Truly, the crew of our little ship is not interested in any other basis for its salvation. It sings with joy:

> The bedrock of my being
> is Christ and his own blood.
> They are my power for seeing
> the true, eternal good.
> The sum of all my living
> is nothing on this earth;
> but what the Lord is giving,
> is of the greatest worth!

That is how it is for us, and that is what our flag clearly indicates. The word *Augustana*—which means "Augsburg Confession"—announces that we are on the side of our dear forebears who in Augsburg in 1530 declared themselves to be against pope and king, who rejected all human rules through which the Roman Church had hidden our Savior from the eyes of sinners, who stood on the Word of God alone, and who knew they could be saved only by grace through faith in Jesus Christ. Consequently, how could our flag draw anyone's eyes away from Christ, since it points directly to him as the only bedrock of our salvation?

Certainly a spirit is blowing through the land, pushing and urging everywhere that the church of the Lord once again become a true church of the Confessions. Could it be, however, that this spirit is the spirit of the age, the spirit of the prince who rules in the air (Eph 2:2)? Who are the ones who have reached out their hands in France and Germany recently in order to tear down the Confessions of our church? Are they not the same spirits who would like to tear the crown of eternal divinity from the head of our Lord Christ? Are they not precisely for that reason the same ones who are so opposed to our Confessions, since they testify so powerfully that Christ is true God, one with the Father, highly praised in all eternity? And once again, who are the spirits who, in our sister Reformed Church in France, pray, sigh, and struggle so earnestly that a banner might be raised again, under which the confessors can gather, those who in truth call Jesus their Lord? The answer is not difficult.

Yet why have a Confession in addition to the holy scriptures? Is it not presumptuous to pay more attention to a human-made confession than to the Word of the living God?

One can answer in this way: the scripture is not a confession, but something much loftier. It is the revelation of God to us. The confession is the human response to it. God sends us his Son and says: "This is my dear Son. Do you believe in him?" We are to answer: "Yes, Lord, I believe." The Word of God demands our confession, and our salvation is connected to it. With his own blood our dear Savior confessed himself to be for us, and so he challenges us to confess ourselves to be for him. "Whoever confesses me before others," he says,

"I will confess before my heavenly father" [Matt 10:32; Luke 12:8], and Paul writes, "One believes from the heart, and so is justified; one confesses with the mouth, and so is saved" (Rom 10:9–10). See also what is written in 1 Peter 3:15 and 1 John 4:2–3.

However, the confession must be drawn from God's Word, like water from the well, otherwise it is no good. In addition, it must be a clear and straightforward confession, so that no rogue can hide behind it. It is not without reason that we sing and pray:

> Lord, heal the deaf that they might hear;
> give speechless ones a voice that's clear—
> the ones who shun confessing free
> what kind of faith might in them be.

Peter's confession (Matt 16:16) was a straightforward, good confession of that kind, and Paul's confession (1 Tim 1:15) was no less magnificent. Whoever can speak in faith the two confessions these men spoke will definitely be saved. Yes, not even this much is required for the salvation of an individual sinner. A while ago a poor, young woman was on her deathbed in a hospital here. Her pastor asked her what, in dying, was the basis for her hope. Her answer was: Jesus Christ. This was a good confession. One can die well with this.

However, what suffices for the individual sinner does not suffice for the church. Christ's church has not only the task of saving individual souls but must also be an example in its life and doctrines of the sacred temple of God, built on the foundation of the apostles and prophets, with Jesus Christ the cornerstone [Eph 2:20–21]. Consequently, it must constantly keep watch that no false building blocks of incorrect doctrine are inserted into the structure and corrupt the temple of God. It is by no means certain that everyone who uses the Word of God for support has the right spirit of faith. It is well known that all false teachers cite the Word of God and that the devil himself said, "It is written" (Matt 4:6). Jesus gave his church his Holy Spirit and promised to lead it in all truth. He thereby laid upon the church the sacred duty of putting before every poor sinner the right doctrine of salvation according to the scripture in a clear, simple, and understandable manner. The church is to set down this doctrine in public confessions of its faith and defend it against all attacks.[2] The church has done this in all the ages in which it has existed: in the first centuries in the Apostolic, Nicene, and Athanasian Confessions of faith in which the basic doctrine of the Christian church, the doctrine of the Holy Trinity, was established; in the age of the Reformation in many outstanding, new testimonies in which primarily the other side of Christian doctrine— the doctrine of sin and grace, of the path on which a poor sinner, through faith alone, is justified before God and saved—was illuminated by the scriptures and cleansed of all human accretions.

Christians are soldiers and Christ's church on earth is an army, for it is called the church militant. Soldiers must have a banner to follow. If the banner is lost, then the situation is not good. Confessions (also called Symbols) are banners. None of the communities of faith that originated in the Reformation has been able to do without a confession. They have all let their banners wave.[3] Some, however, have already lost them in battle. Then their situation is not good, because they are in danger of having their members scatter. Some people have blamed us in particular for saying we are happy about our good banner! Why should we not be happy about it? Christ's name and cross are worked into it, and it is colored with Christ's blood. The testimony of Elector John the Steadfast at the close of the Diet in Augsburg, spoken with a joyful spirit to a large gathering before the emperor, has proved true:

> I know with great certainty that the doctrine contained in
> this Confession is so firmly based in the sacred scriptures
> that even the gates of hell cannot withstand it.[4]

The fact that under this banner one can really battle joyfully and conquer blessedly is demonstrated, if by nothing else, by the great host of sacred musicians who have followed it up with their hymns of faith and victory. Thus, we request that none of our dear readers attribute any false motives to our banner. It is meant only to indicate that we do not shrink from giving a clear confession of

Christ, and, indeed, the same confession with which our forebears made their firm and loyal confession to him.

Several times, too, on account of its brevity and clarity, we have used the word *Lutheran*, and some friends have been even more shocked at this. Yet, they should not be shocked because it is not a partisan term for us. We can get along fine without it, and we gladly join in the words of that courageous confessor from the age of the Reformation, Argula von Grumbach:

> People call us Lutheran, but we are not. We are baptized in the name of Christ, and he is the one we confess, not Luther. We acknowledge that Martin, too, as a faithful Christian, confessed him. God help us that we might never deny this.[5]

What matters for us is Luther's good confession, not his name. In any case, even though Luther himself did not wish for the name,[6] it certainly has been justified and consecrated by history and by the hate and derision laid upon it. Nor should the name be scoffed at in France, where in Paris the gospel's first witnesses, called Lutherans, went to the stake with joy.[7]

In addition, we would like to request our friends not to blame our church leaders or members of our missionary committee for any displeasing comments in this newsletter. They approve of the publication of the little ship, but they are not responsible for its content. Basically, the editors want to allow several co-workers the freedom to determine the publication's content. Our friends ought to get to know us as we are. Hence, in closing, your author will permit himself the following confession, for which he alone takes responsibility.

When I arrived in Paris six years ago, I would have been the first to sign my name in support of the above-mentioned arguments against a specific confession; and, indeed, I would have based my view on the same position as today, that only one thing is necessary.

I did not spend those six years in my study but in constant contact with poor people, struggling to resolve moral and spiritual crises, which certainly cannot be more critical anywhere in the Christian church. The waters of my own affliction and the affliction of others rose far too high in my soul for me to have had time and energy to occupy myself with secondary concerns. Yet, precisely during that time the clear, firm Confessions of our church became valuable and dear to me.

First of all, for my own soul. At the very beginning of the period I had to see several of my closest friends suffer shipwreck of their faith. This happened precisely because in interpreting the scriptures they wanted to rely only on their own minds. They declined the faithful guidance of our church's Confessions. I was very close to plunging into a similar abyss. At that point God sent me a host of poor children; I was to show them the way to their Savior. Since I was in the awkward situation of not knowing where to begin, I took out, for the first time since my youth, Luther's *Small Catechism*, which, in actuality, is a confession document for our people. It helped me find my way. It helped me get into the scriptures. In the scriptures it pointed me to the one thing necessary. As a result I gained a love of the other Confessions, too.

Now I feel very good that as one who cares for God's mysteries I do not have to rely alone on my own insight in the dispensation of Word and sacrament. I do not have to be swayed this way and that by all sorts of doctrinal winds or by deceptions from people addicted to reform [Eph 4:14]. Rather, I have on my side the corroborating testimonies of such a cloud of witnesses regarding the fundamental truths of the Christian faith [Heb 12:1]. These witnesses, calling upon the Holy Spirit, have searched in the *scriptures* for the one thing necessary. Therefore, one can go one's way happily and securely, not because one is relying on human beings, but because one enjoys the well-founded certainty that one stands with both feet firmly in God's Word.

However, the church's firm confession and the church regulations connected with it have also become very important to me for the souls entrusted to me.

One thing is necessary, that sinners be saved; so I add once more: it is difficult for sinners to be saved. The path and gate are narrow and the devil is powerful—everywhere, especially in Paris. There it is not enough to scatter the Word about the cross in homes here and there, or to rouse secure sinners from their sleep with an awakening sermon. The devil would soon take the good seed from the hearts and make the awakened fall back asleep. The awakened souls must also be thoroughly converted, and the converted kept on the narrow way by means of faithful care.

For this to be possible, the widely scattered members must be gathered into stable congregations and strengthened through Word and sacrament for the common struggle against flesh and blood, the devil and the world [Heb 2:14]. Ever anew the one thing necessary must be held before them in a simple and consistent way, and deep in their hearts a solid foundation must be laid for repentance and faith. For such a rescue plan a church with a solid confession is necessary; I am convinced of that. We do not preach Luther and a Lutheran confession to the poor souls whom we gather here, but rather Christ and his cross. We preach Christ until they themselves believe and confess, but we preach the Christ whom our church confesses—not one we have devised. Therein lies a great difference.

Someone might think that a specific confession of this sort constricts the heart and lays a yoke on the shoulders, so that the individual is neither able to breathe freely nor to serve a poor soul in complete freedom. However, I have not sensed this effect in the slightest. Of course, no one can make life's path any wider than our Lord Jesus made it; it is narrow, and few there are who like it so narrow. But this I confess freely: the confession of the church has not been a restriction, any more than God's Word itself, that would have caused me to turn away a single poor, hungry, and thirsty soul, or that would have made me ask: who is my neighbor? In addition, I have never found our church doctrine to repel a soul who is hungry for grace, but rather, because of the doctrine's deep and warm nature, it finds open doors to their hearts.

I have also experienced that our people are drawn to the beautiful liturgies of our forebears, because the congregation itself steps before the Lord in prayer, confession, and with changing melodies of praise, psalms, and wonderful spiritual hymns. Because of their good sense the people reach with both hands for the old, unadulterated, core hymns of our church. We do not forget that we are missionary people. This is clearly demonstrated by the nineteen evening worship services, mostly in German, that we hold weekly, in which God's Word is explained in the very simplest manner. At the same time, we do not withhold the beautiful, rich worship services of our forebears from the souls who gather.

In short, we would like to become everything to everyone everywhere in order to save a few [1 Cor 9:22]. Yet, it is our far greater desire not only to win individual souls, but also to bring entire hosts of poor sinners into eternal life. That is why—that is the only reason why—we wave our banner of faith. No friend of Jesus ought to be annoyed by it, and no enemy shall tear it away from us. We feel very confident that with it we have chosen the better part, which cannot be taken from us. Our conscience assures us that we know and want no other salvation than through Christ alone, and hence we join in the heartfelt prayer:

O, help me regard things
on earth as mere sin,
while one thing is needful:
Christ's blessing to win.

F. Bodelschwingh

FRIEDRICH VON BODELSCHWINGH

The Worker Question

EDITORS' INTRODUCTION: Bodelschwingh's reputation as a social-welfare pioneer emboldened him to speak out on questions of national and political concern. These included topics such as the death penalty, the lottery, dueling, gambling, and drinking. The article that follows,[1] written for the readers of Bodelschwingh's Sunday magazine, *The Westphalian Family Friend*, provides an instructive picture of a pastor engaged in one of the most vexing issues of his day: what can one do in the face of the growing plight of wage earners who, in his words, have "sunk to the level of commodities on the slave market of free competition"?

Unlike the socialist polemicists who proposed to attack the problem through varying degrees of political reform, Bodelschwingh argues that the fundamental problem of the workers—worship of money—can be solved only if the workers serve their proper master, God. This remedy creates, in turn, the challenging need for workers in church and school to oppose the spirit of the day and nurture people in the spirit of Jesus Christ.

The worker question is the severe storm looming more and more threateningly on the horizon, and we can expect it to unleash its terror in this century unless God sends special help. Admittedly, the latest workers' congresses have been more an object of ridicule than anything else, since the heads of the various workers' organizations, themselves like aimless stars in the heavens, have been incapable of providing any reliable direction to the masses they lead. Swearing, bellowing, shattered beer glasses, and finally, people getting tossed out one after the other, form the overall impression an observer gets from these meetings. Meanwhile, the laughter of a conscientious observer soon turns to tears when the observer pays heed to the sounds of profound grief and plaintive cries of pain to be heard through all the chaotic clamor. What alienation from God, and hence, what despair! What hopelessness in the struggle of the throngs of workers for a better lot in life!

The picture of paradise painted for the blind masses is that they can share with the employers or even the capitalists, that they can earn more money with less effort. So should one be surprised if the masses take the bait? Is it not precisely money—naked mammon—with all the earthly pleasures and joys it affords, which industry, the worshiped idol of our century, has enthroned? Strive, above all, for money, lots of it, and then all the happiness a person can hope for will be yours! There is no hereafter, so be blissfully happy here. Spirit and eternity are foolishness; the flesh, material pleasures, temporal happiness—they are the treasures one should run after. This is what the liberal, enlightened sociopolitical experts of the nineteenth century preach. The life of luxury, the stylish, good life is necessary in order for industry to reach its peak. The more that people in their vanity consume, the higher the value of the capital, which then can be rolled over and multiplied all the faster. This is what the person with calloused hands or pale face sees who is stuck at some machine as if one had no will of one's own.

Such persons, in this era when all patriarchal relationships and personal ties are tearing apart, have sunk to the level of commodities on the slave market of free competition. Does it surprise us that such persons, great in offering and selling themselves for the sake of money, become slaves of mammon themselves? Does it surprise us that if they think life is only about money, pleasure, and the here-and-now, they will want to have their share, even if it means by force? Does it surprise us that the Berlin newspaper for workers calls to the preachers of the new blissfulness and those who worship the idol of industry: where is your logic, you pitiful pharisees from the free community and the liberal bourgeoisie, you who have torn the consolation of devout faith away from the people and yet do not want to remove the iron yoke of machines from them? The logic of world history is more rigorous than yours: "Heaven is a thing of the past; the people are justified in laying claim to the earth."[2] Does it surprise us that the party leaders of the masses who no longer believe in God and are no longer afraid of any human authority put these principles into practice with all the fanaticism and terrible consequences of their greedy hearts?

What kind of a dam can we construct in order to hold back the rising, dark-red flood? Nowadays people want to heal every wound with money. They want to cure this century's misery of mammon with mammon. However, one devil does not drive out the other, says the Lord [Mark 3:23]. What good is it if young people of both genders can already earn so much money at fifteen years of age that they no longer need their parents and set up their own turbulent households, only to degenerate into dissoluteness and poverty all the sooner? This is what we see in France and England. The more freely and easily money flows, the more easily and loosely it is squandered, and in the heart alienated from God the appetite for money and pleasure grows and grows.

Naturally, through good laws the state can accomplish some things, and prohibiting work on Sundays, prohibiting child labor, regulating working hours, and so on, are all salutary initiatives. If the state wanted to, it could do even more by regulating the dispensing of alcoholic drinks.[3] The number of pubs, now growing far beyond bounds, and the serving of liquor, which in actuality is subject to no limitations, are wounding our people more seriously than any laws or millions of donors can heal.

In any case, none of these measures will help in the long run. There are neither pills nor powders to prescribe for the misery caused by the service to mammon, which is one and the same with the misery of the worker. The only remedy is the word of him who said: "No one can serve two masters; you cannot serve God and mammon" [Matt 6:24].

The problem of the workers will be solved only through the solution of another worker problem of which Christ speaks when he says: "Ask the Lord of the harvest to send workers into his harvest" [Matt 9:38]. It is clear that the need for workers in the harvest must be remedied first, before the other need will diminish.

Particularly alarming is the lack of good workers in churches and schools. Recently a commission of teachers gathered at Rausingen to study the question of how to increase the number of Christian teachers. Mr. Buschmann, a superintendent of schools, informed them that the number of unfilled positions is growing annually at an alarming rate, while at the same time the schools must accept sixteen- and seventeen-year-old boys. Beyond that came the far more painful news from the teachers in the commission of the vanishing number of teachers in their circles who truly love God's Word. The materialistic spirit of mammon in our century causes fewer and fewer young people to take up the sacred vocation of teaching, a vocation that demands they forgo a great deal. Moreover, the materialistic spirit has already infected most of those who take up the vocation.

Here, in the final analysis, is where we must look for help: "Wake up, O spirit of the first witnesses, in church and school!" [cf. Acts 26:16]. We need workers who, in pulpits and homes, speak without fear to the conscience of the princes of capital and kings of industry in their palaces, as well as to the poor factory laborers and wage earners in their hovels: "You fool, your soul will be required of you tonight. What will happen with all you have prepared? You cannot serve God and mammon" [Luke 12:20; Matt 6:24]. We need workers in schools, above all, that nurture the next generation in the spirit of Jesus Christ, not in the spirit of the times. We need faithful servants of God willing to forgo a great deal, who themselves have found the one thing needful and are able to answer the question: "Simon John, do you love me?" [John 21:15–17]. Who will help pray for such workers? Who will put their hands to the task and enter into the great harvest? [Luke 9:62]. The danger in delaying is indeed great.

FRIEDRICH VON BODELSCHWINGH

Melanchthon
[A Response to the Protestant Union and Rationalism]

EDITORS' INTRODUCTION: The original one-word title does not alert the reader to the fact that this article is a resounding rejection of what Bodelschwingh regards as the Rationalist view held by the Protestant Union, the official confederation of the Lutheran and Reformed confessions imposed in Prussia by Friedrich Wilhelm III in 1817. "Melanchthon," which happened to be the first word of the piece, served as the title when it was published in July 1870 in Bodelschwingh's Sunday magazine, *The Westphalian Family Friend.*[1] One can profitably compare this essay with Fliedner's article on the Apostles' Creed earlier in this volume.

What prompted Bodelschwingh's polemic was the appearance earlier in the same year of a book by Karl Wilhelm Kunis, *Reason and Revelation: The Contradictions Between Faith and Knowledge Treated Scientifically and Philosophically.*[2] Kunis's viewpoint draws the response from Bodelschwingh that the Protestant Union is dishonest when it claims it wants to rid the church of dead doctrines. Rather, Bodelschwingh argues, the real goal of the Union is to get rid of Jesus as the divine Christ. He outlines the contrasting positions that derive from believing that Jesus is either only a human being, which he identifies as the Rationalist view, or the divine-human Son of God. Bodelschwingh attacks the former position because, in his view, it leads to the conclusion that Jesus is nothing more than "the noblest of the noble," a conclusion that does not motivate people to lead a life of compassion. Bodelschwingh explains that those who serve others are those who believe in the God who sacrificed himself for them.

Melanchthon, author of the Augsburg Confession,[3] once said, when accused of being too zealous in his study of theology, "It is clear to me that I never pursued theology for any other reason than to lead a better life."[4] So, too, we answer the Protestant Union when it seeks to overturn the Confessions of the church using concepts about "dead doctrines, unfruitful dogmas that no human intellect can understand and that cannot warm any human heart." The Protestant Union declares: "We know of no other doctrines than those whose power is proved in life. We know of, and desire, no other faith than faith active in love." It is a lie when the Protestant Union tricks the German people with all kinds of empty phrases, as if the Union were about the business of freeing the church from a welter of dead, mortal doctrines. O, no; the Union is concerned only about one single point, namely, the stone that the builders in the high council in Jerusalem rejected, but who nevertheless became the cornerstone. The Protestant Union would very much like to dig the same cornerstone out of the foundation, knowing full well that the whole structure would collapse.

I am fond of recalling a poor Jew who, upon hearing a chaplain's sermon in front of troops at Sebastopol,[5] received the kind of thorn in his heart that Saul had tried to kick against in vain [2 Cor 12:3]. During the crossing to Marseilles the boat encountered extremely dangerous conditions, and in deathly fear the soldier vowed that if he could step on land once more he would ask about Jesus of Nazareth. The man forgot his promise, and in Paris God threw him into bed with such a serious illness that he was taken to a hospital. One day when I was visiting a Protestant patient in the same hospital and was reading from the New Testament, I noticed that the person in the bed next to us had raised his head and, from the look on his face, was listening very attentively. It was the poor Jew. He asked for a New Testament, and then for an Old, in order to find out if the things were true. Though interrupted by horrible suffering, he searched with great enthusiasm for four months. Then I saw him one evening in his bed of pain. His face was beaming with joy, and the words burst out: "He is the one!" He had found his Messiah in Jesus of Nazareth.

Here lies the heart of the issue: Is he the one, or is he not? Is Jesus of Nazareth the Lord whom David, in the Spirit, already called his Lord, and whom he saw sitting at the right hand of God? [Ps 110:1]. Was Thomas right when he sank down before the man with the nail prints on his hands and feet and proclaimed: "My Lord and my God"? [John 20:28]. Did Jesus truly rise from the dead and prove powerfully to be the Son of God in the real, true sense of the word, as he had sworn before Caiaphas? [Matt 26:63–64]. Or is there simply nothing to it? Do I have enough with just Jesus the human being?

I have before me a book that appeared just recently.[6] It is by a scholar in Leipzig who, entirely in the spirit of the Protestant Union, describes the life of the historical Jesus (pages 150–80). He dismisses as mere embellishments of the evangelists Jesus' pre-earthly existence, his supernatural birth, his miracles, his prophecies, his resurrection, his ascension into heaven, in short, everything that points beyond the earth.

It should be noted, however, that he praises Jesus of Nazareth mightily for his fiery soul, his love of others, his modesty and gentleness, his moral purity, and his trust in God. His lofty example had an ennobling effect on the lower classes, to which he belonged. Of course, Jesus let himself be misled by the praise of his followers and, as a result, saw himself as one especially pardoned by God, and he became a little arrogant. This brought about his death. Nevertheless, when all is said and done, he was "the noblest of the noble."

So, in what direction does the author of the book proceed in following up this "noblest of the noble," whose moral purity and greatness of soul he elevates so high, and whose "awe-inspiring religiosity" he praises? We hear the following. First, he proves that matter is eternal; hence, there is no creator, because there was nothing to create. Second, he proves that the human being derives from lower forms of the plant and animal world, finally from apes, and he denies any principal difference between humans and animals: there is no soul, to say nothing of an immortal soul. Third, he proves that there is no personal freedom. The atoms in matter, which attract and repel each other according to eternal laws, and which in this process have developed all the way up to the human brain, continue operating there according to the same laws. One cannot think or act differently than one thinks and acts, otherwise one would be interfering with the eternal laws of matter. It is pure deception for us to imagine that we have a free will to do something good or to avoid doing something evil. Good and evil do not exist at all. Everyone does only what he or she finds most pleasant. This is the only moral dictate: strive for pleasant sensations, yet in a way that does not harm your fellow human beings, for if you harm your fellow human beings you harm yourself and disturb your pleasant sensations. That is how far the tender filaments of feeling in the atoms of the human brain have brought things. What self-interest the natural laws have found!

Aside from the fact that the author launches several caustic attacks full of moral indignation at those who believe in the Bible (if there is no personal freedom he ought to excuse the creeping atoms in the brains of these people), he is fully consistent.

> If it is correct that Jesus of Nazareth was just a human being, then everything supernatural must be deleted from his life. Since there are neither miracles nor prophecies there is also no living God, no creator nor preserver of the world. The eternal laws of nature are our gods. Resurrection and eternal life must be translated into the proper expression, "eternal exchange of matter." Human beings are nothing more than the highest developed blossoms of nature, which also decompose like autumn leaves, with nothing remaining but, at most, a memory of them in the oscillations of the brain atoms of following generations.[7]

If there is no god above nature who can intervene in it freely, then neither can the human being who is the product of the eternal laws of nature. Human life is a clockwork that runs down and with which humans cannot meddle any more than a clock can meddle with its own works. There can be no talk of sin or of freedom of the will. These are the only correct conclusions to be drawn from the sentence: Jesus of Nazareth can only have been a human being like us.

One sees how terribly far apart our paths diverge from this one, first point. If he is not the one—if he is not the Son of the living God in the sense that the scriptures and the church profess—then there is no living God either. Then there is neither heaven nor hell, sin nor grace, guilt nor responsibility, salvation nor damnation, neither resurrection nor eternal life. We all fulfill our life's calling if we arouse in ourselves as many pleasant sensations as possible, while at the same time doing good for our neighbors. The most sophisticated self-interest is the highest morality. This is the dogmatic of the spirit of the times in our illustrious century.

If, on the other hand, he is the one—if he is Jesus Christ, the eternal Son of the living God—then we have a creator and father in heaven, a God who works miracles and hears prayer. Then we have sin and guilt, freedom and slavery, mercy and deliverance. Then we have immortal human souls and a day of resurrection, a judgment seat before which we all must open ourselves. Then we have a new life emanating from God, self-denying love, and Christian virtue, which in the fervent, open struggle of faith subdues sin and death and wrestles for the jewel held up before us by the divine calling in God. Then we have an inheritance for the saints in light, a Jerusalem above, and a Father's house that stands forever.

Do you think these are dead dogmas and statutes that cannot warm the human heart? Obviously our minds do not have the capacity to measure God's love, no more than we can surround the heavens with the breadth of our hand. Hence, it can still be said: "O, what depths both of God's wisdom and understanding! Who has known the mind of the Lord, and who has been his counselor?" [Rom 11:33–34]. Yet, even though God's love and his Son's love are beyond all understanding (Eph 3:19), and even though the great "therefore" (John 3:16) will remain an unfathomable mystery of all sanctified people and angels in all eternity, it is nevertheless precisely this same love that possesses the miraculous power to warm and ignite cold human hearts. Otherwise, what would be left of the power of the Palm Sunday epistle, Philippians 2:5–11, which paints in broad strokes the descent of the Son from his eternal heights to the deepest ignominy of his death on the cross, and then his ascent even as far as the hour of indescribable majesty when all knees in heaven and on earth and under the earth will bow before him? Otherwise what would be left of the words full of the stirring power of love (2 Cor 8:9) that speak of the eternally rich one who became poor for our sake, so that we could become rich through his impoverishment? What if there were nothing to the pre-earthly existence of Christ, nothing to his majesty at the right hand of his Father before the world existed? Just open up our hymnbook. What is it that has caused the harps of sacred singers in all centuries of Christianity to ring out in song, other than this very love? If there were nothing to the preexistence of Christ, who could still sing with Paul Gerhardt:

> The crown of noblest honor
> you bore upon your head,
> but you I greet this hour
> despised and mocked instead.[8]

Or, if there were nothing to the true, eternal divinity of our redeemer, who, then, could still sing with Gesenius (in the magnificent hymn, "When My Sins Grieve Me," and so on):

> "O wonder so unbounded!"
> say those who do observe:
> the master, he was martyred,
> instead of those who serve.
> The one true God, it was but he
> who found me lost and straying,
> and suffered death for me.[9]

Truly, the heart of our hymns, indeed, the heart of our most inspiring hymns, would have to be cut out of the hymnbook if our doctrine were false.

As we know, Rationalism, which sees in Jesus of Nazareth only "the noblest of the noble," only the "blossom of humanity," and praises his example, has been able to produce a veritable flood of splendid hymns about virtue. In these hymns the self-righteousness of one's own heart can be reflected splendidly, ultimately to such a degree that one regards oneself as the noblest of the noble. Yet, a sinful human heart kindled with love for God? That is not a part of Rationalism.

As it is with words, so it is with deeds. Hence, only the person who has been forgiven abundantly can love abundantly [Luke 7:47]. Only the person who can confess with Peter knows the extent to which one has been forgiven: "Know that you have been redeemed neither with gold nor silver, but with the precious blood of Christ, the innocent and spotless lamb" [1 Pet 1:18–19]. These words would be nonsense and foolishness if Jesus were only a human like us. Followers of the "historical Jesus" have always achieved, to be sure, isolated deeds of love that do people some good or affect earthly things. Nevertheless, everyone knows that the Protestant Union and all its precursors have never lifted a finger to save lost souls, never lifted a finger for foreign missions, never lifted a finger for Christian care of the sick, of the imprisoned, of abandoned children, and so forth. All these tasks are a blessed prerogative of those whose hearts have been kindled by faith in the love of him who has loved us forever in his eternal Son.

The Diaconate

Deaconess Pledge

EDITORS' INTRODUCTION: Soon after Bodelschwingh took over the network of facilities known as Bethel, its rapid growth meant that ever more women were needed to serve as deaconesses. Soon Bodelschwingh composed the pledge spoken by each woman taking up the vocation.[1] While the pledge was not unique—Bodelschwingh was acquainted with Theodor Fliedner's pledge for deaconesses at Kaiserswerth, as well as that of Wilhelm Löhe for Neuendettelsau— his words express succinctly how one is to live in community as well as how one is to serve others.

In 1900 Bodelschwingh gave an address at the motherhouse about the pledge he had crafted many years earlier. In it he expressed his understanding of the significance of a woman's decision:

> The early church fathers had the saying, *servitium Christi summa libertas*—in translation, "servitude to Christ is the greatest freedom."…With her vow, made at a sacred place, the sister who is consecrated to the office of serving love takes a joyful, new step into the marvelous freedom of a Christian, and precisely because she has bound herself more firmly to Christ's yoke.[2]

In this volume the pledge serves not only as a window into Bodelschwingh's spirituality, but also as a reminder of the many generations of women dedicated to its simple yet demanding vision.

1. Do you voluntarily resolve to accept as your life's vocation the office of loving service in Christ's church and pledge to fulfill the same in humility, obedience, and faithfulness according to the capacities that God has given you, and to persevere in the same, unless God's will clearly points to another path?

2. Do you, as Jesus Christ's redeemed who have received mercy, pledge to be merciful friends of the poor, sick, lost, and lowly, in the love that Jesus offers those who are saved?

3. Do you furthermore pledge, as consecrated sisters, to be models for the younger sisters in all that is good, teaching and encouraging them through loving words and good example to labor in humility, obedience, faithfulness, and unity of spirit in the work of Jesus?

4. Finally, do you pledge through the power of Christ's obedience to renounce your own will completely, and, as long as your obedience does not require you to do anything against God's will, to be willing and meticulous in your obedience toward the directors of the Mother House, Sarepta, which accepted you as its own with fatherly and motherly love, and which, as long as you do not leave due to your own willfulness, will provide for and take care of you until the end of your life? If so, answer:

Yes, by the grace of God.

Nurturing the Sisters in Truthfulness and Discipline in the Community and Through the Community

Speech at Kaiserswerth at the Sixth General Conference of Deaconess Mother Houses

EDITORS' INTRODUCTION: In 1878, little more than forty years after Theodor Fliedner founded the first deaconess house in Germany, fifty motherhouses were in operation and their leaders gathered for their sixth annual conference at Kaiserswerth. By this time the acknowledged national leader of deaconess work was Friedrich von Bodelschwingh.

In this address to the conference Bodelschwingh examines the challenge of how one is to achieve the purpose of a motherhouse.[1] Rather than taking up issues of training or even administration, as one might expect, he addresses a more fundamental issue by engaging in a probing analysis of spiritual life in community. He maintains that the purpose of a motherhouse is to move the human heart from lying to truthfulness and from defiance of to obedience to Christ. This purpose is a challenge because, as Bodelschwingh contends, impurity and self-will—contradictions to the aim of the motherhouse—are precisely the traits that characterize the human being.

First, Bodelschwingh details a list of factors in a motherhouse that promote impurity and self-will. Then he reviews the means by which the pastor and supervising sisters can combat these negative factors and nurture the deaconesses. A deaconess's growth in the desired qualities depends fundamentally on her acceptance of Christ's forgiveness of sins, because only this contrition produces the humility that, in turn, frees a person from self-righteousness and self-will.

386

FRIEDRICH VON BODELSCHWINGH

Bodelschwingh's careful analysis and detailed recommendations are based not only on his personal experience of presiding over a motherhouse but also on his astute observation and understanding of human behavior.

All people are liars, and their hearts are defiant and cheerless things, says God's Word [cf. Rom 1:18–32]. These words apply to our sisters, too, not only when they stand before the entry gate of a deaconess house, but also when they leave the same in death. Impurity and self-will are enemies with which any poor sinner, even a pardoned sinner, must keep struggling until the hour of death. Ultimately, the question is whether nurturing grace gradually moves the human heart more and more from lying to truthfulness, from defiance of Christ to obedience. A deaconess house definitely does not understand its task if, despite all the activities and work it does for others, this teaching effort is not attended to, or if the institution perhaps sinks to the level of a training institute for play-acting by persons with undisciplined inner lives.

I recall what a friend of mine once said in a sermon on Confirmation Sunday. He ranked Confirmation Day without question above all other days as being not merely troublesome but thoroughly painful. He did this in light of concrete experience that after this day one observes in most children a decided regression on the path to heaven, and progress in only a few.

Who among us deaconess pastors does not become worried every time a young Christian woman arrives at the entry gate of the deaconess house and asks to be admitted into the bond of sisterhood? Will she find in the sisterhood what she needs? Will she find a strong helping hand along life's way, a watch and protection against the enemies of her soul? Will she find the salt of truth and the disciplining love of self-understanding and of surrendering one's self?

Have we not also found that the opposite sometimes occurs? Do we not hear sighs in the deaconess houses from the hearts of poor deaconesses: "Since I crossed the threshold of this house I have gone backward instead of forward!" Is it not true that many a sister in the deaconess house has suffered harm to her inner person?

Let us first of all face this painful issue with courage and ask: is it really possible for a community of deaconesses to promote rather than to inhibit lying, dishonesty, self-will, and lack of discipline? The deaconess house: an institution that teaches impurity and lack of discipline? Certainly a horrible thought, and yet not an impossible one!

If we take a look at the young Christian women who appear at our doors it cannot be denied that the first danger of impurity and false pretenses is particularly great. According to the admission criteria presented to them, and on the basis of which they are examined, they present themselves in order to lead a life of self-denial, obedience, willing poverty, and thankful love to him who first loved them. For his sake alone they want to serve their brothers and sisters. Is this really true? Is not a multitude of secondary aims present, of which the sisters themselves might be unaware? Instead of self-denial, merely a more refined self-centeredness? Instead of obedience—which perhaps had become an aggravation at home—hope for greater independence and for following one's own will? Instead of humility, through which one wants to become less, pride that reaches for greater honor than one would receive as an ordinary young woman? Are such thoughts and words not heard from young sisters when there are menial tasks to be done? "That is suitable for a maid, not for a deaconess. Those people have obviously forgotten who I am!," and so on. Do not deaconesses often seek thanks and praise from others? Or is the predominant wish perhaps for earthly comforts? Sometimes the idea of becoming a deaconess is strenuously pushed on the poorest of children by relatives who have no idea what to do with them, even though the children lack absolutely everything for being a deaconess.

And what other impurities lie in the heart! It has happened to me that girls have applied because they are absolutely unable to get along with their parents and siblings. Others are driven to the door of the deaconess house by weariness with the world, or by the jumble of their life's hopes, or by a tendency to romanticize.

FRIEDRICH VON BODELSCHWINGH

Perhaps already existing impurities such as these suddenly come to light in the community of sisters, or maybe the community simply provides the soil in which the impurities can grow, blossom, and unfold. Is it not true that the moment a poor woman dons the deaconess cap, even though she might have entered in finery, she is immediately regarded more highly in the world and assumes a higher social rank? In fact, from the secular point of view is it not true that the majority of women who enter the deaconess house do not take a step downward to greater poverty and lowliness but a step upward to greater honor in the eyes of others?[2] And how much of the old Adam does a woman not cover up or hide under the deaconess cap in order not to lose the bothersome honor connected with it? What a wide field opens up for spiritual acting! Moreover, this acting is even more likely if the deaconess house exerts in place of inner spiritual discipline only a nice outward discipline that can change unnoticeably into a mere facade of outward rules.

Unfortunately, there is not only a facade in rules of dress, and so forth, but also in Christian talk, which, the less it pervades one's heart, the more it crosses one's lips. Both the salt of truth from God's Word that takes hold of the inner person and the fire of love that warms the person are to outweigh the outward rules and forms of law. Wherever they do not, one finds the kind of community life of impure souls that has not broken away from impurity.

I must confess that when I sometimes come across a young sister who, it is clear, has extremely well-cared-for clothing, very smoothly combed hair, a well-schooled manner in her face, eyes, and speech, and who, only a short time before sat unkempt in the cow stall or at the loom, I shudder because I get the impression that the inner person has lagged far behind the outer. The further the inner heart is alienated from the truth of Christ's love and obedience to him, the more perfect the outward forms can become, so that even experienced pastors can be deceived and take imitation pearls for the genuine thing. It is astonishing, simply astonishing, what Christian-motivated girls can achieve in the art of pleasing pastors. Moreover, such misshapen figures can slip into any deaconess house.

Yes, even the devotional practices of our houses can be misused as tools of play-acting (we know this goes on in excess in Catholic cloisters). Here, too, the most beautiful forms can obscure the content and lull souls to sleep so they think they have the kernel when they have only the shell. Perhaps only a slight spiritual need had been present, and now all of a sudden comes an abundance of spiritual food in devotions and worship services. A person becomes accustomed to it, participates outwardly in everything, and is content. Do our deaconess houses not daily run the dual risk either of letting the salt of truth lose its effect because of outward forms or of killing spiritual hunger by over-saturation with officially prescribed devotional practices, namely, when these are polished off quickly and no time is allowed for quiet reflection?

And how is it with the second point, with the question of one's own will, with promoting genuine humility and willing obedience? O, how many sisters enter the circle of deaconesses and do not have the most precious gift, the most necessary thing, I would say, for a deaconess: a broken heart! Can it even be possible for a person without a broken heart to maintain herself in a community of sisters in which, as one should assume, no sustenance is available for the self-will? Here I must again answer: unfortunately, yes.

I am not speaking of houses where God's Word is entirely missing, and there are such, even though they are not represented among ours. Certainly in such houses the gates and doors are wide open to the lack of discipline, and on the daily agenda are wars in which everyone fights against everyone else. However, it is also possible that even though an outwardly firm discipline and an outwardly meticulous obedience dwell in a house, and even though the law and fear have the upper hand over selfish desires, the heart remains unbroken. A facade, such as the Catholic Church has, breaks no hearts inwardly but merely bends stiff necks for the sake of appearance.

No real freedom from the slavery to one's own will can exist where fear and strictness rather than the truth of love are in charge.

Where they dominate, one will find that as soon as a sister—one who has been obedient merely because of outward fear—achieves a position of leadership, she will impose her self-will all the more against her subordinates. Woe to those young sisters who come under the supervision of a deaconess who has reached her position in such a way. They will have to suffer much without her old Adam really being affected. Yes, such a domineering, self-willed, inwardly undisciplined deaconess will, in turn, cultivate similar successors out of inwardly unbroken sisters.

If what is asserted from the most experienced quarters is true, that deaconesses who get married after many years in the vocation are very seldom happy precisely because they are accustomed to too independent a life, then the assertion is also an admission that the deaconess vocation offers much nourishment for the self-will. For my own part, I tremble when I think of the great host of mostly very young girls who otherwise might have served for many years in jobs with little independence. Yet quite independently they oversee their often large households and must command an entire host of people. O, how many a genuinely humble heart can suffer shipwreck on such a cliff of premature governance by finding too great a pleasure in it. One can observe the danger in cases where, for example, through illness of the supervisory sister a younger one is pressed into service temporarily. O, how sweet the time seems to many of them. However, when they are to step back into simple service in their subordinate position, the bitter lack of willing obedience often becomes painfully obvious! And the older a house becomes, the more painful the experiences become, also with older sisters of whom one would never have suspected it.

Now that we have looked the threatening dangers straight in the eye, it will be all the easier for us to find the correct weapons to guard and protect us. And—praise God—even if the temptations of impurity and self-will are powerful in a deaconess community, the antidotes given us against such afflictions are even more powerful.

Which task, then, is the first to fall to the pastor of the house? O, how he will want to impart properly the word of truth entrusted to him, to apply law and gospel in the proper places, publicly and privately, to bring the salt of truth and the comfort of love close to every individual soul, because only both—in proper proportion and at the same time—can lead people to truthfulness and genuine humbling of the soul. In particular, it will be his task to cause each deaconess, in her own eyes, to be, and want to be, nothing other than what she professes to be: a poor sinner. Second: that she indeed knows of, and seeks no other rescue from her sin, than the forgiveness of sins in the blood of Christ. He will have to punish in earnest not only where he sees a self-chosen sanctity and virtue emerging, but also where a Christianity of feeling begins spreading itself, which would like to establish its peace more on its own experiences and feelings than on the Word of the forgiveness of sins. He will need to track down carefully the hidden impurities and delicate idiosyncrasies that hide under the cover of the beautiful vocation, even as in Zinzendorf's request:[3]

> Sovereign, whom we all are serving,
> —whether from the heart, you see—
> save us through your reconciling
> from a false serenity.
>
> Make us vigilant in heeding
> whether we have hearts sincere,
> whether we embrace your leading,
> whether we are mere veneer.
>
> Under sensitive behavior
> are the depths we could not see
> as we slept in great composure
> in our crude security.

With commanding force he will also have to take the field against the type of arrogance and self-will that often poses quite humbly behind the mask of sensitivity. This sensitivity, which is full of excuses and lacks the peaceable wisdom from above to accept advice gladly, is a real plague in deaconess houses. It is arrogant and counterfeit at the same time. There are sisters who get sick every time they are criticized or cannot have their own way, while wanting to appear as though they are very unassuming, as though they would always like the lowest seat, like to be unrecognized, and so on. Two very sharp, clean, two-edged weapons must be used against such poisonous evil: a deep seriousness about truth, and an even greater measure of urgent love that believes all things, hopes all things, and endures all things [1 Cor 13:7].

As watchman for the entire spiritual direction of the house the pastor must make it a matter of greatest concern that no practices, forfeitures, or sacrifices can be demanded of the sisters that exceed their measure of faith (Rom 12 [:3]), which nourish hypocritical self-praise or mislead the sisters to look down on other co-workers in the kingdom of God—for example, housewives and mothers. All in all, the entire life, work, and suffering of the deaconess must contain nothing other than what, according to the Ten Commandments and the sacred baptismal vow, can be demanded of any other Christians in their vocation and place: never anything self-chosen, exaggerated, or harmful. No tasks can be laid upon the sisters that Christ and his Word do not also lay upon them. I do believe that according to the degree to which the life of faith gains strength in individual sisters they can be expected to take greater tests of love. It is questionable, however, to demand serious tests of love from a weak faith, and one must choose carefully in light of the varying circumstances—strong shoulders for heavy loads. Otherwise you will have backbreaking experiments.

So that the sisters' life of faith can grow the pastor will have to see that time is set aside for them to have quiet reflection. One's life cannot be taken up entirely by hasty Martha-living and by perhaps even more hasty devotions and worship services [Luke 10:38–42]. Without a life of prayer, a true life of prayer, no true life of faith is possible, and without a true life of faith no true life of love is possible.

But he will have to balance the scales not only in regard to the life of faith and love but also in regard to heavenly and earthly bread. By the latter I do not mean primarily the physical eating and drinking, the caring for the body that Paul orders [cf. 1 Cor 6:12–13]. Of course, there are people who already equate the deaconesses here below with angels and who think they require neither sleep nor food. In this regard it can well be the pastor's task to see that the sisters receive what is necessary and salutary so that neither an undisciplined embitterment nor an overly spiritual self-denial is fostered.

However, his responsibility lies far more in preventing a one-sided satiation from spiritual food. He must ensure that care in terms of earthly things goes hand in hand with care in terms of heavenly things for the soul. The sisters do, after all, live on earth, not only in heaven, and they must know and have as much of the earth as suits their vocation and circle of activity. Otherwise they become not only one-sided but also in many cases inwardly false, not only toward themselves but toward those in their care. Once a young, staunch Christian woman who had consumption and was preparing herself with great earnestness for death said to the sisters who were caring for her, and who thought they had to talk to her only about dying and eternity: "You don't always have to talk to the sick only about dying." That is exactly right.

My practice, when young sisters enter, is to demand at first only one pledge of "yes"—the promise of forthrightness. "God allows only the upright to flourish" [cf. Prov 10:16]. I impress upon them how utterly impossible it would be for their work to succeed if they secretly pour out their needs and conflicts not only to the One who knows the heart but to all kinds of people who are not involved, while keeping them secret from us. I tell them that my room and the house-mother's room are open to them at all times in order for them to pour out their needs in confidence, and I ask them to make use of this invitation as freely as they wish. Of course, we, for our part, have to make use of the sister's initial "yes." The sisters must be taken at their word, and this word must be held up before them frequently: "You promised me and gave me your hand on it that you will be forthright." In most cases this promise has been honest, but experience teaches that feminine shyness almost always prevents even the forthright from accepting our invitation.

We have in our hand the most powerful and most compassionate means of nurture: prior to public confession the personal declaration that one intends to go to the Lord's supper. Given the

394

frequent changes of shifts, the great amount of coming and going that often requires the sisters to leave a service just before celebrating the sacrament, and given the often very intense hours they must face, the Lord's supper should be celebrated in a deaconess house no less than once a month.

It goes without saying that I do not equate the personal registration for the Lord's supper with obligatory private confession. It is, of course, good when in small congregations the pastor can absolve each individual penitent personally after the general confession. However, one must handle personal confession itself with great delicacy, making sure that it is totally voluntary. Otherwise it can turn suddenly into its opposite, becoming a means of nurturing hypocrisy.

In contrast, the personal declaration, which can be used by all, is a thing of compassion. It is to be a means of assistance, without being insistent, that helps shy souls in particular to open their hearts to their pastor. The latter will make allowances for the fact that a few sisters are inclined to speak about the condition of their souls, while others, who are in greater need of it, are incredibly reserved. Consequently, the pastor will need to rein in the one who is inclined to spiritual effusion and inspire the other to talk openly.

Also, in order not to deceive himself, the pastor will have to make allowance for the fact that Christian-motivated young women can speak and behave toward their pastors quite differently than they otherwise would. O, how differently young sisters can act when they know they are not being observed, as opposed to when they are under the eyes of the pastor or other superiors. On the other hand, it should be noted that generally the judgment of women by women partly vacillates, is partly too stern, while the judgment of men about women is mostly too mild.

Given these considerations the pastor must act as a caretaker of souls with the individuals who register for communion, and, above all, must work to keep them from bringing any conscious impurity or intentional disobedience to the table of the Lord's supper. At these pastoral conversations he will have to apply the wisdom of not imparting immediately the unfavorable or bad things he has heard from others about the respective sister, but first of all emphasize the favorable and good things others have shared with him. Through this kind of friendly recognition of what is good, one prepares the soil for correction. The sister gains greater desire and courage to confess her sinful acts voluntarily. In contrast, if one starts off with only the accusations one has heard from others, then one arouses bitterness and the sister's determination to justify herself. When the sister confesses voluntarily, he compassionately treats her distress about sin, completely covers her error with Jesus' blood, and completely forgets it, without bringing it up unnecessarily at every opportunity [cf. Heb 9—10]. By doing this he offers the struggling soul an intercessory heart for the good fight [1 Tim 6:12]. Then courage and love of forthrightness will be strengthened mightily in the sister.

The pastor has manifold opportunities in addition to the days of holy communion to nurture the sisters: the hours of instruction, the visits to patients at the sisters' stations, the hours of preparation for consecration, and, above all, the change in shifts, when the sisters are to report to the pastor each time and be accompanied by him in prayer. On his journeys he should never be satisfied with greeting the sisters in common and asking them as a group how things are going. Rather, as far as possible, he should never move on without giving each individual the opportunity to speak with him face to face, reminding her of the pledge of sincerity that she gave. O, how much then comes to light that in the circle of sisters no one was willing to say, or for which the courage was lacking.

Finally, the pastor will have to set an example for the sisters who teach and supervise by not ruling over the sheep entrusted to him but by being a model for them. Regardless of all the authority he has acquired, especially by first submitting himself to the word he preaches, "We have learned that an upright nature is in Jesus Christ" [cf. Ps 92:14–15], he will have to guard himself carefully against being the kind of person who demands respect. Otherwise the anxious person will dare not approach him. Only with a truly compassionate, fatherly, and above all discreet nature that arouses confidence can he actually help plant purity and willing obedience in the circle of sisters. Overall, he must show that it never matters to him to assert only his will but rather to treat each soul in the manner that is best for God's purposes and for the sister's soul.

Of far more importance than the pastor's role in strengthening a truthful and selfless person is the effect of the housemother and of the supervisory sisters, as well as that of the entire sisterhood. What applies to the pastor applies just as well to the housemother and all the sisters in charge of the stations. They cannot want to dominate their co-sisters but must be models for them, not only in their truthful, pure character, but also in the joyous, voluntary way in which they submit themselves to the rules of the house and follow them meticulously. "I have been like a mother to you, just as a nursemaid cares for her children," writes Paul [1 Thess 2:7]. Wherever this motherly, truly compassionate attitude dwells in the supervisory sisters, a truthful and childlike trust is also possible, and the salt of truth and the discipline of love will find a good home.

For the planting and strengthening of trust it is extremely important that one practice the greatest confidentiality. One must take great care not to find fault with one sister in the presence of other sisters—to say nothing of in front of the sick—not to criticize a sister who is not present, and not to speak ill of persons when neither the situation requires it nor the office demands it. Such conversations will, because of busy gossipers, reach the ones affected, and trust is permanently damaged. In addition, a supervising sister will make it her concern that at all times she not only can tell her subordinates the truth with kindness but can also be grateful when she is made aware of her own mistakes.

Flatterers, too, are among the sisters: vipers with poison on their lips. Woe to the supervising sister who tolerates such flattering darlings, who always say what she wants to hear and gloss over their own faults at the expense of others. She must have a switch ready for such flatterers. She must make it very clear that she loves the sister most who openly tells her the truth, even though she herself may be hurt by this truth. She must diligently plant and nurture this attitude: my best friend is the person who tells me my faults without holding back anything, because that helps me in my most difficult struggle, the struggle against my own "I."

What is necessary for a circle of sisters is noted more precisely in John 13:1–17: "As I then, your Lord and teacher, have washed your feet, so you, too, should wash one another's feet." Pure, serving, humble love must, through deeds more often than words, convict one's co-sisters of their wrong. Whenever one applies this means, it will seldom be necessary to go beyond the first disciplinary step that the Lord describes in Matthew 18:14 [sic]: "If your brother sins against you, go and tell him his fault between you and him alone. If he listens to you, you have gained your brother" [Matt 18:15]. Well it is for the house with this spirit, where rarely any of the minor problems of daily life become so important that they must be brought to the director of the motherhouse. Of course, no sinful secrecy should be employed instead.

Neither can we tolerate the attitude of those who say to themselves, "I'm going to avoid burning my fingers; I won't say anything; I won't say anything," when to speak up is to exercise one's duty to be compassionate, and not speaking up is the sin of Cain: "Am I my brother's keeper?" [Gen 4:9].

On the other hand, I think of those sisters who neither have, nor want to have, the wisdom from above that is peaceable and tolerant, and whose behavior thus causes the others to talk about them. I would like to put together a dictionary of caustic sayings to use on the annoying sisters, such as, "I'd really like to thank you for telling on me!" and "Don't you want to make another trip to Bielefeld and leave me behind again?" Would they not be shocked and blush at the ugliness of such words?

Perhaps in disciplinary action the second and third levels of authority must be introduced, so that several co-sisters or even the motherhouse itself must be drawn into the affair. Then the rule must still apply that the process, whether oral or written, may not proceed behind the sister's back, but only after open, prior notification. It is also evident that genuine love, not a passion for gossip, compels these stern measures. In the end, truth spoken in love, even if not recognized immediately, wins the victory.

If none of these means has the desired effect, then it is an act of compassion not only for the house but also for the sister herself to show her the door promptly. Thus, it is still possible for her own soul to find its way. Naturally, it is possible to readmit a sister who has been expelled. However, she can be readmitted only to the same house she had to leave—never to another—because only where the sister shows deep humility can one hope for a blessing.

As far as nurturing the sisters to obedience is concerned, it is of greatest importance that the young sisters see how the older, supervisory sisters live in complete confidence of the motherhouse. They do not criticize its rules unkindly but are convinced, even if they do not comprehend something in them, that it has been considered very carefully before God. Woe to the supervisory sister who is never ashamed of feeling superior to and finding fault with the rules of the motherhouse in the presence of younger sisters.

In regard to devotions, the head sisters clearly must watch that these do not sink to the level of duty but remain genuinely beneficial and refreshing. In order to keep regular devotions firmly on schedule they cannot be too long. If, because of pressing circumstances, the prescribed text cannot be read calmly, then it is better for the supervising sister simply to read the word of the day and leave it at that. Then, at some other time when people can relax, such as in the evening, they can sit together longer around God's Word and also hold a discussion about it. In any event, our wish for devotions is that the sisters receive something from God's Word, that they pray, not just as an outward act, but really pray together and, yes, more than that: the devotions and the life in God's Word must provide an impetus toward a prayer life in spirit and truth. If the devotions do not accomplish this, then they are not being held in the right manner. They must lead to prayer in one's private chamber, and the sisters must be allowed time for this—whether in the morning, the evening, or a quiet half-hour in the afternoon. If the motherhouse does not allow its sisters time beyond the public worship services and common devotions to be alone with God in stillness, it shares the blame if truth and discipline suffer.

In addition to the usual devotions it is certainly good if the sisters can gather at the end of each week or month (we here have chosen the afternoon of the first Sunday for a longer discussion of God's Word). Wherever possible, groups of stations should also get together. On these occasions, after a commentary on the scriptures, the sisters speak openly, for example, about things that can strain or enhance their life together, if such points arise from the reading. If nothing in particular arises, one should not try to force anything out.

Prior to the day of communion the mutual, sisterly discipline should penetrate more deeply. I think it is worthy advice that the little cluster of sisters working at a station get together before the general confession, or perhaps even better, directly after the fresh impression of the warning to the penitents. Then not merely the usual question goes around, "Have you anything against me?" and so on, but rather the more important question: "Tell me openly, have I, in any of my words or actions grieved my Savior, been a disgrace to him, demonstrated impurity, or insisted on my own will?" Supervisory sisters may also direct such questions to their subordinates. Together, troubles of this kind can be brought before God and turned over to him in prayer.

A genuine life of faith, a true life of prayer, cannot remain hidden but must become visible in a life of genuine love. O, the tainted love, O, the merely mechanically memorized and practiced works of love, how cold they are, yes, how injurious. O, how even those on the outside remark, "That is not sincere." O, how even the rules and regulations of the house, how ostensible obedience in an impure heart can be misused and employed as a coverup for inner poverty of love, which is unable to be everything to everyone in order to win a few [1 Cor 9:22]. On such days one cannot be easy on cold hospital assistants and on unkindness of this sort but must bring such things out in the open and look for forgiveness for them in the blood of Christ. "If we say we are in community with him while we walk in darkness, then we are lying and not acting according to the truth. But if we walk in the light, just as he is in the light, then we are in community with each other, and the blood of Jesus Christ, his Son, purifies us of all sin" [1 John 1:6–7].

400

FRIEDRICH VON BODELSCHWINGH

This community—the community formed in the confession of sins and forgiveness in Christ's blood and the community with the Lord Jesus who is our righteousness and strength—must be the foundation for the deaconess community. This community can be strengthened, can grow and blossom especially through the right use of the sacred sacrament of the altar. With every confession and every Lord's supper the deaconess house can become lovelier; purity and holy discipline can grow, and love for one another can become deeper, purer, and more tender.

On this foundation alone grow the kind of friendships that are a source of blessing and can be permitted in deaconess houses. We know that in deaconess houses there are also bad friendships. These are impure, untruthful, licentious, carnal friendships that cause cliques and are the enemy of everything good. Genuine friendships are the ones that come to light under the cross of Jesus, where one is thankful for every act of love that uncovers one's own faults, and where one experiences great joy for the mercy and peace one has in the forgiveness of sins.

It is especially beautiful when, in this kind of friendship—and it can happen not only out at the stations but also in the mother-house—an older, experienced sister becomes fond of a young beginner, is sympathetic to her, shares her difficulties and struggles, now and then takes her into her little room for prayer together, reproves her in the manner of a loyal friend, but also lovingly encourages her, builds her up, and helps her unsteady feet stay on the narrow path. It is wonderful if the younger sister then develops this attitude toward the older one: "I thank you from the heart for everything you say to me. Please don't stop. Do not go easy on me. I know you mean the best for me."

Furthermore, in times of need the older sister will find in this sort of younger sister a brave helper for her own soul and its recovery to complete truthfulness. This is the beautiful, noble path to ever-greater purity and to a loving, disciplined character whose beauty cannot be hidden. Well it is for older sisters who have the reputation that one can entrust the unsteady reed to them without any qualms, and they can give strength to the reed. And well it is for the house that has many such sisters. How many a useful tool that otherwise would be lost for God's vineyard can be retained through such sisters. To be sure, only those will be fit for this work of love who stand firmly in the truth that they themselves live in nothing but the forgiveness of their sins.

Yes, forgiveness of sins in the blood of Christ—therein lies ultimately the only key that frees us from all these problems. We are poor sinners—that is the truth Christ's blood preaches to us—and we stay that way until the end. But this truth sets people free [John 8:32]. The more we recognize and ponder it, the more we free ourselves from all hypocritical self-righteousness and the more truthful we become in all our speaking and doing. Where there is forgiveness of sins, and where one lives daily from the forgiveness of sins alone, there one also finds truly humble and broken hearts. There dies the self-will, one's own evil "I"; there we live according to the example of the dear, victorious champion of the new covenant: "I have been crucified with Christ; I live, yet now it is not I, but Christ living in me, who loved me and gave himself up for me" [Gal 2:20].

Notes

INTRODUCTION

1. The German website for the Bodelschwinghian Institutions of Bethel offers a wide range of information on the institution's history and current activities (see http://www.bethel.de).

2. The most comprehensive biography of Bodelschwingh is by Martin Gerhardt (vol. 1 and vol. 2, part 1), continued by Alfred Adam (vol. 2, part 2), *Friedrich von Bodelschwingh: Ein Lebensbild aus der deutschen Kirchengeschichte* (Bethel bei Bielefeld, 1952, 1958).

3. In 1888 Friedrich Wilhelm succeeded Wilhelm I as Emperor Frederick III, but died of a fatal disease only 100 days after his accession.

4. Gustav von Bodelschwingh, *Friedrich von Bodelschwingh: Ein Lebensbild*, 1st ed. (Bethel bei Bielefeld, 1922), pp. 65–66.

5. Gerhardt-Adam, *Friedrich von Bodelschwingh*, vol. 1, p. 166.

6. Friedrich von Bodelschwingh, *Die Arbeiterfrage*, in *Friedrich von Bodelschwingh: Ausgewählte Schriften*, ed. Alfred Adam, 2 vols. (Bethel bei Bielefeld, 1955, 1964, reprinted 1980), vol. 1, *Veröffentlichungen aus den Jahren 1858 bis 1871*, p. 549.

7. Gerhardt-Adam, *Friedrich von Bodelschwingh*, vol. 1, p. 78.

8. H. W. Koch, *A History of Prussia* (1978, reprinted New York, 1993), p. 279.

9. Ibid., p. 282. See also Hartmut Lehmann, "Friedrich v. Bodelschwingh und das Sedanfest. Ein Beitrag zum nationalen Denken der politisch aktiven Richtung im deutschen Pietismus des 19. Jahrhunderts," *Historische Zeitschrift* 202 (1966): 542–73; and idem, "Bodelschwingh und Bismarck. Christlich-konservative Sozialpolitik im Kaiserreich," ibid., 208 (1969): 607–26.

10. Friedrich von Bodelschwingh, *Von dem Leben und Sterben vier seliger Kinder*, 1st ed. (Ducherow, 1870).

11. Bodelschwingh, *Friedrich von Bodelschwingh*, p. 154; also in Gerhardt-Adam, *Friedrich von Bodelschwingh*, vol. 1, p. 424.

12. Friedrich von Bodelschwingh, *Zur Einsegnung von siebzehn westfälischen Diakonissen*, in Adam, *Ausgewählte Schriften*, vol. 2, *Veröffentlichungen aus den Jahren 1872 bis 1910* (Bethel bei Bielefeld, 1964), pp. 425–30.

13. Friedrich von Bodelschwingh, *Rede über die Herstellung und den Ausbau von Wasserstraßen* ("Speech About the Construction and Extension of

Canals," from the minutes of the Prussian Parliament, Berlin, 1904, col. 4864–75), in Adam, *Ausgewählte Schriften*, vol. 2, p. 560. See also *Mehr Luft, mehr Licht...* ("More Air, More Light..."), ibid., pp. 83–107, which dutifully reports the applause of his supporters and the grumbling of his opponents.

14. Gerhardt-Adam, *Friedrich von Bodelschwingh*, vol. 2, part 1, pp. 143–44.

15. Ibid., p. 53.

COME OUT, JOACHIM, THE SAVIOR IS HERE!

1. Friedrich von Bodelschwingh, *Joachim heraus, der Heiland ist da*, in *Friedrich von Bodelschwingh: Ausgewählte Schriften*, ed. Alfred Adam, 2 vols. (Bethel bei Bielefeld, 1955, 1964, reprinted 1980), vol. 1, *Veröffentlichungen aus den Jahren 1858 bis 1871*, pp. 382–86.

2. Weimar edition, vol. 10, part 1, bk. 2, p. 376. See also *What Luther Says*, p. 976, #3075. Bodelschwingh slightly alters the original.

3. Paul Gerhardt (ca. 1607–76), Lutheran pastor in Berlin, considered to be the greatest hymn writer of the German Lutheran Church after Martin Luther, wrote approximately 130 hymns. The lines Bodelschwingh quotes are from the third verse of Gerhardt's Advent hymn, *"Warum willst du draußen stehen."*

4. Source unidentified. Jerome (ca. 342–420) chose to live in a cave near Bethlehem where he undertook a Latin translation of the Bible known as the Vulgate.

5. Source unidentified.

6. The *Evangelische Missionsgesellschaft in Basel*, or *Basler Mission*, succeeded in 1815 the *Christentumsgesellschaft*, which had been founded in 1780. Hundreds of young men were trained at the missionary school that opened in 1816 and served around the world. Under the leadership of Christian Gottlieb Blumhardt, who served as director from 1816 to 1838, uncle of the social activist Johann Christoph Blumhardt, the Basel Mission became the center of the evangelical missionary movement for almost the entire European continent. The Basel Mission was and is still known for its supra-national and supra-confessional character within Protestantism.

AT THE CONSECRATION OF SEVENTEEN
WESTPHALIAN DEACONESSES

1. Friedrich von Bodelschwingh, *Zur Einsegnung von siebzehn westfälischen Diakonissen*, in *Friedrich von Bodelschwingh: Ausgewählte Schriften*,

FRIEDRICH VON BODELSCHWINGH

ed. Alfred Adam, 2 vols. (Bethel bei Bielefeld, 1955, 1964, reprinted 1980), vol. 2, *Veröffentlichungen aus den Jahren 1872 bis 1910*, pp. 425–30.

2. Bodelschwingh's sermon is based on the motifs of the return of the exiles from Babylon and the rebuilding of the temple and walls of Jerusalem, as reported in 2 Chronicles, Ezra, Nehemiah, Haggai, and Zechariah.

SERMON ON THE ANNIVERSARY OF BETHEL

1. Friedrich von Bodelschwingh, *Predigt am Jahresfeste der Anstalt Bethel*, in *Friedrich von Bodelschwingh: Ausgewählte Schriften*, ed. Alfred Adam, 2 vols. (Bethel bei Bielefeld, 1955, 1964, reprinted 1980), vol. 2, *Veröffentlichungen aus den Jahren 1872 bis 1910*, pp. 454–59.

2. Misericordia Sunday is the Second Sunday after Easter.

ONE THING IS NECESSARY

1. Friedrich von Bodelschwingh, *Eins ist Not*, in *Friedrich von Bodelschwingh: Ausgewählte Schriften*, ed. Alfred Adam, 2 vols. (Bethel bei Bielefeld, 1955, 1964, reprinted 1980), vol. 1, *Veröffentlichungen aus den Jahren 1858 bis 1871*, pp. 114–21.

2. Bodelschwingh notes here: "Whoever is still in doubt that in addition to the scriptures a creed in accordance with the scriptures is really necessary need only note what happened recently in Paris. By a majority vote the Paris Bible Society decided to distribute to those congregations that so desired a version of the Bible worked on by the hand of unbelief in order to excise Christ's divinity from the text as much as possible. Thereupon the minority withdrew from the Paris Bible Society, so that now a society of so-called friends of the Bible remains that, at its own discretion, has dropped a basic doctrine of the Christian church on which our salvation depends. It is not the fault of the church that our creeds have become longer and more detailed than many would like, but rather the fault of false teachers from whom the church must guard its members."

3. Bodelschwingh notes here: "The only exception is a church group in Holland, the Arminians, who wanted absolutely no confession, saying that the scripture was sufficient, but then this church died out after scarcely one hundred years."

4. Source unidentified. John the Steadfast, brother and successor of Luther's first protector, Frederick the Wise, was among the princes who presented the Augsburg Confession to the Diet on June 25, 1530.

5. In a letter by Argula von Grumbach to her cousin, Adam von Töring, document XII in Felix Joseph Lipowsky, *Argula von Grumbach* (Munich, 1801), quoted in Peter Matheson, *Argula von Grumbach: A Woman's Voice in the Reformation* (Edinburgh, 1995), p. 105.

6. Weimar edition, vol. 8, p. 685.

7. The early martyrdoms to which Bodelschwingh refers began in approximately 1523. See Joseph Lecler, *Toleration and the Reformation*, vol. 2 (New York, 1960), p. 14 ff.; also John Foxe, *The Acts and Monuments of the Church: Containing the History and Sufferings of the Martyrs*, ed. M. Hobart Symour (New York, 1850), p. 396 ff.

THE WORKER QUESTION

1. Friedrich von Bodelschwingh, *Die Arbeiterfrage*, in *Friedrich von Bodelschwingh: Ausgewählte Schriften*, ed. Alfred Adam, 2 vols. (Bethel bei Bielefeld, 1955, 1964, reprinted 1980), vol. 1, *Veröffentlichungen aus den Jahren 1858 bis 1871*, pp. 549–51.

2. Source unidentified.

3. Bodelschwingh notes here: "Recently the owner of an ironworks in Norway who has one thousand one hundred employees told me that any bartender who serves liquor after 7:00 P.M. is subject to a fine of five Norwegian talers ($7^1/_2$ Prussian talers). Consequently, the ironworks owner does not pay his employees until after 7:00 P.M., because he is sure the money will get home and cannot be drunk away that evening at least."

MELANCHTHON

1. Friedrich von Bodelschwingh, *Melanchthon*, in *Friedrich von Bodelschwingh: Ausgewählte Schriften*, ed. Alfred Adam, 2 vols. (Bethel bei Bielefeld, 1955, 1964, reprinted 1980), vol. 1, *Veröffentlichungen aus den Jahren 1858 bis 1871*, pp. 613–17.

2. Karl Wilhelm Kunis, *Vernunft und Offenbarung: Die Widersprüche zwischen Glauben und Wissen naturwissenschaftlich-philosophisch bearbeitet* (Leipzig, 1870).

3. Philipp Melanchthon (1497–1560) became Luther's closest associate and took the primary role in writing the Augsburg Confession, which was presented to Emperor Charles V at the Diet in 1530.

4. Bodelschwingh cites here with minor alterations Melanchthon's original Latin and Greek: *"Ego mihi conscius, me nunquam tetheologekenai, nisi ut vitam emendarem."* The quote is from a letter Melanchthon wrote to Camerarius on January 22, 1525, published as letter no. 371 in *Melanchthons Briefwechsel: Kritische und kommentierte Gesamtausgabe*, ed. Heinz Scheible (Stuttgart-Bad Cannstatt, 1995), vol. T2, ed. Richard Wetzel and Helga Scheible, pp. 239–40. See also Karl Matthes, *Philipp Melanchthon: Sein Leben und Wirken aus den Quellen dargestellt* (Allenburg, 1841), pp. 75, 392.

5. The site of a bloody siege during the Crimean War (1853–56). Florence Nightingale's work there was to gain international recognition.

6. Bodelschwingh notes here: "K. W. Kunis, *Vernunft und Offenbarung* (Leipzig: Moritz Schäfer, 1870)."

7. Kunis, ibid., n.p.

8. Paul Gerhardt (ca. 1607–76), Lutheran pastor in Berlin, considered to be the greatest hymn writer of the German Lutheran Church after Luther, wrote approximately 130 hymns. The lines Bodelschwingh quotes are from the first verse of Gerhardt's "Passion Chorale," an adaptation of *"O Haupt voll Blut und Wunden"* ("O Sacred Head Now Wounded") attributed to Bernard of Clairvaux.

9. Justus Gesenius (1601–73), pastor in northern Germany, co-editor with David Denicke (1603–80) of *The New Hannover Hymnal* (1646). Also author of a widely used catechism. The stanza Bodelschwingh quotes is the second verse of his hymn, *"Wenn meine Sünd' mich kränken."*

DEACONESS PLEDGE

1. Friedrich von Bodelschwingh, *Das Diakonissen-Gelübde*, in *Friedrich von Bodelschwingh: Ausgewählte Schriften*, ed. Alfred Adam, 2 vols. (Bethel bei Bielefeld, 1955, 1964, reprinted 1980), vol. 2, *Veröffentlichungen aus den Jahren 1872 bis 1910*, p. 125.

2. Ibid., p. 113.

NURTURING THE SISTERS IN TRUTHFULNESS
AND DISCIPLINE IN THE COMMUNITY
AND THROUGH THE COMMUNITY

1. Friedrich von Bodelschwingh, *Erziehung der Schwestern zur Wahrhaftigkeit und zur Zucht in der Gemeinschaft und durch die Gemeinschaft*, in *Friedrich von Bodelschwingh: Ausgewählte Schriften*, ed. Alfred Adam, 2 vols. (Bethel bei Bielefeld, 1955, 1964, reprinted 1980), vol. 2, *Veröffentlichungen aus den Jahren 1872 bis 1910*, pp. 28–41.

2. Bodelschwingh notes here: "How much, O, unfortunately, how much the sisters are flattered even by sensible Christian people, to say nothing of the insensible children of this world! And what a heart is immune to such fiery arrows!"

3. Count Nicholas von Zinzendorf (1700–1760), leader of the Moravians. Zinzendorf's hymn unidentified.

Suggestions For
Further Reading (in English)

PIETISM

Brown, Dale, *Understanding Pietism* (Grand Rapids, 1978).

Schmidt, Martin, "Pietism," *The Encyclopedia of the Lutheran Church*, ed. Julius Bodensieck, vol. 3 (Philadelphia, 1965), pp. 1898–1906.

Stoeffler, F. Ernest, *The Rise of Evangelical Pietism* (Leiden, 1965), chap. 1.

GERMAN PIETISM

Erb, Peter, *Pietists: Selected Writings* (New York, 1983).

Stoeffler, F. Ernest, *German Pietism During the Eighteenth Century* (Leiden, 1973).

Tappert, Theodore, "Orthodoxism, Pietism, and Rationalism, 1580–1830," *Christian Social Responsibility*, vol. 2, ed. Harold Letts (Philadelphia, 1957), chap. 2.

AWAKENING

Bachmann, E. Theodore, "The Church and the Rise of Modern Society," *Christian Social Responsibility*, vol. 2, ed. Harold Letts (Philadelphia, 1957), chap. 3.

Barth, Karl, *Protestant Theology in the Nineteenth Century: Its Background and History* (New York, 1959; reprinted Valley Forge, 1973), chap. 16.

Groh, John, *Nineteenth-Century German Protestantism: The Church as Social Model* (Washington, D.C., 1982).

Shanahan, William O., *German Protestants Face the Social Question*, vol. 1, *The Conservative Phase, 1815–1871* (Notre Dame, 1954).

Ward, W. R., *The Protestant Evangelical Awakening* (Cambridge, 1994).

Bibliography

I. Works Cited

A. SOURCES BY THE FOUR AUTHORS

Bodelschwingh, Friedrich von

Ausgewählte Schriften, ed. Alfred Adam, 2 vols. (Bethel bei Bielefeld, 1955, 1964, reprinted 1980); vol. 1, *Veröffentlichungen aus den Jahren 1858 bis 1871*, vol. 2, *Veröffentlichungen aus den Jahren 1872 bis 1910*.

"Von dem Leben und Sterben vier seliger Kinder," *Westfälischer Hausfreund*, 1849 (Bethel bei Bielefeld).

Fliedner, Theodor

Der Armen- und Krankenfreund, Quarterly vol. 4, 1849; Quarterly vol. 4, 1853; vol. 80, 1928 (Kaiserswerth).

Die besondere Seelsorge: Eine hohe Pflicht der Pfarrer u. Aeltesten, eine Synodalpredigt über Ap. G. 20, 28 gehalten zu Urdenbach, den 20. August 1834 vor der versammelten Düsseldorfer Kreissynode (Crefeld, 1834).

Diakonissen-Liederbuch, 7th ed., ed. Julius Disselhoff (Kaiserswerth, 1866), selected hymns by Fliedner.

Das erste Jahr-Zehnt der Diakonissen-Anstalt zu Kaiserswerth am Rhein vom Oktober 1836 bis Januar 1847 (Kaiserswerth, 1847).

Haus-Ordnung und Dienst-Anweisung für die Diakonissen in der Diakonissen-Anstalt zu Kaiserswerth, unnumbered ed. (Kaiserswerth, 1852)
Jahrbuch für christliche Unterhaltung (Kaiserswerth, 1849).
Predigt Vater Fliedners am 4. Advent (24. Dez.) 1843 über John. 3, 30, Document No. FL IIa 27, Fachbücherei für Frauendiakonie Düsseldorf-Kaiserswerth (Kaiserswerth, n.d.).

Tholuck, August

Exposition of St. Paul's Epistle to the Romans with Extracts from the Exegetical Work of the Fathers and Reformers, trans. Robert Menzies (Philadelphia, 1844).
Gespräche über die vornehmsten Glaubensfragen der Zeit, zunächst für nachdenkende Laien, welche Verständigung suchen (Halle, 1846).
Die Lehre von der Sünde und vom Versöhner oder: Die wahre Weihe des Zweiflers, 7th ed. (Hamburg, 1851).
Predigten über Hauptstücke des christlichen Glaubens und Lebens, 4 vols., 2d ed. (Halle, 1838–47).
Stunden christlicher Andacht: Ein Erbauungsbuch, 2d ed. (Hamburg, 1841).

Wichern, Johann Hinrich

Ausgewählte Schriften, ed. Karl Janssen and R. Sieverts, 3 vols. (Gütersloh, 1956–62).
Fliegende Blätter aus dem Rauhen Hause, ed. Johann Hinrich Wichern, series 3, 1846–47 (Hamburg).
Gesammelte Schriften D. Johann Hinrich Wicherns, ed. J. Wichern and F. Mahling, 6 vols. (Hamburg, 1901–08).
Die innere Mission der deutschen evangelischen Kirche: Eine Denkschrift an die deutsche Nation..., ed. Martin Gerhardt (Hamburg, 1933).
Der junge Wichern: Jugendtagebücher Johann Hinrich Wicherns, ed. Martin Gerhardt (Hamburg, 1925).

Sämtliche Werke, ed. Peter Meinhold, 8 vols. (Berlin and Hamburg, 1958–80).

B. ABOUT THE FOUR AUTHORS

Bodelschwingh, Friedrich von

Bodelschwingh, Fritz (Friedrich), *Aus einer hellen Kindheit*, 13th ed. (Bethel bei Bielefeld, 1977).

Bodelschwingh, Gustav von, *Friedrich von Bodelschwingh: Ein Lebensbild*, 1st ed. (Bethel bei Bielefeld, 1922).

Gerhardt, Martin, vol. 1, continued by Alfred Adam, vol. 2, *Friedrich von Bodelschwingh: Ein Lebensbild aus der deutschen Kirchengeschichte*, 2 vols. (Bethel bei Bielefeld, 1950, 1958).

Fliedner, Theodor

Fliedner, Georg, *Theodor Fliedner: Sein Leben und sein Wirken*, 3 vols. (Kaiserswerth, 1908–12).

Gerberding, G. H., *Life and Letters of W. A. Passavant, D.D.* (Greenville, 1906).

Gerhart, Martin, *Theodor Fliedner: Ein Lebensbild*, 2 vols. (Düsseldorf-Kaiserswerth, 1933, 1937).

Schaff, Philip, "Fliedner, Theodor," in *The New Schaff-Herzog Encyclopedia of Religious Knowledge*, vol. 4 (New York, 1909): 333–34.

Sticker, Anna, *Florence Nightingale, Curriculum Vitae, with Information about Florence Nightingale and Kaiserswerth* (Düsseldorf-Kaiserswerth, 1965).

———, *Theodor Fliedner*, 2d ed. (Kaiserswerth, 1959).

———, *"...und doch möchte ich nur meinem Sinn folgen...": Friederike Fliedner, Stifterin der Kaiserswerther Diakonissenanstalt* (Offenbach/Main, 1986).

Tholuck, August

Barth, Karl, *Protestant Theology in the Nineteenth Century: Its Background and History* (New York, 1959; reprinted Valley Forge, 1973), chap. 16.

Flückiger, Felix, *Die protestantische Theologie des 19. Jahrhunderts*, vol. 4, installment P of *Die Kirche in ihrer Geschichte*, ed. Bernd Moeller (Göttingen, 1975).

Hirsch, Emmanuel, *Geschichte der neueren evangelischen Theologie*, vol. 5 (Gütersloh, 1949), pp. 103–15.

Kähler, Martin, "Tholuck, Friedrich August Gottreu," *Realencyklopädie für protestantische Theologie und Kirche*, vol. 19, ed. Albert Hauck, 3d ed. (Leipzig, 1907): 695–702.

Sack, Karl Heinrich, *Geschichte der Predigt in der deutschen evangelischen Kirche von Mosheim bis auf die letzten Jahre von Schleiermacher und Menken*, 2d ed. (Heidelberg, 1866).

Weigelt, Horst, *Erweckungsbewegung und konfessionales Luthertum im 19. Jahrhundert, untersucht an Karl v. Raumer*, in *Arbeiten zur Theologie*, ed. Alfred Jepsen, Otto Michel, and Theodor Schlatter, 2d series, vol. 10 (Stuttgart, 1968).

Witte, Leopold, *Das Leben D. Friedrich August Gottreu Tholuck's*, 2 vols. (Bielefeld and Leipzig, 1884, 1886).

Wichern, Johann Hinrich

Beyreuther, Erich, *Geschichte der Diakonie und Inneren Mission in der Neuzeit*, 3d ed. (Berlin, 1983).

Gerhardt, Martin, *Johann Hinrich Wichern: Ein Lebensbild*, 3 vols. (Hamburg, 1927–31).

Shanahan, William O., *German Protestants Face the Social Question*, vol. 1, *The Conservative Phase, 1815–1871* (Notre Dame, 1954). No second volume appeared.

Wittenborn, Erich, *Johann Hinrich Wichern als Sozialpädagoge, dargestellt an seiner Rettungshauserziehung* (Wuppertal, 1982).

II. Other Bibliography

PIETISM

Arndt, Johann, *Vom wahren Christentum* (Berlin, 1712). English trans.: *True Christianity*, trans. Peter Erb (New York, 1979).

Benz, Ernst, "Pietist and Puritan Sources of Early World Missions (Cotton Mather and A. H. Francke)," *Church History* 20 (1951): 28–55.

Bergendoff, Conrad, *The Church of the Lutheran Reformation* (St. Louis, 1967), chap. 12.

Berman, Harold, *Law and Revolution: The Formation of the Western Legal Tradition* (Cambridge, 1983).

Beyreuther, Erich, *Der geschichtliche Auftrag des Pietismus in der Gegenwart: Drei Fragen an Pietismus und Kirche* (Stuttgart, 1963).

———, *Geschichte des Pietismus* (Stuttgart, 1978).

Brastberger, Immanuel Gottlob, *Evangelische Zeugnisse der Wahrheit zur Aufmunterung im wahren Christentum* (Reutlingen, 1758).

Brecht, Martin, and Klaus Deppermann, *Der Pietismus im achtzehnten Jahrhundert*, vol. 2 of *Geschichte des Pietismus* (Göttingen, 1995).

Gäbler, Ulrich, ed., *Der Pietismus im neunzehnten und zwanzigsten Jahrhundert*, vol. 3 of *Geschichte des Pietismus* (Göttingen, 2000).

Gawthrop, Richard, *Pietism and the Making of Eighteenth-Century Prussia* (Cambridge, 1993).

Gerdes, Egon, "Pietism: Classical and Modern," *Concordia Theological Monthly* 39 (1968): 257–68.

Greschat, Martin, "Zur neueren Pietismusforschung," *Jahrbuch für Westfälische Kirchengeschichte* 65 (Bielefeld, 1972): 220–68.

———, ed., *Zur neueren Pietismusforschung* (Darmstadt, 1977).

Hinrichs, Carl, *Preußentum und Pietismus: Der Pietismus in Brandenburg und Preußen als religiös-soziale Reformbewegung* (Göttingen, 1971).

Irwin, Joyce, "German Pietists and Church Music in the Baroque Age," *Church History* 54 (1985): 29–40.

Kaiser, Gerhard, *Pietismus und Patriotismus im literarischen Deutschland: Ein Beitrag zum Problem der Säkularisation* (Wiesbaden, 1961).

Knox, Ronald, *Enthusiasm: A Chapter in the History of Religion with Special Reference to the XVII and XVIII Centuries* (Oxford, 1950).

Langen, August, *Der Wortschatz des Deutschen Pietismus*, 2d ed. (Tübingen, 1968).

Lehmann, Hartmut, *Pietismus und weltliche Ordnung in Württemberg: Vom 17. bis zum 20. Jahrhundert* (Stuttgart, 1969).

Ohlemacher, Jörg, "Das Reich Gottes in Deutschlands Bauern: Ein Beitrag zur Wortgeschichte und Theologie der deutschen Gemeinschaftsbewegung," *Arbeiten zur Geschichte des Pietismus* 23 (Göttingen, 1986).

Olsson, Karl, "What Was Pietism?" *The Covenant Quarterly* 28 (1970): 3–14.

Pietismus und Neuzeit: Jahrbuch zur Geschichte des neueren Protestantismus (Bielefeld and Göttingen, 1974–).

Pinson, Koppel S., *Pietism as a Factor in the Rise of German Nationalism* (New York, 1934; reprinted, 1968).

Schmidt, Martin, *Pietismus*, 2d ed. (Stuttgart, 1978).

Schneider, Hans, "Der radikale Pietismus in der neueren Forschung," *Pietismus und Neuzeit: Jahrbuch zur Geschichte des neueren Protestantismus* 8 (Göttingen, 1982): 15–42.

Skarsten, Trygve R., "The Doctrine of Justification in Classical Lutheran Pietism: A Revisionist Perspective," *Trinity Seminary Review* 3 (1981): 20–29.

Spener, Philipp Jakob, *Pia Desideria*, ed. Theodore Tappert (Philadelphia, 1964).

Stephan, Horst, *Der Pietismus als Träger des Fortschritts: In Kirche, Theologie und allgemeiner Geistesbildung* (Tübingen, 1908).

Stoeffler, F. Ernest, ed., theme issue entitled "Pietism, a Much Maligned Movement, Re-examined," *Christian History* 5, no. 2 (1986). See in particular the articles by F. Ernest Stoeffler,

"Can These Bones Live?" pp. 9–12; C. John Weborg, "Reborn in Order to Renew," pp. 17–18, 34–35, and "The Roots and Branches of Pietism," p. 19; and Gary Slatter, "Moving on Many Fronts," pp. 20–22.

———, *Continental Pietism and Early American Christianity* (Grand Rapids, 1976).

———, *German Pietism During the Eighteenth Century* (Leiden, 1973).

———, *The Rise of Evangelical Pietism* (Leiden, 1965).

Strom, Jonathan, "Problems and Promises of Pietism Research," *Church History* 71 (2002): 536–54.

Tersteegen, Gerhard, *Crumbs from the Master's Table*, trans. Samuel Jackson (London, 1837). The original title: *Geistliche Brosamen, von des Herrn Tisch gefallen, von guten Freunden aufgelesen, und hungrigen Hertzen mitgetheilt: Bestehend in einer Sammlung verschiedener Erweckungs-Reden weyland von Gerhard Tersteegen zu Mülheim an der Ruhr gehalten*, 2d ed. (Solingen, 1772).

Wallmann, Johannes, *Der Pietismus* (Göttingen, 1990).

Weber, Otto, and Erich Beyreuther, eds., *Die Stimme der Stillen* (Kaiserswerth, 1959).

Weigelt, Horst, "Interpretations of Pietism in the Research of Contemporary German Church Historians," *Church History* 39 (1970): 236–41.

———, "Johann August Urlsperger, ein Theologe zwischen Pietismus und Aufklärung," *Zeitschrift für Bayrische Kirchengeschichte* 33 (1964): 67–105.

———, *Der Spener-Hallische Pietismus*, vol. 4, part 1, *Pietismus-Studien*, in *Arbeiten zur Theologie*, series 2:4 (Stuttgart, 1965).

AWAKENING AND ITS CONTEXT

Aland, Kurt, ed., *Pietismus und moderne Welt* (Witten, 1974). See "Awakening."

Ashby, Leroy, *Saving the Waifs: Reformers and Dependent Children, 1890–1917* (Philadelphia, 1984).

Baumer, Franklin L., *Religion and the Rise of Scepticism* (New York, 1960).

Benrath, Gustav Adolf, "Einige Bemerkungen zur Zeitschriften-literatur der Erweckung," in Gäbler and Schram, *Erweckung am Beginn des 19. Jahrhunderts*, pp. 197–204.

Beyreuther, Erich, "Neue Forschungen zur Geschichte der Deutschen Christentumsgesellschaft," *Theologische Literaturzeitung* 81 (1956): 355–58.

————, *Die Erweckungsbewegung*, vol. 4, part R:1 of *Die Kirche in ihrer Geschichte: Ein Handbuch*, ed. Kurt Dietrich Schmidt and Ernst Wolf, 2d ed. (Göttingen, 1977).

————, "Erweckungsbewegung," *Die Religion in Geschichte und Gegenwart*, vol. 2, 3d ed. (Tübingen, 1958), cols. 621–29.

————, *Frömmigkeit und Theologie: Gesammelte Aufsätze zum Pietismus und zur Erweckungsbewegung* (Hildesheim, 1980).

————, *Geschichte der Diakonie und Inneren Mission in der Neuzeit*, 3d ed. (Berlin, 1983).

Bigler, Robert, *The Politics of German Protestantism: The Rise of the Protestant Church Elite in Prussia, 1815–1848* (Berkeley, 1972).

————, "The Rise of Political Protestantism in Nineteenth Century Germany: The Awakening of Political Consciousness and the Beginnings of Political Activity in the Protestant Clergy of Pre-March Prussia," *Church History* 34 (1965): 423–44.

Bradfield, Margaret, *The Good Samaritan: The Life and Works of Friedrich von Bodelschwingh* (London, 1961).

Brakelmann, Günter, *Die soziale Frage des 19. Jahrhunderts*, 5th ed. (Bielefeld, 1975).

————, *Kirche und Sozialismus im 19. Jahrhundert: Die Analyse des Sozialismus und Kommunismus bei Johann Hinrich Wichern und bei Rudolf Todt* (Witten, 1966).

Brecht, Martin, ed., *Die Basler Christentumsgesellschaft*, in *Pietismus und Neuzeit* 7 (Göttingen, 1981).

————, "Spätpietismus und Erweckungsbewegung," in Gäbler and Schram, *Erweckung am Beginn des 19. Jahrhunderts*, pp. 1–22.

Buchholz, W., and W. Köllmann, eds., *Raum und Bevölkerung in der Weltgeschichte*, vol. 2 (Würzburg, 1955).

Christianson, Gerald, "J. H. Wichern and the Rise of the Lutheran Social Institution," *The Lutheran Quarterly* 19 (1967): 357–70.

Christensen, Torben, *Origin and History of Christian Socialism 1848–54* (Aarhus, 1962).

Christophe, Paul, *L'Église de France dans la Révolution de 1848* (Paris, 1998).

Conser, Walter, Jr., *Church and Confession: Conservative Theologians in Germany, England, and America, 1815–1866* (Macon, 1984).

Dru, Alexander, "The Reformation of the Nineteenth Century: Christianity in Germany from 1800 to 1848," *The Dublin Review* 226 (1952): 34–45.

Eisenblätter, W., "Erweckung," *Historisches Wörterbuch der Philosophie*, ed. Joachim Ritter, vol. 2 (Basel, 1972), cols. 732–33.

"Erweckung/Erweckungsbewegungen," *Theologische Realenzyklopädie*, vol. 10, ed. Michael Wolter and Gertrud Freitag-Otto (Berlin and New York, 1982): 205–20.

Fullbrook, Mary, *Piety and Politics: Religion and the Rise of Absolutism in England, Württemberg and Prussia* (Cambridge and New York, 1983).

Gäbler, Ulrich, *"Auferstehungszeit": Erweckungsprediger des 19. Jahrhunderts. Sechs Porträts* (Munich, 1991).

———, ed., *Der Pietismus im neunzehnten und zwanzigsten Jahrhundert* (Göttingen, 2000).

Gäbler, Ulrich, and Peter Schram, eds., *Erweckung am Beginn des 19. Jahrhunderts* (Amsterdam, 1986).

Geiger, Max, "Das Problem der Erweckungstheologie," *Theologische Zeitschrift* 14 (1958): 430–50.

———, *Aufklärung und Erweckung: Beiträge zur Erforschung Johann Heinrich Jung-Stillings und der Erweckungstheologie* (Zurich, 1963).

Gerhardt, Martin, "Innere Mission und christlich-soziale Bewegung," *Zeitschrift für Kirchengeschichte* 51 (1932): 281–304.

————, *Ein Jahrhundert Innere Mission: Die Geschichte des Central-Ausschusses für die Innere Mission der deutschen evangelischen Kirche* (Gütersloh, 1948).

Geuze, Matthijs Dirk, "Some Remarks on Revival, Its Terminology and Definition," in Gäbler and Schram, *Erweckung am Beginn des 19. Jahrhunderts*, pp. 23–32.

Ginzberg, Lori, *Women and the Work of Benevolence: Morality, Politics, and Class in the Nineteeth-Century United States* (New Haven, 1990).

Gooch, G. P., *Germany and the French Revolution* (London, 1965).

Grane, Leif, *Die Kirche im 19. Jahrhundert: Europäische Perspektiven*, trans. Monika Wesemann (Göttingen, 1987).

Grauvogel, Gerd, *Theodor von Wächter: Christ und Sozialdemokrat* (Stuttgart, 1994).

Greschat, Martin, "Die Erweckungsbewegung: Versuch einer Übersicht anhand neuerer Veröffentlichungen," *Jahrbuch für Westfälische Kirchengeschichte* 66 (1973): 97–148.

————, ed., *Theologen des Protestantismus im 19. und 20. Jahrhundert* (Stuttgart, 1978).

————, *Das Zeitalter der Industriellen Revolution: Das Christentum vor der Moderne*, in *Christentum und Gesellschaft*, vol. 11 (Stuttgart, 1980).

Groh, John, *Nineteenth-Century German Protestantism: The Church as Social Model* (Washington, D.C., 1982).

Helmstadter, Richard, ed., *Freedom and Religion in the Nineteenth Century* (Stanford, 1997).

Hobsbaum, Erich, *The Age of Revolution* (London, 1962).

Hoover, Arlie, *The Gospel of Nationalism: German Patriotic Preaching from Napoleon to Versailles* (Stuttgart, 1986).

Hope, Nicholas, *German and Scandinavian Protestantism, 1700–1918* (Oxford, 1995).

Ibbeken, Rudolf, *Preußen 1807–1813* (Berlin, 1970).

————, *Preußen 1807–1813. Staat und Volk als Idee und Wirklichkeit. Darstellung und Dokumentation* (Cologne, 1970).

Janz, Oliver, *Bürger besonderer Art: Evangelische Pfarrer in Preußen 1850–1914* (Berlin, 1994).

Junkin, Edward, *Religion versus Revolution: The Interpretation of the French Revolution by German Protestant Churchmen, 1789–1799* (Austin, 1974).

Kantzenbach, Friedrich Wilhelm, *Zwischen Erweckung und Restauration: Einige Kapitel aus der unbekannten Kirchengeschichte des 19. Jahrhunderts* (Gladbeck, 1967).

————, *Gestalten und Typen des Neuluthertums: Beiträge zur Erforschung des Neokonfessionalismus im 19. Jahrhundert* (Gütersloh, 1967).

————, *Die Erweckungsbewegung: Studien zur Geschichte ihrer Entstehung und ersten Ausbreitung in Deutschland* (Neuendettelsau, 1957).

————, *H. E. von Kottwitz und die Erweckungsbewegung in Schlesien, Berlin und Pommern* (Ulm, 1963).

Koch, H. W., *A History of Prussia* (London, 1978; reprinted New York, 1993).

Kouri, E. I., *Der deutsche Protestantismus und die soziale Frage, 1870–1919: Zur Sozialpolitik im Bildungsbürgertum* (Berlin, 1983).

Kramer, Rolf, *Nation und Theologie bei Johann Hinrich Wichern* (Hamburg, 1959).

Kretschmar, Georg, *Der Evangelisch-Soziale Kongress: Der deutsche Protestantismus und die soziale Frage* (Munich, 1972).

Krummacher, Friedrich Wilhelm, *Blicke ins Reich der Gnade* (1825), trans. R. F. Walker, *A Glimpse of the Kingdom of Grace* (New Ipswich, 1993).

Kupisch, Karl, *Die deutschen Landeskirchen im 19. und 20. Jahrhundert*, vol. 4, part 2 of *Die Kirche in ihrer Geschichte: Ein Handbuch*, ed. Kurt Dietrich Schmidt and Ernst Wolf (Göttingen, 1966).

————, *Das Jahrhundert des Sozialismus und die Kirche*, 2d ed. (Berlin, 1975).

————, *Kirche und soziale Frage im 19. Jahrhundert*, in *Theologische Studien*, ed. Karl Barth and Max Geiger (Zurich, 1963).

————, *Quellen zur Geschichte des deutschen Protestantismus (1871–1945)* (Göttingen, 1960).

————, *Vom Pietismus zum Kommunismus: Zur Jugendentwicklung von Friedrich Engels*, 2d ed. (Berlin, 1965).

————, *Zwischen Idealismus und Massendemokratie: Eine Geschichte der evangelischen Kirche in Deutschland von 1815–1945* (Berlin, 1955).

Lahrsen, Ingrid, *Zwischen Erweckung und Rationalismus: Hundtwalcker und sein Kreis* (Hamburg, 1959).

Lamberti, Marjorie, "Lutheran Orthodoxy and the Beginning of Conservative Party Organization in Prussia," *Church History* 37 (1968): 439–53.

Latourette, Kenneth Scott, *The Great Century in Europe and the United States of America A.D. 1800–A.D. 1914* (New York, 1941), vol. 4 of *A History of the Expansion of Christianity* (New York, 1937–45).

Lehmann, Hartmut, "Bodelschwingh und Bismarck: Christlich-konservative Sozialpolitik im Kaiserreich," *Historische Zeitschrift* 208 (1969): 607–26.

————, "Pietism and Nationalism: The Relationship Between Protestant Revivalism and National Renewal in Nineteenth-Century Germany," *Church History* 51 (1982): 39–53.

————, *Das Zeitalter des Absolutismus: Gottesgnadentum und Kriegsnot* (Stuttgart, 1980).

Lütgert, Wilhelm, *Die Religion des deutschen Idealismus und ihr Ende*, vol. 2 (Gütersloh, 1926).

Macchia, Frank, *Spirituality and Social Liberation: The Message of the Blumhardts in the Light of Württemberg Pietism* (Metuchen, 1993).

Mahling, Friedrich, *Beiträge zur Geschichte der Entwicklung der Inneren Mission* (Hamburg, 1898).

Maier, Hans, *Revolution und Kirche: Studien zur Frühgeschichte der christlichen Demokratie, 1789–1901*, 5th ed. (Freiburg, 1988), 2d ed. (Freiburg, 1965), trans. Emily Schossberger, *Revolution and Church: The Early History of Christian Democracy, 1789–1901* (Notre Dame, 1969).

BIBLIOGRAPHY

Maser, Peter, *Hans Ernst von Kottwitz: Studien zur Erweckungsbewegung des frühen 19. Jahrhunderts in Schlesien und Berlin* (Göttingen, 1990).

———, "Ein Modell diakonischer Arbeit in der frühen Erweckungsbewegung: Vorbild für die innere Mission," in Gäbler and Schram, *Erweckung am Beginn des 19. Jahrhunderts*, pp.169–82.

Massanari, Ronald, "True or False Socialism: Adolf Stoecker's Critique of Marxism from a Christian Socialist Perspective," *Church History* 41 (1972): 487–96.

Maurer, Wilhelm, *Aufklärung, Idealismus und Restauration*, 2 vols., in *Studien zur Geschichte des neueren Protestantismus*, ed. Heinrich Hoffmann and Leopold Zscharnack, 13–14 (Giessen, 1930).

McLeod, Hugh, *Piety and Poverty: Working-Class Religion in Berlin, London and New York, 1870–1914* (London, 1996).

Meissner, Erwin, *Der Kirchenbegriff Johann Hinrich Wicherns* (Gütersloh, 1938).

Mickel, Wolfgang W., ed., *Geschichte, Politik und Gesellschaft*, vol. 1 (Berlin, 1988).

Mildenberger, Friedrich, *Geschichte der deutschen evangelischen Theologie im 19. und 20. Jahrhundert* (Stuttgart, 1981).

Nowak, Kurt, *Geschichte des Christentums in Deutschland: Religion, Politik und Gesellschaft vom Ende der Aufklärung bis zur Mitte des 20. Jahrhunderts* (Munich, 1995).

Ohl, J. F., *The Inner Mission* (Philadelphia, 1913).

Oldenberg, Friedrich, *Johann Hinrich Wichern: Sein Leben und Wirken*, 2 vols. (Hamburg, 1884–87).

Orr, J. Edwin, *The Eager Feet: Evangelical Awakenings, 1790–1830* (Chicago, 1975).

———, *The Light of the Nations: Evangelical Renewal and Advance in the Nineteenth Century* (Grand Rapids, 1965).

Paletschek, Sylvia, *Frauen und Dissens: Frauen im Deutschkatholizismus und in den freien Gemeinden 1841–1852* (Göttingen, 1990).

Penzel, Klaus, "Philip Schaff: A Centennial Appraisal," *Church History* 59 (1990): 207–21.

Petrich, Hermann, *Johann Hinrich Wichern: Leben und Wirken des Herolds der Inneren Mission* (Hamburg, 1908).

Pönnighaus, Klaus, *Kirchliche Vereine zwischen Rationalismus und Erweckung: Ihr Wirken und ihre Bedeutung vornehmlich am Beispiel des Fürstentums Lippe dargestellt* (Frankfurt/Main, 1982).

Postgate, R. W., ed., *Revolution from 1789 to 1906: Documents Selected and Edited with Notes and Introductions* (London, 1920; Harper Torchbook edition, New York, 1962).

Prelinger, Catherine, *Charity, Challenge, and Change: Religious Dimensions of the Mid-Nineteenth-Century Women's Movement in Germany* (New York, 1987).

—————, "Religious Dissent, Women's Rights, and the *Hamburger Hochschule für das weibliche Geschlecht* in Mid-Nineteenth-Century Germany," *Church History* 45 (1976): 42–55.

Rahlenbeck, H., "Johann Hinrich Wichern," *Realencyklopädie für protestantische Theologie und Kirche*, vol. 21, 3d ed. (1908): 219–24.

—————, "Johann Hinrich Wichern," *The New Schaff-Herzog Encyclopedia of Religious Knowledge*, ed. S. M. Jackson, vol. 12 (New York, 1912): 345.

Reardon, Bernard M. G., *Religion in the Age of Romanticism: Studies in Early Nineteenth Century Thought* (New York, 1985).

—————, *Religious Thought in the Nineteenth Century* (Cambridge, 1966).

Rohr, Donald G., *The Origins of Social Liberalism in Germany* (Chicago, 1963).

Ross, Ronald, *Beleaguered Fervor: The Dilemma of Political Catholicism in Wilhelmine Germany* (Notre Dame, 1976).

—————, *The Failure of Bismarck's Kulturkampf: Catholicism and State Power in Imperial Germany, 1871–1887* (Washington, D.C., 1998).

Saeger, R., *F. W. Krummacher, Gottfried Daniel Krummacher und die niederrheinesche Erweckungsbewegung zu Anfang des 19. Jahrhunderts* (Berlin, 1935).

Schnafel, Franz, *Deutsche Geschichte im neunzehnten Jahrhundert*, 2d ed., vol. 4, *Die religiösen Kräfte* (Freiburg, 1951).

Schoeps, Hans-Joachim, *Aus den Jahren preußischer Not und Erneuerung: Tagebücher und Briefe der Gebrüder Gerlach und ihres Kreises 1805–1820* (Berlin, 1963).

————, *Das andere Preußen: Konservative Gestalten und Probleme im Zeitalter Friedrich Wilhelms IV,* 3d ed. (Berlin, 1964).

Schroeder, Paul, *The Transformation of European Politics, 1763–1848* (Oxford, 1994).

Seeburg, R., "Erweckung," *Realencyklopädie für protestantische Theologie und Kirche*, vol. 5 (Leipzig, 1898), pp. 486–88.

————, "Die soziale Frage und der Preußische Staat," in *Preußisches Jahrbuch 1874*, published in *Quellen zur Geschichte der sozialen Frage in Deutschland*, vol. 2, ed. E. Schraepler (Göttingen, 1957).

Staehlin, Ernst, *Die Christentumsgesellschaft in der Zeit der Aufklärung und der beginnenden Erweckung: Texte aus Briefen, Protokollen und Publikationen* (Basel, 1970).

Stephan, Horst, *Geschichte der evangelischen Theologie in Deutschland seit dem Idealismus*, 3d ed., ed. Martin Schmidt (Berlin, 1973).

Sticker, Anna, *Theodor und Friederike Fliedner* (Wuppertal and Zurich, 1989).

Stupperich, Robert, ed., *Vom biblischen Wort zur theologischen Erkenntnis: Hermann Cremers Briefe an Adolf Schlatter und Friedrich v. Bodelschwingh 1893–1903* (Bethel, 1954).

————, *Wort und Wahrnehmung: Briefe Adolf Schlatters an Hermann Cremer und Friedrich v. Bodelschwingh* (Bethel, 1963).

Taylor, Anne, *Visions of Harmony: A Study in Nineteenth-Century Millenarianism* (Oxford, 1987).

Thier, Erich, *Die Kirche und die soziale Frage. Von Wichern bis Friedrich Naumann. Eine Untersuchung über die Beziehungen zwischen politischen Vorgängen und kirchlichen Reformen* (Gütersloh, 1950).

Tiesmeyer, L., *Die Erweckungsbewegung in Deutschland während des 19. Jahrhunderts*, 4 vols., 2d ed. (Kassel, 1905–12).

Valentin, Veit, *1848: Chapters of German History*, trans. Ethel Talbot Scheffauer (London, 1940).

Vidler, Alec, *The Church in an Age of Revolution* (Baltimore, 1961).

Waterman, A. M. C., *Religion, Economics, and Revolution: Christian Political Economy, 1798–1833* (Cambridge, 1991).

Weeks, Andrew, *German Mysticism from Hildegard of Bingen to Ludwig Wittgenstein* (Albany, 1993).

Weiser, Frederick, *Love's Response: A Story of Lutheran Deaconesses in America* (Philadelphia, 1962).

Welch, Claude, *Protestant Thought in the Nineteenth Century*, vol. 1, *1799–1870* (New Haven, 1972).

Wendland, Walter, "Erweckungsbewegung," *Die Religion in Geschichte und Gegenwart*, vol. 2, 2d ed. (Tübingen, 1928), cols. 295–304.

———, *Erweckungsbewegungen in Deutschland* (Berlin, 1926).

———, *Das Erwachen religiösen Lebens in Berlin im ersten Drittel des 19. Jahrhunderts* (Berlin-Steglitz, 1925).

Wentz, Abdel Ross, *Fliedner the Faithful* (Philadelphia, 1936).

TWENTIETH CENTURY AND GENERAL

Ahlstrom, Sydney E., "Religion, Revolution and the Rise of Modern Nationalism: Reflections on the American Experience," *Church History* 44 (1975): 492–504.

———, *A Religious History of the American People* (New Haven, 1972).

Clark, Kenneth, *Civilisation: A Personal View* (New York, 1969).

Diephouse, David, *Pastors and Pluralism in Württemberg, 1918–1933* (Princeton, 1987).

Drummond, Andrew L., *German Protestantism Since Luther* (London, 1951).

Fehler, Timothy, *Poor Relief and Protestantism: The Evolution of Social Welfare in Sixteenth-Century Emden* (Aldershot, 1999).

Groh, John, "The Kingdom of God in the History of Christianity: A Bibliographical Survey," *Church History* 43 (1974): 257–67.

Hale, J. Russell, "Lutherans and Social Action," in *The Lutheran Church in North American Life*, ed. John E. Groh and Robert H. Smith (St. Louis, 1979), pp. 100–131.

BIBLIOGRAPHY

Hendrix, Scott, "Rerooting the Faith: The Reformation as Re-Christianization," *Church History* 69 (2000): 558–77.

Hürten, Heinz, *Verfolgung, Widerstand und Zeugnis. Kirche im Nationalsozialismus. Fragen eines Historikers* (Mainz, 1987).

Kraus, Hans-Joachim, *Die biblische Theologie: Ihre Geschichte und Problematik* (Neukirchen-Vluyn, 1970).

Lindberg, Carter, *Reformation Initiatives for the Poor* (Minneapolis, 1993).

————, "The Liturgy After the Liturgy: Welfare in the Early Reformation," in *Through the Eye of a Needle: Judeo-Christian Roots of Social Welfare*, ed. Emily Hanawalt and Carter Lindberg (Kirksville, 1994), pp. 177–91.

————, "'There Should Be No Beggers Among Christians': Karlstadt, Luther, and the Origins of Protestant Poor Relief," *Church History* 46 (1977): 313–34.

Mackintosh, Hugh Ross, *Types of Modern Theology: Schleiermacher to Barth* (London, 1937).

Macmillan, Kerr D., *Protestantism in Germany* (Princeton, 1917).

Marty, Martin, *Religion and Republic: The American Circumstance* (Boston, 1987).

————, *The Modern Schism: Three Paths to the Secular* (New York, 1969).

————, "When the Forms Began," *Dialog* 4 (1965): 21–26.

McGiffert, Arthur C., *Protestant Thought Before Kant* (New York, 1911).

McNeill, John T., *Christian Hope for World Society* (New York, 1937).

————, *Modern Christian Movements* (Philadelphia, 1954).

Nichols, James Hastings, *History of Christianity, 1650–1950* (New York, 1956).

Scharpff, Paulus, *Geschichte der Evangelisation* (Gießen, 1964).

Smith, Helmut Walser, *German Nationalism and Religious Conflict: Culture, Ideology, Politics, 1870–1914* (Princeton, 1995).

Strauss, Gerald, "Success and Failure in the German Reformation," *Past and Present* 67 (1975): 3–63.

————, *Luther's House of Learning: Indoctrination of the Young in the German Reformation* (Baltimore, 1978).

Wagar, Warren, ed., *The Secular Mind: Transformations of Faith in Modern Europe. Essays Presented to Franklin L. Baumer* (New York, 1982).

Ward, W. R., *Theology, Sociology and Politics: The German Protestant Social Conscience, 1890–1933* (Bern, 1979).

Williams, Rowan, *Christian Spirituality* (Atlanta, 1979).

Wischnath, Johannes, *Kirche in Aktion: Das Evangelische Hilfswerk 1945–1957 und sein Verhältnis zur Kirche und Innerer Mission* (Göttingen, 1986).

Index of Names

Index of Places

Index of Topics

Other Volumes in This Series

Abraham Isaac Kook • THE LIGHTS OF PENITENCE, LIGHTS OF
HOLINESS, THE MORAL PRINCIPLES, ESSAYS, LETTERS, AND POEMS
Abraham Miguel Cardozo • SELECTED WRITINGS
Albert and Thomas • SELECTED WRITINGS
Alphonsus de Liguori • SELECTED WRITINGS
Anchoritic Spirituality •ANCRENE WISSE AND ASSOCIATED WORKS
Angela of Foligno • COMPLETE WORKS
Angelic Spirituality • MEDIEVAL PERSPECTIVES ON THE WAYS OF ANGELS
Angelus Silesius • THE CHERUBINIC WANDERER
Anglo-Saxon Spirituality • SELECTED WRITINGS
Apocalyptic Spirituality • TREATISES AND LETTERS OF LACTANTIUS,
ADSO OF MONTIER-EN-DER, JOACHIM OF FIORE, THE FRANCISCAN
SPIRITUALS, SAVONAROLA
Athanasius • THE LIFE OF ANTONY, AND THE LETTER TO MARCELLINUS
Augustine of Hippo • SELECTED WRITINGS
Bernard of Clairvaux • SELECTED WORKS
Bérulle and the French School • SELECTED WRITINGS
Birgitta of Sweden • LIFE AND SELECTED REVELATIONS
Bonaventure • THE SOUL'S JOURNEY INTO GOD, THE TREE OF LIFE, THE
LIFE OF ST. FRANCIS
Carthusian Spirituality • THE WRITINGS OF HUGH OF BALMA AND GUIGO
DE PONTE
Catherine of Genoa • PURGATION AND PURGATORY, THE SPIRITUAL
DIALOGUE
Catherine of Siena • THE DIALOGUE
Celtic Spirituality •
Classic Midrash, The • TANNAITIC COMMENTARIES ON THE BIBLE
Cloud of Unknowing, The •
Devotio Moderna • BASIC WRITINGS
Early Anabaptist Spirituality • SELECTED WRITINGS
Early Dominicans • SELECTED WRITINGS
Early Islamic Mysticism • SUFI, QUR'AN, MI'RAJ, POETIC AND
THEOLOGICAL WRITINGS
Early Kabbalah, The •
Elijah Benamozegh • ISRAEL AND HUMANITY
Elisabeth of Schönau • THE COMPLETE WORKS
Emanuel Swedenborg • THE UNIVERSAL HUMAN AND SOUL-BODY
INTERACTION
Ephrem the Syrian • HYMNS
Fakhruddin 'Iraqi • DIVINE FLASHES

Other Volumes in This Series

Other Volumes in This Series

Other Volumes in This Series

The Classics of Western Spirituality is a ground-breaking collection of the original writings of more than 100 universally acknowledged teachers within the Catholic, Protestant, Eastern Orthodox, Jewish, Islamic, and Native American Indian traditions.

To order any title, or to request a complete catalog, contact Paulist Press at 800-218-1903 or visit us on the Web at www.paulistpress.com